AMERICAN SOCIETY

A Critical Analysis

AMERICAN SOCIETY

A Critical Analysis

Edited by

Larry T. Reynolds
CENTRAL MICHIGAN UNIVERSITY

James M. Henslin
SOUTHERN ILLINOIS UNIVERSITY—EDWARDSVILLE

DAVID McKAY COMPANY, INC./NEW YORK

AMERICAN SOCIETY: A CRITICAL ANALYSIS

Copyright © 1973 by David McKay Company, Inc.

Second Printing, March 1974

All rights reserved, including the right to reproduce
this book, or parts thereof, in any form, except for
the inclusion of brief quotations in a review.

ISBN: 0–679–30006–6

Library of Congress Catalog Card Number: 72-96708
Manufactured in the United States of America

Interior Design by Angela Foote

Cover Design by Jane Sterrett

For our colleague
Janice M. Reynolds

ABOUT THE EDITORS

Larry T. Reynolds is an associate professor of sociology at Central Michigan University. He received his Ph.D. in sociology from Ohio State University in 1969; his areas of intellectual interest are sociological theory and the sociology of knowledge. He has contributed articles to *Sociometry, Sociological Focus, Journal of Value Inquiry, American Sociologist* and numerous other journals and books in the social sciences. Professor Reynolds is the co-editor of *The Sociology of Sociology: Analysis and Criticism of the Thought, Research, and Ethical Folkways of Sociology and Its Practitioners* and the author of the forthcoming book *Sociology As Social Product: An Introduction to the Basic Styles of Sociological Reasoning.*

James M. Henslin is an associate professor of sociology at Southern Illinois University. In 1967 he received his Ph.D. in sociology from Washington University. His areas of interest are the sociology of sex, social psychology, sociology of religion, sociology of everyday life, and deviance. He has contributed many chapters to books on sociology as well as articles to social science journals such as *American Journal of Sociology* and *Social Problems.* He is the editor of *Down to Earth Sociology.* Professor Henslin is also the editor of *The Sociology of Sex* and the co-author of *Introducing You to Sociology* (both forthcoming).

ABOUT THE CONTRIBUTORS

Martin Glaberman, a production worker in the auto industry for twenty years, is a lifelong student of working-class politics and has been active in the radical movement for forty years. He has contributed articles to *Antioch Review*, *Radical America*, *International Philosophical Quarterly* and numerous other journals on the Left. He has been editor of *Correspondence* and *Speak Out*.

George P. Rawick, associate professor of sociology at Empire State College, is a historian-sociologist with a longstanding interest in working-class politics. He is the author of the forthcoming book *The American Slave: A Composite Autobiography*.

John C. Leggett, sociologist-political scientist, is author of *Class, Politics and Race* and of the forthcoming book *Party and Class: The Politics of Race*. He is associate professor of sociology at Livingston College–Rutgers University.

Richard L. Rising teaches sociology at City College of New York and is completing his Ph.D. in sociology at City University of New York, Graduate Center. His prime areas of interest are the sociology of poverty and the military establishment.

Dusky Lee Smith, associate professor of sociology at McMaster University, has written numerous articles on the sociology of science. He has contributed articles to *Activist*, *Catalyst*, *Science and Society* and *Liberation*.

David Bartelt, assistant professor of sociology at Glassboro State College, is interested in sociological theory, social psychology, and the sociology of religion. He is currently preparing a manuscript on the sociology of knowledge.

Janice M. Reynolds, assistant professor of sociology at Central Michigan University, is interested in the social organization of medical institutions. She is the editor of *The Sociology of Sociology: Analysis and Criticism of the Thought, Research and Ethical Folkways of Sociology and Its Practitioners*.

Ted R. Vaughan, associate professor of sociology at the University of Missouri, is primarily interested in the sociology of intellectual life. He has contributed articles to *Social Forces*, *Social Problems*, and *American Sociologist* and is author of the forthcoming work *Critical Sociology*.

Eric Grønseth, associate professor of sociology at the University of Oslo, is interested in the structure of the family in varying types of society. A collection of his articles on the family is published in the volume *Familie, Sansvalitet Der Samfunn*. At present he is engaged in researching families where both husband and wife are engaged only half-time in occupational life.

Leon Shaskolsky, assistant professor of sociology in the school of criminology at Tel Aviv University, holds degrees in both sociology and law. His areas of interest are the sociology of law and the sociology of knowledge.

PREFACE

This volume is a collection of original essays tied together by a common theme and intended for use in courses dealing with American society, social organization, social problems, and principles of sociology. The book obviously presents a different perspective on our contemporary society than is to be found in the great majority of sociology texts. As such this volume can be used as either a substitute for such standard texts or in conjunction with them for those interested in exposing students to antiestablishment as well as establishment sociology's analysis of the American social order.

Following an introductory statement outlining the general perspective adhered to by the contributors to this volume, the book is divided into two basic parts. Part I deals with the master institutions of market society: the economic, political, and military orders. We assume, as did C. Wright Mills, that it is within the upper echelons of these three institutions that the real power in American society resides. We find ourselves in further agreement with Mills' thesis that the highest reaches of the economic, military, and political orders interlock and overlap to form a military-industrial-political complex or what Mills termed *The Power Elite*. We do not, however, assume that the political, military, and economic institutions are equally dominant, powerful, or influential. While recognizing the overlapping, reinforcing, and even near-symbiotic nature of the relationship between these three institutions, we argue the thesis that the economic institution is *the* master institution of American society.

Part II deals with American society's scientific, religious, medical, educational, familial, and legal institutions. C. Wright Mills was of the opinion that the economic, political, and military institutions had pushed the other social institutions off to the side of human history and had either relegated them to a position of minor importance or had made them subservient to the needs of the military-industrial-political complex. The argument presented here is that these *secondary institutions* generally serve the needs and follow the dictates of American society's economic order and have become, in our words, mere *appendages to the market.*

A word of warning is perhaps in order with respect to our use of the term "market." We are not seriously contending that the United States is a market society as that term is employed by classical economics. Such contention is best left to political reactionaries, individualistic sociologists, and the heirs to political economy. In the strict political economy sense of the term, market or "free market" society is a social fiction—it never existed. In a looser sense, market society as a short-lived product or commodity-centered phenomenon ended in the late 1800s with the shift from laissez faire to corporate capitalism. One could with some degree of accuracy, however, argue that American society is a market society dominated by a few corporate giants. It is nonetheless probably better to say that we live in a society whose principal form of social organization remains, in a very real sense, the short-term, depersonalized, specific, and atomistic contract but whose dominant structural feature had become the acendancy of large-scale, bureaucratic organizations. In short, we live in a corporate capitalistic society of organizational bureaucracy. We still prefer to use the term market because we feel that in the minds of beginning student readers of this manuscript, this term more than the vague terms "organizational" or "bureaucratic" will clearly, directly, and immediately point to both the dominance of American society's economic sector and to the primacy of the provisioning relationships in the determination of human affairs. And that, after all, is the central thesis of this book.

LARRY T. REYNOLDS
Mt. Pleasant, Michigan

JAMES M. HENSLIN
Edwardsville, Illinois

CONTENTS

Introduction

Larry T. Reynolds

> *Sociology, which of all sciences should benefit man most, is in danger of falling into the class of polite amusements, or dead sciences.*
>
> LESTER FRANK WARD

> *As Ward realized in his day that sociology was dying, the more astute and discerning student of today understands that sociology has been well prepared for its grave. The pallbearers are mainstream or Establishment sociologists.*
>
> DUSKY LEE SMITH

Establishment Sociology

One key observation on the content of contemporary American sociology has led to the publication of this work: a great deal of what passes for the sociological study of American social life, structure, and problems consists of totally astructural analysis.[1] American sociology has rather consistently failed to either see or carry out the full implications of the fact that it is the principal way in which man relates to man, that is, his form of social organization, which is the prime cause of both his actions and his history. Instead, the majority of American sociologists, whose work is a curious and peculiarly American admixture of ultraconservative and superliberal ideology,[2]

1

apparently feel that the basic cause of social behavior and human history is either (1) personality, human nature, and other intraindividual phenomena that occasionally reach the level of intragroup (small group) interaction;[3] or (2) culture—variously referred to as the social order, the normative order, and/or systems of beliefs, values, or rules.[4] Most frequently the key or principal cause of social phenomena is conceived as a combination of human nature, a la Adam Smith[5] or George C. Homans,[6] and culture, a la Emile Durkheim[7] or Pitirim Sorokin.[8] Such reasoning also tends to be aeconomic, apolitical, and lacking in "guts," especially in the sense that economic and political phenomena constitute the guts or basic processes of the larger social life of American society. In short, American academic sociology fails to see that it is neither that bio-psychic entity known as personality nor the apparatus through which meaning is molded into our daily activities, but social organization that gives constancy or patterning to social life.

Sociologists who are perpetrators of astructural analysis are likewise champions of "the problem-centered." They seek to understand, explain, and even to change—in the "tinkering" sense of the term— phenomena that are the mere results or end products of larger structural relationships. They have minimal awareness, it would seem, of those larger institutional arrangements that systematically and regularly produce the results that so pique their liberal consciences. What they fail to grasp they obviously do not intend to change[9]—although their reticence may not be due so much to their failure to comprehend as to their deep-seated commitment to American society's status quo.[10] Discussing the problems approach of Harry Bredemeier and Jackson Toby,[11] two highly orthodox representatives of the sociological establishment, the unintentionally humorous Samuel Stouffer, himself a mainstream empiricist of note, informs us that they "love America and American institutions." Perhaps there is a modicum of truth in the old cliché that it is easier to worship that which forever retains its mystery.

Nevertheless, these mainstream sociologists have some understanding of larger institutional arrangements or "society," but only in the idealized form of its actual manifestations. This idealized form is referred to as the normative order—society is regarded as it was by Saint Simon[12] and Durkheim,[13] that is, as the mere application of a system of ideas. Mainstream sociologists take the charter of American society—its pronouncements about and definitions of itself—as if it constituted reality, rather than merely the reality of the American establishment—a reality held to because, as Marx would note, such belief is functional (i.e., it serves their purposes). In spite of their imperfect, indeed farcical, understanding of larger social forces, these "larger forces," again in their idealized form, remain the standards or models. Any disruption of or deviation from them defines the very existence of what they consider to be a social problem.

To these chivalrous cultivators of a dead science, as Dusky Smith calls them,[14] social problems are nothing more nor less than that which impedes the functioning of the "smooth society." [15] Their answer to Lindner's question—Must You Conform?—is a resounding yes. For establishmentarians such as S. N. Eisenstadt, the very existence of a social problem can be defined as the individual refusing or otherwise failing to conform to the role that society has readied for him.[16] These "just men of sound reason" apparently cannot conceive that the smooth society and its supportive institutions are the true culprits, or that what they refer to as the real problems are simply the products of the smooth society of corporate democracy functioning at its healthiest and best.

For those who sail the placid waters of the mainstream, social problems are not naturally occurring phenomena flowing from the very nature of the larger American social structure; they are unnatural, pathological anomalies—anomalies capable of correction within the confines of the present system. From the perspective of these "good citizens," no matter how repressive a given society, those who fail to conform to its norms are deviants, troublemakers. Society, a la Big Brother, the collective conscience, or the American Dream, is the sole criterion by which human beings are to be judged. For Marshall Clinard,[17] persons who do not conform to norms tolerated by "society" are deviants. It seems to matter little that the end product of the smoothly functioning society may be the equally smooth grinding up of Homo sapiens.

It is bad enough when an analytical abstraction such as "society," or more directly, "norms" or "values"—they are aften used as if they were interchangeable terms—is proposed as the criterion for judging men and women, but these sociologists go one step further:

their analytical abstractions are not so abstract. What they mean by human society turns out to be a fairly new social construction, the nation-state—in this case that geographic-political unit known as the United States of America. According to Weinberg,[18] a social problem is nothing more or less than what is "objectionable" when "viewed in the context of American standards of living, values, and institutions." In effect, when these sociologists chant that what is good for society is good for its members, they mean that what is good for the United States is good for its citizens. Couple this with their proclivity to equate society with its ruling class, and it translates still more freely into the old adage, "What's good for General Motors is good for the country and what's good for the country is good for you and me"—save for the fact that General Motors now must share federal moneys with the giant defense industries, a point few "sunshine sociologists" care to dwell on. This coterie of high-status, fat-contract, big-cat apologists, as Martin Nicolaus[19] calls them, receive their research funds from either big government or big industry; as they are reluctant to bite the hand that feeds them, precious little study of the political or economic institutions in American society is undertaken. While these courteous gentlemen purport to be value-free, their services to the corporate order are anything but cheap. The general irrelevance of their sociological work with respect to alleviating the suffering of the masses leads them to spend their well-paid careers in a vain attempt to demonstrate the empirical superiority of a system of values to which they themselves just happen to subscribe.

And so while sociology has fallen into the realm of polite amusement or dead science, this pious cloister of priestly technocrats remains as one additional barrier to the creation of a viable study of man.

Antiestablishment Sociology

Yet, many sociologists have turned or are beginning to turn away from, the sociological establishment—from the perspectives of structural functionalism, exchange theory, symbolic interactionism, and social action theory. As Shaskolsky tells us, many of these paradigms simply represent different aspects of the same reality; they are in part utopian schemes written in the present tense.[20] They share ideological homogeneity in that each apologizes for corporate democracy[21]—one in its organic manifestations and the others in its individualistic ramifications. These theories are, to use paradoxically enough Mr. Cooley's phrase, but two sides of the same coin. So, sociologists are turning away from the conservative organic culturology of Talcott Parsons,[22] Robert Merton,[23] and Robert Nisbet[24] and toward the *new sociology* of Irving Louis Horowitz[25] and the *reflective sociology* of Alvin Gouldner;[26] from the individualistic exchange theory of George Homans[27] and Peter Blau[28] and toward the *critical philosophy* of Herbert Marcuse[29] and the *genetic structuralism* of Lucien Goldmann;[30] and from the liberal social psychology of Erving Goffman,[31] Harold Garfinkel,[32] and Howard S. Becker[33] and toward the *critical interactionism* of John Seeley,[34] the *old or classic sociology* of C. Wright Mills,[35] and the *radical sociology* of Karl Marx.[36]

This "turning away" has also been accompanied by the belated appearance of several self-critical and self-reflective essays[37] joining themselves to the earlier works by Mills[38] and Bramson.[39] Furthermore, recent years have witnessed the publication of a number of antiestablishment volumes intended for graduate and undergraduate consumption in such courses as introductory sociology,[40] social problems,[41] methodology,[42] race relations,[43] and social theory.[44]

The present work furthers this trend. It contains, in varying degrees depending in large measure on who authors a particular chapter, differing elements of the critical philosophy of Marcuse, the new sociology of Horowitz, the reflective sociology of Gouldner, and the self-conscious sociology of Mills. But the overriding theoretical framework for all the contributors is the critical-radical sociology of Karl Marx. Of course, Marcuse, Horowitz, and Mills are all in a sense and to a varying degree heirs to the legacy of Marx—the legacy of scientific socialism. This book is also constructed from the vantage point of sociology's social protest tradition, and as such it has two basic objectives: (1) to heighten the student's understanding of American society by providing a radical analysis of its institutions; and (2) by so doing, to increase the reader's awareness of the essence of critical or radical sociology.

Obviously, little can be said in this brief introductory chapter regarding the structure of American society. Cliché or not, the chapters that follow speak for themselves. Some may also argue that the student gains a better understanding of radical sociology by reading radical analyses of concrete social phenomena than by reading a necessarily skimpy discussion of what a radical analysis, and hence radical sociology, looks like in principle. I sympathize to a certain extent with this view, but there are two basic reasons for not employing it in this volume:

1. Quite possibly the student's grasp of radical sociology is best enhanced by his first being confronted with a skeletal outline of sociological radicalism, which is then "fleshed out" by the presentation of a concrete radical analysis of the student's own society.

2. It will no longer suffice to have students read "radical analyses" of specific social events and processes as the sole means of coming to grips with sociological radicalism. One has only to attend a sociological convention or read selected books and articles by certain prominent "scholars" to understand why. Quite simply, it is becoming progressively more fashionable to refer to oneself as a "radical" sociologist. This deception, which hopefully is only self-deception, is now being practiced by representatives from all walks of establishment sociology as an unconscious exercise in repressive tolerance. Arthur Godfrey is peddling a revolutionary new detergent; Lewis Coser is peddling conflict theory.[45] While conflict theory is not necessarily radical sociology, it is a small step from passing oneself off as a conflict theorist to passing oneself off as a radical sociologist. Obviously, an establishment sociologist who calls himself something he is not still provides a conventional analysis of the specific social phenomenon he is forced to deal with. No understanding of critical sociology is imparted by reading the works of such authors. In light of the above, a brief outline of the basic features of radical sociology is clearly called for in this introductory chapter.

Radical Sociology

This discussion of the rudiments of radical sociology[46] is of necessity very brief and perhaps hopelessly general. Brief so that the reader will not long be prevented from getting to the analyses provided by the contributing authors, and general enough to embrace a number of key issues on which the contributors share a common point of view. At the same time, no author need feel hemmed in, dictated to, or in other ways prohibited from exercising his own creative interpretation and application of the general paradigm.

Table 1 sets the general parameters of the discussion by delimiting the specific topic to be dealt with.[47] Although I have included for comparative purposes an outline of sociology's major theoretical traditions, I intend to discuss only the radical or organizational perspective. Even here, not all items posted in the diagram will be taken up and those that are shall be dealt with in a parsimonious manner. From those topics cataloged, I wish to direct attention only to radical sociology's (1) image of man, (2) locus of causal priority, (3) image of society, (4) system of logic, and (5) problematic aspects of social life. In the course of discussing these five items, I also hope to at least touch lightly upon such topics as class interests served and the nominalism-realism issue.

IMAGE OF MAN

What is meant when we say that the radical sociologist views man as being both subject and object? Quite simply, it means that men are seen as conjointly constructing their lives and in the process their "constructions," such as society itself, "come back" to constrain, impose restrictions, and give direction to man's activities. Yet, the relationship does not stop here. Man reacts to his own constructions, and that reaction is not always—if indeed it *ever* is—a totally supportive one. Man in association with his fellow man rejects, rebuilds, or in other ways either alters or destroys his own social artifacts. Furthermore, his gigantic creations, e.g., society, are constructed in such a way that they embody those very elements that will lead to their own breakup—a breakup again effected at the hands of conjointly acting men. The relationship between man and his constructs, between man as subject and as object, is itself a kind of dialectical relationship. Therefore, sociological radicalism does not, as does sociological conservatism, see man as a passive billiard ball set in motion only by forces external to himself. Neither is man the "captain of his own ship" or the "master of his destiny" as the liberal-individualists assume. This is, of course, not to deny that man can be and indeed does become more of an object in some societies than in others.

CAUSAL PRIORITY

Sociological radicalism sees the ultimate cause of human activity and the prime mover in human history to be social organization

TABLE 1. *Basic Styles of Sociological Reasoning*

INTELLECTUAL TRADITION	ORGANIC	INDIVIDUALISTIC	ORGANIZATIONAL
Political response to the industrial revolution	conservative	liberal	radical
Image of man	object	subject	subject–object
Causal priority/reality principle	culture	personality	social organization
Image of society	organic analogy	flux and/or aggregate model	totality of interested relationships
Nominalism-realism issue	classic realism	nominalism	transcendent realism
Theory-method relation	social cultural theory/social psychological methodology	social psychological theory/social psychological methodology	social organizational theory/social organizational methodology
Key concepts	culture norms values function community consensus anomie dysfunction	personality the actor interaction status authority communication deviation maladjustment	social organization social structure differential power differential interest class consciousness alienation class conflict history
System of logic	deductive	inductive	dialectical
Problematic aspects of social life	*social order* consensus integration differentiation evolution	*adaptation* motivation adjustment deviation fluxuation	*social change* class consciousness internal contradiction systemic conflict revolution

—that is, the basic, principal, or characteristic way in which man is related to man. These relationships are of prime importance as they transpire within the confines of the provisioning institution, regardless of whether that provisioning institution is the Trobriand kinship net with its imbedded economy or one such as the American institution which is a separate social institution characterized by short-term, depersonalized, specific, and atomistic contractual relationships. Sociological radicalism does not contend, therefore, that ideas (part of culture) precede and lead to action. Rather, as the following quotations suggest, the social protest tradition employs a large-scale variant of the action-leads-to-ideas formula:

> In the creation and development of institutions, ideas reflect institutions as much as they shape them. To understand this relation, it is often more profitable to pursue the analysis from institutions to ideas, than to argue from ideas to institutions. But the investigation of the ideological service of major concepts and dicta—of, for example, the academic dictum, "knowledge for its own sake"—goes against our rationalist grain. The liberal-rationalist tradition derives action from ideas; for us ends precede means, motives precede acts, and values precede institutions, both in time and in logic. Pragmatically and in the short term, motives and values may be an adequate guide to behavior. However, if the questions are expanded to include the origins of motives and ideas (and if the problem is precisely change), it is more often illuminating to view ideas as the "dependent variables." [48]

> I do not mean to suggest that ideological transformations give rise to social ones. Only the reverse is in fact true. [49]

> It is not the consciousness of men that determines their existence, but, on the contrary, their social existence determines their consciousness. [50]

As culture is seen as ultimately determined by structure or organization, so too is character—as evidenced by the following discussion of the class-linked nature of personality traits:

> In modern industrial societies the routine workers learn to make the drives toward security and a higher living standard most completely expressive of their selves; and what they har-

bor of other drives is channeled into those two consuming working-class hungers. To an individual worker, for example, to be a "success" is to have job security. In the jobs and occupations that are the lot of the routine worker, the elite drives really play a secondary role. This is primarily because since there is a very definite limit on how far the routine worker can rise in his work, expansion, achievement, and the rest have little emotional meaning for him. The aspirations of the elite, as we shall see, have no limit; for them expansion is a passion yearning in the flesh.

What the American industrial system does not offer the routine worker can be appreciated best by contrast with what it does offer one of its elite groups, scientists and engineers. By the same token, the personality *deprivations* of the average worker can be appreciated by a view of the personality *expectations* of this elite.[51]

I would point out at this juncture that the radical's assumption that social organization begets personality is not identical to nor a simple variation on the conservative's conception of man as a totally determined, internally consistent being—a position strongly criticized from the basically individualistic standpoint of Dennis Wrong.[52] Rather, as the following critique of the oversimplified conception of the American slave's personality as somehow "infantilized" or "Sambo-like" reveals, contradictions inherent in society become inherent in human personality:

> . . . the slave struggles against the master by struggling with his own internal dilemmas. The social struggle begins, in an immediate sense, as a struggle within the slave and only then becomes externalized and objectified. Therefore, unless the slave is simultaneously Sambo and revolutionary, Sambo and Nat Turner, he can be neither Sambo nor Nat Turner. He can only be a wooden man, a theoretical abstraction . . . the most important problems inherent in the study of plantation production based on slave labor can be solved only by an analysis of the class struggle between master and slaves; such analysis must begin with the self-activity of the slaves themselves. . . . This is not to argue that the slave was in no sense Sambo. A man is Sambo precisely when he is at the very point of being the rebel. Rebel he must be, but self-confident he is not. The greatest of

all abolitionist leaders, the ex-slave Frederick Douglass, tells repeatedly in his autobiography that when in the very act of fleeing, he was not only afraid—he also felt he was doing something wrong. Everything seemed to tell him that he was incapable of being a freeman; but at the same time, everything told him he must be a freeman. Unless we understand the contradictory nature of the human personality in class societies, we can never portray reality.[53]

IMAGE OF SOCIETY

For the individualistic paradigm, society is a fluid, constantly changing, amorphous *name* which they apply to a collectivity of individuals. There is no reality over and above that of the concrete individual. For the organicist, society is a stable, wholistic phenomenon whose integration is based upon people's subscription to a common ethic, to a system of shared beliefs and values. Society by the conservatives' estimate is greater than the sum of its individual members; over and above the conglomeration of concrete individuals lies the press, the restraining influence of a common culture, a normative order, or a collective conscience—all of which precede the individual's entry into society and survive his departure.

Critical sociology, like organicism, sees society as somehow greater than the total number of individuals it embraces. In rejecting the pure fluidity or "society as nebula" model of the individualists, the radical argues again in common with the conservatives, that contemporary society has an integrated or stable quality to it. But there is a crucial difference between the images of society held by radicals and by conservatives. The radical sociologist, at the same time that he acknowledges the integrated nature of society, also argues that society is process—that it has a processual (historical) character. Furthermore, sociological radicalism argues that society's integration rests upon a different basis from the one the organic tradition sees. The source of social cohesion is not a common culture but the binding relationships among men. Stability as such flows from a condition of social organization and not from a situation of cultural consensus. Society is the totality of these interested or binding relationships. Generically society is nothing more or less than a set of social relations—relations by means of which people construct their lives. A definition of contemporary society which appears to flow from this generic definition views "Society as a contested struggle between groups with opposed aims and perspectives." [54] In order for this definition to be consistent with a radical perspective, however, the word *groups* must not be translated into *status* groups. The Weberian definition of society as an arena of competing *status groups* is not what I am talking about. The specific set of relations which give focus to the radical scholar's attention, as exemplified in the following quotation, are the relations of production:

> In order to produce, they (human beings) enter into definite connections and relations with one another, and only within these social connections and relations does their connection with Nature, i.e., production, take place. . . . These social relations between the producers and the conditions under which they exchange their activities and share in the total act of production will naturally vary according to the character of the means of production.[55]

The character of the means of production, therefore, determines what the *type* of society will be. In capitalistic society the relations of production are precisely property relations. This system of relations determines the class structure of society. And the conflict between these classes gives to society its processual character and moves history along.

Such a conception of society, that is, as a binding set of historically conditioned relationships, appears logically consistent with an image of man that in dialectical fashion sees him as both subject and object, and that sees social organization as the ultimate cause of human behavior and social history.

It follows from this definition of social life that society per se is not seen as oppressive. In fact, radical sociology argues that apart from structured relations with others, Homo sapiens as Homo sapiens do not exist. This, I take it, is what Horton means when he informs us that the conflict perspective has an "Immanent conception of society and the social relationship; men are society; society is the extension of man; the transcendence of society is tantamount to the alienation of man from his own social nature." [56] Man's "salvation" does not lie in his total freedom and autonomy from others; he is not in his basic nature the social atom liberal individualists have historically taken him to be. He simply appeared "atomlike" within the context of early market society. Man is no more an atom than the contractual relationship which makes him appear as such is the aboriginal unit of social organization.

SYSTEM OF LOGIC

I do not wish, nor do I think it possible, to take up here such issues as what generally is dialectical reasoning and what is the precise nature of dialectical logic. These questions require fuller explication than is possible here. Rather, I simply wish to remark on the congruence between one's image of man, image of society, and statement of causal priority and the way man reasons—that is, his system of logic. If a person assumes, as organicists such as Durkheim did, that (1) the whole is greater than the sum of its parts—that culture is superorganic and superordinate over those individuals who live under and by it; and (2) that the concrete individual is a mere mirror of this overriding cultural order, that he is nothing but an object, and that "people are what they are because the social order is what it is"—then it is not at all difficult to see that his system of logic is in essence deductive. This is the system employed by the conservatives. They reason from the group to the individual; from the general to the specific.

Conversely, if one contends, as Adam Smith did and George Homans does (1) that reality is resident only in the concrete individual; and (2) that society is nothing more than the totality of its individual members, and that "society is what it is because people are what they are"—then he is reasoning from the individual to the group, from the specific to the general. Inductive logic is the logic of the individualistic tradition.

It is, however, not quite so easy to see the hookup between the images of man and society, the locus of causal priority, and the *system of logic* that characterizes critical sociology. But if one looks, for example, at Rawick's previously cited description of the American slave as being part Uncle Tom-like and part Nat Turner-like and notes the corresponding contradiction in the exploitive system producing such human character, and if one notes Marx's conception of society as a battleground of warring "haves" and "have-nots"—he begins, I think, to see that such an image of man and of society has within itself a decidedly dialectical quality. If one reasons that major traits of human character call forth in persons embodying them traits that in point of fact are their antitheses; that every social order in the epoch of prehuman history is predicated upon a principle of social organization that contains within itself as its thesis the basis of its own demise, its antithesis; and that the emergence of any social class logically implies (as it must) the existence of another class, and that that other class has (as it will) interests diametrically opposed to it— then his conception of man and society and of social causation dictates that his attendant logic system be dialectical.

PROBLEMATIC ASPECTS OF SOCIAL LIFE

A problematic aspect of social life is one that, because it is naturally occurring and nonpathological, must be scientifically explained. A glance at the outline of the basic styles of sociological reasoning reveals that those aspects of social life—alienation, internal contradiction, class conflict, revolution—that radical sociology considers normal or naturally occurring, at least in contemporary society, are perhaps best placed under the general heading of *social change*. Each item listed under this heading is a contributing or potentially contributing factor to the process of large-scale social change—in fact more than one of these problematic aspects is, in and of itself, a form of social change.

Manifestly *not* assumed is that the social system tends to equilibrium—dynamic or otherwise—that individuals tend to par, or that the natural state of objects, particularly animate ones, tends to rest or inertia. Rather, some form of change is held to be both inevitable and desirable—be it the cataclysmic variety supported and brought on through *class conflict* or that variety brought about through the *confrontational* politics of the *classless* society.

Alienation, man's estrangement from self and others in general and his disenfranchisement from the productive process in particular, is a potential mechanism for social change. And radical sociology's focusing on alienation as a substantive area of inquiry is in large measure dictated by alienation's change-evoking possibilities. Alienation is assumed to be a desirable state of affairs to the exact extent to which the larger society is assumed to be rotten. As a social as opposed to a psychological state, alienation, particularly among those in society's lower strata and/or in socially marginal positions, is regarded as both natural and desirable. In the last analysis, of course, alienation, again as both natural and desirable phenomena, is not restricted to that social class which suffers most under an oppressive social order, but radiates throughout the entire social structure. Alienation likewise speeds along the working out of those internal contradictions that the system itself generates and that, through the vehicle of class conflict, may ultimately bring about that system's demise at the hands of a social revolution. Here again, the point is that the major "problematic aspects" of social life for sociology's social protest tradition are best summed up under the larger rubric of social change.

Radical Sociology's Value Commitment

It is perhaps best to conclude this chapter with a brief look at the value commitment of radical sociology. To discuss this value commitment separately is not to suggest that it is not part of radicalism's intellectual structure; on the contrary, it is the very basis for it.

If I pose here two basic questions, Knowledge for What? and Knowledge for Whom? the first becomes the easier to answer. Although a number of radical sociologists give credence to the legitimacy of laying to rest one's own intellectual curiosity as *one* basis of thought and research, there appears to be unanimity in the assumption that what is really sought is the production and creation of a system of knowledge that alleviates human suffering and enriches the human condition.

Some, but perhaps not too much, difficulty arises when we address the second question. The question of knowledge for whom becomes simply a question of whose suffering we alleviate and whose condition we labor to enrich. Sjoberg and Vaughan inform us:

> Our argument is that sociologists must strive to legitimize their actions in terms of their contributions to "the dignity of man" principle. . . . To what group or groups does modern man (or the sociologist) owe his loyalty? We have reasoned the sociologist's loyalty is to mankind at large.[57]

Yet, Gouldner tells us:

> A sociology of the underdog is justified because, and to the extent that, his suffering is less likely to be known and because—by reason of his being underdog—the extent and character of his suffering are likely to contain much that is avoidable.[58]

Does the radical sociologist, then, owe his loyalty to some abstract humanity in general or should his allegiances be to a historically specific social class, namely, the oppressed classes of contemporary societies? The answer is both. The difference appears to be one of orientation in time. The concern for the welfare of humanity proper on the part of most radical sociologists is a future-oriented one. The concern for the suffering of society's "have-nots" is an immediate concern for the here and now. There is a dilemma here. For while it is manifestly true that man does not live by bread alone, it is criminal to focus one's total attention upon this fact when people are starving. On the other hand, a total ignoring of the "beyond bread" aspects of a common humanity leaves one in the most unenviable position of all: that of not having an alternative system of truly cooperative relationships that coincide with man's basic nature available to supplant the currently oppressive one. It will not do to have radical sociologists spending 100 percent of their time engaged in either of these two pursuits.

The need to serve the interests of the nonruling class appears to me both manifestly desirable and obvious. The need to profess loyalty to humanity in general appears equally so—but not because Alvin Gouldner tells us that rich people suffer too.[59] It is in fact only through the study of "humanity as a whole" that a reasonable future can be contemplated and indeed planned. The liberals have left us in a lurch. In their initial hyperindividualistic reaction to feudalism's conception of natural, God-given differences between supposedly "superior" and "inferior" classes of people, the liberal's doctrine that "all men are created equal" degenerated into the notion that *all men are created equally nothing*. The radical scholar must ask and answer the question: *Created equally what?* What are the common parameters of our basic humanity, what is it that we all share in common, what is that common human nature which exists beyond and above our biology? This, I take it, is what Noam Chomsky,[60] Claude Levi-Strauss,[61] and a growing number of radical scholars have set out to answer.

Lastly, in addition to directing his energies against the interests of the ruling class and on behalf of humanity in general and oppressed classes in particular, the radical sociologist must profess a profound sense of loyalty to himself. The basic reason behind this posture of self-loyalty is the fact that theory and method are inextricably bound together in the tradit'on of sociological radicalism. One practices what he preaches. And because he does, he is held accountable for his scientific pronouncements. This notion of accountability is the essence of praxis; it may well be the essence of radical sociology itself.

NOTES

1. This brief description of establishment sociology has profited from a manuscript by Dusky Lee Smith, "The Costs of Corporate Democracy: A Tentative Approach to Social Problems," 1968.

2. See Leon Shaskolsky, "The Development of Sociological Theory in America: A Sociology of Knowledge Interpretation," *Ohio Valley Sociologist* 32, no. 3 (Spring 1967): 11–35.

3. See, for example, George C. Homans, "Bringing Men Back In," *American Sociological Review* 29 (December 1964): 809–18.

4. See, for example, Talcott Parsons, *The Social System* (Glencoe, Ill.: Free Press, 1951).

5. Adam Smith, *An Inquiry Into the Nature and Causes of the Wealth of Nations* (New York: Modern Library, 1937).

6. George C. Homans, *Social Behavior: Its Elementary Forms* (New York: Harcourt, 1961); in this volume Homans sets forth his image of man as a pigeon with a pocketbook. This image is almost enough to make one wish that Homans would "Bring Men Back In," but apparently he is not able to.

7. Emile Durkheim, *The Division of Labor in Society*, trans. George Simpson (Glencoe, Ill.: Free Press, 1947).

8. Pitirim Sorokin, *Social and Cultural Dynamics*, 4 vols. (New York: American Book, 1937–41).

9. Perhaps no single work as clearly typifies sociology's fervent commitment to the status quo as does Russell Dynes et al., *Social Problems: Dissensus and Deviation in Industrial Society* (New York: Oxford University Press, 1964). The authors are apparently so convinced of the naturalness of what-

ever happens to be the status quo that a subheading of their "theoretical" chapter reads simply: The "Cause" of Social Problems—Social Change.

10. The following social problems texts can be characterized as identifying with the current American status quo of corporate democracy: Robert K. Merton and Robert Nisbet, *Contemporary Social Problems* (New York: Harcourt, 1971); James M. Reinhardt, Paul Meadows, and John M. Gillette, *Social Problems and Social Policy* (New York: American Book, 1952); Edward McDonagh and Jon Simpson, *Social Problems: Persistent Challenges* (New York: Holt, 1965); Harry C. Bredemeier and Jackson Toby, *Social Problems in America* (New York: Wiley, 1960); Marshall Clinard, *The Sociology of Deviant Behavior* (New York: Holt, 1963); S. Kirson Weinberg, *Social Problems in Our Time* (Englewood Cliffs, N.J.: Prentice-Hall, 1960); and Earl Raab and G. J. Selznick, *Major Social Problems* (New York: Harper, 1964).

11. Bredemeier and Toby, *Social Problems in America*, pp. 146–47.

12. See Felix Markham, ed., *Saint Simon: Social Organization, the Science of Man and Other Writings* (New York: Harper Torchbooks, 1964).

13. Emile Durkheim, *The Elementary Forms of the Religious Life*, trans. Joseph W. Swain (New York: Collier, 1961).

14. Smith, "Costs of Corporate Democracy."

15. For an excellent discussion of the mainstream, smooth-society sociologists see Dusky Lee Smith, "The Sunshine Boys: Toward a Sociology of Happiness," *Activist* (Spring 1964): 166–77.

16. S. N. Eisenstadt, *Comparative Social Problems* (Glencoe, Ill.: Free Press, 1964), p. xiv.

17. Clinard, *Sociology of Deviant Behavior*, p. 22.

18. Weinberg, *Social Problems in Our Time*, p. 4.

19. Martin Nicolaus, "Text of a Speech Delivered at the American Sociological Association Convention, August 26, 1968," *American Sociologist* 4 (May 1969): 154–56.

20. See Shaskolsky, "Development of Sociological Theory in America."

21. See Alvin W. Gouldner, "The Sociologist as Partisan: Sociology and the Welfare State," *American Sociologist* 3 (May 1968): 103–16.

22. See Parsons, *Social System*.

23. See Robert K. Merton, *Social Theory and Social Structure* (Glencoe, Ill.: Free Press, 1957).

24. See Robert Nisbet, *The Sociological Tradition* (New York: Basic Books, 1966).

25. See Irving Louis Horowitz, ed., *The New Sociology: Essays in Social Science and Social Theory in Honor of C. Wright Mills* (New York: Oxford University Press, 1965).

26. See Alvin W. Gouldner, *The Coming Crisis of Western Sociology* (New York: Basic Books, 1970).

27. Homans, *Social Behavior.*

28. Peter Blau, *Exchange and Power in Social Life* (New York: Wiley, 1964).

29. See Herbert Marcuse, *One-Dimensional Man* (Boston: Beacon Press, 1964).

30. See Lucien Goldmann, *The Human Sciences and Philosophy,* trans. Hayden V. White and Robert Anchor (London: Jonathan Cape, 1969).

31. See Erving Goffman, *The Presentation of Self in Everyday Life* (New York: Doubleday, 1959).

32. See Harold Garfinkel, *Studies in Ethno-methodology* (Englewood Cliffs, N.J.: Prentice-Hall, 1967).

33. See Howard S. Becker, *Outsiders* (New York: Free Press, 1963).

34. See John Seeley, *The Americanization of the Unconsciousness* (New York: International Science Press, 1967).

35. See C. Wright Mills, *The Power Elite* (New York: Oxford University Press, 1956). For Mills' own summary of the classic tradition in sociology see his *Images of Man: The Classic Tradition in Sociological Thinking* (New York: Braziller, 1960), pp. 1–17.

36. See Karl Marx, *Das Kapital* (Chicago: Regnery, 1954); *The Eighteenth Brumaire of Louis Bonaparte* (New York: International Publishers, 1926); *A Contribution to the Critique of Political Economy* (Chicago: Kerr, 1904); and Karl Marx and Friedrich Engels, *Manifesto of the Communist Party* (New York: International Publishers, 1922); and *The German Ideology* (New York: International Publishers, 1947).

37. See Gouldner, *The Coming Crisis of Western Sociology;* Robert Friedrichs, *A Sociology of Sociology* (New York: Free Press, 1969); and Larry T. Reynolds and Janice M. Reynolds, eds., *The Sociology of Sociology: Analysis and Criticism of the Thought, Research and Ethical Folkways of Sociology and Its Practitioners* (New York: McKay, 1970).

38. C. Wright Mills, *The Sociological Imagination* (New York: Oxford University Press, 1959).

39. Leon Bramson, *The Political Context of Sociology* (Princeton, N.J.: Princeton University Press, 1961).

40. See Charles H. Anderson, *Toward a New Sociology: A Critical View* (Homewood, Ill.: Dorsey Press, 1971); and Maurice Zeitlin, *American Society Inc.* (Chicago: Markham, 1970).

41. See Steven C. Deutsch and John Howard, eds., *Where It's At: Radical*

Perspectives in Sociology (New York: Harper, 1970); Robert Perrucci and Marc Pilisuk, eds., *The Triple Revolution: Social Problems in Depth* (Boston: Little, Brown, 1968); and Frank Lindenfeld, ed., *Radical Perspectives on Social Problems* (New York: Macmillan, 1968).

42. See Gideon Sjoberg and Roger Nett, *A Methodology for Social Research* (New York: Harper, 1969).

43. See Sidney Willhelm, *Who Needs the Negro?* (Cambridge, Mass.: Schenkman, 1970).

44. See Irving Zeitlin, *Ideology and the Development of Sociological Theory* (Englewood Cliffs, N.J.: Prentice-Hall, 1969).

45. See Lewis A. Coser, *The Functions of Social Conflict* (New York: Free Press, 1954).

46. This discussion of radical sociology is principally informed by Larry T. Reynolds and Janice M. Reynolds, *Sociology As Social Product: An Introduction to Sociological Reasoning* (New York: McKay, forthcoming).

47. This composite diagram is drawn from a number of sources the most important of which are (1) lectures on social theory delivered by Ted R. Vaughan and Roger G. Krohn at Ohio State University in the mid-1960s; (2) John Horton, "Order and Conflict Theories of Social Problems as Competing Ideologies," *American Journal of Sociology* 71 (March 1966): 283–99; and (3) Werner Stark, *The Fundamental Forms of Social Thought* (Bronx, N.Y.: Fordham University Press, 1963).

48. Roger G. Krohn, *The Social Shaping of Science* (Westport, Conn.: Greenwood Publishing, 1971), pp. xvii–xviii.

49. Claude Levi-Strauss, *The Savage Mind* (Chicago: University of Chicago Press, 1966), p. 117.

50. Karl Marx, *A Contribution to the Critique of Political Economy* (Chicago: Kerr, 1904), pp. 11–12.

51. Jules Henry, *Culture Against Man* (New York: Vintage Books, 1963), pp. 30–31.

52. Dennis Wrong, "The Oversocialized Conception of Man in Modern Sociology," *American Sociological Review* 26 (April 1961): 183–93.

53. George Rawick, "The Historical Roots of Black Liberation," *Radical America* 2, no. 4 (July–August 1968): 2–5.

54. Horton, "Order and Conflict Theories."

55. Thomas Bottomore and Maximilien Rubel, eds., *Karl Marx: Selections From His Sociology and Social Philosophy* (New York: McGraw-Hill, 1964), p. 146.

56. Horton, "Order and Conflict Theories."

57. Gideon Sjoberg and Ted R. Vaughan, "The Sociology of Ethics and the Ethics of Sociologists," in *The Phenomenon of Sociology: A Reader in the Sociology of Sociology,* ed. Edward A. Tiryakian (New York: Appleton-Century-Crofts, 1971), pp. 273–375.

58. Gouldner, "Sociologist As Partisan," p. 107.

59. Ibid.

60. Noam Chomsky, *Language and Mind* (New York: Harcourt, 1968).

61. Levi-Strauss, *Savage Mind.*

PART I

The Master Institutions of Market Society

1

THE
ECONOMIC
INSTITUTION

Martin Glaberman
and
George P. Rawick

From Free Enterprise to the Welfare State

One distinctive characteristic of capitalism is that it is revolutionary. It does not develop slowly, evenly. It undergoes massive, irregular, rapid changes. As Marx and Engels wrote:

> The bourgeoisie cannot exist without completely revolutionizing the instruments of production, and thereby the relations of production, and with them the whole relations of society. . . . Constant revolutionizing of production, uninterrupted disturbance of all social conditions, everlasting uncertainty and agitation distinguish the bourgeois epoch from all earlier ones. All fixed, fast-frozen relations, with their train of ancient and venerable prejudices and opinions, are swept away, all new-formed ones become antiquated before they can ossify. All that is solid

melts into air, all that is holy is profaned, and man is at last compelled to face with sober senses his real conditions of life and his relations with his kind.[1]

It need hardly be noted that since these lines were written there has been no diminution of disturbance, uncertainty, and agitation. What does need to be discussed is the forms these disruptions have taken and the directions in which they have led. This implies that capitalism must be looked at historically, in its development, to be seen whole and in truth. The statistical summary and the sociological survey deal with facts that are quite transient and can thus lead to misleading conclusions.[2]

In this century, World War I provided the first major turning point, an international crisis so great that capitalism could not overcome it without substantial structural changes. In the United States, however, these were both concealed and delayed because one consequence of the crisis was to shift decisive power to the United States. A defeat for capitalism on a world scale thus appeared as a victory for one national capitalism. With the Great Depression, however, and immensely accelerated by the catastrophe of World War II, the tendencies inherent in the new stage of capitalism arose in increasing number.

Monopoly capitalism reached a climax in World War I. It is commonly said that this war provided the impetus for a technological revolution. In point of fact the working class always provide the impetus for a technological revolution: technological change is designed to cheapen or degrade or control or eliminate labor. Nevertheless, what the war made possible, because of the huge sums the government poured into research and production, was the capital accumulation that made the technological revolution a reality.

The development of the chemical industry was crucial both to the development of new products and the refinement of old ones. Combined with this was the harnessing of electric power which transformed the refining of ores for the metallurgical industries and the drilling of wells and refining of oil in the growing petroleum industry. The new technology resulted in substantial changes in the organization of production, that is, the relationships between human beings at the point of production. "Electricity made much more efficient the 'straight-line' system of production, the conveyer belt and the assembly line." [3]

The assembly line, key to industrial development in the 1920s and 1930s, is not simply a rational organization of work. It is above all a social relationship between classes. That relationship was best typified by the Ford Motor Company, masters of the assembly line. First, it was the prototype of totalitarian organization within the framework of the factory. Spies, secret police, and thought control all foreshadowed, within the limits of one huge factory and the city built around it, the total political-social-economic organization of fascism. Second, it was the much-publicized five-dollar day; that is, the new technology imposed a new level of exploitation upon the workers.[4] The workers responded with a resistance that in turn produced more rational and totally organized repression. At the same time, the new level of exploitation made possible the higher wage and living standard that has become the hallmark of the American worker.

But the contradiction is not overcome that simply. We were talking, not of development, but of crisis. And the crisis consisted in part in the fact that social control of the working class and accumulation of the necessary capital got beyond the capacity, not only of Henry Ford, the last of the free enterprisers, but even of such newer monopolies as General Motors, U.S. Steel, and Du Pont. What began in World War I and attained momentum in the next major crisis, the worldwide depression of the 1930s, was the shift from monopoly capitalism to state capitalism.

Even so careful and, in Marxist terms, orthodox an observer as Lenin was aware of the shift, and soon after the publication of his classic work on monopoly capitalism, *Imperialism*,[5] he was writing of state-monopoly capitalism and state capitalism.[6] Writing half a century after the first volume of *Capital* was published, Lenin found sufficient changes within the framework of capitalism to call it a new stage. It would be a contradiction of Lenin's most fundamental beliefs to pretend that, over a half-century later, no further significant changes had taken place.

With much less precision and perception the ideologists of capitalism worked their way to an understanding of what was happening. The innovator was John Maynard Keynes who became the theorist of welfare-state capitalism.[7] He was followed in this country by the economists and social theorists of the New Deal—Adolph A. Berle, Gardiner C. Means, and their heirs and assigns such as Galbraith, Heilbroner, and many others. Berle noted:

> In reality, [the American] economy is organized and is controlled, though until recently this fact has received surprisingly little public attention.
>
> Pulling together and establishing control over the economic forces by which the United States has been propelled were largely the result of initiatives taken by President Franklin D. Roosevelt in 1933. Upon the base he laid, an institutional structure was erected. Existence of the structure was formally recognized by the Congress of the United States when it passed the Employment Act of 1946.[8]

It should be noted before we proceed that the crucial weakness of bourgeois ideology is not that it cannot see significant change after it has taken place. The weakness lies in the fact that it assumes each change to be the last—the final adjustment that will henceforth assure eternal stability. This is discussed further later on in this chapter. First, we must document "pulling together and establishing control."

People tend to forget how relatively recent was the acquisition by the federal government of substantial power to manage the economy. Gardiner C. Means indicates that the program of Roosevelt's first hundred days was of crucial significance.[9]

> Probably the most basic single reform was that of the monetary system and the establishment of monetary management by government. To this end, bank deposits were guaranteed; gold was drawn from the bankers and the public into the hands of government; monetary banking was separated from investment banking; money in the economy was released from rigid internal relation to gold by the abrogation of the gold clause in public and private debts; the domestic economy was separated from a rigid relation to the world economy by the abandonment of the gold standard and the rejection of the stabilization proposals of the London Economic Conference. . . . What is immediately important is that this basic reform of our monetary system made monetary management a practical instrument of government.[10]

Going off the gold standard did not, of course, end the dependence of money on gold and the determination of the value of gold in production as divulged by the international gold market. But it did make that dependence more distant and indirect and thus gave the American (and other) governments some room to maneuver. Related to the substantial monetary reform was a reform in the credit structure, again involving massive intervention by the federal government in the control of credit and in the determination of the availability of credit.

Establishment of the principle of federal responsibility for a system of social security took longer to make good in practice but became a significant instrument for control of the economy. (Roosevelt even manipulated the Works Progress Administration [WPA] rolls to swing elections, padding the rolls in the weeks before election day and slashing them brutally after the votes were in.)

The massive intervention in agriculture on all levels had far-reaching consequences. Crop control, financial subsidies, and other supports were but one element. Another was to make the government the prime accumulator of capital in an industry in which the units of production were too small to have any effect. Rural electrification, the Tennessee Valley Authority (TVA), and the building of the great dams in the western United States transformed the technological basis of agriculture; it made possible the introduction of machinery on a large scale and the exclusion of manual labor. A third element was the extension of the functions of land grant colleges, the colleges of agriculture and engineering, providing the "research and development" that highly centralized basic industry arranges to some extent for itself. (Research and development now depends in greater measure on governmental resources than ever before—particularly in those fields that reflect the new stage of capitalist technology, atomic energy and electronics. The contradiction with the outmoded ideology of free enterprise was overcome by the overwhelmingly military context of most research. This development transformed American colleges from simply training centers for the managerial elite to integral components of capitalist production.)[11]

Fundamental changes in American agriculture resulted. Although the preamble to every bill passed by Congress to date referred to the objective of preserving the family farm, the reverse occurred. Farming was industrialized. Labor was reduced to an absolute minimum. Minimum capital requirements for farming rose to levels far beyond the means of the ordinary working-class or lower-middle-class family. The financial structure of the agriculture industry changed to the point that the term "tenant farming" was completely transformed in meaning. In the 1930s it used to be a sign of poverty; today it is a sign of wealth. The wealthy or corporate farmer rents his neighbor's land because his own capital is much more fruitfully invested in machinery than in land.

Hand in hand with control over money and credit the government began to use fiscal policy to achieve changes in employment, the market, production, etc. Taxation was no longer mainly for revenue; it also served for a variety of economic purposes.

> The social and economic legislation of the mid-1930s created, while preserving the rhetoric of a free enterprise system, what was in reality a mixed-enterprise system. And this process was accelerated in the 1940s, under the impetus of wartime controls, allocations, and regulations. . . . This process brought about a real ambiguity in concepts of private enterprise and enterprise that was, to use a formerly fashionable phrase, affected with a public interest. Thus, government began the process of regulation of such previously private matters as the manner in which a corporation could distribute its securities and raise its capital, of the manner in which it could hire and fire its employees and, on occasion, of the prices at which it could buy and sell—even whether and to whom it could sell. Much of that bundle of rights which constitutes private property was, by the end of the 1930s, substantially in the hands of the government. World War II, the Korean war, new concepts of the ability and indeed the duty of government to manage the economy, accelerated the process and dimmed the distinctions between the affairs of private business and those of government.[12]

"The public interest" is a most ambiguous phrase and should not be permitted to confuse the reality of what was happening. Brad Wiley has noted that "The New Deal era represented the beginning of a decisive shift in both the extent and nature of government intervention in the market." [13] But he makes it very clear that this did not succeed in ending unemployment and solving the human problems of the depression:

Thus if the New Deal neither promoted economic recovery nor established as permanent practice the new fiscal role of government in the economy, what was the significance of the Roosevelt programs mentioned earlier with respect to these occurrences? What the New Deal did accomplish was to establish the political precedent that legitimated the new economic function of government. More concretely it established the administrative machinery and pool of personnel and techniques necessary to run the new kind of government. Among other things this meant turning to the universities and professionals to staff the new agencies and bureaus. What the New Deal did then, rather than to promote recovery, was to provide the iedological and technical basis for government participation in the wartime and postwar recovery of the economy.[14]

What began as a response to the crisis of the Great Depression was further developed in response to the crisis of World War II. The government assumed direct control over production, a control it never entirely relinquished in the postwar years. And what is in some ways equally significant, worldwide changes in popular temper forced the codification of wartime governmental planning into peacetime objectives, such as full employment and growth in national productivity, which would have been unheard of only a few years before.

Andrew Shonfield has summarized some of the features of Western capitalism in the postwar years:

1. There is the vastly increased influence of the public authorities on the management of the economic system. This operates through different mechanisms in different countries: in one the control of the banking system is decisive, in another it is the existence of a wide sector of publicly controlled enterprise. In all of them the government's expenditure has been enormously enlarged and determines directly a large segment of each nation's economic activities.

2. The preoccupation with social welfare leads to the use of public funds on a rising scale. . . .

3. In the private sector the violence of the market has been tamed. . . .

5. The characteristic attitude in large-scale economic management, both inside government and in the private sector,

which has made itself increasingly felt during the postwar period, is the pursuit of intellectual coherence. Its most obvious manifestation is in long-range national planning.[15]

To be sure, the theorists of state capitalism overreach themselves. Shonfield says: "Governments have therefore been given time to learn how to intervene with increasing skill, without causing disaster in the course of educating themselves." [16] Not quite. The planning skills and sophisticated institutions of France under de Gaulle were not adequate to prevent the catastrophe (for French capitalism) of the revolt of 1968.

The internal changes in American and Western capitalism were paralleled by external changes. The forms, although not the essence, of imperialism do change. The basic changes are two: investment and politics.

Changes in the movement of capital were indicated by Michael Barratt Brown.

> In previous periods the whole capital movement has been private, but today about half of the $12 billion movement of the last few years has been public—loans and aid both of governments and of the international institutions. Most of the public capital has gone to the developing lands, but less than a half of the gross movement of private capital: and the private capital movement has been growing faster in the past five years.[17]

> An important part of the recent flow of funds has consisted of Government aid and loans. This has amounted to about a third of the total for Britain and nearly two thirds for the United States. Of the private investment only a small part is now portfolio investment by private individuals—about 12 per cent in Britain, 20 per cent in the U.S.A. The rest of the private investment (today more than half) is direct investment and reinvestment by companies in their subsidiaries overseas. This is the significant new development.[18]

Robert L. Heilbroner summarized the changes in American economic imperialism:

> In 1897, 59 percent of American foreign direct investment was in agriculture (plantations), mining, or railways; by 1969 this figure had dropped to 11 percent. Conversely, in 1897 only 15

percent of our overseas direct investment was in manufacturing; this has jumped to over 40 percent today. . . . In 1897, 54 percent of our overseas direct investment was in the underdeveloped parts of the world, the remainder in the European-Canadian developed areas. Today the balance has swung the other way. Sixty-four percent of our foreign direct investment is now in Canada, Europe, and Oceania and only 36 percent in Asia, Africa, and Latin America. More striking, of the increase in American foreign direct investment during the last decade, almost three-quarters was located in the developed world.[19]

These economic changes have interesting consequences in military and diplomatic policy that should not be too difficult to detect. The marines no longer land solely to protect American private investments. They are now called upon to land anywhere in the world where American capitalism *in general,* that is, in its abstracted, stratified form, feels threatened, directly or indirectly.

Political changes add another dimension to the problem of imperialism. The basic political fact of the post-World War II world has been the colonial revolution, the achievement of national independence by most nations of the world. The consequences of this are manifold and contradictory. Methods of imperialism that were generally successful in the years before World War I have had to be revised considerably. Even though independence is very often political only, and does not extend to economic and social independence, yet the movement as a whole has weakened imperialism and lessened its flexibility, if only by bringing millions of formerly silent people into the international political arena. As indicated earlier, however, the general weakening of imperialism is concealed (at least for Americans) by the fact that the United States has replaced the more traditional imperialist powers as the overwhelming world-imperialist power.

The indoctrination of American intellectuals with the ideology that social science consists of "the counting of things" has left most of them unprepared to understand how the nose of American imperialism, the most powerful in history, can be tweaked by communists in Asia or colonels in South America. The weakness in methodology which makes it impossible for the American academic community to understand peasant movements is only an extension of its inability to see its own working class. The theorists of welfare-state capitalism (or corporate liberalism, if you prefer) begin with two abstract categories, private enterprise and government. Since forms of ownership or control are decisive to them, they interpret the movement from "private enterprise" (a social form that is never private and rarely enterprising) to government regulation and control as a movement of substance and, therefore, as a way to overcome the admitted weaknesses and difficulties of capitalism. They never stop to think that "private enterprise" is a relationship between people[20] and the movement to another form of ownership or control may change the form without changing the substance.[21] According to this ideology, "private enterprise" is not subject to popular control and is therefore bad; government is subject to popular control and is therefore good.

Radical economists have done their share to contribute to the mythology of capitalism by their uncritical acceptance of the distinction between the "public" and "private" sectors. Within carefully defined limits, of course, the distinction has validity. But "public" is one of those ambiguous words that seems to mean "for the public good." And that is something else again. On the one hand, there is nothing private about private enterprise. As Marx noted many years before the appearance of the huge modern international corporation, production is *social*. Even the division of profits is social and is the consequence of many factors, of which ownership is only one. One must be careful, however, not to confuse "social" with socialistic or democratic or majority or any other such irrelevant term.

On the other hand, there is nothing public about the public sector. Unless, of course you accept as gospel your high school civics textbook, nothing about the modern capitalist state should lead anyone to believe that it is anything other than capitalist. In other words, the "public" of the public sector should not be confused with the American public of more than 200 million souls. It is the much more limited public of the collectivity of the American capitalist class. Everything else is appearance only, and is intended so to be. To put it differently, the Philadelphia Navy Yard, for most purposes, is rather less public than General Motors, or, at any rate, no more public. The governmental sector of the economy and the government as a whole *tends* (and only tends) to speak with the relatively unanimous voice of American capitalism. The nongovernmental sector *tends* (and only tends) to be somewhat more fragmented and more representative of the divisions within the capitalist class. The divisions within the capitalist class are of considerable interest to the capitalists themselves. These are divisions of profits, of power, and of points of view. But these divisions should be of only minor interest to the rest of us.

In *Imperialism* Lenin disputed Kautsky, the German social democrat, for calling imperialism a *policy* of the capitalist state, rather than a *stage* of capitalism. There is an implication of the reformist Kautskian viewpoint in the neo-Marxian insistence that power goes only one way, that the corporations control the state with no element of the reverse being true. The implication, of course, is that the state, as such, is neutral. Remove the control of the corporations and the capitalist state can become the instrument of the people. Such decisions as whether a contract goes to Boeing or Lockheed, or whether Lockheed, largest of the defense contractors, survives at all, are *political* decisions that used to be made in corporate boardrooms.

Lost is the concept, well-buttressed by facts, that class rule was never limited to the ownership of property, has always involved control of the state, and has never depended on the physical, mental, or financial well-being of any or all members of the ruling class.[22] The nationalization of British coal or French automobile plants or Peruvian oil may have made particular capitalists unhappy; it may even have destroyed some. But it did not change class relations where they matter—at the point of production.

The American Working Class

We must retrace our steps to get rid of some crucial distortions in the picture thus far.

At the turn of this century, when the giant monopolies were being formed (Standard Oil in 1899, U.S. Steel in 1901) they represented more than the simple pooling of financial resources to destroy competition. These resources embodied technological improvements designed to eliminate some workers and to change the character of work, making the remaining workers, in Marx's famous phrase, "an appendage of a machine." [23] In the steel industry, for example, new processes—chemicals that could be measured more carefully and fuels that could be burned at more controllable levels—reduced the skill level of the steelworker. The master steelmaker no longer judged the quality of the steel or the timing of the process by his visual judgment of the molten metal's color. It was timed for him by a chemist and an engineer—or, more precisely, by a foreman.

This process occurred in all kinds of occupations, particularly basic industry. Always the new technology was described as making work easier. In a very narrow sense it did: work always became lighter physically and less demanding mentally. But it also, and inevitably, became more demanding, more demeaning, more degrading. In an auto engine plant in 1940 a worker had to wrestle with crankshafts that weighed over one hundred pounds and with engine blocks that weighed much more than that. But he could shut his machine off for a few minutes when he had to go to the toilet. On an automated line in 1970 a worker may lift no crankshafts and push no engine blocks—but he cannot go to the toilet without asking his foreman for permission and without having a relief man take his place on the line while he is gone.

The alienation of factory life is all-pervasive and has been well documented in sociological literature.[24] Even the press has been forced to acknowledge working-class alienation. *Time* informs its readers that "Western industry long ago disproved Karl Marx's prediction that the workingman would become ever poorer in a capitalistic state. [Quoting Marx accurately was never one of *Time*'s strong points.] But it has yet to prove wrong his less well remembered forecast that workers would become progressively more alienated from their jobs." [25] What has been less well documented is that alienation is not simply a passive resignation to exploitation. Life at the point of production is a constant struggle. What workers do (or are prepared to do), what managers do, what governments do—all are conditioned by the struggle that takes place on the shop floor.

The basic form of organization in production is totalitarian and hierarchical.[26] This is true in strong union shops as well as in open shops. The union contract and company rules combine to require of the industrial worker a kind of obedience that can otherwise be found only in kindergartens and prisons. You cannot enter or leave the plant without permission, except at shift change. You cannot leave your job without permission. You cannot leave your department. You cannot walk around the plant. Grown men have wet their pants because foremen would not give them time to go to the toilet. And in 90-degree weather men have been unable to get a drink between jobs because they could not reach the water cooler, 10 yards away.

> The American system of jurisprudence assumes innocence and the state must prove guilt. In industry it appears that the opposite is the case. Workers are required to submit to whatever decisions management may make, and only after having done so can they protest by filing a grievance.[27]

Where, then, is the affluent worker? Isn't the average worker ready to accept this exploitation in exchange for a house, a car, and a color television set? Or is this a modern myth?

To begin with, affluence is not payment for suffering. It is payment for struggle. To the extent that American workers share in the goods produced by this society, it is the result of massive battles and continuous wars, going back over a hundred years, marked by violence, looting, destruction, strikes large and small, on a level that puts the record of any other major industrial country to shame.

In addition, the increased living standards of American workers do not in any sense reduce the level of exploitation. The proportion the American worker receives of the value he produces has steadily declined. What that value can buy has gone up because of a technology that reduces the value of all commodities. As a result, although money wages have increased over the years and real wages have also increased, by cheapening commodities, relative wages (i.e., relative to what workers produce) have declined.[28]

It might be well at this point to dispose of an almost universally held fiction that a relationship exists between wages and productivity, that wages can increase only to the degree that productivity increases. This view is put forward by economists, by management, by government, and by labor leaders. Even apart from this overwhelming weight of authority, it *seems* reasonable. After all, where else are higher wages to come from if not from increased productivity? The answer, of course, is from profits. But the theory has one justification —pegging wage increases to increased productivity (speedup) justifies the contract deals by which labor leaders barter increased discipline over the workers for financial benefits. The alleged relationship between wages and productivity is false in theory and false in fact. Without massive struggles, workers' wage increases tend to fall behind gains in productivity. With massive struggles, wages rise far beyond what productivity gains would indicate. In the late 1930s, for example, general gains in workers' wages (both nominal and real) had no relation to productivity whatever. Workers simply took by force a larger share of the pie, that is, of the total value they produced. And that is where wage increases always come from: the share of the total product of labor which had previously been appropriated by capital.

But the class struggle that determines the nature of life at the point of production is infinitely more complex than a battle over dollars and cents and fringe benefits. In times of rapid technological change, such as the period before World War I or the period of substantial automation in the 1950s, the working class becomes transformed. It is not simply that particular workers lose their skills. Numbers of workers are thrown out of the working class altogether; new workers are brought in to replace them. Old plants are shut down; new plants are built to accommodate the new technology and the new workers.

As a result, associations built up among workers over the years are broken; knowledge gained about the intricacies of production become outdated. New associations have to be formed, new knowledge accumulated. That is what class consciousness is about, and it is not something one is born with by virtue of having working-class parents. Labor under capitalism, as Marx often noted, is cooperative; this is what imposes class solidarity on workers, not as an absolute, not in all times and all places, but as an overriding tendency. And the greater the technological advances made, the greater is the required cooperation. It should be carefully noted that this cooperation is not a voluntary attribute of the workers (which can as easily be withdrawn) but an objective attribute of the process of production. It should also be noted that cooperation in the process of production concerns the manipulation of *things*. It never concerns the manipulation of *people*—one of the most corrupting forms of work in capitalist society.

After they enter a factory, workers find out about one another:

who is glib and good at negotiating, who is strong and brave and good at blocking a plant gate or beating up a scab, who is astute as a tactician, who is a public speaker, etc. Workers also find out about the work process and the equipment: it is there to control them but it is always possible to turn the tables. In production on an individual machine, the worker finds out what makes it run. The same elementary investigation also tells him what makes it stop running. So the worker is able to have the machine running as smoothly as possible to make the work more manageable—or he can arrange for the machine to break down when he needs an extra break or is harassing a foreman.

Transfer the situation to the intense cooperation of an assembly line and two changes tend to take place. It takes a little longer for workers to begin to sabotage the line for an occasional rest period because they have to be sure of those who are working around them. But the control and the struggle is moved to a wider arena than that afforded by one worker on one machine. The control can easily extend beyond the confines of one plant. In 1969 there was a wildcat strike at the Sterling Stamping Plant of the Chrysler Corporation, fifteen miles outside Detroit. The workers on the picket line were aware of the dependence of Chrysler plants around the country and abroad on their production. They knew that on the first day of their strike three main plants in Detroit would also have to shut down; on the second day, the Windsor, Ontario, plant; on the third day, the plant in St. Louis. And so on.

The description of certain kinds of rank-and-file action introduces new elements into the picture.

> I don't know if anybody has participated in a wildcat strike. Working class democracy, working class action, is a very unique and distinctive thing. It takes several forms. One of the forms which is very frequent, and the kind that short wildcats usually take is that you're working on a machine or on a line and you see some people coming down the aisle heading toward the time clock. And you look up, and it isn't lunch time and it isn't quitting time and there are too many people to be going to the tool crib. So you know they're leaving the plant. So what you do, literally, is shut your machine. If you've got tools, you put them in your toolbox; you lock your box and you wipe your hands

and you walk out; you punch out. You have no idea what's happening, none whatsoever. All you know is that the plant's being struck; and the sight, visually, is fantastic. You see a factory melting away until the last man is out the door. Then you go outside and say, "What the hell's going on?" "Oh, such and such happened." And then you might say, "Well, great; it's about time. We've been taking this shit for too long." Or you might say, "What kind of nonsense is that? You mean you walked out for that?"

The point I'm getting at is when you get outside you might find that you support the strike or you oppose the strike, but the basic characteristic of the working class is that first you strike. Unless everybody strikes, there's no meaningful action. . . .

But there's a peculiar element in that. To shut your machine down in full confidence that everybody else is, is not an instinct that you're born with. When you get out of the womb, you don't know how to run a wildcat strike. It comes from a long period of experience in a particular plant, a knowledge of the particular form of production, of your particular workmates on the whole and what you can expect of them and what they can expect of you. . . . You've got to know all of these things. And it takes a long time to develop, because it's not developed in terms of formal education; it's developed in terms of living experience.[29]

The American worker is the most intensely exploited worker in the industrial world. The rates of production he is required to accept, the tensions, the alienation he is subjected to, have no equivalent elsewhere. In this context, to treat the American worker as if he has been bought off by a house in the suburbs, a car, and a television set is not simply to ignore the reality of the deadly class struggle that is a feature of factory life. It is to treat him as an inferior being, incapable of human feelings and responses. To a British worker at the beginning of the nineteenth century the fact that he lived in a miserable hovel was all of one piece with the fact that he worked twelve hours a day in a dark, miserable plant. But to a man or woman who can see the physical reality of what modern society can provide—what kind of sense can it make to enter that plant every morning for the rest of his life to be subjected to that totalitarian system?

The totalitarian tendency of capitalist production cannot be separated from the resistance of the working class.[30] This resistance takes historically recognizable forms.

> A whole new layer of workers, the result of the economic development, burst into revolt in the CIO. The CIO in its inception aimed at a revolution in production. The workers would examine what they were told to do and then decide whether it was satisfactory to them or not. This rejection of the basis of capitalist economy is the preliminary basis of a socialist economy. The next positive step is the total management of industry by the proletariat. . . .
>
> Because it was not and could not be carried through to a conclusion, the inevitable counterpart was the creation of a labor bureaucracy. The history of production since is the corruption of the bureaucracy and its transformation into an instrument of capitalist production, the restoration to the bourgeoisie of what it had lost in 1936, the right to control production standards. Without this mediating role of the bureaucracy, production in the United States would be violently and continuously disrupted until one class was undisputed master. . . .
>
> The bureaucracy inevitably must substitute the struggle over consumption, higher wages, pensions, education, etc., for a struggle in production. This is the basis of the welfare state, the attempt to appease the workers with the fruits of labor when they seek satisfaction in the work itself. The bureaucracy must raise a new social program in the realm of consumption because it cannot attack capitalism at the point of production without destroying capitalism itself.[31]

The changing relationships in production result in changing forms of organization as old forms become transformed into their opposite. Craft unions are superseded by industrial unions. But these in turn become bastions of capitalism. The process is often very deceptive and leaves its participants in confusion.

The putting of stewards and committeemen on full time on the shop floor, for example, was an early objective of worker-militants. It was intended to prevent discrimination against union spokesmen by foremen who isolated militant stewards and gave them the worst jobs. On full time a steward could patrol his district and see that contract provisions weren't violated. From a means of making the steward available to the workers, however, full-time union representation was transformed into a means of making representation unavailable to the workers. Committeemen wandered around the plant, even left the plant, and were much more difficult to find when needed than were foremen. What began as protection of the committeeman from the company ended as protection of the committeeman from the workers.

A similar transformation is evident in the dues check-off, originally intended to remove company pressure from the union. Foremen in the early union days made it difficult for stewards to collect union dues and encouraged the lazy and the cowardly not to pay dues. Under the check-off, the company deducts union dues from each worker's paycheck and turns a lump sum over to the union every month. From a means of avoiding company pressure on the union, the check-off has become a means of avoiding rank-and-file pressure on the union, for it is no longer possible for a worker to air his beefs when the steward comes around to collect his dues each month. No one cares what the worker thinks anymore.

But the basic transformation has occurred in the contract itself. Originally the document in which the victories of the workers were recorded, it has become the document under which the worker is disciplined. The more detailed the worker's rights, the more specific have become his duties—above all, the duty to obey the company rules. It is possible to document how, as the union contract has become longer, more detailed, and more legalistic, the union representative has changed from a rank-and-file militant to a legalistic politician. The legalistic intricacies of the modern labor contract call for specific talents to service the disputes it engenders. Militancy is not one of those talents.

The increased bureaucratization of the union hierarchy, the changing personnel that has increasingly separated itself from the rank-and-file worker, is not particularly a matter of subjective ill will. Even the most militant shop steward finds himself enforcing the union contract, that is, disciplining workers when they get out of line. The result has been the transfer of the fundamental division between capital and labor into the organizations of labor themselves. More and more, the gulf between workers and union leaders widens. Workers increasingly look elsewhere than to the union for any serious attempt to grapple with their fundamental problems. They are experimenting with new forms of organization to bypass the restraining force of the union.

The most common form of struggle is the wildcat strike, the incidence of which has risen in the years since World War II. The pressure of the wildcat strike has in turn forced an increase in the number of legal, authorized strikes as union leaderships run to keep in front of their members and desperately seek to avoid losing control altogether.[32] The first signs of organizational forms that go beyond the traditional union caucuses have also begun to appear. In the Detroit area (and spreading to other parts of the country) the League of Revolutionary Black Workers has been organizing directly on the shop floor and has called strikes in its own name.

It is difficult to judge when working class practice at the point of production learned to by-pass the union structure in dealing with its problems, and to substitute (in bits and pieces) a new organizational form. It was clear to me, with my year stay in an auto motor plant (Detroit area, 1968), that the process had been long underway. What I find crucial to understand is that while sabotage and other forms of independent workers' activity had existed before (certainly in the late Nineteenth Century and with the Wobbly period), that which exists today is unique in that it follows mass unionism and is a definite response to the obsolescence of that social form. The building of a new form of organization today by workers is the outcome of attempts, here and there, to seize control of various aspects of production. These forms are beyond unionism; they are only secondarily concerned with the process of negotiation, while unionism made that its central point. Just as the CIO was created as a form of struggle by workers, so, out of necessity, that form is being by-passed and destroyed now, and a new organizational form is being developed in its place. . . .

There is planning and counter-planning in the plant because there is clearly a situation of dual power. A regular phenomenon in the daily reality of the plant is the substitution of entirely different plans for carrying out particular jobs in place of the rational plans organized by management.

On the very casual level, these substitutions involve, for example, a complete alternative break system of workers whereby they create large chunks of free time for each other on a regular basis. This plan involves a voluntary rotation of alternately working long stretches and taking off long stretches. Jobs are illegally traded off, and men relieve each other for long periods to accomplish this. The smuggling of men through different areas of the plant to work with friends is yet another regular activity requiring no small amount of organization. . . .

The coexistence of two distinct sets of relations, two modes of work, and two power structures in the plant is evident to the worker who becomes part of any of the main plant areas. But that co-existence is the object of constant turmoil and strife; it is hardly an equilibrium when considered over time. It is a struggle of losing and gaining ground. The attempt to assert an alternative plan of action on the part of workers is a constant threat to management. . . .

Within these new independent forms of workers' organization lies a foundation of social relations at the point of production which can potentially come forward to seize power in a crisis situation and give new direction to the society.[33]

Poverty and Crisis

We have thus far assumed the validity of the claim that the American working class is affluent. Our purpose was twofold: (1) we wanted to emphasize the decisive importance of production and the position held by the working class in society as a consequence of its position in the process of production; and (2) we were concerned that the revolutionary impulses that exist in the working class not be sought in terms of poverty and despair but in terms of the nature of work under capitalism. Having said that, however, it is necessary to state categorically that poverty and unemployment are problems that capitalism has been unable to solve.

In 1933 Franklin D. Roosevelt noted that one-third of the nation was ill housed, ill clothed, and ill fed. Forty years later, years that saw the acquisition and use by the federal government of tremendous economic power, the situation is essentially the same as it was at the beginning of the Great Depression.

In a 1964 report, the President's Council of Economic Advisers used a cash income of less than $3,000 in 1962 as a poverty line for families of two or more persons, and an income of less than $1,500 for unattached individuals living alone or with nonrelatives. The council estimated that between 33 million and 35 million Americans were by this standard living at or below the boundary of poverty.

Economist Leon H. Keyserling established a baseline of less than $4,000 for families (in 1960 dollars) and less than $2,000 per year for unattached individuals. In addition, Keyserling realistically added a category of "deprivation," those who lived in a constant situation of economic insecurity, unable to meet adequate living standards and as a result living a marginal social existence. Much of the latter, we might add, is dedicated to the struggle to avoid slipping farther down, through males taking additional jobs, moonlighting, or through women accepting low-paying jobs (even though most of their wages have to go for baby-sitters) to bring in a margin of income that will mean the automobile or washing machine or television will not be repossessed. Keyserling estimated 77 million Americans lived in families comprising these two categories in 1960—about 38 percent of the total population.

Poverty is not spread equally across the population. The aged, families headed by women, nonwhites, and rural-farm families bear a heavy share of poverty. In 1960, 39.6 percent of families headed by someone over 65 had incomes of less than $2,500; 70.5 percent of such families were below $5,500. In 1960, 38 percent of families headed by a female had incomes of less than $2,500; 70.9 percent of such families were below $5,500. In 1960, 28.6 percent of nonwhite families had incomes of less than $2,500; 70.9 percent of such families were below $5,500. In 1960, 34.5 percent of rural-farm families had incomes of less than $2,500; 71 percent of such families were below $5,500. The situation for nonwhites has been steadily worsening. In 1959 nonwhites comprised slightly more than one-fourth of the poor; in 1966, about one-third were poor; by 1970, close to 40 percent were poor. The percentage of the poor found among the aged and rural-farm families remained roughly constant from 1960 to 1970; the number of poor families headed by females increased slightly.

While many of the poor suffer from chronic unemployment and are aged, women, and nonwhites, a large number of the poor in America, contrary to popular belief, are hard-working people employed full-time or nearly full-time. Nearly one-third of all families living in poverty in 1964 were headed by a person who worked 50–52 weeks a year at a full-time job. If we concentrate only on families headed by males under sixty-five, the percentage of poverty families with a fully employed person comes close to 50 percent. And if we include among the working poor those who work an average of 35 weeks per year, and exclude the aged and families headed by women, close to 70 percent of all poverty families can be accounted for in any typical year. Unemployment, of course, compounds the problem.

> Over 11 million American workers were jobless and looking for work at some time during the prosperous year 1966. This was almost four times the average number (2.9 million) unemployed in any one week of the year. The total number out of work during 1967 was probably somewhat higher. . . . About four times as many workers had 5 or more weeks without work during 1966 as is suggested by the monthly data. . . . Any complacency as to the limited impact of extended unemployment among men in the central age groups, who are generally the most employable and have the heaviest family responsibilities, should be ended by these data. Close to 1.3 million men aged 25 to 44 had 5 or more weeks of unemployment during 1966, almost six times the number (226,000) shown by the monthly surveys. . . . Clearly, the number of men of prime working age who are severely affected by joblessness is much higher than is indicated by the monthly unemployment data. And, to a lesser degree, the same is true for women.[34]

Nonwhites make up a much larger proportion of the unemployed than do whites. Blacks account for about 25 percent of the long-term unemployed although they are only 11 percent of the workforce. There has been no significant improvement in this situation in the past decade. In many areas fully 40 percent of young black men are to be counted at all times among the long-term unemployed. Some do not even show up in the official unemployment figures because they have given up actively seeking work.

Statistics for poverty and unemployment cannot convey any conception of the quality of life involved, the costs to human beings, or the fact that in most social services (medical services, education, transportation) American capitalism provides the poor considerably less than any other major capitalist power. Even financial and monetary costs are higher for the poor. It has been estimated that for the poor as much as 50 percent of income goes toward taxes (income, sales, property, excise, etc.) making a mockery of the whole concept of graduated income taxes. Added to that are the inordinate costs of credit for those whose economic existence is largely marginal.

While there is no doubt that one's chance of being poor is greatly increased if he is part of a household headed by an aged person, a woman, a nonwhite, an ill or disabled individual, or someone with poor education and few job skills, poverty as a social reality is not caused by old age, by desertion, by separation or divorce, by death of the breadwinner, by being nonwhite, by being ill and disabled, or by lack of education and job skills. If everyone who headed a family was white, male, between the ages of twenty-five and fifty-five, in good health and physical condition, with a college education and adequate social and job skills, virtually the same amount of poverty would exist as there is at present. There would also be the same number of auto workers, car-wash workers, street cleaners, etc. Items such as age, sex, race, health, and education only help to determine which particular individuals will be poor; they have little, if anything, to do with the fact that the American economic and political system has as a central feature the poverty or near-poverty of at least two-fifths of the nation.

Constant poverty combined with cyclical crises during which unemployment and the problems of unemployment become catastrophic are an inherent feature of American capitalism. Marx drew as a major conclusion of his study of capital the existence and growth of "an industrial reserve army." This is not the same as the unemployed. It includes people who in a sane society would take a normal part in the useful activities of that society but who are excluded from such activity under capitalism. Women are the major such category, closely followed by the nonwhite population and by the young. Sometimes consciously, sometimes unconsciously, the industrial reserve army is manipulated so as to be both controlled (i.e., not a source of serious unrest) and available when needed. At the beginning of World War II, for example, women were urged to imitate "Rosie the Riveter" and enter the world of industrial production. As soon as the war ended, all the resources of governmental, educational, entertainment, and journalistic institutions were directed to convincing women that their place was in the home. A similar phenomenon has, over the past few generations, tended to raise the age of independent employment for the young, with growing emphasis on schools that act both as prisons for the unruly and trainers of surplus workers and technicians. During World War II, 50,000 American Indians were enticed into war production and then forced out when they were no longer needed. Work camps, the army, welfare agencies, and the like all act as organizers of the industrial reserve army.

Although in the immediate sense, poverty is caused by low or no wages for the individual poor, it is important to understand that unemployment and depressions are not caused by the inability of workers to buy back what they produce (the classic theory of underconsumptionism). Marx developed his theory of crises in *Capital*, assuming throughout that all commodities produced were sold. Why, then, are there crises and unemployment? As we noted earlier, all technological improvement is directed against the working class. The basic drive of capitalism, and the reason for its fantastic ability to expand productivity, is the drive to expand means of production at the expense of living workers, to replace workers with machines. As a result, the most characteristic and crucial industries in capitalist society are the industries that produce production goods, so-called heavy industry, rather than consumer-goods industries. (Some industries, such as the auto industry, straddle the two areas in producing "heavy" consumer goods.)

A glance at American industry will show where the overwhelming bulk of large-scale capital is invested—and, to be specific, overinvested. It is in metals, mining, machinery, and the like. In the area of capital-goods production there is an inherent tendency toward overproduction. The Great Depression started, not in consumer-goods industries, but in steel, which was the first industry to be hit by large-scale layoffs. Workers in clothing, food processing, and related consumer-goods industries did not feel the layoffs until after steel, machine tooling, building, and other industries that primarily serve the needs of capital expansion were hit. The depression of 1970–71 in Detroit has devastated the tool and die industry. It is capital expansion that suffers first.

To put the matter another way: capital does not expand to increase the number of commodities available to society (although that may be a consequence of expansion) but to increase productivity. The very function and purpose of expansion of capital is to get rid of workers. The only thing that prevents this from being an absolute and continuing catastrophe is the relative expansion of population and of markets and the appearance of new needs and new industries. In this context, war production acts as a safety valve since it is entirely waste production. But this must be modified by the inevitable side-product of war production—advances in technology which ultimately hasten the process of increasing the industrial reserve army.

The new planning and other economic powers of government can organize unemployment in a more sophisticated way and can level, to some degree, the extremes of the business cycle. But as long as the prime object and purpose of capitalism is the expansion of capital (i.e., profit, in its total Marxist sense) it cannot do away with the vast areas of poverty and with the specific problems of unemployment, underemployment, insecurity, and starvation.

Some of the limits are indicated by Appalachia:

> Pockets of hunger remain in the hollows of Appalachia despite the Nixon Administration's pledge to put an end to hunger and malnutrition, and after nearly a decade of massive Federal aid to the distressed region.
>
> Ten years ago, the coal counties of West Virginia, eastern Kentucky and western Virginia—the core of Appalachia—were on the brink of disaster. Tens of thousands of idle miners and their families faced starvation.
>
> Today, bigger Social Security payments, black lung benefits and a vastly expanded food stamp program have enabled most of the poor to stave off hunger and to subsist in cheerless deprivation.
>
> Yet thousands of families lack even enough money for food stamps. And the school lunch program, which provides free or reduced-price lunches to 6.6 million needy children throughout the nation, does not reach another estimated one million to three million children who need it.[35]

Anyone who thinks that this problem cannot be solved because of the money being spent on the Vietnam war is practicing simple self-deception. Poverty, like imperialist war, goes back a long way before Vietnam, and both will continue as long as capitalism exists.

Capital and Labor

In the 1950s a major offensive against the American working class was launched under the name of automation. It was the period of technological innovation. Old concentrations of workers (such as the huge Rouge plant of the Ford Motor Company) were broken up or reduced. New plants were built embodying the new technology. Wage increases and fringe benefits were regularly won by the leaders of the great industrial unions. But the democratic heritage, which some of them had still maintained, was rapidly eroded. The unions became one-party states. Union contracts extended regimentation and control over the membership and a discipline rivaling that of preunion days began to appear in the plants across the nation.

This was the period when theories about the disappearance of the working class or theories about the "new" working class first appeared.[36] In point of fact, the industrial working class did not decline in size, although it did decline in numbers relative to the population as a whole. Infinitely more crucial than size was the fact that the industrial working class still resided at the points of production and transportation and communication and thus could exert effective control in areas decisive for all of society.

One factor that those who predicted the imminent disappearance of the working class failed to recognize was the inability of capitalism to solve its own problems. The technological development of capitalism poses for the capitalists a problem of size. The masses of capital required to implement the new technology fully are simply not available. Marx indicated this problem when he developed his theory of the falling rate of profit.[37] This theory holds that all value and therefore all surplus value (profit) is produced by labor. The more technologically advanced capitalism becomes, the greater the proportion of nonvalue-producing constant capital (means of production) required to put relatively lesser amounts of variable capital (labor) in motion. Since the rate of profit is determined by the ratio of profit (surplus value) to total investment (constant plus variable capital), as the proportion of constant capital continues to rise, so the rate of profit must tend to fall. Since total amounts continue to grow, this does not mean that the mass of profit declines—only that the rate gets smaller. Nor does Marx treat this as an absolute—he records various countertendencies which can slow up or reverse the process. But he states that in the long run the tendency of the rate of profit to fall will assert itself.

This theory has been the source of considerable debate among Marxists and between Marxists and non-Marxists. Attempts have been made to prove its validity and attempts have been made to disprove its validity. The fact is that the theory is not statistically verifiable and was not intended to be. Marx's category of profit is equal to the total surplus value, that is, to all that is produced and not returned to the workers, no matter how it is used in the short or long run (e.g., taxes, legal fees or salaries, advertising costs, depreciation). This is not the place to get into that controversy. Suffice it to say that Marx's theory of the falling rate of profit remains entirely valid as a theoretical or conceptual tool. The mass of capital employed to achieve a certain mass of profit must be constantly enlarged. What that critical mass must be will vary with the technological makeup of each particular industry.

For example, when the auto industry embarked on substantial automation in the 1950s, some industrial giants found themselves unable to maintain the pace. Packard, Hudson Motors, Murray Body, giants in most other contexts, went down the drain. Hudson is now a huge parking lot for a complex of Chrysler plants and the Packard plant has become a network of stores, warehouses, and small factories. One effect of the shortage of capital that burdens modern capitalism is the tendency toward conglomerates. That tendency is in part the result of a search for greater stability which diversification can help produce. But it is also the result of the accumulation of masses of capital that are too small to be useful in basic industry but are adequate for other purposes such as financing hotel chains, book publishing, retail enterprises, and so forth. It is the basis for the contradictory phenomenon of the simultaneous capital shortage and surplus. But the shortage is more significant than the surplus. John F. Kennedy campaigned against the Republicans and the Eisenhower record on the issue of the shortage of capital, that is, on the failure of the American economy to grow at the rate required to maintain its international position.

Even the giants, for example, General Motors and Ford, could not automate the working class completely. Old concentrations of workers were scattered somewhat and a period of learning, of trial and error, had to take place before workers could work out their response to the new relationships of production. But certain facts are now emerging. In an industry such as the auto industry, the new forms of production are more integrated, not less, and as a result smaller groups of workers now have greater power than ever before. In place of the huge concentrations of workers at the Rouge plant of Ford or the Dodge main plant of Chrysler (now Hamtramck Assembly) there are now such plants as the Sterling stamping plant of the Chrysler Corporation (just outside Detroit), the Mansfield, Ohio, stamping plant of General Motors, the Twinsburg, Ohio, stamping plant of Ford, none of them employing as many as ten thousand workers, yet each of them capable of shutting down the bulk of the work done in their corporations. Moreover, the workers involved are perfectly aware of their relationship to the flow of production and have, in each case, used their power. The technology that took stamping operations from the Dodge plant and the Chrysler plant and the Plymouth plant and concentrated it at Sterling reorganized the forms of workers' struggles, but it could not put an end to the fundamental relationships in production and the ability of workers to organize their struggles in a new framework.

The so-called new working class is in a similar position. The expansion of automation in banking, insurance, and in general office work has resulted in the expansion of clerical work. But it is clerical work of a new kind. The stenographer is now a dictaphone operator. The bookkeeper is now an IBM machine operator. Thousands upon thousands of these new workers are now indistinguishable from factory workers except that their jobs are cleaner and better lit. It is only a matter of time before consciousness catches up with objective reality.

That process of catching up has made itself evident in other industries. Nothing represents the "new" working class better than public utility workers. Gas, electric, and phone company workers have the security and prestige presumed to go with middle-class consciousness. They also suffer the difficulty of working in industries that are almost totally automated. The Bell System not too many years ago announced that automatic long-distance dialing had become general enough for the company thenceforth to be strikeproof. What has happened instead is that in every major utility strike in the Midwest in the last ten years there have been reports of violence, the cutting of wires, the dynamiting of valves and switches, and so on. The idea that workers will respond to a new technology by giving up whatever power they may have is a conception unique to employment managers and middle-class radicals. Utility workers have not yet felt the need to restore to their arsenal an old tactic—the sit-in. What company, no matter how automated, is impervious to that form of struggle, widely used in the 1930s and revived and polished by black students in the 1960s?

Social Class and Its Contradictions

No class, least of all any class in a society as huge and complex as the United States, is a simple homogeneous unit. All sorts of divisions and contradictions appear. The stratification of production has led to a fusion and interchange between national political figures and the apex of the corporate elite. The appearance of Rockefellers, Kennedys, Harrimans, and, on a lesser corporate level, Romney, Roosevelt, C. E. Wilson, McNamara, and the like in the political arena is evidence of two things: (1) the substantially greater importance of politics for business and finance, and (2) the most sophisticated spokesmen for capitalism have learned to look beyond the profit requirements of their own corporate holdings. The commonly used term, corporate liberalism, reflects that development but distorts its meaning. There is nothing liberal in the fact that the strategy and tactics of the capitalist class have finally left the eighteenth century and have been brought into some correspondence with the needs (of capitalism) of the twentieth.

Ever since the Civil War, the American political structure has been totally inadequate to the task of providing rational and reasonably efficient capitalist government. Its decentralization, balance of powers, and mythology of weak government place inordinate power in institutions such as the Senate (or, even more narrowly, the committees of the Senate) and the major political parties wherever the middle layers of the capitalist class are overrepresented. These layers (with the addition of some of the Neanderthal oil magnates) seem unable to see beyond their own narrow regional and corporate interests, leading to such hilarious contradictions as Vice-President Spiro Agnew denouncing the "eastern establishment" (i.e., the apex of corporate and financial power in the United States) for being too permissive and too liberal. It leads to the further contradiction of the New York financial community favoring a withdrawal from Vietnam to put an end to the constant drain—financial, political, and moral—of a war that is impossible to win while the next layers of the corporate elite, joined with the military hierarchy in the "military-industrial complex," press for the continuation of old-fashioned jingoism.

The contradictions within the capitalist class are real. The contradictions between politics and economics, between inherited political forms and the needs of a modern capitalist state, are also real. But they can be understood only as elements of a larger totality. C. Wright Mills was groping toward that reality in his conception of a power elite, that is, that American capitalism has developed new forms and that final power no longer rests with the corporation board rooms but is shared with the national executive. The proportions in various industries of production dependent on government order have been growing.

> In the United States at the end of the fifties more than nine tenths of final demand for aircraft and parts was on government, overwhelmingly military, account; as was nearly three fifths of the demand for non-ferrous metals; over half the demand for chemicals and electronic goods; over one third the demand for communications equipment and scientific instruments; and so on down a list of eighteen major industries one tenth or more of whose final demand stemmed from government procurement.[38]

The problems of Lockheed and Boeing are indications that some corporations, at least, despite their existence as independent corporate entities, are largely political creations of the federal government.

But it is not as customer that the power of the state is felt most

crucially. It is as investor of capital: in building plants and other facilities (or financing their construction); in financing the tremendous
expansion of higher education to train the fantastically great number
of technicians required by the new technology; in financing directly
by the government or indirectly through academic institutions the
research and development that private capital cannot manage; in
the vast systems of subsidies to most American industries; in the manipulation of credit and interest rates; in its intervention in labor relations—in all these and more the government approaches ever
closer to Engels' "ideal personification of the total national capital."
No one should be misled. The fact that air force generals and union
bureaucrats have been given a share of the power does not make that
power any less capitalist; it is still the power of the rulers over the
ruled.

The working class has its own share of contradictions. Divided
by skill, industry, region, age, sex, race, national origin, religion—it
seems a wonder that such a thing as a "working class" exists at all.
Often enough the divisions explode with a ferocity that destroys class
solidarity. Race riots are one obvious example. Others are divisions
within the union over demands that benefit older workers vs. demands that benefit younger workers; discrimination against women
by male workers—the list can be continued and has to be a part of
any analysis of the American working class. But here, too, the divisions must be subsumed under a greater totality.

After four hundred years of slavery and officially propagated
racism it would be a miracle if racist attitudes did not permeate the
American working class, particularly since, often enough, these attitudes bring concrete financial rewards. Consider, then, the overriding force of cooperative production which has constantly miti-
gated that racism (or nationalism or sexism) and made it possible for
workers to reach frequent peaks of class militancy and solidarity. An
indication of what is involved can be given by citing the notorious
Democratic party primary in Indiana in 1964 wherein George Wallace swept such industrial centers as Gary. What is most significant is
the duality: in the primary, when workers were free to vote their racial prejudices, they voted for Wallace. In the election, when the totality of economics and politics was at stake, workers did not vote for
the candidate who most closely embodied Wallace's racism. They

did not vote for Goldwater. They voted for Johnson and the Democratic party as the traditional embodiment of liberalism and social welfare. The election returns in both 1964 and 1968 showed that Wallace was a middle-class, not a working-class, candidate. The distribution of the Wallace vote outside the Deep South showed that his basic strength lay with the lower middle class, traditional source of fascist legions.

There has rarely been (outside the South) a strike situation in which class solidarity did not assert itself. This is true in mass production, basic industry. The picture changes and the conflicts become more serious when you enter the skilled trades which have been exclusionist and privileged for generations.[39] The only possibility of dealing with such situations is through confrontation and struggle by those workers who are excluded from particular trades and occupations, or from equal pay and upgrading.

But another element is involved. The American working class has always contained substantial numbers, sometimes majorities, of blacks, foreign-born, women, and youth. The composition of the working class tends to gravitate toward the most disadvantaged sections of society. As a consequence, the makeup of the workers of certain key industries is undergoing change. Municipal transportation in several major cities has become largely black. In the powerful auto industry, the majority of workers in the Detroit metropolitan area are now black. In addition, about 40 percent of the auto workers are now young, hired within the last ten years. Similar developments are taking place in other industries, although not at the same pace.

However you interpret these developments, whether as a process of whites escaping from alienated, exploitative work or of blacks forcing their way into major industrial occupations, the consequences are the same. Black workers are no longer dependent on white support to make major attacks on the real centers of power in the United States. This same fact also provides the basis for cooperation in the struggle against capitalism for the control of the shop floor. In situations where the majority (or a strategically placed minority) of the workers are black, or Spanish-speaking, or female, the multiple exploitation of these workers tends to reduce the significance of divisions in the working class and contributes instead to greater militancy, revolutionary explosiveness, and the assumption of leadership over less active workers.

In the spring of 1968 several middle-aged Polish women from the trim shop of the Chrysler Hamtramck plant in the Detroit area, fed up with the company's failure to solve certain specific local grievances, linked arms in front of the plant gate during the lunch hour in an attempt to shut the plant down. A few young black men joined them. The plant was closed for several days. During that period, one year after the Detroit rebellion, the Dodge Revolutionary Union Movement (DRUM) was organized. By July DRUM was calling strikes in its own name; it shut the plant down several times that summer.[40]

The dynamics of the class struggle is sometimes difficult to comprehend. In ordinary, relatively peaceful times, the weight of the more conservative sections of the class seems quite great. What is not so evident is that this weight can be effective only when little is happening. Like most conservative influences, it thrives on inactivity. When militant or revolutionary activities break out, led, as they always are, by the most exploited sections of the working class (the young, blacks, women) the influence of the more conservative workers disintegrates. It does not provide a counter center. The large majority of workers remain inactive or follow behind those who lead. Workers in factories are very aware of this reality. Older workers will often express their own limitations (e.g., concern for a family or fear of losing seniority) and indicate that the initiative will have to come from the young.

The reality of revolutionary movements in the industrial world, whether ghetto riots in the United States or the 1968 revolt in France, is that they originate with the poorest, most exploited, least organized people—and the rest follow. In France it was women aircraft workers and young male workers, outside the control of the unions, who started the movement. The organized communist workers of Renault and the others followed. When a massive struggle is under way, the divisions within the working class tend to heal, or are at least held in abeyance.

Another difficulty in viewing the class struggle from the outside is the universal misconception of the nature of working-class consciousness. Middle-class intellectuals, whether students, academics, or revolutionaries, tend to view consciousness in middle-class terms, that is, as a formal statement of views on political questions. They do not see that the essential ingredient of working-class consciousness is activity, and that often there is an apparent contradiction between words and deeds. How many antiwar activists, for example, are aware of the fact that more war production has been halted or delayed by the ordinary activity of the American working class than by all the antiwar demonstrations put together? Major strikes at Olin-Mathieson, North American Aviation, and several railroads during the Vietnam war years came close to triggering government intervention. These were not, of course, strikes against the war. What they indicate, however, is that when workers are forced to choose between patriotism and class interest, they will usually choose class interest (and consider it patriotic).

Similarly, during World War II auto workers in a secret ballot, voting in the privacy of their own homes, voted 2–1 to retain the no-strike pledge. In this, the ideal sociological survey, workers seemed to put patriotism over class interest. Before you jump to this conclusion, however, try to explain why these same auto workers, in this same period, wildcatted all over the place. What seemed reasonable to them while they listened to the casualty reports over the radio did not seem at all reasonable to them the next day in the factory when confronting a foreman.

It would be worth remembering these little-known words of Marx:

> Both for the production on a mass scale of this communist consciousness, and for the success of the cause itself, the alteration of men on a mass scale is necessary, an alteration which can only take place in a practical movement, a *revolution*; this revolution is necessary, therefore, not only because the *ruling* class cannot be overthrown in any other way, but also because the class *overthrowing* it can only in a revolution succeed in ridding itself of all the muck of ages and become fitted to found society anew.[41]

In short: revolutions create revolutionary consciousness, not the reverse.

Which brings us back where we started. "One distinctive characteristic of capitalism is that it is revolutionary. . . . There has been no diminution of disturbance, uncertainty and agitation." And as long as capitalism can neither stabilize nor control its own system, it cannot eliminate the sources for insecurity and unrest and it cannot do away with those sections of the population that have the power to transform society.

NOTES

1. *Communist Manifesto*, in Karl Marx and Friedrich Engels, *Basic Writings on Politics and Philosophy*, ed. Lewis S. Feuer (Garden City, N.Y.: Doubleday, 1959), p. 10.

2. Very often they are worse than misleading; they are unintelligible. "The paradox about the economy is that, depending entirely on how one looks at it, it is in marvelous shape or it is in near-crisis. . . . The situation would be funny if it weren't so serious. Here we are 55 years after the foundation of the Federal Reserve System and economists cannot even agree on which financial indicators to use to decide whether money is 'easy' or 'tight.' Believe it or not, last spring and summer the Federal Reserve Board, to a man, was convinced that their policy was one of anti-inflationary restraint, while a powerful outside school of economists and one of the 12 Federal Reserve Banks (the St. Louis bank) was convinced that policy was, in fact, highly expansionary and even inflationary." Edwin L. Dale, Jr., "The Dreadful Economic Choice That Faces Mr. Nixon," *New York Times Magazine*, 24 November 1968.

3. Thomas C. Cochran and William Miller, *The Age of Enterprise* (New York: Harper, 1961), p. 304.

4. "Roughly, we may attribute the decisive change in the American economy to the last part of the nineteenth century and the first part of the twentieth century, taking 1914 as a convenient dividing line. After World War I the Taylor system, experimental before the war, becomes a social system, the factory laid out for continuous flow of production, and the advanced planning for production, operating and control. At the same time there is the organization of professional societies, management courses in college curricula and responsible management consultants. Between 1924 and 1928 there is rationalization of production and retooling (Ford). Along with it are the tendencies to the scientific organization of production, to closer coordination between employers, fusion with each other against the working class, the intervention of the state as mediator and then as arbiter.

"For the proletariat there is the constantly growing subdivision of labor, decrease in the need of skills, and determination of the sequence of operations and speed by the machine. The crisis of 1929 accelerated all these processes. The characteristic, most advanced form of American production becomes Ford. Here production consists of a mass of hounded, sweated labor (in which, in Marx's phrase, the very life of society was threatened); and opposed to it as a class, a management staff which can carry out this production only by means of a hired army (Bennett) of gangsters, thugs, supervisors who run production by terror, in the plant, in the lives of the workers outside production, and in the political control of Detroit. Ford's regime before unionization is the prototype of production relations in fascist Germany and Stalinist Russia," C. L. R. James, *State Capitalism and World Revolution* (3rd ed.; Detroit: Facing Reality Press, 1969), pp. 39–40.

5. Lenin, *Selected Works*, vol. 1 (Progress Publishers, 1967), pp. 673–77.

6. "To make things even clearer, let us first of all take the most concrete example of state capitalism. Everybody knows what this example is. It is Germany. Here we have 'the last word' in modern large-scale capitalist engineering and planned organization, *subordinated to Junker-bourgeois imperialism.*" Lenin, " 'Left-Wing' Childishness and the Petty-Bourgeois Mentality," in ibid., vol. 2, p. 697. Lenin quoted this and other passages from this article in an article, "The Tax in Kind," published in 1921. Ibid., vol. 3, p. 587. Cf. "The Marxian analysis of capitalism still rests in the final analysis on the assumption of a competitive economy." Paul A. Baran and Paul M. Sweezy, *Monopoly Capital* (New York: Monthly Review Press, 1966), p. 4.

7. See Paul Mattick, *Marx & Keynes* (Boston: Porter Sargent, 1969).

8. Adolph A. Berle, *The American Economic Republic* (New York: Harcourt, 1965), p. vii.

9. Gardiner C. Means, *The Corporate Revolution in America* (New York: Collier, 1964), pp. 30–37.

10. Ibid., pp. 30–31.

11. How easily a new necessity becomes transformed into a management ideal is shown by the following: "Ideally . . . the production of useful new knowledge should be financed collectively through the government, and the results made available to potential users free of charge." Harry G. Johnson, "The Efficiency and Welfare Implications of the International Corporation," in *The International Corporation*, ed. Charles P. Kindleberger (Cambridge, Mass: Harvard University Press, 1970), p. 36. Miracle of miracles—collectivism becomes an ideal of free enterprise!

12. Seymour J. Rubin, "The International Firm and the National Jurisdiction," in ibid., p. 185.

13. Brad Wiley, "The Myth of New Deal Reform," in *Up Against the American Myth*, ed. Tom Christoffel, David Finkelhor, and Dan Gilbarg (New York: Holt, 1970), p. 145.

14. Ibid., p. 147.

15. Andrew Shonfield, *Modern Capitalism* (New York: Oxford University Press, 1965), pp. 64–65.

16. Ibid., p. 64.

17. Michael Barratt Brown, "European Capitalism and World Trade," in *Socialist Register 1966* (London: Merlin Press, and New York: Monthly Review Press), p. 137. See also Michael Barratt Brown, *After Imperialism* (London: Heinemann, 1963; rev. ed., 1970); Hamza Alavi, "Imperialism Old and New," *Socialist Register 1964*; Michael Kidron, *Western Capitalism Since the War* (London: Weidenfeld & Nicholson, 1968; rev. ed., 1970).

18. Brown, "European Capitalism and World Trade," pp. 147–48.

19. "The Multinational Corporation and the Nation-State," *New York Review of Books*, 11 February 1971, p. 22. The universal, almost instinctive, use of the word "our" to describe the foreign investments of GM, IBM, Standard Oil, et al., undoubtedly imbues us with the warm glow of affluence.

20. "To the [producers] the relations connecting the labor of one individual with that of the rest appear, not as direct social relations between individuals at work, but as what they really are, material relations between persons and social relations between things." Marx, *Capital*, vol. 1 (New York: International Publishers, 1967), p. 73.

21. "In the trusts freedom of competition changes into its very opposite —into monopoly; and the production without any definite plan of capitalistic society capitulates to the production upon a definite plan of the invading socialistic society. . . . In any case, with trusts or without, the official representatives of capitalist society—the state—will ultimately have to undertake the direction of production" (p. 103). "But the transformation, either into joint-stock companies and trusts or into state ownership, does not do away with the capitalist nature of the productive forces. In the joint-stock companies and trusts this is obvious. And the modern state, again, is only the organization that bourgeois society takes on in order to support the external conditions of the capitalist mode of production against the encroachments as well of the workers as of individual capitalists. The modern state, no matter what its form, is essentially a capitalist machine, the state of the capitalists, the ideal personification of the total national capital. The more it proceeds to the taking over of productive forces, the more does it actually become the national capitalist, the more citizens does it exploit. The workers remain wage-workers—proletarians. The capitalist relation is not done away with. It is rather brought to a head" (p. 104). Engels, *Socialism: Utopian and Scientific*, in Marx and Engels, *Basic Writings*. This short work was first published in 1882, the year before Marx's death. The larger work of which this was a part, popularly called *Anti-Duhring*, was published in 1878 and quite familiar

to Marx. These facts make it very difficult to understand the following: "Engels, in some of his own writings after Marx's death and in editorial additions to the second and third volumes of *Capital* which he prepared for the printer, commented on the rapid growth of monopolies during the 1880's and 1890's, but he did not try to incorporate monopoly into the body of Marxian economic theory." Baran and Sweezy, *Monopoly Capital*, p. 5. Engels is already discussing the tendency toward state capitalism as inherent in capitalism and Baran and Sweezy can barely discern monopoly!

22. "If the crises demonstrate the incapacity of the bourgeoisie for managing any longer modern productive forces, the transformation of the great establishments for production and distribution into joint-stock companies, trusts, and state property show how unnecessary the bourgeoisie are for that purpose. All the social functions of the capitalist are now performed by salaried employees." Engels, *Socialism*, p. 103.

23. *Capital*, 1:708. ". . . within the capitalist system all methods for raising the social productiveness of labor are brought about at the cost of the individual laborer; all means for the development of production transform themselves into means of domination over, and exploitation of, the producers; they mutilate the laborer into a fragment of a man, degrade him to the level of an appendage of a machine, destroy every remnant of charm in his work and turn it into a hated toil; they estrange from him the intellectual potentialities of the labor-process in the same proportion as science is incorporated in it as an independent power; they distort the conditions under which he works, subject him during the labor-process to a despotism the more hateful for its meanness; they transform his life-time into working time, and drag his wife and child beneath the wheels of the Juggernaut of capital."

24. See, for example, Robert Blauner, *Alienation and Freedom* (Chicago: University of Chicago Press, 1964); Georges Friedmann, *Industrial Society* (Glencoe, Ill.: Free Press, 1955, 1964); Paul Romano and Rita Stone, *The American Worker* (Detroit: Facing Reality, 1947, 1969); Alexander R. Heron, *Why Men Work* (Stanford: Stanford University Press, 1948).

25. *Time*, 9 November 1970, p. 74. Marx's prediction of the *relative* impoverishment of the worker is contained in the following sentence (among other places): "It follows therefore that in proportion as capital accumulates, the lot of the laborer, be his payment high or low, must grow worse." *Capital*, 1:708-9.

26. "An industrial army of workmen, under the command of a capitalist, requires, like a real army, officers [managers], and sergeants [foremen, overlookers], who, while the work is being done, command in the name of the capitalist. The work of supervision becomes their established and exclusive function." Marx, *Capital*, 1:364. "The technical subordination of the workman to the uniform motion of the instruments of labor, and the pecul-

iar composition of the body of workpeople, consisting as it does of individuals of both sexes and of all ages, give rise to a barrack discipline, which is elaborated into a complete system in the factory, and which fully develops the before mentioned labor of overlooking, thereby dividing the workpeople into operatives and overlookers, into private soldiers and sergeants of an industrial army." Ibid., 1:463. "Upon the basis of capitalist production, the social character of their production impresses itself upon the mass of direct producers as a strictly regulating authority and as a social mechanism of the labor process graduated into a complete hierarchy. This authority is vested in its bearers only as a personification of the requirements of labor standing above the laborer." Ibid., 3:1027. Any discussion of the fantastic extension of bureaucracy in modern industrial society that does not begin here, that is, at the point of production, is doomed to superficiality.

27. Seymour Faber and James W. Rinehart, "Structural Sources of Working Class Political Unrest" (Paper presented at the Society for the Study of Social Problems, Washington, D.C., 1970).

28. ". . . output per worker has risen 471% from 1899 to 1966, while the average real purchasing power of the wages of these workers before taxes has risen only 345% in the same period of time. This means that their relative position in production is only 73% of what it was in 1899. This 73% . . . would be dramatically lower if taxes were taken into consideration." Jeffrey D. Gilbert, "A Critique of Kolko's *Wealth and Power in America*" (Unpublished paper, 1970), p. 14.

29. Martin Glaberman, *Theory and Practice*, (Detroit: Facing Reality, 1969), pp. 15–16. See also a remarkable discussion of a collective effort by workers in an auto plant to redesign an engine, and failing that, to destroy it, in Bill Watson, "Counter-Planning on the Shop Floor," *Radical America* 5, no. 3 (May–June 1971).

30. "We do not claim that directing attention to the generation and absorption of surplus gives a complete picture of this or any other society. And we are particularly conscious of the fact that this approach, as we have used it, has resulted in almost total neglect of a subject which occupies a central place in Marx's study of capitalism: the labor process. We stress the crucial role of technological change in the development of monopoly capitalism but make no attempt to inquire systematically into the consequences which the particular kinds of technological change characteristic of the monopoly capitalist period have had for the nature of work, the composition (and differentiation) of the working class, the psychology of workers, the forms of working-class organization and struggle, and so on. These are all obviously important subjects which would have to be dealt with in any comprehensive study of monopoly capitalism." Baran and Sweezy, *Monopoly Capital*, pp. 8–9. It is difficult to understand how one can study the generation of surplus without studying the labor process. Where in the world do our radical economists think the surplus is generated—in corporate board rooms? They do

an injustice to Marx. His study of the labor process did not occupy a central place (side by side with other significant subjects). It was the heart of his analysis of capitalism. But, take heart! Baran and Sweezy continue: "Our neglect of the labor process does not, however, mean that this book is not concerned with the class struggle. For a number of reasons . . . the class struggle in our time has been thoroughly internationalized." Ibid., p. 9. Well, if they will not deal with the American working class, perhaps they will deal with the international working class? Not quite; it is all a deception: "The revolutionary initiative against capitalism, which in Marx's day belonged to the proletariat in the advanced countries, has passed into the hands of the impoverished masses in the underdeveloped countries who are struggling to free themselves from imperialist domination and exploitation." Ibid., p. 9. So, it is not that they will not deal with the American working class—it is that they are writing it off. Through the ambiguity (in this case) of the term "class struggle," they replace the struggle of an industrial working class with that of a national peasantry.

31. James, *State Capitalism and World Revolution*, pp. 40–41.

32. "Blue collar anger has burst out this year in the worst epidemic of strikes since just after World War II, and in the form of hardhat riots in New York City, St. Louis and elsewhere. This year postal employees have gone on strike for the first time in history, city workers have stomped off the job in Cincinnati, and tugboat crewmen and gravediggers have struck in New York. Municipal employees in San Francisco and Atlanta, rubber workers in Akron, and teamsters across the country—all have walked out. In this year's first nine months, the U.S. lost 41.5 million man-days through strikes, up 32% from the equivalent period last year." *Time*, 9 November 1970, p. 69. These figures do not include the massive GM strike which took place in the last three months of 1970.

"Company bargainers fret over rising membership rejections of contracts negotiated by the union leadership. A Chicago dairy, whose Teamster Union members this year turned down four contracts, blames attempt by younger workers to wrest control of the union from older leaders." *Wall Street Journal*, 26 December 1967.

"One of management's shibboleths through the years has been the charge that 'union bosses' were exercising too much authority over rank-and-file members. In the face of an increasing trend toward contract rejections by members, however, some employers are reassessing their earlier view and privately expressing dismay at the way union democracy is working. . . . Nationally, according to a study made by the Federal Mediation and Conciliation Service, there has been a rise in contract rejections in recent years." Damon Stetson, "The Rejected Contract," *New York Times*, 2 December 1968.

"The fact is that during the first six months of 1967 U.S. industry experienced more strikes than in any comparable period since 1953. At the same time, the tempo of rank-and-file rejections of proposed contract settlements also rose. In the first half of 1967, one of seven settlements was turned down by the workers involved—a 20 per cent increase over the same period in 1966. . . . The 40 and under group is the fastest growing segment of organized labor, already making up about half of all union membership. Of that half, one out of two workers is under 30." Thomas G. Ayers, "The Bargaining Table—Must Government Sit In?" Chicago *Sun-Times*, 7 January 1968.

33. Watson, "Counter-Planning," pp. 77, 82–85.

34. *Manpower Report of the President, including Report on Manpower Requirements, Resources, Utilization and Training by the U.S. Department of Labor* (Washington, D.C.: Government Printing Office, 1968), p. 18. Quoted in "The Permanent Job Shortage," by Tom Christoffel, in *Up Against the American Myth*, p. 262.

35. Homer Bigart, "Many in Appalachia Hungry Despite U.S. Aid," *New York Times*, 18 June 1971, p. 20.

36. These theories come from sources such as Marcuse's *One-Dimensional Man* (Boston: Beacon Press, 1964).

37. Marx, *Capital*, vol. 3, pt. 3.

38. Kidron, *Western Capitalism Since the War*, p. 50.

39. "Imperialism has the tendency to create privileged sections also among the workers, and to detach them from the broad masses of the proletariat." Lenin, *Imperialism*, in *Selected Works*, 1:760.

40. Martin Glaberman, "Black Workers Organize Dodge Plant," *Guardian*, 23 November 1968, p. 5. Also see Robert Dudnick, *Black Workers in Revolt* (*Guardian* pamphlet, 1969).

41. Karl Marx and Friedrich Engels, *The German Ideology* (Moscow, Progress Publishers, 1968), p. 87.

2

THE
POLITICAL
INSTITUTION

John C. Leggett

Is the State Overwhelming?

The state[1] is never neutral. Along with its beneficiaries, it leans
to one side.[2] Especially is this true when the businessman's state in-
tervenes to socialize its citizens in market society.[3] In this context, the
state leans on people's heads, and I will focus on how this is done, but
before doing so, I would like to make some preliminary remarks on
the nature of the state.

The state is rightly regarded as an ideology-producing institution,[4] and it is likewise the most powerful of disseminating agents. As
that organization which claims for itself a monopoly of violence
within a given territory, it insists upon the prerogative of regulating

the flow of information to all its potential taxpayers and future war personnel.[5] Others are also earmarked for concern, but crucial is the way in which state elites investigate, regulate, and, when necessary, punish the nonelites. Nor are the political elites without a bias on class and scrutiny. In a context where land, labor, and goods are produced for profit with a minimal amount of state regulation,[6] the businessman's state focuses its attention on public schools and scrutinizes texts and teachers of privately run educational institutions.[7]

The state interests itself in the flow of all information, and when necessary the state threatens what it does not own or regulate in the realm of the mass media.[8] In a more paternal way, the state directly communicates to families, private police, churches, and like secondary institutions, for it expects obedience, within limits, from these institutions.[9] The state thereby becomes a primary creator and paternal distributor and censor of information, including mystified accounts of its own nature as well as behavior.[10] As masker of its own design, the state distributes ideology, not all of it, but a good deal of those ideas that justify and obfuscate the relationships between the state and all other institutions; between the state and all persons in the society; between the propertied who strive to command and staff the state,[11] and the propertyless who are taught to obey.

The businessman's state acts to accommodate the demands of an economy geared to the use and exhaustion of human and other resources in order to produce predictable levels of profit, high levels of corporate longevity (and prestige) as well as the successful promotion of executive careers.[12] Indeed, the business executive becomes an important owner of investment capital, a person whose prestige, wealth, and knowledge make him eligible to become a potential occupant of official positions within the state. There he can act to enhance his private career, corporate obligations, personal honor, and private fortunes. The businessman's state, then, is run by propertied directors of organizational power.[13]

In its regulatory actions, the state rejects and often suppresses counterideologies, that is, formulas which question the legitimacy of state control and private property. Above all, the state disallows the serious dissemination of utopian visions on societal alternatives. For example, the businessman's state prefers to vanquish a positive portrayal of communism in the public school system, for the state's leaders view a competitive vision as potentially subversive to both its power, which it perpetuates, and to the economic interests, which it serves.[14] The businessman's state looks askance at those ideas that might in any way dissolve the ideological glue that supplements the organizational force, for the directors of the state are aware of the integrating function of ideas propounded by the state and ancillary institutions. Thus, for example, to the degree that people accept the myths of supply and demand and are unaware of the chicanery of administered pricing, they misperceive a reality defined by state elites as resting upon the moral principles of the free marketplace. To the degree that masses[15] are inaccurate in perception, but in agreement with this and related legitimating myths, the state defines them (as these masses define themselves) as loyal to this order, hence they are less likely to take actions subversive of both state authority and private ownership of the means of production.[16]

Given the signal importance of ideologies for political control, what are their content and how are they received? Here we are concerned with both content of themes and forms of dissemination used to control populations seemingly predestined to internalize ideologies favored by the state. Previous major formulations on this matter of mental guidance by the state have portrayed a state striving to maintain a monopoly of violence and hence of day-to-day control through the distribution of myths to a readily brainwashed population. *The mass is generally depicted as being passive recipients at the end of a string of institutional disseminators.* From Marx through Mosca, Pareto, and Michels to Lasswell,[17] this theme recurs. *Paradoxically, these same writers have commented on the conditions under which the subordinate classes break with state ideologies, formulas, derivations and myths and move towards the creation of revolutionary countersymbolism and revolutionary organizations.*[18] We must concern ourselves with the resolution of this seeming contradiction by approaching the problem developmentally.

The State Must Shift Gears

Concern with the resolution of this contradiction moves me to explore the following thesis: *how the state formulates its justifications, and how the state uses force to maintain political control, depends to a high degree on whether state myths[19] are in fact being accepted by the mass found within the subordinate classes.*[20]

By definition, mass acceptance of state myths is to a high degree dependent upon whether the mass is located within a period of political equilibrium or revolution. During moments of equilibrium, the well-reasoned justification of political pluralism complements a state policy of repressive tolerance—with a modicum of state violence. During the early periods of revolutionary unrest, however, mass acceptance of state formulas wanes, as masses shift to utopian concern on alternate state[21] formulas. At this time, the state both persists in its commitment to political pluralism and attempts to coopt its critics. Furthermore, the state relies increasingly upon shockingly illogical judicial, executive, and administrative non sequiturs. In this context, the state uses violence more frequently, as well as indiscriminately, to punish those deemed beyond the pale of state acceptance.

If the businessman's state fails and the socialist revolution proves successful, that is, if the alternate state becomes the official state, the revolutionary state will momentarily foster the dissemination of formulas consistent with the revolutionary aspirations of the great majority of the masses. Subsequently, the contradictory demands of revolutionary defense negate many of the gains—and myths—associated with the struggle against inequality. Finally, when there occurs a sharp domestic reaction against the alleged excesses and extremes of revolutionary behavior, there follows the slight possibility of rejuvenation of revolution and the achievement of equality through continuous struggle against those forces associated with the new inequality. At this point the state may well pursue a myth of "cultural revolution" and use a modicum of violence to revitalize the revolution.

Let me express this idea in another, more general way. It is true that masses generally accept state myths, especially those on the inevitability of inequality, presented to them by the state through the mass media, religious institutions, schools, families, prisons, and the like—in short, by the institutional network. But not always.[22] Admittedly during moments of stable equilibrium,[23] the state and ancillary institutions find little opposition to the successful flow of general ideologies on how the society is organized, what are the societal alternatives, and how the state can ensure the ideological status quo. By contrast, during protorevolutionary and revolutionary periods, ideology runs smack into the continuous and popular opposition of both *counterideology* and *utopian construction*[24]—counterideology depicts the damned present, while utopia incompletely designs the revolutionary future. Confronted with these increasingly accepted expressions from below, the state expresses itself through ideological reformulation and increased violence.

The collision between ideology and utopia frequently occurs within the context of a political battlefield, and generally when one attempts to analyze the soldiers of struggle, one falls back upon the anthropomorphizing of class categories. Many speak of the proletariat standing up, or a coalition of peasants, intellectuals, and workers as well as progressive bourgeoisie coming together, and so forth. We talk about coalition politics as if whole groups were allied. In fact, we know better, for what we observe over and over again are bits and pieces of classes, status groups, and generations coalescing. This being the case, class analysis makes little sense unless refined. Sections of classes may participate or lead in a struggle, but we should not confuse the part with the whole and indeed go so far as to attribute individual characteristics to an analytic category or real group.

The Clusters: Moral Core, Eschatological Radicals, Ambivalent Partisans, Deliberate Radicals, and Quiescent Dumb

Clusters of political allies draw their membership from various sections of classes, status groups, and generations: the crucial sources of group behavior.[25] In our time, we can observe over and over again how in one corner are the heterogeneous forces of economic conservatism and cultural traditionalism. Together these forces constitute the "moral core":[26] the key carriers of societal folkways and mores, the unconscious purveyors of upper-class beliefs and values, the dreary reciters of eternal verities which hang like albatrosses around the necks of those political movements that seek revolutionary change. Although led by an overwhelming majority of those who monopolize the strategic resources of society, the moral core includes, as it rests upon, a sizable segment of those whom corporate wealth oppresses. For, as Frantz Fanon has indicated, it is normal for many who suffer repression—even the double exploitation of class-racial manipulation meted out by the white man in the black colonies—to identify with their oppressors as a way of adapting to circumstances in which the oppressed are without a revolutionary alternative.[27]

This mental set remains among the oppressed as a form of cultural residue, one based upon a previous adaptation maintained long after the society has passed from a condition of near equilibrium to one of revolutionary flux. As such, the loyalty of these victims functions to legitimate the moral core's leadership and myths. What better way to make a suspect group respectable than to have its most depressed segment testify its loyalty through continued identification and even emulation;[28] after all, the affluent leadership can't be all that bad, since many miserable ones subscribe to it.

Flagrantly and at times "scandalously"[29] opposed to the moral core are the "eschatological radicals." Drawn from many classes but especially the petite bourgeoisie and young working classes, these persons bring a total indictment against the corrupt present, call for the creation of a revolutionary presence on all matters, see and demand bipolarization now, fully expect the forces of revolution to triumph soon, live part of the future within their ongoing countercommunities, pen the rough outlines of the new society, and thereby justify the casualties of ongoing and pending armed struggle. The eschatological radicals turn out to be visible at all times in societies in which market economy exists—in part because some are publicly adopted by the more cosmopolitan members of the establishment.[30] But they become most obvious when a society moves away from ready adjustment of various parts to a period of rapid and near-total reorganization. During these moments, their numbers grow as does the din and influence of their revelations.

Somewhere in between the moral core and the eschatological radicals are those who are both ideological and utopian: the "segmental partisans"—persons who have compartmentalized their minds to accept (1) portions of justifications of the present, (2) indictments of the ongoing, and (3) formulations on revolutionary alternatives. One moment allied with the moral core, segmental partisans consistently admonish those who violate the principles of the past; yet at the next moment they sarcastically and inconsistently derogate the parameters of the very institutions whose rules and principles

they had only recently defended.[31] Segmental partisans express contradictory statements, but many of their criticisms run deep. According to segmental partisans—a sizable minority of whom are intellectuals—the state sets boundaries around institutions that behave
within prescribed limits to socialize and thereby damn to irrational
perdition the very ones whose "autonomous rationality" must be
achieved if the moderate goals of the segmental partisans are to be
realized.

Sometimes out of despair, the segmental partisans will identify
with the goals of the eschatological vanguard, if not its careening
style.

However confused the segmental partisans may be, it becomes
the task of egalitarian movements to vanquish their central inconsistencies and to bring the ambivalent ones over to the side of accepting
revolutionary utopias, which the converted can later help to sharpen.

To win the segmental partisans is no routine activity, and from
the point of view of many within the radical movement, this task
should *not* fall to the eschatological radicals, for they alienate most
persons, including one another. Through default, the job generally
falls to the "deliberate radicals." Their relative calmness in the art of
persuasion complements their insistence on viewing people's political
beliefs as falling on a continuum. Indeed, deliberate radicals believe
that persons can move up a scale from conservative to radical under
the pressure of current events, participatory involvement, critical
friendship, and political self-analysis. All these considerations press
the deliberate radicals to be flexible but firm when dealing with persons who have internalized a chunk of both the mores of the past and
the utopian vision of the future.

The deliberate radicals best handle the guidance of the ambivalent partisans through situations in which the ambivalent will do as
much as they can for a particular cause and where the predictable
repression of the state will anger them to do more to solve the particular problem; it is the task of the deliberate radicals to help interpret
these events as both they and the ambivalent partisans pass through
crises loaded with potential for radicalization.[32]

But to lead in such a way demands subtlety and perhaps an element of guile, qualities scarcely known among the eschatological
radicals in search of immediate apocalypse. The deliberate radicals

do not accept such a vision of forthcoming events, and above all they reject the related and dichotomous distinctions between the saved and the damned. The deliberate radicals eschew any theory of cataclysmic bipolarized immediacy, the belief that it is necessary for everyone to choose sides *now* in order to achieve a propertyless, classless, statusless, and stateless society a few historical moments from the present.

Deliberate radicals propound a firm but patient evolutionary view on when and how revolution can take place. They believe that if and when a particular sequence of conditions and processes occurs —and revolutionaries should help to shape and accelerate it by widening the breadth of revolutionary inclusion—then in all probability a successful revolution will follow. This calculating and activist approach leads many others to view the deliberate radicals as cautious manipulators. This view is correct. They are. They are generally persons with a vision and a long-term view on how best to relate to people in order to resolve inimical contradictions.[33]

Their consciousness reveals itself as totally different from the perspectives of the "quiescent dumb." These uninvolved ones seem singularly mindless. They act as persons whose cortical areas have been dulled by the litany of all institutions, so that their perspectives become antiscientific, especially in the realm of nonwork relations.[34] What characterizes these people is the absence of the mind-lodging and mind-sorting and scientific using of elementary information on the relationship between state power and modified market economy. Their minds appear to be incapacitated, unable to think in terms of how the state and private property systematically control and exploit their own lives. For them their fortunes ride on chance, luck, and/or cosmic dictation. It is this group which makes a contribution to the old regime, but the contribution is ordinarily analogous to giant logs blocking a beach about to be traveled by an assault group.

The quiescent dumb are not part of the moral core, for they carry and practice few traditional values. Quite frequently they believe little or nothing that lies beyond the bounds of their privatized, family-centered lives. Largely unknown to themselves, they are frequently cynics or pessimists, people who do not vote and in general do not believe in the pluralistic formulas on political participation. They do not attend church or school, except when necessary.[35] Nor do they subscribe seriously to myths on the life hereafter, not to mention the life before passage. In the United States today these people seldom apprehend television materials even though their TV sets may be on for hours every day. They seldom read newspapers, books, or magazines, but when they do, they comprehend information only in a very limited number of areas and only in the most concrete sense; it is as if they are incapable of gathering materials from which they might be able to generalize about who controls their lives. Nor do they share moral core beliefs on the presumed goodness to be derived from an understanding of public issues. Generally they are out of it—and they are many. Yet they are sometimes in it, and then they can be significant, for during political crises many of them can be activated by the defenders of the status quo to leave their political lethargy and to speak and act on subjects they only minimally understand.[36] The quiescent dumb derive from all classes, status groups, and generations. They are by no means drawn exclusively from the lesser proletariat, some of whom are both highly informed and committed.[37]

These are the principal actors who troop about the stage of politics during both moments of equilibrium and revolution. But they do not move through time as if its stages were without differentiation. For time includes its periods, and if we are to understand it, we must at the very least schematize its trajectory. And in our time to do so demands that we make relevant distinctions between the periods of stationary equilibrium and those associated with total cultural revolution: (1) the Period of Stationary Equilibrium, or the pre-prodromal period, (2) the Prodromal Period itself, (3) the Coming to Power of the Radicals, (4) the Period of Encirclement, and (5) Thermidor —the Period of Reaction.[38]

The Period of Stationary Equilibrium

The stage of stationary equilibrium lends itself to analysis, since most people know their slots and act out their roles predictably. Here institutions function much as the structural-functional sociologists tell us they do.[39] Traditions permeate as they radiate from family, church, and school and prove consistent with the beliefs of the state. The hierarchical order gives ample indication of timelessness. The upper classes bask in the generally unquestioned brilliance of their own intellectual and material opulence. Contradictions exist, but they are readily ignored at the very moment that their sources remain hidden by lack of either cataclysmic uplifts or detectable microseisms.

Discontent remains largely personalized, seldom articulated behind a mantle of self-congratulation and self-celebration heaped upon the upper and middle classes by their scribes. C. Wright Mills observed this phenomenon during the 1950s when he dealt with the art of upper-class celebration and the "end of ideology." Almost alone he announced how social science intellectuals had set aside their radical critiques of the 1930s to posture before the academic foundations and educated publics the themes of collective arrival and pervasive happiness.[40] The conservative formulation was clear: capitalism had solved its internal problems and would tackle foreign hangups with both analyses bereft of Marxism and programs developed by a reformed capitalism dependent upon both a subsidized scientism without bias and a new conservative ethic with traditional warnings against man's presumptuousness. In these celebrated analyses,[41] mass unemployment had ceased, modified market economy had equilibrated, and people had won democratic political representation. Domestic class strife had ended, and what remained to be solved were problems of nonrevolutionary consequence. Put on the agenda were problems of man's alienation from work and self, plus the need to re-create religiosity.[42] Daniel Bell's *End of Ideology* and his damning article-length review of C. Wright Mills' *Power Elite* (published in the regular article section by the *American Journal of Sociology*[43]) exemplified the two sides of the ideological coin: (1) celebration of private property and its alleged pluralistic political context, and (2) damnation of those who would suggest that power was not pluralistic but both concentrated and pyramidal in the context of an institutionalized socialization of a politically inconsequential mass. Mills' counterideological formulations had stung the celebrators, and their cobralike response smacked of the subsidized, vengeful overkill.[44]

Long before Mills' piercing analysis of the power elite made its way into the hands of graduate students (and for many of us that was his most influential, however imperfect, work) Marx had noted that

the ideology of the ruling class stamps the mentality of all.[45] None
can escape.

This conditioned, indeed wholly determinist, view of man has
seemed most applicable during intervals of historical lassitude, moments when trade unions make predictable gains, class struggle
barely simmers, class-racial minorities acquiesce, and the younger
generation both slumbers to the purr of success and moves to the demands of career, with its daily, weekly, monthly, and yearly rounds
chunked in terms of predictable time intervals from birth to death.
Society seems to assume the symmetrical, cyclical quality of a primitive world described by a British cultural anthropologist like Radcliffe-Brown.[46]

Here, then, the propertied do not fear the clarion call of revolutionary social movements but rather through gelded intellectuals
command a near-monopoly over formulations that redound to the
pecuniary and power interests of the upper classes. And this monopoly provides a limited pluralism which cannot escape a conservative
mood. For throughout the writings of intellectuals an implicit assumption of hierarchy and order penetrates. Terms are defined to
express vertical integration among parts, a mapping commensurate
with the pyramidal order of groups in the society. A fairly accurate
intellectual outline of the reality does emerge. Yet an element of un-
truth remains, for the unpleasant is generally avoided, while the recent past whenever ugly is characterized as a deficiency resulting
from the maniacal efforts of the crazed prophet, the power-bent agitator, or the "true believer." [47] A typological, empirical, and deductive view of the world stands as the best way to comprehend the social order.[48]

Of course, even under these conditions, there is conflict, and
consciousness, most notably among the upper classes, for the internal
subsections *do* jockey through their political parties for greater state
control and intellectual hegemony. There are disputes at the top
among the moral core[49] as to what morality is and who are its articu-
lators.

The conservative and progressive subsections of the establishment[50] express their differences and commonalities in a variety of
ways, but perhaps of most interest is the way in which they compete
to give the quintessence of meaning to particular cultural symbols

presented through the mass media; the way in which they in their own distinctive ways overlook certain problems by neglecting to categorize them, and hence, to damn the oppressed persons thereby subjected to conceptual vagueness. This categorical obscurity allows the oppressed in question to wallow in the residual category of things to be dealt with eventually, that is, when the oppressed make trouble. For until these subjects rise and use their own injuries and deaths to publicize their collective case, they are seldom the object of concern and categorization among the elite and their ciphers.[51] Unless these rebellious acts occur, the moral core publicists make less than readily apprehensible problems which then go beyond the comprehension of most; the mass must settle for casual stereotypes as the basis for understanding events and people at the bottom.[52]

When the full formulation does occur, the moral core differs among themselves also on the creation of countersymbols to be used to define the problems of recent past as well as the ongoing present. In setting up this definition, they disagree on the epistemology best used to intrigue intellectuals already bored by the analytic shabbiness that abounds during these periods. Among the concerned intellectuals is an absence of consensus on how to redefine cognitively the societal landscape—whether in terms of the fairly pleasant abstraction which portrays a general picture but obfuscates particular social problems, or the particular problems and hence palpable objects, which invite the uninvited and dissenting exposé.[53]

For the progressives found at the edge of the moral core, society may well appear corrupt, perhaps damnable, if only because of the silence of most intellectuals on social problems. For these dissenters, a sizable readjustment of the society may seem in order. Clearly the needs of the poor, the minorities, and the young are being sidestepped by the state and glossed over by the mandarin intellectuals.[54] Meanwhile, the traditional ways of thinking through or around problems may appear to dissenting intellectuls to be suffering from the presence of mental arteriosclerosis and the absence of developmental schema, conflict models, and dialectical analyses.[55]

These complaints do not seriously disrupt the ongoing order, but they keep alive criticisms and find their best expressions through plays, poems, and the limited circulation of nonacademic journals distributed among dissenters.

But the value criticisms occur within the frame of cognitive acceptance. The very cognitive categories of thought used by the critics, the seemingly nonvalued portions of their perspectives, assume a multitiered form,[56] as when persons assign themselves and others through their religions to the position of lambs led by a sheepherder, or when a person nondeliberately stares at a number of cars in a parking lot and absentmindedly ranks his own vehicle in relation to them, or when he sees others of his kind, ranks them preferentially, and jealously places himself in tiered order. At all levels and in every way, intellectuals make invidious, many times hostile, comparisons. These symbol specialists thereby semiconsciously emulate the very ones whom they simultaneously both reject and honor.

A hierarchical conception of the world finds greatest acceptance among the nondissenting spokesmen on the verities of inequalities. For these moral core conservatives, the differential distribution of wealth, power, and prestige are not inequities, since those genetically unqualified are ineligible for generous public concern on matters of what they fail to get. Yet the unqualified should not be ignored entirely by the responsible. The genetically shortchanged are unfortunate and are to be helped paternally, not through a foredoomed redistribution of wealth, but through the timely gift from on high.[57] The ideology reeks with prejudice and self-edification.

From the point of view of the moral core conservatives, *inequities* (and *not* the victims) are fortunate results. Inequities recompense as they motivate those whose achieved abilities *merit* differential rewards. These in turn ensure subsequent and high motivation among those others who are also intellectually endowed.[58]

For the moral core, especially those of conservative background, nothing is more odious than the demands for egalitarian freedoms, economic equality, and untempered justice. In their eyes, freedom should mean the right of each class or status group to take full advantage of its peculiar rights, duties, and privileges: rights are packaged and bundled according to one's station. Those at the top inherit the rights to privilege, and the honors of responsibility, while those in the middle and certainly those at the bottom, as a matter of course, have progressively fewer rights, more duties, and harder, less rewarding, responsibilities.[59] To the conservative, the weakening of these hierarchical bonds threatens civilization.

And economic equality? It is transparently impossible. It is the intellectual creation of the daft demagogue who would substitute in place of tempered mercy and the free marketplace both societal chaos and unscrupulous personal aggrandizement. Sexual equality is impossible, for God built inequality into his order when he created man with strength and created woman from a mere part of man, giving her less strength and thereby making her less able to compete. Complementing this inequality of physique is the uneven distribution of naked intelligence: some were and are inherently dumber, especially women, since they have never had to compete and hence submit to the laws of survival of the fittest. Since the date of pristine creation, these intrinsic inequalities among persons have resulted in the differentiation of the ordinary masses from the gifted eminent, the unrewarded mediocrity from the talented wealthy, the closeted female absurdity from the masculine success. The conservative views as natural and good the correlation between the gifted gentleman and leisurely affluence.[60] He also believes that this sifting process would fail to occur without the threat of economic inequality. Later we will have occasion to discuss how certain deliberate radicals have accepted this position.

Untempered justice? Justice becomes untempered and hence reprehensible when the personal digression of the elite, the judgment and choice of the accomplished, are absent from the interpretations of law. In turn it is nothing more than a firm expression of mores derived from centuries of experiences sifted by the elite and sanctified by the proper laws—be they those of God, supply and demand, or survival of the fittest.[61]

During this period of stationary equilibrium, nothing appears more repulsive to the conservative than the elimination of the right of the upper classes to express punishment through wrath or mercy. Nor do many deny them this right, for they accept the upper-class tautology on legitimate wisdom: when people have intellect, they and only they become qualified to judge others and to temper justice with wisdom. When people have intellect, it is because of genetic superiority brought naturally to fruition; with realized superiority they rule; their rule is a sign of their intellect and hence they and only they should temper justice with wisdom.

The mass acceptance of mythical wisdom ebbs noticeably during the beginnings of revolution. Then, the eschatological and the deliberate radicals begin to recruit from the ambivalent partisans and the moral core, indeed to turn on a small but growing portion of the quiescent dumb, as radicals put together counterideological formulations and utopian constructions. These in turn force the state to rely less on myth and more on force to maintain political control under conditions of loss of state legitimacy.[62]

The Prodromal Stage

On the level of ideas, the hallmark of the early prodromal stage is the growing popularity of counterideologies and utopian theories. Initially, the principal expression of counterideology is dissent, although confrontation[63] later provides greater basis for an airing of grievances against the system. During the earlier phases of this period, what takes place are the beginnings of deterioration of establishment and ruling-class myths. State power[64] is questioned but not yet seriously threatened, as it moves increasingly to rule through force. What does become obvious is the propensity of the state to use violence to maintain a society marked by great spans of differences in the realms of power, prestige, and wealth. Lack of understanding proves of little political significance, for as conflict increases, the issues and biases voiced by the participants become increasingly clear-cut. The issues are debated. The Left and its friends win the arguments but lose the decisions made by the state. For now its key figures are not only biased but frightened by those whom the state judges to be subversive. The state backs away from a policy of repressive tolerance—from a policy of cultural and political charity—for the state elite now associate the growing popularity of cultural and political revolutionary currents with the demise of the legitimacy of the state, its procedures, and its key personnel, namely, themselves. Under these circumstances, the administrative and judicial non sequiturs, in some cases massive in form and quality, grow in popularity and replace the well-constructed justifications so common among elite decision-making bodies such as courts and university committees during the stage of political equilibrium. Indeed, the state settles more frequently upon the use of deliberate physical injury as a way of ensuring political control.[65]

State efforts to solve social problems fail. Parallel to failure in state collective problem solving, protestors begin to pass increasingly, however unevenly, from dissent to confrontation, and during this passage to articulate utopian perspectives quite discrepant with those of the well-heeled and intellectually well-oiled found at the center of the moral core. It is then that ideology comes under full counter-ideological attack, for along with the appearance of utopian outlines stiletto-like diagnoses pierce faltering social institutions.[66] The pyramidal hierarchies within these organizations are correctly portrayed as inept, corrupt, venal, and hypocritical by *conservative, bureaucratic standards*. As exposé piles on revelation, the institutional hierarchies are shaken. Indeed, the analyses are those of angered and often young denunciators sensitized to contradictions. The young novelists, painters, poets, playwrights, composers, scientists, and social scientists in ever greater numbers move against institutions depicted as faulty if not deformed.

Demonstrations and fierce repression alternate with moments of quasi equilibrium. It is then that the locus of ultimate power and institutional accommodation becomes more obvious, as the state transparently and ironically attempts to use institutions now filled with internal strife to bring about an end to conflict. This effort requires the use of shootings, gassings, and murders of institutional members.[67]

Even state terror sometimes fails to quell civil disobedience and to return secondary institutions to their normal, subordinate position. The chief of state depends increasingly upon indiscriminate killing and thereby violates his own rules and subsequently earns the image of bile-laden. In cartoons, he often assumes an indecorous posture, with protruding gut and varicose veins.

The issues become somewhat clearer, although there is pronounced vacillation between support for either rebellion or revolution.[68] The debate remains somewhat clouded because the progressive captains of the old core, wherever and whenever they can, move to try to solve problems through programs designed to coopt critics.

Yet even when cooptation works, reformers appear to be predoomed to defeat, for their programs fail to alleviate let alone get to the root of problems.[69] The state is thereby stymied in its efforts to resolve contradictions. Rather, it increases grievances articulated increasingly by a poor drawn from quiescence and dumbness to activism and consciousness by charismatic.leadership which makes clear for the oppressed their worsened conditions.[70] The leaders put into speech and prose the masses' deepest beliefs, feelings, hates, and desires.

The net result is the movement of a growing portion of the population from moral core obsequiousness to open struggle. Indeed, the modern state often fosters international war in an effort to postpone reform and justify repression at the very moment that it exploits its victims, the poor, who pay for the war through the taxes, inflation, selective service, their lives, and induced unemployment.[71] All reek havoc with the poor who come increasingly to support[72] sporadic bombings, lootings, and quasi insurrections.

What further upsets the leadership of the moral core is the movement of many of the poor from the moral core and the quiescent dumb to the categories of ambivalent partisans and from there to deliberate radicals and even eschatological Reds. Moving, too, are many who have been ambivalent partisans for most of their lives, as when noted professional scholars denounce the state.[73]

The state leadership suffers a loss of legitimacy within an increasingly wider circle of the oppressed and their alienated allies, for with affluence-poverty comes growing consciousness, empathy, sympathy, and trained ability of young intellectuals to dissect the hypocritical and to react against the oppressors of the down-and-out.[74] Not that all intellectuals trod this path,[75] but many, enough certainly, swing over to champion the poor in order to become part of a vociferous minority capable of becoming an organized and revolutionary majority.

This mutual criticism moves toward becoming total castigation on both sides, as first a miniscule and then a noticeably large number within every institution—and at all levels and interstices—begin to choose sides and criticize accordingly. These critics spend a good deal of time correcting conservative misdiagnoses and articulating alternative ideological forms. The radicals[76] take the lead to point out that the system does not suffer from poor leadership and maladministration but rather built-in, structural faults which cannot be changed in proper time unless revolutionaries hasten the demise of the entire system.

On the level of utopian construction, the eschatological radicals appear torn between refusal to sketch the new society and a desire to make clear what the new society is all about. Wishing to avoid the predictable rigidities of prism construction, hoping to rely upon the oppressed themselves to construct through spontaneous struggle what is soon to be achieved, these particular counterelites[77] flounder until forced by criticism to initiate the intellectual constructions of the future. Still they hesitate to depict fully, for the process of design would in some ways replicate the very elitism they wish to abolish. This fear they recognize but dimly; nonetheless, it proves sufficient either to halt their efforts to depict utopia, or to result in a hazy sketch of an ideal society. Rather than turning to the gigantic demands of constructing a grand picture, they favor the demolition of the sagging present and leave the future to popular, spontaneous creation.[78]

By contrast, the deliberate radicals begin to portray the future. They emphasize such matters as which classes and class-racial groups will reconstruct a society now torn by struggles just this side of civil war and revolution. What will be the relative strength of the state during the immediate postrevolutionary period as well as stages beyond? [79] To deal with this problem, revolutionaries sometimes call constitutional conventions and carefully draw up statements declared to be alternatives to the present ones which do not work.[80] The radicals pose important questions. How will oppressed minorities organize themselves for the new society? Crucial here is the debate among the radicals on the acceptable form of class-racial pluralism during the transition to socialism as well as its form immediately after the demise of the businessman's state.[81] What will be the relative strength of progressive and radical classes during the revolutionary transition and beyond? In answering this question revolutionaries sometimes go so far as to adopt a ratio scale of measurement and allocate points to the revolutionary worth of the various classes.[82] What will be the fate of classes and status groups currently identified with the old regime? Heatedly debated is whether they shall enjoy any rights whatsoever after the radicals take power. What will happen to the old ideologies that have helped to hold the oppressed in bondage? [83] The radicals disagree on whether the new revolutionary institutions will allow detached treatment of castigated ideologies once the revolutionaries have formed a new state.

What remains largely unspecified is the *pace* of these changes as well as how persons will engineer them and what will be the cost; when will all forms of potential repression disappear; how will the revolution handle the predictable Thermidorean reaction?

Of little interest but of great importance to the revolutionary movement is the question of what will happen after military victory to those people's councils, soviets, radical trade unions, and neighborhood groups, all created during the period of coming to power. Will they continue to be significant after the old state has been beaten or will the new state abolish these new forms and take over their activities? Radicals sidestep this question for fear of even greater division during a moment when there is a great need to avoid issues that will further exacerbate differences within the revolutionary movement. Rather, efforts are made to seek issues that will unite. In short, although the deliberate radicals prove more articulate on utopian construction, they leave much unsaid.

And while people muse over the future, events often move swiftly, for it is entirely possible for a revolutionary vanguard to find itself at the head of a general revolutionary movement running rapidly toward the elimination of the power of the older order without any clear idea of what concretely is to be achieved and how soon the tasks of state reconstruction will be upon them. This lack of intellectual presence disenchants some, but indiscriminate state oppression generates greater numbers of revolutionaries than the cadre can alienate because of their intellectual and organizational clumsiness.[84]

The Coming to Power of the Radicals

If and when revolutionaries take power,[85] they must translate utopia into ideology while fighting to maintain the revolution now being attacked from without as well as within. During this period of setting up revolutionary institutions and disseminating new ideologies, the radicals define the moment of grasping power as that delicious interval of historical arrival when all the old inequities are buried. Obvious celebrants are the people themselves operating, however momentarily and imperfectly, their own steel mills, power plants, railroads, farms, banking organizations—all come under the people's hegemony.[86]

Less apparent but visible are parallel efforts made to destroy the old cognitive structures. Old calendars are dismissed. Alphabets are revised. Certain genetic models are downgraded. Particular mathematical models are spurned, while others are celebrated. Antiquated terms are either abolished or invested with new meaning. Eliminated are old forms of address that signified hierarchy; people refer to one another either as citizens or as comrades. Whole areas of cognitive thought hitherto ignored by the state are given categorization to benefit those until recently oppressed; for example, the reclassification of diseases accompanies new programs against the bacteria, rodents, viruses, and insects slated for elimination.[87]

The state momentarily ceases to be a monopolizer of violence— for it has rivals in the people's militias—but rather becomes, however briefly, the near-perfect vehicle of change for the good. The new state is different. This state reflects the expressed aspirations of the former victims by striving to realize an egalitarian society. For the first time, full equality becomes visible at the end of a long road to be traversed and worked by the labor of those devoted to realization of total reconstruction through the eighteen-hour day.[88]

To travel this surface demands the suspension of static mentality. The new state ideology calls for the succession of a system of thought in which everything is in the process of becoming. The new cognitive categories avoid hard-and-fast definition—including propositional testability—in a world of delectable dialectical flux. Definitions of reality become malleable as never before in the living memories of participants, as people sense a new freedom based upon release from the old hierarchical categories. The laws of collective becoming through comradely struggle replace those of frozen stasis through obsequious adaptation. What begins to crystallize is a vision of the radical man, the person who defies as he defines and supplants the bourgeois laws of psychology and sociology. A fresh perspective becomes dominant: dialectical principles supplant in importance the old natural laws on mind and sociation. To promote understanding, the applicants of revolutionary theory circumscribe less general areas of human action than did their academic predecessors in order to lend credence to propositions having less generality but more specificity (not testability) and hence revolutionary effectiveness when implemented.[89]

The Period of Encirclement

When the reformist revolutionaries falter, the radicals assert their power, as the foreign enemies of the revolution continue to use military force and internal espionage to smash the adolescent revolution. At this point the high incidence of casualties force the revolutionary leadership to make more explicit *why* the sacrifice must continue.

In this context the deliberate radicals face an awful dilemma: if the revolution is to succeed in breaking encirclement,[90] the dwindling forces of revolution must be coordinated militarily on a dozen fronts by a vanguard party;[91] but to impose coordination is to tighten the reins of authority, for that is what coordination denotes. Yet to concentrate and centralize authority at the expense of local revolutionary impulse and locally controlled trade unions, soviets, and workers' councils means to destroy the vitality of the very revolutionary institutions people have just learned to use (and to misuse) in order to control their own lives.

The suppression of these new institutions occurs. With their demise goes the promise of group freedom from future state repression once the people's armies have destroyed the encirclement. The suppression stuns, for after all, the vast majority of revolutionary partisans want participatory democracy to last forever.[92]

Yet the demands of revolutionary military success during that historical moment take precedence over the maintenance of revolutionary institutions capable of maintaining a democratic impulse within the revolution.[93] New state power consolidates as it passes whole hog to the vanguard party and its leadership, who in turn become the leaders of both the Red Army and the new moral core.

This sacrifice of people's control proves both tragic and comical when Thermidor later descends among those who have survived and led the revolutionary struggle against encirclement, for ironically, the victims of Thermidor often prove to be the very ones who had only recently made the decision to suffocate the people's institutions;

the only institutions that might have been able to protect the deposed had these workers' councils, radical trade unions, and people's soviets been allowed to survive.[94]

At this pre-Thermidorean juncture, state ideology justifies power concentration but contradicts utopian depictions on the necessity of continued decentralization of power within liberated territories. Lost in a wave of rhetoric on postponement is people's control from the bottom up. This defeat angers as it humiliates, depresses, and dehumanizes those few grass-roots militants who have survived the earlier fights against the bourgeois state and marketing system. In many cases they become further disillusioned when the new state depicts them, of all people, as adventurers and ultraleftists to be placed in the counterrevolutionary category; until then this rubric had been used only to subsume the enemies of revolution lodged within the old moral core, the guts of the ancien régime.

What survives during periods of purge is the commitment to build a new society, now without institutions capable of doing so. Efforts are made and celebrated as consistent with the old counter-ideology and utopian perspective. A brave new effort is made to impress a skeptical outside world, as many revolutionaries and their foreign apologists discuss the revolution as if no repression had happened.[95] These reconstructions include an effort to build equality into many relationships. Illustrative are activities to create equality in an army without distinctions in dress but differences in rank; the use of the language of equality at work but within the shells of recently powerful trade unions (and workers' councils as well as soviets); the practices of equality in treatment of the two sexes in a political world in which top positions of state power are all but devoid of women.

Yet celebrated changes do take place. Not all is fully contradictory. During the phase of war communism,[96] especially its later moments, equality becomes the guiding idea and to some degree a living thing for progressive sections of all classes, status groups, and generations. Seemingly unshakable cultural and personality rigidities do fall, as drug addicts become disciplined gun carriers, prostitutes become warriors, ex-professors become revolutionary staff members, and diligent peasants work as comrades with former professors. Paradoxically, the new state admonishes conservatives for their lack of revolutionary élan at the very moment the latest elites resurrect new bureaucratic controls and prepare the way for the acceptance of the classical conservatives formulas on why inequality persists.

During the final phase of war communism against foreign encroachment, the distinction between the saved and the damned moves to another level of discussion: what is left-wing? People's lives ride on this definition, as the new state imposes a terror to relieve the society of those who might betray the revolution to foreign enemies and domestic desperados. The new rulers prefer to circumscribe the definition of "Left" to include commitment to the maintenance of the new state, and within it, the eventual realization of economic equality through common state ownership and fraternal relations. By contrast, the receding anarchosyndicalists insist upon equal access to political decision making in state government through control of their own organizations. The state should be controlled by the soviets, the workers' councils and the trade unions. For anarchosyndicalists, these organs should be resurrected and given state power.[97]

In all revolutions the local anarchosyndicalists, whatever their particular designation might be, argue that unless the people can reconstitute this control, they will be unable either to eliminate the economic inequities that survive or to preempt those that would undoubtedly arise in the absence of democratically controlled trade unions, workers' councils, soviets, and neighborhood groups. Without these kinds of popular controls, all forms of social stratification would reemerge, so that those having the greatest state power through occupation of top decision-making positions would use this power to increase their incomes and embellish their reputations. The indictment is complete: in the absence of grass-roots governance what would crystallize would be a span of rewards different in form but similar in content to that of the old regime. Thus, yesterday's leftist-intellectual leadership would become tomorrow's right-wing: a new moral core replete with state power, great wealth, false honor plus the unearned reputation of being new and hence potentially progressive.[98] Thus those who objectively oppress through unbridled state power obviously win—enough to make cynics of those who had hoped and died for more.[99]

Thermidor

Thermidor is the realization of the anarchosyndicalist nightmare, not a delusion, for the objective passage of a revolution into the beginnings of Thermidor proves unmistakable. Those spent through struggle become ready for an exhausted examination of what is happening around them, for although ennui permeates those not decimated by struggle, this collective torpor does lend itself to contemplation. They observe the new leaders, captains of the new revolution, who haltingly justify in backhanded fashion how they as vanguard leaders have gained a disproportionately large amount of power, wealth, and prestige for themselves.

Justifications of the new inequities abound. Revolutionary leaders describe the present inequities as part of a passing phase and hence of passing interest. Temporary maldistributions of good food, clothing, housing, education, and the like are rationalized as being temporary inconveniences. What occurs among the revolutionary rank and file is a growing awareness of how the new captains of revolutionary institutions are driving new and better vehicles, sending their children to better schools, speaking a more precise language, treating ordinary citizens with bureaucratic disdain, circumspectly admonishing proletarian minorities for their alleged boorishness, eating much of the better (and scarce) food, garnering more of their share of scarce beverages, consuming a larger portion of the scarce and high-quality durable goods, using a disproportionately large share of the high-quality fuels, holidaying at spas used only recently by the leadership of the old regime, earning inordinately large incomes even though the leaders do not create value, compromising with the old ruling classes and their cultural symbols by reinstituting old religious symbols, calendars, workweeks, personal designations, and even some forms of private property.[100]

In the context of new inequalities now institutionalized, the new moral core[101] generally and eventually falls back upon the old structural-functional theories of social stratification. One argument proves particularly popular: to the inherently talented go the trained capabilities—and the necessary rewards. In the new society, the state must fulfill certain economic functions if it is to survive. To survive, it must cull from the mass those who are most talented. The state must then train them for important positions in the economy. But to select the talented and to train them demands that the state reward both them and their imaginations. How? The state must make known its rewards during training periods for the promising young, so that they will forgo pleasures and give themselves to educational training in order to maximize personal pleasures once the training is completed and the functionally important jobs are obtained. The intellectuals thereby articulate a theory of the state with overtones of Social Darwinism.[102]

Other responses of the new revolutionary elites to the new inequalities stress revolutionary lag. There are those who accept the new inequities as momentary, distasteful but inevitable. They deliberately rationalize an expanding span of rewards by saying that the span will disappear at a later moment. They say these things without indicating precisely when the shrinking of the span will begin. Whatever the rationalization, what appears fullblown are justifications of social stratification under conditions of state ownership of the means of production and tight state control of ideological dissemination. Suppression of utopian alternatives generally becomes total.

Not content with the demise of equality and the introduction of its stratified successors, old-time revolutionaries sometimes intervene. Generally their doing so is to no avail, for their numbers are few and their actions irrelevant, since to revitalize revolutionary institutions requires the recruitment of numerous comrades now found within institutions padded with the fat of limited radical success: the seizure of state power and the enjoyment of its pecuniary rewards.

On occasion, however,[103] a handful of the revolutionary old guard can and do unite with Red youth to attack those members of the middle generation who have faltered and flatulated. When the new alliance occurs, and if it receives positive endorsement of the state, its members sometimes create a general social movement[104] and move out within every institution to smash what they deem to be counterrevolutionary cultural values and activities, that is, Thermidorean commitments and actions that contravene the egalitarian aspirations of the original utopia. The Red alliance directs liberation struggles in schools, trade unions, government bureaus, collective farms, mines, factories, and universities—wherever people suffer from the reappearance of the old forms cloaked in the new revolutionary jargon. An effort is made by the anti-Thermidorean coalition of the revolution to disseminate through printed leaflets, seized newspapers, chalked blackboards, scrawled walls, and local bulletin boards a simple message: revitalize and refurbish now to avoid the path which normally leads full circle to total cultural revolution from below. The attack is aimed against "functional necessity" and "human nature." On the question of functional necessity, the Red alliance revolutionaries argue that the revolution knows no necessities other than the need to rejuvenate revolution or to allow it to drift until it becomes necessary to destroy the *new* regime. On the level of human nature, a sustained effort is made to indicate the frailties of collective problem solving when both the tracings of the past inequities remain and the present structures foster elitism.

Illustrative is the cultural revolution in China.[105] There, a coalition of new moral core irregulars—Mao and Chiang Ching (Mao's wife) among them—united with a large section of youth to revitalize all of China. Perhaps nowhere was this effort more obvious and perhaps more successful than in the universities, a favorite bastion and source of elitism in all societies. Recent accounts indicate a thoroughgoing effort to erase the built-in propensity of the universities to recruit from the favored classes. Rather, the Red alliance and the rejuvenated state now dispense a university ideology and practice more in keeping with the needs of the lower classes and an egalitarian division of labor.[106]

But the Chinese success is the exception. Furthermore, there is the distinct possibility that the Chinese state could regress to the predictable pattern of pressing for inequalities. The Chinese state could follow the Russian example and justify the growth of inequities once Mao is dead by citing the need to create an unequal reward structure in order to motivate persons to meet state goals. The state could then move against those revolutionary-egalitarian groups without the institutional base of people's councils.[107] The fatal ingredient in the Chinese revolution remains what it has always been: the absence of people's continuous control over their own state through their own revolutionary institutions. In the long haul, the vanguard party and Mao's charisma will not be enough.

Conclusions

1. How the businessman's state formulates its rationalizations and how the state uses force depend on whether state myths are being accepted by the subordinate classes.

2. During moments of equilibrium, the state emphasizes political pluralism and repressive tolerance while deemphasizing the actual use of state violence; in effect, ideology plays the key cohesive role.

3. During the prodromal period of revolution, there is at first a slightly discernible, and then later a totally visible, decline in the ability of state ideologies to integrate the population; the businessman's state persists, nonetheless, in its praise of the myth of political pluralism, introduces the technique of massive cooptation of critical rebels, depends less upon reasoned argument, and uses violence more frequently if less discriminately; the state engages in this shift, in large part because a large and growing portion of the mass rejects the state's political formulas and engages in rebellious and revolutionary action.

4. If and when a revolutionary state is created, it will momentarily propagate political formulas consistent with the revolutionary aspirations of the great majority of the turned-on masses who indeed take action to control the new state through people's councils; the state dares not ignore the very ones upon whom the state leaders depend for their continued occupancy of state power positions.

5. Under conditions of encirclement and war communism, with their contradictory demands for both (a) military defense of the revolutionary republic through *greater concentration* of state power *and* (b) people's struggles for the maintenance and extension of a new democratic and *decentralized* system of workers' councils, autonomous trade unions, and grass-roots soviets—many of the egalitarian achievements of the revolution are lost.

6. During the Thermidorean period, there occurs the slight possibility of rejuvenating the drive for equality—as in the Chinese cultural revolution—but the "short haul" recrudescence of revolutionary egalitarianism may well be followed by the "long haul" giving way to the reconstruction of autonomous, authoritarian, bureaucratic elites—unless the people themselves are able to create and di-

rect on a continuous basis their own institutions, and through them, that most powerful of institutions, the revolutionary state.

NOTES

1. In this analysis I refer primarily to the businessman's state, the state in which the corporate- and banking-propertied dominate. Many of my remarks could apply to socialist and other state forms as well, however. In the last part of this paper I discuss revolutionary states of the nonbusinessman's variety. For discussions on the nature of the state, see Lawrence Krader, *Formation of the State* (Englewood Cliffs, N.J.: Prentice-Hall, 1968); Frederick Engels, *The Origin of the Family, Private Property, and the State* (New York: International Publishers, 1942); Morton Fried, "On the Evolution of Social Stratification and the State," in *Culture in History*, ed. Stanley Diamond (New York: Columbia University Press, 1960), pp. 713–31; Gerhard Lenski, *Power and Privilege* (New York: McGraw-Hill, 1966), esp. pp. 43–93; Ralph Miliband, "The State and Revolution," *Monthly Review* 21 (April 1970): 77–90; Reinhard Bendix, *State and Society* (Boston: Little Brown, 1968); John Porter, *The Vertical Mosaic* (Toronto: University of Toronto Press, 1966), pp. 3–28, 201–558; and of course Vladimir I. Lenin, *The State and Revolution*, vol. 7 (New York: International Publishers, 1943), pp. 5–111.

2. Many social democrats would like to view the state as a neutral mechanism, one which can be steered by the party in power to achieve socialism whenever social democrats take power; however, they generally resist the temptation to go all the way. Immediately after coming to power, they must make a decision on how to relate to the holders of capital; either to move for their eventual expropriation or to settle for their continuation and to set thereby the norm for relating to capital throughout the period of social democratic governance. See David Horowitz's "Introduction" in his *Corporations and the Cold War* (New York: Monthly Review Press, 1969), p. 13. See also C. Wright Mills, "The Structure of Power in American Society," in *Power, Politics and People*, ed. Irving Louis Horowitz (New York: Oxford University Press, 1963), p. 25; and Herbert Marcuse, *One-Dimensional Man* (Boston: Beacon Press, 1964), p. 2.

3. Market society is different from free-market economy. Market society is one in which profit is derived from the flow of land, labor, and goods. Free-market economy occurs when there is an unfettered flow of land, labor, and goods, as for example, in England in the mid-nineteenth century. See Karl Polanyi, *The Great Transformation* (Boston: Beacon Press, 1957), esp. pp. 163–219.

4. I assume that the businessman's state is a crucial institutional com-

ponent of international capitalism. For a global analysis of the relationship between the bourgeois state and international capital, see Oliver Cox, *Capitalism as a System* (New York: Monthly Review Press, 1964).

5. The state elite concern themselves with the behavior of others as well, especially during moments of perceived threat to the state. Crucial during these periods more than others is the way in which the officials of state investigate, threaten, and punish potential dissenters. For an excellent analysis of campus repression of academics—as they correctly perceived this repression—during the 1950s, see Paul F. Lazarsfeld and Wagner Thielens, Jr., *The Academic Mind* (Glencoe, Ill.: Free Press, 1958).

6. In modern bourgeois democracies, it is often the regulated who regulate the regulators. The state will on occasion attempt to reform the behavior of giant corporations, banking groups, and utilities, only to find later that the very boards established by the state to accomplish the regulatory tasks become staffed and almost completely controlled by representatives of these economically and politically powerful groups. For a lucid discussion of how this redesign of purpose and function occurs, see G. William Domhoff, *Who Rules America?* (Englewood Cliffs, N.J.: Prentice-Hall, 1967), esp. pp. 12–114, 132–37.

7. Illustrative are the periodic firings of teachers judged disloyal to a state during a period of perceived emergency, as during the early 1950s in the United States.

8. State threats against establishment newspaper reporting, such as the *New York Times*, abounded during the 1960s and early 1970s. During the Cuban missile crisis in October 1962, for example, a White House memo, not too veiled in its concern over the detailed reporting of the period by the *Times*, asked the press and broadcast media to use "caution and discretion" in handling data deemed vital to national security. See *New York Times*, 25 October 1962, p. 25; 1 November 1962, p. 5; 17 November 1962, p. 1; 21 November 1962, p. 1; 1 December 1962, p. 26.

In 1967–68, before and during the Tet offensive in Vietnam, U.S. military representatives opened up against all U.S. newsmen in Vietnam by saying that U.S. newsmen might face courts-martial for disobedience of orders (armed forces have legal jursidiction over American civilians working in Vietnam under military auspices). *New York Times*, 16 February 1967. For related *Times* news stories, see *New York Times*, 25 February 1967, p. 29; 2 April 1967, p. 30; 1 June 1967, p. 1; 1 July 1967, p. 11.

After Nixon's election in the fall of 1968, the president-elect named H. G. Klein as director of communications for the executive branch of government, a new post giving Klein apparently "unusual powers over all government information services." *New York Times*, 26 November 1968, p. 1; 29 November 1968, p. 58. Shortly after taking office Nixon moved to tighten policy on withholding military data that might be of intelligence value to the enemy. *New York Times*, 27 February 1969, p. 2; 16 March 1969, p. 17.

In the fall of 1969 the Nixon Administration initiated a systematic intimidation of the media. Beginning on November 13, Vice-President Agnew charged that three TV networks let producers, newscasters, and commentators give "highly selective and often biased presentation of the news." *New York Times*, 14 November 1969, p. 1. Three days later President Nixon's communications director, H. G. Klein, commenting on Vice-President Agnew's criticism of news coverage, widened administration criticism of coverage to include all news media. *New York Times*, 17 November 1969, p. 1.

On November 20, Agnew broadened the attack on the media to include newspapers, particularly the *New York Times* and *Washington Post*. *New York Times*, 21 November 1969, p. 22. Shortly thereafter *Newsweek* quoted an Agnew aide as saying that the attack on TV and press was a "carefully organized" campaign. *New York Times*, 24 November 1969, p. 31. The International Press Institute indicated that Vice-President Agnew's attacks on press and TV were the "most serious threat to press freedom" in the Western world, and went on to say that the most serious aspect of the attacks was the implication that they were inspired by President Nixon. *New York Times*, 1 January 1970, p. 6. The idea of a Nixon strategy was further reinforced by Attorney General John Mitchell's policy of issuing subpoenas for unedited files and unused pictures of the news media. *New York Times*, 1 February 1970, p. 1. For related news stories see *New York Times*, 4 February 1970, p. 1; 6 February 1970, p. 1; 4 April 1970, p. 1; 11 August 1970, p. 1.

9. We sometimes forget that the principal arms of the state are bureaucrats whom most people detest and armies which most persons fear. And for good reason: these two groups have ultimate control over much of our lives.

10. Crucial, for example, is the cloudy information available in the United States on the control structure of such powerful state agencies as the Central Intelligence Agency and the Federal Bureau of Investigation. Generally, only intellectuals have an informational understanding of these two groups, and even then, the information and hence analyses are limited. Nonetheless, such glimpses are useful. See, for example, G. William Domhoff's "The Military, the CIA and the FBI," found in his *Who Rules America?*, pp. 115–32.

11. The relationship between property and state occupancy has been analyzed by a number of writers, most notably C. Wright Mills in his *The Power Elite* (New York: Oxford University Press, 1959). Also see Domhoff, *Who Rules America?*; G. William Domhoff, "Who Made American Foreign Policy, 1945–1963," in Horowitz, *Corporations and the Cold War*, pp. 25–70; and William Appleman Williams, "The Large Corporations and American Foreign Policy," in ibid., pp. 71–104.

12. Perhaps the best discussion of corporate and executive expectations

can be found in Paul Baran and Paul Sweezy's *Monopoly Capital* (New York: Monthly Review Press, 1966), esp. pp. 14–51. For a discussion of the waste of human resources, see their discussion in ibid., pp. 112–367.

13. Perhaps this is Domhoff's major contribution to our understanding of the relationship between the propertied and state power. See, for example, his analysis of "The Military, the CIA and the FBI," in *Who Rules America?*, pp. 115–31. For a discussion of the way in which executives are wooed by corporations through promises of stock in corporations, see also Gabriel Kolko, *Wealth and Power in America* (New York: Praeger, 1962), pp. 9–45; and Mills, *Power Elite*, pp. 269–97.

14. Many governments pride themselves in screening their teacher applicants for signs of potential disloyalty and firing those who had earlier passed the loyalty tests but who later indicated a potential disloyalty to the principles advocated by the state. The signing of a loyalty oath by no means shields a professor from future harassment by the state while employed as a civil servant.

15. By *masses* is meant those without state power other than the recurrent right to opt for one of several candidates already chosen for them.

16. The mesmerizing quality of myths has been discussed by a number of writers, but seldom more acutely than by Gaetano Mosca in his *The Ruling Class* (New Class: McGraw-Hill, 1939), pp. 62–146; for a comparative analysis of Mosca and Pareto's contributions on the understanding myths, political formulas, and derivations, see James H. Meisel's *The Myth of the Ruling Class* (Ann Arbor: University of Michigan Press, 1958); also pertinent is George Sorel, *Reflections on Violence* (Glencoe, Ill.: Free Press, 1950), pp. 136–201. Perhaps most relevant is Harold Lasswell's eclectic writings on the power of myths, and their use by those who seek to obtain and retain state power. See his "Politics: Who Gets What, When and How," in *The Political Writings of Harold D. Lasswell* (Glencoe, Ill.: Free Press, 1951), pp. 311–25; also see Harold Lasswell and Abraham Kaplan, *Power and Society* (New Haven: Yale University Press, 1950), pp. 103–41; 240–84.

17. In compressed form are T. B. Bottomore and Maximilien Rubel's excerpts from Marx on "The State and Law" in their *Karl Marx: Selected Writings in Sociology and Social Philosophy* (London: Watts, 1956), pp. 215–30; see also Karl Marx, *The 18th Brumaire of Louis Bonaparte* (New York: International Publishers, 1963), pp. 15–16. Mosca's analysis of mass as object of manipulation can be found in his *Ruling Class*, esp. pp. 50–69; Pareto's views on this matter are not that different from Mosca's, according to Meisel in his *Myth of the Ruling Class*, pp. 14–21. Roberto Michels clearly enunciated his view of the common man as inevitably doomed to the forces of manipulation in his discussion of the Iron Law of Oligarchy; see Michels' *Political Parties* (Glencoe, Ill.: Free Press, 1949), esp. pp. 365–408. Finally Harold Lasswell presents a similar view in his "Politics," pp. 295–341, 375–91, as well as Lasswell and Kaplan's *Power and Society*, pp. 103–41.

18. Again we can cite the existence and lengthy quotations from Bottomore and Rubel, *Karl Marx*, pp. 231–40. In Mosca's *Ruling Class*, there are references to the conditions associated with "revolution," pp. 199–221, while Pareto's theory of "the circulation of the elite" argues that the ending of that circulation paves the way for revolution. See T. B. Bottomore, *Elites and Society* (London: Watts, 1964), pp. 42–62. Finally, the concluding substantive chapter in Lasswell and Kaplan's *Power and Society*, pp. 240–84, deals exclusively with conditions and processes associated with revolution.

19. By *myths* are meant ideologies concerned with the nature of power, wealth, and prestige. These ideologies may or may not be deliberately construed. When deliberately construed, myths are *particular;* when part of the general culture and not traceable to the design of particular persons, these myths are *general.* When myths demand a qualitative change in society— such as the myth of the general strike under conditions of capitalism—myths may be either particular or general, but in any event they are *transcending*.

20. By *subordinate classes* are meant those groups that relate to the means of production in ways other than to derive most of their income from investment.

21. *Alternate state* actually refers to groups that give every indication of either becoming a new state or relating themselves to other organizations that indicate such an organizational propensity. An example of an "alternate state" would be a soviet of workers, peasants, or soldiers that had assumed functions ordinarily ascribed exclusively to the state. The "attacking group" would include collectivities such as a vanguard party. For the pathfinding discussion, see Vladimir I. Lenin, "A Dual Power," in James H. Meisel and Edward S. Kozera, *Materials for the Study of the Soviet System* (Ann Arbor, Mich.: George Wahr, 1953), pp. 7–9.

22. It is useful to include as part of one's analysis not only the class structure but the institutional network as well, for clearly the state and the propertied classes depend heavily upon institutions to maintain political control.

23. By *moments of stable equilibrium* are meant those periods when the economy is able to provide full or near-full employment for all or nearly all sectors of the adult population. My conception of equilibrium is consistent with Bukharin's. See Nikolai Bukharin, *Historical Materialism* (New York: Russell & Russell, 1965), p. 130.

24. Crucial in understanding ideology is the distinction among ideology, counterideology, and utopia. By *ideology* is meant those ideas that justify the extant system of property, power, and prestige. Ideology may be particular, as when a person deliberately fabricates myths; or general, as when a group unconsciously creates ideas which justify, obscure, conceal and/or rationalize real relationships in the realms of power, property, and prestige. By *counterideology* is meant ideas—whether particular or general—aimed at dele-

gitimating the extant rules, beliefs, values, and authorities in the realms of property, power, and prestige. *Utopia* consists of ideas that sharply question the ongoing structure of stratification by expressing beliefs diametrically opposed to the present. By way of illustration, a utopian vision under conditions of capitalism would call for the elimination of private property, the withering away of the state, and the creation of a society with status based upon collective service. For a discussion of ideology and utopia, see Karl Mannheim, *Ideology and Utopia* (New York: Harcourt, 1936), pp. 55–108, 192–263.

25. If nothing else, empirical sociology established, during the 1930s, '40s, '50s, and '60s, the way in which occupational position, occupational status, ethnic rank, and religious status—as well as educational and income prestige—together determined how people voted, how they made love, where they lived, what they ate, what they drank, how they played, how they spoke, what they read, what they watched, whom they visited, which organizations they joined, and what their children thought and did.

26. My use of the term *moral core* does not mean that I approve of them or their morality.

27. Fanon's discussion of the Frenchified West Indian in relation to his mother country, France, would be appropriate. See Frantz Fanon, *Black Skin, White Masks* (New York: Grove, 1967), pp. 19–20. By contrast, the same author indicates how the colonized can move once revolutionary conditions exist. See his *Studies in a Dying Colonialism* (New York: Monthly Review Press, 1965). Indeed, revolution becomes a means of divesting the colonized of his propensity to identify with the oppressor, the central thesis of Fanon's most well known work, *The Wretched of the Earth* (New York: Grove, 1966).

28. Thorstein Veblen was one of the first to note the propensity of the lower classes to identify with as they emulate the upper classes. See his *The Theory of the Leisure Class* (New York: Mentor, 1963), esp. pp. 33–80.

29. What scandalizes the moral core is the countercultural behaviour of many eschatological radicals. Dress style, "vulgar" speech, sexual promiscuity, esoteric food beliefs, illegal drug use, "excessive" geographical mobility, and the like embarrass, enrage, and scandalize those more cramped in life style.

30. What is needed is a definitive study of the relationship between the eschatological radicals and their upper-class patrons. Without their support, the eschatological radicals could barely survive the harassments of the police, the courts, and the bill collectors.

31. What I have in mind are liberal publications such as *The Nation* and *The New Republic*.

32. The potential for radicalization should not be confused with radicalization, for often struggle activities lead to demoralization of all participants, especially when the protestors lose.

33. Useful is the distinction between inimical and antagonistic contradictions. By *inimical contradictions* are meant those structural antagonisms that occur within one's own camp, one's own struggle group. By contrast, *antagonistic contradictions* have reference to those antagonisms that occur between one's own struggle group and the enemy camp.

34. At times it would seem, in many parts of the United States, as if a cultural norm pressed people to think rationally while at work and nonrationally once beyond its confines. This observation is simply conjecture, but it would appear that many persons insist upon their right to apply one set of criteria while at work—generally some form of deductive thought—and another set of criteria for thinking while away from the workplace—beliefs in sloppy free association and the massive non sequitur.

35. Compulsory school attendance now exists for many college students who obey both the demands of their parents on mobility and the demands of the labor market on work postponement.

36. In the United States during the 1940s, '50s, and '60s, pollsters and survey organizations discovered time and again that significant minorities of those interviewed were unaware of such basic information as the name of the president of the United States, the senators or governors of their states, and whether France was a republic or a monarchy. Of interest, too, was the propensity of persons to know a good deal about subjects that did not exist.

37. Of recent interest is the propensity of the low-income and lessor educated blue-collar workers to organize into unions, neighborhood groups, and the like. Those who participate in these struggles, especially, become well informed and quite involved in the political process. Examples would be hospital workers, garbage collectors, grape pickers, and the like.

38. For a discussion of periodization schema much like my own, indeed, I drew my categories largely from their works, see Lyford P. Edwards, *The Natural History of Revolution* (New York: Russell & Russell, 1965); Crane Brinton, *The Anatomy of Revolution* (New York: Vintage, 1965).

39. For a discussion of one such model, that of Talcott Parsons, and a critique of this approach, see Alvin W. Gouldner, *The Coming Crisis of Western Sociology* (New York: Basic Books, 1970), esp. pp. 167–338.

40. C. Wright Mills' most famous work in this regard was his *The Sociological Imagination* (New York: Grove, 1959). But part of this attack appeared earlier in his *Power Elite*, especially in his discussion of the "military ascendancy," pp. 198–224. Even before *The Power Elite* had appeared, Mills had begun to dissect the new conservatism in his "The Conservative Mood," published in 1954. It can be found in Irving L. Horowitz, *Power, Politics and People: The Collected Essays of C. Wright Mills* (New York: Oxford University Press, 1962), pp. 208–20.

41. The most celebrated analysis was, of course, Daniel Bell's *End of*

Ideology, especially the essay by that title. See his *End of Ideology* (Glencoe, Ill.: Free Press, 1960), pp. 369–75.

42. Bell's brilliant essay "Two Roads From Marx: The Themes of Alienation and Exploitation in Socialist Thought" appeared in ibid., pp. 335–68. The concentration of religiosity proved popular in much of sociology during the 1950s. Since the civil rights movement of the 1960s, interest in the subject has waned.

43. Daniel Bell, "The Power Elite Reconsidered," *American Journal of Sociology* 64 (November 1958): 238–50.

44. C. Wright Mills delivered a general reply to these criticisms. See his "Power Elite: Comment on Criticism," *Dissent* 4 (Winter 1957): 22–34.

45. See, for example, Bottomore and Rubel's selections in their *Karl Marx*, pp. 135–38.

46. Illustrative would be A. R. Radcliffe-Brown's *The Andaman Islanders* (Glencoe, Ill.: Free Press, 1948).

47. The assumption is clear: if only the true believer would cease to indulge his ego in efforts to remake the world, societal problems would occur less frequently and be less severe. Pertinent here are Gerhard Lenski's summary remarks on the conservative mentality as it approaches this problem. See Gerhard Lenski, *Power and Privilege* (New York: McGraw-Hill, 1966) p. 29.

48. The professional journals of sociology, social psychology, and psychology in the United States have smacked totally of this orientation.

49. It makes little sense to assume that the upper classes are homogeneous in membership and outlook when in fact all evidence indicates otherwise, at least in the United States during this century.

50. By *establishment* is meant those groups which have a monopoly of the strategic resources of the society, be they land or capital. The establishment differs from the *ruling class*, a category that refers to the political elite, namely, those who exercise state power. The members of these two categories are by no means coterminous, although there may well be considerable overlap of membership and positive, symbiotic relations between various role occupants.

51. Illustrative was the impact of the civil rights movement during the 1960s. Above all, it made the "invisible poor" visible.

52. To repeat, the mass refers to those who do not wield state power. Hence, the mass may well include many relatively well-off members of the middle class. Those at the bottom we may refer to as the lower classes—the lesser blue collar or the lesser mass—clearly persons without not only state power but without influence over the state *unless* they participate in revolt or revolution.

53. For example, in the United States during the late 1950s and early 1960s, a number of critical exposés appeared, most notably Michael Harrington's *The Other America* (New York: Macmillan, 1962).

54. See an excellent analysis of the new warfare-state intellectuals, the professorial advisers to the U.S. state, in Noam Chomsky, *American Power and the New Mandarins* (New York: Pantheon, 1969), pp. 23–158.

55. An illustrative criticism would be Ralf Dahrendorf, "Out of Utopia," *American Journal of Sociology* 64 (September 1968): 115–27.

56. Bendix and Lipset have written on the hierarchical perspective common to nineteenth-century conservatives. See Reinhard Bendix and Seymour Lipset, eds., *Class, Status and Power* (Glencoe, Ill.: Free Press, 1953), p. 9.

57. This tradition goes back at least as far as Speenhamland. See Polanyi, *Great Transformation*, pp. 77–85, 280–88.

58. The functional theory of social stratification has few peers to Kingsley Davis and Wilbert Moore's formulation. See their "Some Principles of Stratification," *American Sociological Review* 10 (April 1945): 242–49.

59. See Bendix and Lipset, *Class, Status and Power*, pp. 9–10.

60. T. B. Bottomore's introductory paragraphs to his discussion of the conservative and egalitarian positions on equality would seem appropriate. See Bottomore, *Elites and Society*, pp. 122–23.

61. The demands for justice are answered by conservatives in their counterconceptualization on "survival of the fittest." For a discussion of Darwin and Spencer on these materials, see Marvin Harris, *The Rise of Anthropological Theory* (New York: Thomas Y. Crowell, 1968), pp. 108–216.

62. By *loss of state legitimacy* is meant the vast majority of the mass no longer view the state as having ultimate authority. In a more dynamic sense, the phrase can refer to the continued decline in such recognition after a majority have already taken this position. People's alienation from the state in this regard should also deepen, thereby lessening popular legitimacy of state authority.

63. By *dissent* is meant to be critical but to stop short of institutional obstruction. By contrast, *obstruction* has reference to efforts made to curtail or to stop the normal functioning of part or all of an institution. For a discussion of the related topics of "Non-Violence and Armed Defense," see Martin Oppenheimer and George Lakey, *A Manual For Direct Action* (Chicago: Quadrangle, 1965), pp. 114–23.

64. *Power* has reference to A coercing B to act against B's own interests. *State power* simply designates the unit of coercion, real or potential. This approach to power is very similar to the one advanced by Max Weber in his discussion of structures of power. See H. H. Gerth and C. Wright Mills, *From*

Max Weber: Essays in Sociology (New York: Oxford University Press, 1946), pp. 159–79.

65. Few have surpassed L. P. Edwards and Crane Brinton's analyses of the increased and unwise use of state force during the late prodromal period. See Edwards, *Natural History of Revolution*, pp. 38–67; Brinton, *Anatomy of Revolution*, pp. 67–91.

66. Illustrative would be Beaumarchais' uncensored libretto in Mozart's *The Marriage of Figaro*, a direct attack on the ancien régime immediately prior to the French Revolution. See Brinton, *Anatomy of Revolution*, pp. 67–68.

67. Batista's government, the dictatorial regime of Cuba immediately prior to the coming to power of Fidel Castro's "alternate state," reportedly killed 20,000 political suspects and prisoners between 1952 and 1959. Many of these were innocent, even by Batista's criteria. See Leo Huberman and Paul M. Sweezy, *Cuba: Anatomy of a Revolution* (New York: Monthly Review Press, 1961), pp. 28–29.

68. By *rebellion* is meant mass action to revitalize the state by attempting to press it to conform to an ideal model presumably approached by the state during an earlier period. By *revolution* is meant the mass acting to go beyond reform of the state to the substitution of one form for another: republic for monopoly, monarchy for monopoly, and so forth. This discussion and distinction derives mainly from the writings of E. J. Hobsbawm. See his *Primitive Rebels* (London: Manchester University Press, 1959), pp. 1–12.

69. Some "problems" are structural in two senses: they stem from relationships among groups, while these relationships defy easy alteration.

70. "Making it real" demands mass participants at gatherings addressed by charismatic leaders who by definition have this ability. For the classical discussion of charisma, see Max Weber's "The Sociology of Charismatic Authority," in Gerth and Mills, *From Max Weber*, pp. 245–52.

71. Illustrative are the Great Basin poor—whites, Chicanos, and Indians; California Central Valley poor; the Appalachian mountaineers; the big-city racial minorities, at least their poorer members. The list could be extended to include one-fifth to one-quarter of the U.S. population associated with state exploitation. Maurice Zeitlin's *American Society, Inc.* (Chicago: Markham, 1970) contains an excellent section on poverty in the United States; see pp. 151–221.

72. *Support* has reference to lending aid, all the way from abject silence but attitudinal backing, through vociferous dissent to total and continuous participation in struggle.

73. Hans Morgenthau recently penned an acidic and incisive attack on the U.S. state by analyzing the way in which a state-corrupted university

system further alienates many of the young in his "Reflections on the End of the Republic," *New York Review of Books* 15 (24 September 1970): 38–41.

74. It has been said that one of the contradictions of the modern university system is its propensity to train students to think critically about institutions and then not to expect them to apply this critical perspective to corporations and other institutions that have "merged" with the university. For a keen theoretical appraisal of the merger but lack of understanding of the contradictions involved, see Clark Kerr, *The Uses of the University* (Cambridge, Mass.: Harvard University Press, 1964).

75. Intellectuals are as heterogeneous in composition and attitude as the working class. Unfortunately, we sometimes refer to intellectuals as if they were a homogeneous group, as a bloc committed either one way or another. In fact, groups such as sociologists—about whom stereotypes are legion—are highly differentiated in terms of both background and predisposition. Alvin W. Gouldner and J. Timothy Sprehe have demonstrated this pattern in their study of 3,440 sociologists. There was an absence of anything approaching concensus on such fundamentals as: (1) values and social science, (2) emphasis on the scientific method, (3) the social role of sociologists, (4) the role and value of social theory, (5) evaluation of the sociologist, (6) attitudes toward the profession, (7) the metaphysics of sociologists, (8) people and publics. See their "The Study on Man: Sociologists Look at Themselves," *Transaction* 2 (May–June 1965): 42–44.

76. When referring to *radicals,* what I have in mind are persons fully committed to fraternal equality in all areas; popular, democratic control over all institutions including the state; full and continuous equality in the realm of the distribution of wealth and power; prestige differentiation as the basis for rewards for those who participate in egalitarian, libertarian activities promotive of group welfare. Admittedly, few radicals meet all these criteria. Hence, it is necessary to think in terms of a continuum for the purposes of placing radicals next to one another relative to the two poles of a continuum which would simultaneously incorporate the mentioned criteria.

77. By *counterelite* is meant those members of the mass who take the lead in both establishing counterstates—such as soviets and their equivalents—and eliminating extant state organizations. Before October 1917, Lenin, for example, was a member of the Russian counterelite, as was Mao before the People's Liberation Army established full state hegemony on the Chinese mainland.

78. This propensity predisposes eschatological radicals to accept the mass spontaneity conception of revolution. A leading and articulate exponent of this approach was Rosa Luxemburg. For a comparative discussion of her analysis, see J. P. Nettl, *Rosa Luxemburg*, vol. 2 (London: Oxford University Press, 1966), pp. 786–827.

79. An interesting and critical analysis of this problem has been presented by Miliband in "The State and Revolution," pp. 77–90.

80. See *Black Panther*, 12 September 1970, p. 3.

81. Mao in his "coalition government" (1945) followed a cultural self-determinist position in keeping with the writings of Lenin. See Conrad Brandt, Benjamin Schwartz, and John K. Fairbank, *A Documentary History of Chinese Communism* (Cambridge, Mass.: Harvard University Press, 1952), p. 313. For Lenin's classical formulation on the subject, see his "On the Right of Nations to Self-Determination," found in Vladimir I. Lenin, *Lenin: Selected Works* (New York: International Publishers, 1943), pp. 249–93. Also see Bertram D. Wolfe, *Three Who Made a Revolution* (Boston: Beacon Press, 1955), pp. 578–90.

82. Mao was very explicit on the giving of credits: "To give credits where they are due, if we allot ten points to the accomplishments of the democratic revolution, then the achievements of urban dwellers and the military units rate only three points, while the remaining seven points should go to the peasants in the rural revolution." See Brandt, Schwartz, and Fairbank, *Chinese Communism*, p. 83.

83. By way of illustration, see ibid., pp. 456–59, esp. p. 456, which presents portions of Mao Tse Tung's "On the People's Democratic Dictatorship." Also see Franz Schurmann, *Ideology and Organization in Communist China* (Berkeley, Calif.: University of California Press, 1968), pp. 17–104.

84. Useful in understanding the dynamic flow of persons into revolutionary organizations and perspectives is Emile Durkheim's ideas on normal rates of activity. Durkheim has observed that any society, given its structure, will generate a typical, predictable rate of homicide, suicide, and the like, barring of course, a serious alteration of societal structure, in which case the dependent rate will also change. See Emile Durkheim, *The Rules of the Sociological Method* (Glencoe, Ill.: Free Press, 1950), pp. 47–75. Today U.S. society contains sufficient and heady structural contradictions to produce a high incidence of potential rebels and revolutionaries despite, indeed, perhaps in part because of, the schools, the churches, the mass media, and the like. Given my earlier definition of institutions, I wonder at what point institutions pass over to become essentially nonintegrative, and hence noninstitutional, for the state. So does Ronald Reagan puzzle over this problem.

85. I have skipped the whole question of the conditions under which the radicals take state power. This others and I have done elsewhere. See John Leggett, Richard Apostle, Al Baronas, David Driscoll and John Magney, "Total Cultural Revolutions, Class-Racial Consciousness and Current U.S. Insurrections: Revolutions Abroad and Insurrections at Home" (Paper read before the annual meeting of the American Sociological Association, 1967).

86. In almost every total cultural revolution—revolutions which call for changing everything, from substructure through superstructure—the subordinate classes erect grass-roots controls over their revitalized and newly

created institutions. George Orwell, for example, has vividly depicted Barcelona in mid-1936, when the Spanish revolution had not yet taken a turn to the "right" in order to foster a "united front." See his *Homage to Catalonia* (New York: Harcourt, 1952), esp. chaps. 1 and 5. Equally lucid descriptions of the Spanish workers' takeover can be found in Noam Chomsky, "Objectivity and Liberal Scholarship," in *American Power and the New Mandarins* (New York: Pantheon, 1969), pp. 76–80. Also see E. H. Carr, *The Bolshevik Revolution: 1917–23*, vol. 2 (New York: Macmillan, 1952), pp. 55–146, 394–97.

87. Perhaps the best illustration was the attack made by the Chinese Revolution on disease, for the attack was a cultural blow against the old ways of relating to insects, rodents, and other disease carriers. Mass participation in highly intense, antidisease campaigns was also encouraged by the Chinese state. For a brief overview of the Chinese Communist antidisease program, see Edgar Snow, *The Other Side of the River* (New York: Random House, 1962), pp. 301–16.

88. The exhaustion of revolutionary participants has generally not received its deserved analysis. One author who has written with great insight on the matter, however, was E. H. Carr. See his *Bolshevik Revolution*, pp. 193–98; E. H. Carr, *The Interregnum 1923–24*, vol. 4 (New York: Macmillan, 1954), pp. 39–85.

89. For the classical discussion of the utopian mentality, see Mannheim, *Ideology and Utopia*, pp. 192–263.

90. *Encirclement* refers to a revolutionary stiuation in which the insurgent forces of revolution are in fact geographically surrounded by hostile military forces intent on immediately smashing the forces of revolution and occupying liberated turf through concerted, continuous military and violent means. An example would be the invasion of Red Russia between 1919 and 1922 by British, French, Japanese, White Russian, and American military forces committed to the physical elimination of recently liberated turf. That was an extreme case, documented by a number of writers, including the best known biographer of the Red Army's then (1919–20) commander-in-chief. For an excellent biographical description of Leon Trotsky and the fledgling Red Army struggle during this period, see Isaac Deutscher, *The Prophet Armed: Trotsky: 1879–1921* (New York: Oxford University Press, 1963), pp. 325–522.

Lesser encirclement may also occur as when hostile military groups sit external to the revolution, perched and ready, always threatening, to smash the revolution through military means. In this sense, the Cuban revolution, except during the Bay of Pigs fiasco (1961), has weathered lesser encirclement.

91. By *vanguard party* is meant a political organization that acts on the basis of democratic centralism. J. I. Simmons and Barry Winograd, in their *It's Happening* (Santa Barbara: Marc-Laird Publications, 1966), p. 146, pre-

sent a useful and general definition of democratic centralism. For the classical study of the vanguard party, particularly on how democratic centralism
works, see Selznick, *Organizational Weapon*, p. 1–73. Carr discusses at length
Lenin's role in shaping the Bolshevik party as the prototype of the vanguard
party through the application of the principles of democratic centralism in
his *Bolshevik Revolution*, pp. 3–44, 184–249.

92. This is not to deny the inherent oligarchical tendencies in all large-
scale organizations such as large unions and full-scale people's militias. Perhaps one answer to the problem of oligarchy, a beginning, would be to concentrate on the development of smaller-scale organizations. Seymour M.
Lipset, Martin Trow, and James Coleman found that oligarchy was absent
from a union (the International Typographical Workers' Union) where the
locals were small, the membership skilled and educated, the group culturally
homogeneous, and the membership highly involved in off-work associational
activities which brought the work colleagues and their families together. In
short, the creation of continuous "primary group ties" among sophisticated
equals within an organization whose limited size makes possible direct participation in collective problem solving lends itself to the avoidance of the
iron law of oligarchy. See Lipset et al., *Union Democracy* (New York: Doubleday Anchor, 1962) esp. pp. 1–16.

93. Crane Brinton discusses at length the tremendous difficulties faced
by a new revolutionary government both surrounded by foreign and hostile
armies and bedevilled by domestic breakdowns in food supplies, transportation, public utilities, home fuels, and the like. See his *Anatomy of Revolution*,
pp. 176–204.

94. Ironically, Leon Trotsky, by far the most important decision maker
in the Russian Revolution, called successfully for the smashing of the Kron-
stadt sailors' soviet by the Bolshevik armies, the dissolution of independent
trade unions and the regimentation of labor, only to find himself later on
without the kind of support those associations could have given him during
his fight with Stalin. See Carr, *Bolshevik Revolution*, 2: 198–245; Deutscher,
Prophet Armed, pp. 325–522; Isaac Deutscher, *The Prophet Unarmed* (New
York: Oxford University Press, 1959), pp. 1–394.

95. An exception in the Russian case was Bertrand Russell. See his *The
Practice and Theory of Bolshevism* (New York: Simon & Schuster, 1964).

96. The period of war communism largely coincides with the condition
of encirclement, for war communism refers to actual military struggle
against foreign military armies and domestic insurgents. The period of war
communism does not coincide with the phase of lesser encirclement. See
Carr's discussion of war communism in his *Bolshevik Revolution*, 2: 272–73.

97. For a useful discussion of Russian workers who feared the growing
power of the Bolshevik state and demanded decentralized autonomy of
workers' councils, soviets, trade unions at the very moment Trotsky (Lenin

and others) was working around the clock as commander of the Red Army to coordinate the scattered and badly mauled resources of the new republic. See Carr, *Bolshevik Revolution*, 2: 223–27; Carr, *Interregnum*, 4: 394–98.

98. See Max Nomad's discussion of Waclaw Machajski's analysis of this problem in Nomad's *Aspects of Revolt* (New York: Bookman, 1959), pp. 96–117.

99. Perhaps Max Nomad has answered as well as anyone the question of why embark on revolution if so many revolutionary gains, made at such a tremendous price, are almost immediately lost. See his discussion of "permanent revolt," ibid., p. 15. Also see Brinton, *Anatomy of Revolution*, pp. 237–64.

100. See Edwards, *Natural History of Revolution*, pp. 186–209; Brinton, *Anatomy of Revolution*, pp. 205–36.

101. Yesterday's irregular revolutionaries have a propensity to become tomorrow's regular state bureaucrats after others have paid with their lives for revolutionary success. See Nomad, *Aspects of Revolt*, pp. 99–100.

102. For the explication of such a theory, see Davis and Moore, "Some Principles of Stratification"; also we should observe how Stalin's labor code enunciated in the mid-1930s provides for wages consistent with the functional theory. See "Stalin: The Argument for Wage Incentives" (1935), in Meisel and Kozera's *Materials for the Study of the Soviet System*, pp. 220–21; also pertinent is E. H. Carr's discussion of "Labour" in his *Socialism In One Country: 1924–1926*, vol. 1 (Harmondsworth, England: Penguin, 1970), pp. 388–447, esp. pp. 401–6.

103. Just when these rare occasions occur, however, remains unclear. Analytically, what is necessary is a general theory on the conditions and processes which promote the rejuvenation of a revolutionary movement.

104. Herbert Blumer has presented a useful distinction between a general and a specific social movement. See his "Collective Behavior," in Alfred McClung Lee, *New Outlines in Sociology* (New York: Barnes & Noble, 1946), pp. 199–214.

105. For a general discussion of the Chinese "cultural revolution," see Morton H. Fried, "Those 'Mad' Chinese," *Nation* 204 (27 February 1967). Also see Joan Robinson, *The Cultural Revolution in China* (Baltimore: Penguin, 1969); Franz Schurmann and Orvell Schell, *Communist China*, vol. 3 (New York: Vintage, 1967), pp. 607–36; Schurmann, *Ideology and Organization in Communist China*, pp. 582–92; editorial, "China's Cultural Revolution," *Monthly Review* 18 (January 1967): 1–18; editorial, "Understanding the Cultural Revolution," *Monthly Review* 19 (May 1967): 1–16; E. L. Wheelwright, "The Cultural Revolution in China," *Monthly Review* 19 (September 1967): 22–34; Branko Bogunovich, "The Victor Can Only Be Mao Tse-tung," *Monthly Review* 19 (January 1968): 31–36.

106. For an analysis of the cultural revolution in China's leading uni-

versity, see Victor Nee with Don Layman, "The Cultural Revolution at Peking University," *Monthly Review* 31 (July–August 1969): 11–91. Recently Han Suyin has skillfully depicted the impact of the cultural revolution on China's universities (*New York Times*, 21 September 1970, p. 41).

107. *People's councils* here refers to ongoing and powerful workers' councils, autonomous trade unions, and workers', peasants', intellectuals', and soldiers' soviets.

3

THE MILITARY INSTITUTION

Richard L. Rising

Surely one of the greatest failures of twentieth-century man has been his demonstrable inability to control the instruments of his own design. Among his many instruments, the military institution should be singled out as most critical for human existence—for should man's existence cease it will be because of, and not despite, the military institutions of the various nation-states. The twentieth century, like no other century in man's existence, has witnessed the formidable expansion of the engines of destruction and their widespread application. This is not to say that the military institution confers no benefits upon mankind—as in all things it provides a mixed blessing. Nevertheless, this institution remains most critical if for no other reason than the consequences of mistakes and imperfections in the institution. Barring the conscious idiocies of man, the random factor of accident is omnipresent.

Because of the absence of a major conflagration between the European powers from 1815 to 1914, historians often refer to the nineteenth century as the "100 Years' Peace." [1] If this appellation is taken as true, then the twentieth century may well be called the 100 Years' Death—should any chroniclers of the event survive. The capacities and efficiencies of mass annihilation need no accounting here—they are facts of our existence, and well-known facts at that. The forces making for militarism, however, are increasing the opportunities for extinction, and within this milieu of increasing militarism lies the age-old scenario of human tragedy.

The basic *fact,* if not spirit, of the twentieth century has been the inexorable growth and development of the American Empire, backed as always by military might. This development outshadows all other events of modern times. Indeed, one could go so far as to insist that this event *is* Modern Times. Admittedly, the growth of empire and treasure has had certain beneficial by-products, especially in *American* standards of living—but it has had its costs as well. In a very real way, the standards of living that we, you and I, enjoy as members of a particular nation-state empire, and the gadgets we have learned to "need," have been and are still being paid for by the major portion of the planet's population and resources. Nationals of the United States represent a scant 5 percent of the world's population yet they consume 35 percent of its resources. Clearly, pause and perspective are indicated.

At this writing a major political and sociological interest in the condition of the environment and the maintenance of its ecological balance exists—a crude but fashionable attempt to return to a determination of the social structure by "natural law." In my opinion a much more serious question deserving of everyone's efforts is the growth of militarism in every crevice of the world's social organization. As one casts about the globe, he finds that more and more nation-states increasingly direct and structure their social order by the rifle bolt than by any other means. Today, fully two-thirds of the governments of Latin America are ruled directly by the military—and a substantial proportion of the remainder cannot lift the proverbial finger toward economic development without taking full recognition of the military's "needs," "desires," "goals," and "class preferences."

In Asia one notes the presence of several foreign powers, principally the United States, who rule through force of arms and military alliances. Only recently, for example, has Japan been released from the constraints imposed by a U.S. occupation, and then only after the Japanese constitution had been made acceptable to the United States—a condition reminiscent of the force-fed Platt Amendment thrust upon Cuba at the end of the Spanish-American War. The "government" of Taiwan needs little attention; few are unaware of the prototypical military dictatorship existing there—the efforts of the American China Lobby notwithstanding. Thailand, Burma, Pakistan, Afghanistan, Iraq, Ceylon, Vietnam, Cambodia, and Laos round out the Asian list of nations dominated by their military structures. In short, in all of Asia only China, India, and Japan could be said to have nonmilitarily controlled governments, and even this contention is by no means free of its critics and their arguments, as a glance at any daily tabloid quickly reveals.

Africa requires only passing attention. Virtually every government in Africa south of the Sahara relies upon its military directly for political life. This of course does not include those areas that are still the "property" of some other nation and are either in the throes of liberation wars or illegally occupied, e.g., Angola and Southwest Africa respectively.

In an area generally held to be the birthplace of civilization and the potential for human freedom, the Mediterranean Basin, the military is the dominant political force—Portugal, Morocco, Spain, Greece, Turkey, Israel, Eygpt, Syria.

Such is the sorry state of current human affairs. Militarism has not only stifled economic development, for which it could perhaps be forgiven, but it has also stood by whenever possible to set limits on human political freedom. This latter is the crime for it denies the opportunity of change. The English have a saying that sums this up quite nicely: "Underneath every uniform an Englishman smells a tyrant." Human institutions are not sturdy and durable but weak and frail, and the means by which they are abridged or abrogated is only too available and too facile. One has only to observe the recent (1970) suspension of civil liberties guaranteed by the Canadian constitution in response to minor provocation to see just how easily the democratic experiment can fail.

Whether the pursuit of concerned students should be to eliminate the major consequence of weak political and social institutions —militarism—or to create a new set of institutions free of economy and army is a sociological question of the first order. Moreover, and perhaps most important, it is a question that calls for serious inquiry into the very nature of the military institution. Most political scientists would argue that this institution, being manmade, is susceptible of control by man. A doubtful observation, empirically speaking. Doubtful because I fear that historically there is ample evidence attesting to the critic's contention that institutionalized militarism, once initiated, acts out a natural history of destruction, a course that cannot be reversed by the *same* institutional arrangements that brought it into existence. Unfortunately, the doctrine of irreversibility of social processes, whether conceived in an "evolutionary" or "dialectical" framework, cannot be taken up here. This will have to be accepted for now as an unsubstantiated assumption.

Any serious examination of the military which has as its goal the rectification of a "pathological" institution demands a blueprint for change. The best plans, I believe, can be constructed from a counter-systems model.[2] As conceived here, a counter-systems model is a mental construct consisting of the dialectical mental process of conjuring up the exact opposite of the existing structure and then treating this as an ideal type analytically and as a worthwhile goal politically. Such an endeavor rises or falls depending upon our ability to identify, describe, and otherwise understand the existing structure. Thus, a necessary step in constructing such a model is a thoroughgoing *description* of the subject and especially, though not exclusively, its negative features judged from some point of view. With particular reference to institutions this point of view is inescapably the tenets of philosophical humanism—a certain metaphysical (social-psychological) reality regarding the struggle for a beneficial state of the human condition. Put more simply, the raising of levels of living throughout the world, and the promise implied therein. Although the goal, in my opinion, is an ethical one, the method employed is essentially critical and hence negative, if not altogether strident. Most readers will complain about using so negative an approach. To them, I respectfully apologize for the iconoclastic methodology, but at the same time I offer a challenge. Can alternate means of viewing total institutions which are composed of monolithic, linear, and *irreversible* social processes be created?

Military and Economy

Beginning with the first orchestrations of the industrial revolution, and the concomitant growth of nation-state realpolitik, the economic institution has increasingly become both the cause and the effect of the growth of militarism. For years, historians and students of diplomatic relations have argued ceaselessly over the basic question of whether or not trade follows the flag or vice versa. By *flag* I mean elementary, or virginal, imperialism wherein trade is introduced and sustained by force, e.g., China, 1870–1900. The argument, however, is moot in the *real* world. It is moot simply because it no longer matters which variable precedes which in time. Gabriel Kolko has made this point clear in *The Roots of American Foreign Policy*.[3] Rather than become immersed in a welter of endless (and sterile) debates over establishing the causal primacy of merchant or gun, it is better to recognize (or admit) that the two are inextricably interwoven. Thus it is better to ask "Who profits?" than to become involved in the endless quest for causes per se.

Nonetheless, shunting aside questions of precedence does not bar us from a rightful concern over the incestuous relationship that exists between merchant princes and armies. The *primary* institution in any society is the form of economic organization predominating in that society. Today that means one of three variant forms of capitalism: state, corporate, and welfare.[4] The economic organization is the primary institution because it *determines* not only the social organization, including the ideological and psychological structure of that society, but it also structures and extends the very institutions that keep its dominant form of social organization intact. Failing this it goes under. The military is the basic supportive and maintaining structure or institution. It should be constantly kept in mind that the military is nearly always subordinate to the economy if not always subordinate to the political structure. This difference is the source of much confusion, especially in Latin American affairs. In many Latin

American cases, the military appears to have chosen or at least changed sides in the class war. These apparent preferences are only superficial and can best be understood and explained in terms of conflict between elite groupings and potential ownership rather than a desire to alter the economic structure of the society. That is, the military has opted for either membership on the team, a change of players, or simply the right to decide who plays and who doesn't, but not a change in the game itself. Once this principle is clearly grasped, much of the ideological arguments about democratic political viability vs. the tyrannies of the military falls into perspective. Indeed, in many Latin American countries, the military has been more instrumental in promoting economic development than any other sector.

The economic institution has over the last hundred years increasingly required a further monopolization and maximization of the conditions making for "orderly" markets. That is, the military has attempted or is employed to bring stability, certainty, and predictability into the operations of the marketplace—such is a necessary condition for acquiring, building, keeping, and otherwise enjoying an empire. This "requirement" however is not sui generis à la Talcott Parsons. It is decidedly not a "systems" requirement, that is, a functional imperative for system survival. *No* real system meets every Thursday and consciously decides its needs and fate. Reification is unwarranted. Rather, this "requirement" is a practical and real one stemming from strong historical antecedents. Analytically it is twofold.

First, the need for stability and predictability is a direct consequence of the increased politicization and liberation of consciousness stemming from the growth of rationalism—the singular accomplishment of the Enlightenment. This increased consciousness in turn led to the growth and proliferation of nation-states, and incidentally established a necessary condition of worldwide conflict—competitors. As an ancillary process the growth of rationalism also enlarged the need for internal social control structures in society on a scale hitherto unknown, namely, repressive justice for nonowners and restitutive justice for owners.[5] Nation-states conceived from a conflictual point of view presuppose a measure of stable relations both externally and internally, at least at some unspecified minimal level in order to participate in the world community.

Second, and concomitantly, the need for stability was (and is) a necessary condition of incipient capitalism. Capitalism is a historical process—not instant riches. Historically it is a long-drawn-out process of ascetic accumulation and reinvestment. Such a process, in order to exist and thereby succeed, must be secure in the promise that all will end well—that perseverance will triumph, that deferred wishes and gratifications will be rewarded financially (if not spiritually!). On the ideological front, however, owners cannot realistically offer themselves these promises, nor peddle them to others, save by owning or controlling the structures that vouchsafe stability and predictability in the marketplace. Promises can best be believed when the more tangible "sign" of a compliant military is present to guarantee them.[6]

This essay's central contention is that the military is the commonly used device for maintaining international and national stability in and between markets. An understanding of the importance of the military institution in the nation-state, thus providing a cornerstone for constructing a counter-systems model, would scarcely be complete without detailing the diverse roles this instrument plays vis-à-vis the economy. A simple cataloging of the dispensations of violence by this institution, or the insistence that this institution monopolizes violence, is insufficient.

U.S. society and its history provide the best illustrations. But it should be noted that other would-be and successful empires have practiced the same infamies. The United States however, the country most familiar to us and the country that constitutes the greatest offender, second only to Victorian Britain, has left a good historical track to follow.

The Military as Stabilizer

One component of an "orderly" market is the stability of political influence and trade privileges that allows of long-term planning, such as decisions about whether or not to invest in nonmovable assets. This is usually brought about by controlling one's competition rather than by a direct interference in the internal affairs of other nations. This is not always so, however, and with regard to the United States it is decidedly not so. The U.S. State Department has evolved many ways to control competition in behalf of U.S. business interests, as we shall see. Indeed it is impossible to draw a clear line of demarcation between the State Department and U.S. business interests.

Armies are called upon to protect "national interests." This much is an obvious, tautological, and timeless verity. Less obvious is precisely what the interests being "protected" really are—the credibility gap being what it is. The question, "Protected from what?" should be asked after the speech and press release of every war office. Strip away the superficial rhetoric—the "national interest," "protect," or "self-determination"—or read between the lines of the *Wall Street Journal* and the residue looks suspiciously like nascent imperialism or at best some variant form of neocolonialism. The history of *Yanqui* imperialism in the Caribbean is an adequate demonstration of the role of the military in the pacification of market conditions. The principal lesson to be learned from the twentieth-century version of the Monroe Doctrine is simply that the United States will use military force to maintain or gain trade privileges. (Other conclusions concerning the quest for raw materials are discussed later.) In short, "national interest" has often meant trade privileges, which is simply another way of saying exclusive or monopolistic rights to sell (and buy) in a certain area. This is the hard fact that empires face— capturing and protecting markets.

CASE: THE CARIBBEAN

In 1904, the World Court ruled that those nation-states that had attempted to collect debts from other nations by force had, and would in the future have, prior claims over those that had not. Significantly this litigation arose involving a Caribbean nation.[7] The ruling, in conjunction with the then current interpretation of the Monroe Doctrine, is generally credited with launching the United States along imperialist paths. It is a more logical explanation than the earlier and nonsensical ideological explanation of Manifest Destiny. As a historical continuity, it should by no means go unnoticed that this period parallels the drive toward industrial maturity of U.S. corporate capitalism. The events that followed on the heels of the court's ruling form a classic profile and provide rich data on the early stages of corporate imperialism. However, lest the impression be created that the court's ruling became the precipitant "cause" of U.S. intervention, it should be noted that the ruling was used as an ex post facto justification for events that had already taken place, e.g., in Panama, or that were envisioned as future U.S. policy. In any event the rationalization of the events that followed was at least straightforward, as was the custom in those days:

> Chronic wrongdoing . . . may force the United States, however reluctantly . . . to the exercise of an international police power.

> —Theodore Roosevelt
> December 6, 1904

The "chronic wrongdoing" referred to by Roosevelt was the incurring of *debt*, which in its turn was the consequence of aggressive trade policies by U.S. and European business concerns in the Caribbean. A key element of U.S. foreign policy during this period was "dollar diplomacy." Dollar diplomacy consisted of the State Department's delineating special areas of U.S. concern and then encouraging U.S. business to invest in these areas under full guarantees of either reimbursement for lost moneys or the supplying of troops to protect assets and rights. Generally, the policies thus initiated took the form of loans and credits which were never made with the intention of securing repayment in normal and customary ways. Rather, repayment became the securing of leaseholds, exploration rights, mineral rights and concessions, territorial cessations, military alliances, the installation of friendly governments, the bandishment of undesirable politicos, and the like, instead of cash and usury. Between dollar diplomacy and vigorous trade practices it was little wonder that Caribbean finances became what they were—chaotic.

The solution to the chaos thus engendered was the landing of troops. In the relatively short span of roughly twenty-five years, ca. 1900 to 1925, the United States invaded with regular military forces no fewer than eight nations of the Caribbean and "leaned on" several others to "protect" those *invaded* nations' interests (see table 1). These interests were publicly defined by the Department of State as the exclusion of European economic hegemony assuming, correctly, that economic troubles involving European powers (i.e., banks)

TABLE 1. *United States Military Adventures
in the Caribbean*, 1900–70

COUNTRY	INVADED BY U.S. TROOPS	DIRECT U.S. FINANCIAL SUPERVISION
Cuba	1898–1902 1906–09 1917–22 1961[a]	
Dominican Republic	1913 1916–24 1966–present	1905–41
Haiti	1914–34	1916–41
Nicaragua	1909–10[b] 1912–25 1926–33	1911–24
Mexico	1914 1916–17	
Honduras	1923[b]	
Panama	1903 1921	
Guatamala	1954[b]	

[a] By troops paid, trained, armed, and transported by the U.S. Central Intelligence Agency.

[b] Intervention in a revolution on the side of a conservative aristocracy attempting to overthrow a legitimate democratically elected government unfriendly to U.S. interests. In all three cases, U.S. warships blocked government supplies and reinforcements. Much the same can be said to have occurred in the Dominican Republic in 1966, with some minor qualifications.

would bring European troops to collect the debts (which now consisted of collecting other things than money) and to rectify trade
"imbalances." Accordingly, the debts, thanks to successful military
operations, were transferred from European to American banks. In
addition, "corrupt" Customs officials were replaced, constitutions
were rewritten by the Navy Department, leaseholds and military
bases were secured, trade areas were guaranteed, and friendly governments were installed. All in all, a precursor of the antipollution

campaign could be said to exist: the ideological and economic pollution of Europeans had been ended in what subsequently proved to be the new Yankee Lake. According to Richard Hofstadter, an astute American historian of this period, "By 1924, the U.S. was taking an active part in directing the financial policies of ten Latin-American nations, and was prepared to exert financial pressure or land troops if the need arose." [8]

These events struck a new chapter in the annals of modern imperialism. Prior to this, the era of "gunboat diplomacy," another name for dollar diplomacy, nations had invaded one another for fun and profit and had rationalized their mutual barbarities as conferring the "benefits" of Western civilization on the "pagans" and "heathens"—a duty, as it were. Dollar diplomacy was not appreciably different, save that it offered a new Janus-faced justification. The rationales provided by the administrations of McKinley, Theodore Roosevelt, Taft, and Wilson attained new heights in the world history of hypocrisy, in addition to constituting the touchstone of U.S. policy for the past seventy years. First, the State Department quietly and privately explained to the victim that the intervention was in his (the invaded nation's) best interest—that it was good for him—that at the very least it was but a temporary and necessary evil in order to prevent enslavement by other economic powers. (In 1910 it was enslavement by European bankers; in 1960 it was enslavement by the international communist conspiracy.) Publicly, on the other hand, the U.S. State Department proclaimed U.S. support for the principle of self-determination of peoples. The net consequence of this schizoid policy was that self-determination was curtailed (or heavily mortgaged) and U.S. business interests were advanced.

During all these goings on, the military dutifully acted out the important role of excluding and regulating nation-state competitors under the guise of aid and assistance. By upholding the principle of self-determination they made the victims safe for U.S. business exploitation. On a scale of world historical values, seldom has a nation acted so capriciously or hypocritically—but, then again, the right to make ill-mannered justifications is but one of the many dividends of empire. If the Caribbean adventures sound somewhat analogous with recent events, whether they be "incursions" into Vietnam, the Dominican Republic, Lebanon, Cambodia, Laos, etc., then so be it.

Little has changed in U.S. foreign policy in the ensuing years save the dramatis personae.

> SAN JOSE, COSTA RICA (AP) April 25, 1970: Several thousand students battled police yesterday after legislators approved a huge contract with a U.S. mining concern [Alcoa]. President Jose J. Trejos signed the contract 47 minutes after Congress had given it a third and final approval. Then, in a nationwide broadcast he said that "Communist elements tried to abuse the civic spirit of students, provoking the riots in the center of the city." Under terms of the contract Costa Rica is to supply nearly $11 million to build a highway and dock facility for use by Alcoa. The contract grants a 25-year concession.
>
> —*York Gazette & Daily*

MODERN WORLD STABILITY

By today's norms, it is considered "bad form" to go rudely crashing about someone else's country in search of money and prestige. It is in even worse form to do so with uniformed troops. Yet the demiurge for market stability remains. This does not mean that the power-holding nation-states, and here I mean principally the United States, do not continue to act out the role of bully-on-the-block by taking by force of arms what is denied them by other means, but rather politics being what they are it is much nicer all around if you can save your military for the "final solution," should that become necessary.

The modern way to maintain marketplace stability represents a considerable advance over the "land-the-marines" method. Yet the modern way remains closely tied to military means. Moreover, it is a true advance in the history of capitalism because it has brought the military and the economy ever closer to one another—an inseparable sharing of roles as it will probably turn out. Some authors would call this a new form of imperialism and presently there exists no compelling reason to substitute a neologism here.

This neoimperialism consists in building technological constituencies, or dependencies, by the sale of arms and other materials of war and play-war.[9]

These dependencies create strong bonds, principally because of twentieth-century technological complexity. With the purchase of modern U.S. weapons systems comes a reliance upon U.S. technical advisers and instructors who must teach not only the weapons' maintenance and technical use, but also their tactical and strategic deployment—a *major political role for the military*. Foreign military officers must often be brought to the United States for training, thus cementing ties further, not to mention that these training visits carry with them the added impetus for future arms sales because the trainees are invariably "let in" on the next generation of weapons systems. This latter is the well-known drummer's device for creating new "needs."

> Since World War II over 20,000 Latin-American officers, including some present commanders, and soldiers have received training in the United States or in the three military schools in the Canal Zone. That training, aside from its purely professional aspects, had been intended to acquaint them with the American political philosophy.
>
> —Tad Szulc, *New York Times*, 1970

> [The Military Assistance Program has] through the end of 1969 trained more than 202,000 foreign military personnel in the United States and 95,000 others overseas. In the 1970 fiscal year, 4,757 officers from 44 countries were trained in the United States and 3,953 abroad under grant aid.
>
> —*New York Times*, 1970

A modern military machine, whether deployed in battle or not, nevertheless continually exhausts its supplies of spare parts in rapid succession. As yet, the various arms-producing nations do not strive nor pretend to make their systems compatible with one another. That is, they do not make them amenable to loyalty-less standardized replacement parts (or ammunition, for that matter). Thus a dependency of considerable proportions is created simply by regulating the supply of spares to client states. A good example of this is seen in NATO, a quasi-international organization wherein many weapons systems have been standardized. In instances where the United States does not license European producers to manufacture weapons and parts, competition has set in; for example, Fabrique Nationale makes M-16 rifles and ammunition. Competition does to capitalism what arteriosclerosis does to the body's blood supply; once it sets in, international allegiances are strained. France, for example, one of the world's principal arms salesmen and once the strongest supporter of NATO, found little or no market (save its own armed forces) in NATO for its Mirage system interceptor replete with extensive backup systems; and the British have also felt the crunch in attempting to peddle their Hawk missiles.

Finally, a dependency is created, a debtor dependency, through the credit arrangements surrounding the purchase of arms. Few nations can pay cash for arms. South Africa is about the only country that consistently pays in cash, and they pay in gold. The other two potential cash customers, also gold payers, are the USSR and Sweden, and they generally manufacture their own weapons. It is in the nature of credit agreements that the terms can be tailored and usually quite easily adjusted to political goals. Moreover, the terms can always be renegotiated or canceled as conditions warrant. Additional flexibility can be found in the method of repayment; for example, payment can be in leaseholds, rights, trading privileges, military bases, and the like.

The military establishments around the world do not sit idly by while their foreign offices hit the hustings to sell weapons and construct policy. Rather, the major militaries of the world, at the incessant prodding of manufacturers, take an active role in selling weapons. As a matter of fact they are so deeply engaged in weapons sales and policy formation that the various foreign offices have long since cried for help in curbing these practices.

CASE: PENTAGON AS FINANCIER

Direct sales of arms by the Pentagon and U.S. manufacturers now run to $6.7 billion annually (although some sales are made by producing companies, they are initiated and passed upon by the Pentagon).[10] This figure does not include the tens of millions of dollars in military property that the Defense Department gives away in Thailand and Vietnam. The figure for 1970 arms sales abroad was $5.3 billion, thus indicating a full 25 percent increase in one year alone, and this at a time when Defense repeatedly said it was scaling down its arms sales! The U.S. Congress, in a faint-hearted attempt to stem this flow, enacted legislation limiting the amount going into Latin America to $85 million per year. This "shotgun" approach was necessitated by the Pentagon's refusal to give country-by-country totals, even in secret session. If Congress cannot lay hands on the statistics, it is obviously more difficult for members of the public or scholars to do so. Thus, most reported figures should be revised upward. Whatever the *true* figure—and we will more than likely never find it out—the magnitude is truly cosmic.

As an interesting side effect, the act of limiting arms sales to Latin America has had fortunate ramifications on the West Coast of Latin America, the area containing the bulk of Latin America's mineral wealth. Peru, Bolivia, and Chile have turned away from their dependence on U.S. arms, thus weakening policy ties with the United States. The speed with which these countries withdrew from the U.S. policy orbit bespeaks volumes about the weapons linked dependencies.

> Last year the highly nationalistic military government of Peru expelled a 70-man United States military advisory mission that had worked closely with the armed forces. Later though, Peru admitted seven officers and enlisted men to oversee the use of American equipment, as required by United States laws providing military aid.
>
> —*New York Times*, 1970

Other than ineffectual congressional Band-Aid-type attempts of limitation, the sale of arms by the Pentagon is unacquainted with limit or restraint. Nevertheless, directly sold and financed arms sales by the Pentagon and its suppliers is not the only way that arms find their way to countries that do not need them and cannot afford them from an economic development point of view (not to mention that the selling of arms sometimes pours gasoline on raging nationalistic border disputes, thereby threatening world peace).

Various means are available to the Pentagon ranging from their own Military Assistance Credit Account through the dealings of the Export-Import Bank to the basest form of hypocrisy yet practiced— the financing of sales through the Food for Peace program. In all cases the financing is initiated, arranged, and guaranteed by the Pentagon. An additional source of financing, which unfortunately cannot be taken up here, is that which comes from Agency for International Development counterpart funds. Counterpart funds arise

from the mutually shared profits derived from the sale of U.S. manufactured goods abroad, the importation of which has been financed
by AID loans. The host country is "free" to spend its share of the
profits on military equipment while the United States uses its share
to bribe foreign officials and pay off its agents.[11]

The Military Assistance Credit Account is a revolving fund
managed by the Pentagon for the purpose of financing arms sales to
poor-credit-risk nations—countries that obviously have no need for
arms. Currently this fund amounts to over $400 million. Ten per-
cent of the repayments made under this program are returned to en-
large the fund. These moneys are not lent directly however, but
rather used as a 25 percent reserve requirement to vouchsafe loans
made through the Country-X account at the Export-Import Bank.
This yields a multiplier of 4 which, when translated to full dilution,
means that the Pentagon can theoretically extend $1.6 billion in
credits to poor-credit-risk nations (i.e., underdeveloped countries
that must suppress legitimate liberation movements), and that the
loan will be guaranteed by the Treasury for the full amount. These
loans are made without General Accounting Office and congressional scrutiny. The full extent of this account's use is not known. But
it is known that:

> Between mid-1965 and June 1967 alone, the bank had ex-
> tended $604 million in Country-X loans to the Defense Depart-
> ment, and was planning to extend an additional $1 billion in
> the following two years. From 1963 to 1967 military sales to un-
> derdeveloped countries increased thirteenfold through the use
> of this revolving fund.[12]

The Export-Import Bank finances arms sales in either of two
ways, depending upon a client's credit rating. The first way, described above, is the Country-X account that is used for poor risks.
For the more affluent country, there is direct-interest-bearing financing. For some strange and unexplained reason, this financing is at
very low rates of interest for an international loan. The low rate is
obviously either a subsidy in behalf of foreign policy objectives or a
discounting of the goods in order that they might "clear the market"
or, probably, both.

> . . . direct loans, usually at Defense Department request [were
> made] to low risk countries such as Austria, Great Britain,

Italy, and Australia. These loans were made on a five- to seven-year medium-term basis at an interest rate of approximately 5.5 percent per year. The first two loans by the bank were in 1963 when $163 million went to Austria and Italy, which at the time were arguing for control over parts of the Tyrol. From FY 1963 to FY 1967 slightly more than $1 billion of the $1.6 billion were direct loans such as this.[13]

By the end of fiscal year 1967 the Ex-Im Bank had on-lent $1.6 billion to 17 countries. Fourteen of these countries are classified by the United Nations as underdeveloped. This enormous outpouring of credit financing took place over the relatively short span of just three years.

TABLE 2. *Source of Financing for U.S. Arms Sales to Foreign Powers*

SOURCE	PERCENT OF SALES
Pentagon directly	70
Export-Import Bank	20
Military Assistance Credit Account	10

Recent congressional hearings (1971) have shown that the Food for Peace program is being used to generate moneys with which to buy arms. Disclosures revealed that $143.8 million had been set aside in foreign currencies for "defense purposes." [14] This is an extremely small amount as military expenditures go, but nevertheless instructive in the virtues of Department of Defense thinking about its role in economic development. It is almost a certainty that the full extent of the abuse has yet to be revealed.

As a new form of imperialism the closer connection between the military and the economy represents an unequivocal advance. From a purely military point of view, there is the enviable advantage of possessing intimate knowledge of a potential enemy's weapons capabilities because, first, you sold him hand-me-down equipment and, second, you know the condition of that equipment at time of sale. In sum, it makes military contingency planning much easier and considerably less problematic.

From an economic standpoint the advantages lie in being able more easily to regulate, articulate, calibrate, and tune the economic structure to a finer pitch in terms of industrial output. Technically speaking there is scant difference between producing cars or tanks, trucks or planes. The vast industrial machine confronts this as a minor retooling problem and thus can be ready to produce those products that have ready markets. That is, they can tread the thin line between consumer production and military production at their own choosing. The opportunity of a balanced industrial production, one that would smooth out the vagaries of the business cycle, thus becomes more real and promises internal political security to those who would learn to play such a complex instrument skillfully.

Another benefit to be found in the U.S. arms sales system is that it eliminates an embarrassing problem: what do you do with obsolete military equipment? Concomitantly it also encourages the research and development sector of the economy by clearing out the previous inventions. Hence, because military equipment comes in "generations," an endless production cycle is set in motion. Presumably there is a *limitless* demand for newer and more sophisticated weapons, because no nation ever feels secure knowing that his neighbor may be able to purchase superior equipment. One only has to observe the market for the sold-and-resold arms from the First World War to realize that nations constantly strive to match the sophistication of their military's arms with their ability to purchase newer and better systems.

Another benefit of selling technologically aging weapons is that the goods thus produced and sold *do not necessarily* have to be destroyed in a war in order to maintain demand and full employment in the industrial producing nations. Rather, technological obsolescence can in a very real way lessen the impact of wars generated by excess production. This is one point that the otherwise excellent *Report from Iron Mountain*[15] fails to take up and thus constitutes a gap in this compelling essay on the inevitability of twentieth-century wars as the mainspring of contemporary economic life.

Other, less obvious benefits accrue to the nations of arms sellers. From the point of view of nation-state realpolitik, the political alliances forged and the rights obtained through negotiation are immensely popular with finance capital looking for a friendly working environment. Interestingly enough, nations have often gained by their "gifts" and sales of arms what they could not get for cash on the line. Military bases, oil exploration rights, leaseholds, shipping concessions (most U.S. military aid programs specify that the goods be shipped in American "bottoms"), investment protections such as guarantees and bonds against expropriation, and similar advantages come immediately to mind.

Finally, one by-product of this has certainly been the closer connection between the State Department and the Department of Defense, and their counterpart organizations in other nations have experienced the same movement. In 1910, for example, one could not separate, even analytically, the United Fruit Company from the State Department; today, one can barely manage to delineate Defense from State.

In most countries the Defense Department influences more policy, or is in a position to influence more policy, than does the State Department. Ranging from negotiations for the acquisition of bases and local supplies to many intimate contacts with the future generation of military and political cadres (especially with district politicos because U.S. troops are never stationed in capital cities), the military men stationed in a foreign country are much more involved on a day-to-day, face-to-face basis with the framers of foreign and domestic policy than is the State Department's representative. Moreover, and most importantly, the military, because it handles millions of grant-in-aid and self-maintenance dollars while stationed in a foreign land, becomes extremely familiar with the banking, currency, and financial systems, and their principals, in the host country. All in all, they receive a much clearer picture of the host nation than does the State Department official who attends embassy parties and depends on English-speaking servants for his knowledge of the country.

The Military and Modern Imperialism

The classic definition of imperialism involved elements of the military venturing abroad in search of raw materials and then con-

quering these materials by applying their arts. The halcyon days of
the late nineteenth century witnessed the greatest and final surge of
this phenomenon. Today the military plays little overt role in capturing supplies of raw materials. The means of acquisition are now
more economic than forceful. Nevertheless, the military still plays a
large enough role to merit brief space here because of the implications of future stresses and strains.

Modern economic imperialism is based on the following economic facts of life. First, countries who wish to enter into a twentieth-
century standard of living, generally the so-called Third World
countries, face a series of problems set by the nation-states that are
developed both militarily and economically. In the nineteenth century nonindustrial countries had no choice in the matter—armies
came and took away whatever they pleased. Today, however, a
would-be "civilized" nation must *buy* the products, the manufactured
goods, the demand for which is ever increasing, of the twentieth century or face internal political upheavals at unacceptable levels. The
catch is that they must buy these products with an acceptable foreign
currency—never their own—which today means the almost catholic
American dollar, and to a lesser extent, pounds sterling or Deutsch-
marks. To lay hands on foreign currencies, commonly called "exchange," they must offer something for sale. What is available and
what does the potential buyer want? Under conditions of modern
imperialism these two separate questions have merged into one:
what can I get for my product that "they" say I must sell?

In general only two products are available to an "underdeveloped" country: agricultural products and unprocessed mineral resources. Hitherto raw materials in the form of crude oil, ores, etc. did
not provide the foreign exchange necessary for social and economic
development; indeed, they rarely offered a meagre existence for the
population because most Third World nations did not own these resources to begin with. Only recently has ownership shifted to the
rightful owners, and then only by outright seizure or coercion of one
sort or another.

Offering commodities on the world market is the cruelest way
imaginable, but the only way, to raise foreign exchange. It invariably forces a nation, if it is not already in such a position, into a one-
crop economy.[16] Consider for a moment how prices are set and by

whom. Even in the agriculturally rich United States, prices are set in cities by wholesalers and not by farmers and producers. Price structures for commodities vary considerably because of wildly fluctuating demand for such goods, and abundance in good years brings its own penalty in the form of lower prices. These conditions obtain in even greater severity in *world* markets where countries who sell commodities nearly always find a buyer's market and hardly ever a seller's market. As an example, an American can buy bananas at 15¢ per pound, coffee at 89¢ per pound, and gasoline for 40¢ a gallon, while a European pays $1 per pound for bananas, $2 per pound for coffee, and upward of 90¢ per gallon for gasoline.[17]

In a very real way foreign exchange must be wrung out of the backs of the agriculturists. The peasant producer must somehow be induced (a sometime employment for the military) to give up his surplus and at the same time be paid less than the world market price by his government or its agents. In return he sees little benefit because the foreign exchange "earned" by his government—in most cases paltry, and in all cases precious—through his labor power goes into objects that are light-years removed from his needs. If his government does not spend it all on military toys and adventures—it invariably will spend some of it that way—then it will spend it on national prestige items such as dressing up and glorifying the capital city, or "show the flag" with a national airline operated with tremendous losses. Perhaps it will maintain a $10 million a year United Nations mission in New York. Or it will put the money into heavy industry, such as automobile production in a country that has no decent roads or petrol. Barring these idiocies, it may decide to invest in education by using the exchange to purchase education abroad for its prize (i.e., aristocratic) students; if so, it then promptly loses the students to the attractions of permanent residence in the Western world. And, as a last resort, the money has a curious way of finding its way to Switzerland, as if money were the legendary lodestone.

A concluding note on this subject is illustrative of the desperate situation faced by countless millions. Simply stated, when and if all the above obstacles are overcome—and on a few occasions they are —the resulting gain has been consumed by natural increase of the population. All in all, not a very encouraging prospect for the multitudes of the world. It certainly comes as no surprise, then, that the nations that *have* will do all they can to *keep*—the fall from the top is too far. Actually, the surprising fact is that nations have not done more to climb higher to a more secure perch.

With the increase of one-crop economies throughout the world, the military enters into the equation because the injustices outlined above invariably produce major political "instabilities." A one-crop economy is a two-way street, a fact that is often overlooked. Just as the nation that has only one crop to sell can scarcely tolerate political turmoil, neither can the nation-state that looks to only one or two suppliers do so. Reduction in present supply, or uncertainty in future supply, stands to drive the price up, a cost that in turn is passed on to the consumer and increases the probability of selected unemployment and price increases in the industrial nations. Hence the political instability engendered in an underdeveloped nation has repercussions in the more advanced industrial nations. The consequences of this would be catastrophic for world capitalism were it not for the military.

Small nations could with very little effort cause political troubles out of all proportion to their size and resources for the large industrial nations. The latter are highly vulnerable because of the complexities of the division of labor which maintains their richly structured social organization. Nevertheless, this advantage of "being backward" has not been utilized to any appreciable extent because most economically advanced nation-states stand ready to use their military establishments to ensure that Third World social and political movements are kept in hand. Usually they have only to *brandish* their military might rather than apply it—a feature that mercifully cuts down on the wear and tear of peasant populations which, while not bespeaking much for the human condition, nevertheless represents a step above cannibalism. In any event, the United States and other nations have demonstrated on numerous occasions that they will use their military to halt revolutionary movements and protect aristocratic elite throughout the world.

> The United States flew a planeload of weapons including mortars and machine guns to Trinidad yesterday at the urgent request (!) of the government there, which is seeking to put down a military mutiny reportedly inspired by Black Power elements.

Simultaneously, a six-ship naval squadron was dispatched to Trinidad on President Nixon's orders to be ready to evacuate American citizens if their safety appeared to be endangered. The arms requested by the government of Prime Minister Eric Williams to equip the national police and loyal members of the 600-man Trinidad army after mutineers seized the country's only arms depot at the Chaguaramas Military Base, a one-time U.S. naval base, according to the State Department.

—*York Gazette & Daily*, 1970

In sum, neoimperialism and neocolonialism have become the arts of military brinksmanship with the initiative resting squarely on the industrially advanced nations. This is only fair: the advanced nations set all the conditions; they set all the prices for raw *and* finished materials; they establish all the terms of credit; and they set the transportation costs both to and from market. By dictating the conditions that create subservient client-states, they stand to reap all the consequences both internationally and domestically of instability in these vassal states. Thus the readiness to threaten and apply violence must be ever-present in the thinking of world "statesmen."

CLASSIC IMPERIALISM REVISITED

It may be premature to exclude classic imperialism from a twentieth-century existence. The American position in Southeast Asia is, for some, an example of classic imperialism.[18] It was first believed that the United States was there to get the rubber that Michelin was forced to abandon. Later it was believed that large deposits of tin were present in this region, and while the United States could (then) get all the tin it needed from Chile and Bolivia, it was nevertheless important to deny access to China. Currently, a more feasible hypothesis is in fashion—one that carries with it, in lieu of firm evidence, at least greater deductive credence. It now seems reasonable to argue that *oil* may have instigated, or at least account for continued, U.S. intervention in Southeast Asia. Geopolitically speaking, were China to obtain a confident source of oil it would advance her industrial power at the expense of U.S. "security" and more importantly at the cost of endangering a fossil fuel-driven society which considers the world and its resources its oyster. Any map of Southeast Asia showing U.S. oil leases lends some evidence—admittedly weak evidence—to the suspicion that the United States is in Southeast Asia for the oil. The possibility of a connection has yet to be seriously investigated. Existence of oil leaseholds, whatever pattern they may evince on a map, is not proof of wrongdoing. As a first approximation of such research, however, I believe this connection will be established. The history of the United States with regard to oil is not honorable. An intense U.S. concern with oil can be found in the daily news of the past twenty years covering every part of the world. Lately the U.S. scramble for oil has become more frantic. Present geological knowledge indicates that a full 70 percent of the world's known oil reserves lies within a region containing many countries that are unsympathetic to U.S. interests, i.e., the Middle East. The task of delineating the history of the United States and oil is as difficult as the cleansing of the Augean stables.[19]

> Mr. Trezise [Assistant Secretary of State for Economic Affairs] also said the Government was concerned that "in an emergency oil fields in Western Canada would be almost without reserves" to supply U.S. needs. In response to reporters' questions, however, he also emphasized that "it would be a mistake to say Canada agreed to the U.S. action [i.e., the instituting of an oil import quota for Canada]."
>
> —*Wall Street Journal*, 1970

Future prospects of imperialistic encroachment can be forecast for those areas that possess mineral wealth. The United States, for example, is seriously lacking in certain rare earth minerals. These minerals are absolutely necessary for any nation that would commit its affairs to electronics. What the United States will do to obtain these resources can only be the subject of imaginative conjecture. And major metals, from the U.S. point of view, are not all that secure either. Accordingly:

> Over half the known world reserves of manganese are in Russia and China, and most of the remainder is in Brazil, India, Gabon, and South Africa. South Africa and Rhodesia account for nearly all the world's chromium reserves, Cuba and New Caledonia for half the nickel, China for over two-thirds of the tungsten, and Chile, Northern Rhodesia, Congo, and Peru for well over two-thirds of the foreign copper reserves. Guyana has

about six times the American reserves of bauxite, and China has three times, while Malaya, Indonesia, with Bolivia and the Congo possessing most of the balance. Only zinc and lead, among the major metals, are in politically stable regions, from the American point of view.[20]

Obviously, the problem of resource allocation and acquisition is not endemic to the United States; rather, the rapidly industrializing countries of Western Europe and Japan face similar problems. The Japanese, for example, had this problem once before. The solution then was the Greater East Asia Co-Prosperity Sphere. Preliminary steps in this direction by the United States and others is not an unreasonable expectation for the near future—the consequences of inaction for the empire would be monumental. As Kolko concludes on this point:

> It is extraordinarily difficult to estimate the potential role and value of these scarce minerals to the United States, but certain approximate definitions are quite sufficient to make the point that the future of American economic power is too deeply involved for this nation to permit the rest of the world to take its own political and revolutionary course in a manner that imperils the American freedom to use them. . . .
>
> To suggest that the United States could solve its natural shortages by attempting to live within its raw materials limits would also require a drastic reduction in its exports of finished goods, and this the leaders of the American system would never voluntarily permit, for it would bring profound economic repercussions for a capitalist economy in the form of vast unemployment and lower profits.[21]

The Military as "Hit Man" in Society

This section briefly essays the role of the military in its various domestic costumes. Once again, the United States is preeminent, but it is only one example, and the conclusions and descriptions can be applied to all nation-states in some degree or other. The definition of the military institution is broadened here to include units of the National Guard, but it does not include units of the civil police, specially trained riot police, sheriff's units, and the like.

At the outset the reader should be aware that this separation of the military from the economy and its immediate needs is only an analytical convenience. Domestic order is always tied to the economic interests in society; it is simply not as apparent. Moreover, the military is almost always ordered into civil strife by civilian authorities in industrial countries, and these authorities have as their "significant" or "generalized other" the economic interests of owners.

THE MILITARY AND ORGANIZED LABOR

The history of organized labor in the United States, a long and turbulent one, can be divided into two periods: 1880–1935 and 1935–present.

In the first period, labor strove not so much to overturn the system (although they were often accused of this) or even to reform it along political lines, as to secure recognition and the right to organize—simply to be allowed into the ballgame. The history of this first period is bloody and deadly—Pinkerton guards shot workers and federal troops broke heads and strikes in addition to increasing the mortality rates of strikers. This period yields an unbroken record of involvement by the military in strikebreaking activities. The worst abuses by the military came around 1905–10 in actions against the Industrial Workers of the World (IWW).

The barbarities of strikebreaking were not limited to federal troops, however; they had the support of "honest" citizens. In 1910, after a prolonged and bitter strike in Prescott, Arizona, by the IWW, the "honest" citizens formed a vigilante group and seized 1,100 men, women, and children associated or thought to be associated with the IWW. They loaded and locked them into cattle cars and shipped them into the New Mexico desert without food or water. Thirty-six hours later federal troops arrived and "rescued" them by removing them to a concentration camp in New Mexico where they were never seen nor heard from again.[22] Abuses of this type were unfortunately all too common. The infamous Palmer Raids of the early 1920s were directed at organized labor, especially in the city of Buffalo.[23] The captains of American industry had long held a European outlook on trade unionism, regarding unions as some type of unwashed garden-variety Bolshevism. The military found little opposition to its mission among the population of Buffalo or any other

American city. Labor was a minority group and the dominant values in both the military and citizenry were the same.

The second labor era began with the passing of the Wagner Act in 1935, a key piece of New Deal legislation that, among other things, extended the right to organize to unions. Nevertheless, this act did little to convince business that labor had legitimate interests and, moreover, that these interests were no different in effect from the dream-wishes of corporate capitalism. Conflict made possible by the Wagner Act was postponed until the post-World War II period although a few skirmishes took place in the late 1930s. After the war, however, the government continued its policy of using the military to break strikes—Truman's seizure of the railroads and running them with federal troops is one of the better remembered examples. Twenty years later the government will still call out troops to break strikes—witness the breaking of the 1970 mail strike in the major cities. And in 1971 the mayor of New York threatened his civil service unions with federal troops in a successful attempt to break their legitimately called strike.

Even though a major piece of legislation purported to change the relationship between government and labor, no difference in consequence can be found. The reason for dividing the history of labor into two periods is not to show the noblesse oblige of the New Deal. Rather, this division reflects a change of style in the application of military force to an essentially domestic economic problem. This change of style consisted of justifying the use of troops as necessary for the *public good* rather than the earlier rationalization (when one was even given) of unequivocal support for the businessman. Tactically this shift in emphasis was effected by no longer allowing governors, courts, and employers to invoke federal troops but by increasing the control from Washington. Especially during the 1950s, the federal government made it plain that states could no longer count among their states' rights the sole control of the militia by "federalizing" the militia virtually every time it was called out. One could today summarize labor relations by saying that *established* labor has learned not to confront the naked power of the state; hence, the military seldom is used in traditional labor disputes. *Novice* unions have not learned this lesson, however, and even if they did, as the last to organize they face the hardest task.

THE MILITARY AND POLITICAL DISSENT

Aside from the fact that Army Intelligence maintains nearly one thousand investigators to keep track of the political activities and beliefs of large numbers of U.S. citizens and elected officials; and ignoring the fact that the army maintains computerized dossiers at Fort Meade on undisclosed millions,[24] the military still shoulders a major responsibility for quelling large-scale political movements and suppressing segments of the population who fail to show proper respect for the majority and its "consensus." Among this group of ne'er-do-wells, the military regards blacks and students as prime suspects, preferring to leave small political groups to the FBI or other civil police.

In examining the decade of the 1960s, one finds overwhelming and unimpeachable evidence of *increasing* use of federal troops in maintaining the dominant social order. What had on the surface often appeared to be riotous conduct by aggrieved minorities, and hence merely superficial, actually constituted a more serious threat to the continued existence of the state as then constituted than the outward concern shown for private property and the damage thereof. In my opinion the state saw the danger and promptly moved to meet it.

Historically speaking, one would be hard pressed to distinguish between the purpose and application of troops in Watts in 1965 and Hungary in 1956; or between Czechoslovakia in 1969 and Kent State University in 1970. Wherein lies the difference? In both cases nearly the full power of the state was engaged. It is quite clear that the military plays an important role in maintaining domestic order. For the past ten years the National Guard has been called out daily in some city of the United States to maintain domestic order—hardly a training exercise when the Delaware National Guard has patrolled the streets of Wilmington for over two years!

The largest and most frequent call for troops since the Civil War, however, has revolved around the Vietnam war protests. It has ranged from a full-scale mobilization of a full division of elite paratroops in 1968 for the Democratic National Convention in Chicago, to lesser degrees of shock-troop mobilization to "protect" Washington from peace demonstrators. After a decade of mass demonstrations in Washington, the local police are at long last relieving the military of its police-type chores, but only after they had transformed their units into military-type organizations, the efficiency of which can be judged by the speedy arrest of over ten thousand demonstrators engaged in open-street tactics, a difficult task for even the most sophisticated military unit.

It is safe to say that universities and ghettos constitute a serious antithesis to the established order. Had it not been for the continuous and increasing application of military—not civil—force, the government might very well have become ineffectual, especially in the period since 1965. The prognosis, notwithstanding a cessation of the Vietnam war—for there will be other Vietnams—points in the direction of an ever increasing reliance on the military to maintain civil order culminating in an ultimate suspension of constitutional liberties. This forecast is a grim one, but I think not unreasonable. The American drift into fascism has often been remarked upon by disinterested observers.

Moreover, most revolutionary groups today accept this definition and thus breathe the life of the self-confirming prophecy into it insofar as the speed of the transition is concerned. Reiterating, I believe that the evidence of the past ten years is quite clear: the federal government, regardless of political party, has not been hesitant or stayed its hand in the full application of institution-maintaining violence.[25] The elite have a corner on the violence market, and the stakes are very high.

Summary

I have thus far described, albeit briefly, several roles that the military is called upon to perform as part of its "mission." These roles are modern roles, very different ones in substance from classic nineteenth-century roles. The consequences of the sophistication of the military and its extensions into the economic, political, and social structure of the nation-state is that increased totalitarian coordination of the social structure is no longer the novelistic threat of *1984* but rather a very real prospect.

I offer no brief for optimism—the outlook is hazy. A volunteer army? Such a reformed institution would in all probability eliminate the military's salient features, e.g., mobility escalator for the lower class, while becoming aristocratic in composition and more repressive in means; and much more entwined in the economy.

The Great Refusal? This hypothesis, advanced by Marcuse, foresees the internal collapse of capitalism because the nascent youth revolution is based on a disdain for "things" and instead places a premium value on "people." The hypothesis further proposes that when people cease buying the material production of corporate capitalism, and assuming that the world markets will shrink as more countries begin to attain finished goods-producing status, then the conditions making for internal irresolvable political troubles will have been established. Unfortunately Marcuse's deus ex machina has been denied by the buying habits of today's amorphous, turned-on, tuned-out *a*political youth generation. One has only to observe the expenditures for minor "protest" items, such as antiestablishment dress style or music, to realize that this is but a pipedream.

The only hint of optimism, if indeed it can be called that, has also been voiced—rather faintly and cautiously—by Marcuse. He maintains, and I join with him in the *hope,* that the Third World can *somehow* (?) stop the major industrial powers from stealing that which is the birthright of all—the world's natural resources. Should that happy day arrive, then the resulting collapse of corporate capitalism in the American, Japanese, and European societies would bring about a new society. It is in this collapse that the promise of a new society, a true alternative, a counter-system, lies. Most of all, the promise of a new economic order is found in the construction of a society organized for the sustenance of people rather than the production of "needs" and "things"—a society that would truly maximize conditions, allowing man to develop his capacities to their biological maximum. Without this promise we are condemned to the exigencies of living in an increasingly armed and dangerous world.

NOTES

1. Karl Polanyi, *The Great Transformation* (Boston: Beacon Press, 1957), chap. 1.

2. I am indebted to Gideon Sjoberg for the concept of "counter-system"; however I accept responsibility for the Idealism contained within my definition of the term.

3. Gabriel Kolko, *The Roots of American Foreign Policy* (Boston: Beacon Press, 1969).

4. The difference between state, corporate, and welfare capitalism is demographic. In a society characterized as state capitalism there is but *one* capitalist—the state itself; under corporate capitalism there are more capitalists, usually they occupy a strata in the society; and finally, under conditions of welfare capitalism (not to be confused with the social movement of American business in the late 1920s) *everyone* in the society is a capitalist, in that each has a material interest in the preservation of the status quo.

5. These are Durkheim's terms, but certainly not his intended usage. With regard to my usage of "owners" and "ownership," the long-standing but spurious argument over whether or not *control* of the means of production is decisive as opposed to mere ownership is of no consequence simply because it does not matter in the first place. The dramatis personae of the Managerial Revolution have *no separate interest* that can *long* be defended against the ultimate fact of ownership backed by the state and its monopoly of violence.

The last remaining argument vis-à-vis *control* insists on the sovereignty of the small stockholder in America (and elsewhere). This is little more than an obfuscatory excursion into metaphysical idealism. Domhoff, for example, conservatively reports that 65 to 80 percent of publicly held stock is in the hands of the top 1 percent of the population. See G. William Domhoff, *Who Rules America?* (Englewood Cliffs, N.J.: Prentice-Hall, 1967), p. 45.

6. This does not eliminate the possibility, of course, that the elite can come to believe in their own propaganda and act upon it; still, the process has to start someplace and the prior support of a military can lend considerable credence to the "rightness" of the pursuit. Vietnam fits quite nicely into this mold.

7. The litigation arose out of a German threat to "spank" Venezuela and the Cipriano Castro regime there after the Germans and the British had managed to get the countries financial position into a muddle.

8. Richard Hofstadter, *The United States* (Englewood Cliffs, N.J.: Prentice-Hall, 1957), p. 680.

9. "Play-war" or peacetime war can be as destructive of equipment as "real" war—only it does so in different ways. The generational change of weapons is accelerated under peacetime conditions because of a *lack* of battle testing, thus vitiating certainty of effect—the stock-in-trade of the military. The same thing can be said of the construction of contingency planning; imperfect knowledge dictates constant change—a circular response is initiated which, with a greedy industrial production behind it, proceeds at a high ve-

locity. Finally, nations make *wholesale* changes in their weapons during peacetime, not during war, and this also tends to increase the generational velocity of weapons systems.

10. *San Francisco Chronicle*, 3 February 1971.

11. Kolko, *Roots of American Foreign Policy*, pp. 69–70.

12. George Thayer, *The War Business* (New York: Simon & Schuster, 1969), p. 213.

13. Ibid., p. 212.

14. *San Francisco Chronicle*, 3 February 1971.

15. *Report from Iron Mountain on the Possibility and Desirability of Peace*, with introductory material by Leonard C. Lewin (New York: Dial Press, 1967).

16. Most economists welcome this trend because it supports their central doctrine of "comparative advantage," i.e., each nation should produce that which it is most suited to produce and in turn give up the policy of self-sufficiency in all else.

17. These figures are only approximate and illustrative of the differences in magnitudes.

18. My own personal opinion is that Vietnam was a colossal policy blunder brought about by the W. I. Thomas dictum of the self-confirming prophecy. But once there, the United States "discovered" other "reasons" for being there, and I think oil is one of these.

19. See Robert Engler, *The Politics of Oil* (New York: Macmillan, 1961). This comprehensive work is somewhat dated now, but nevertheless a good work to start the study of oil and its servants.

20. Kolko, *Roots of American Foreign Policy*, p. 53.

21. Ibid., pp. 53–54.

22. This event has received scant attention in scholarly or journalistic circles. The challenge of discovery remains.

23. Elwin H. Powell, "Reform, Revolution, and Reaction: A Case of Organized Conflict," in *The New Sociology*, ed. Irving Louis Horowitz (New York: Oxford University Press, 1965), pp. 331–56.

24. *San Francisco Chronicle*, 27 January 1970.

25. This is not the argument of classical or theoretical fascism; that is, I do not wish to suggest that the state "decays" because it hesitates to use force, nor am I suggesting that governments must keep their "muscles" in good shape by perhaps having a "splendid little war" every so often, as Theodore Roosevelt once maintained. The state does bare its teeth to greater or lesser extent depending upon the state of the population's consciousness of their true condition—and none doubt the fact of those teeth.

The fact that governments fall by force of arms in the face of indecisive action on their part, however, stems from mistakes they make that cannot be attributed to their *hesitancy* to use force but rather from their *inability to command* force at decisive moments.

PART II

Secondary Institutions as Supportive Appendages to the Market

4

THE SCIENTIFIC INSTITUTION

The Knowledge-Producing Appendage

Dusky Lee Smith

Contemporary folklore and mythology notwithstanding, science-technology (a more appropriate expression than "science" since science and technology have converged to the degree that they are now mutually parasitic) is not some ahistorical, telepathic, asocial, or metaphysical "stuff" exempted from sociohistorical tugs and tosses, from the pulls and pushes of daily living. Far from transcending the sociohistorical practice, science-technology is, instead, deeply intwined with the market economy and the humanistic heritage which serves as a vital impetus, as key and indispensible ingredient for society's raison d'être.

Physical Science and the Humanistic Heritage

The humanistic heritage of the United States—emphasizing the worth and dignity of the individual as well as his potential ability to influence his life fate, stressing the development of a social situation in which the individual personality is of major concern and where a high degree of self-autonomy can be realized, professing that self-realization is a viable part of the human condition and confirming the necessity for a public policy founded on rational and understandable laws—has been based on the assumption that individual men are or can be rational, and as rational beings they are to have equal voices in the determining of public policy.

Science-technology's integration into the practices of North America is partially illustrated through its close ties with the humanistic heritage which is officially used as a guideline. The blending of science-technology with the values of humanism is openly admitted yet, at the same time, paradoxical claims are made for a value-free and neutral inquiry. The assumption that science-technology is value free is denied by some of its practice which is usually oriented toward humanitarian goals—for example, the preservation of human life. When scientists-technologists were looking for the "cause" of malaria they could have defined the "cause" as "bad blood." Malaria could then have been cured by draining the blood from the victim who could not live with or without the blood. Since human life is valued by these scientist-technologists, and blood is essential to that life, the "cause" was discovered somewhere else. If the life of the Anopheles mosquito is ever held as sacred as human life, then the value-free, objective, and neutral "cause" will be "discovered" somewhere else.

Science-technology is supposedly a value-free technique which is, nevertheless, placed into a humanistic tradition as "the conscience of mankind" and the perpetrator of "permanent progress."[1] Science-technology generates a "proper" balance between the material, emotional, mental, and spiritual aspects of the human personality; it shifts, in the words of George Sarton, "man's center of maximum response from the purely physical and emotional toward improved reasoning and understanding. This is the path to wisdom and spiritual advancement that must be trod if man is to become a balanced entity." [2] Science-technology assists in freeing men from fear, anxiety, and frustration and initiates an appreciation of beauty. In short, it brings about happiness, since it "takes its place beside religion and art as one of the great humanizing influences of mankind." [3] North America "has become able to afford such luxuries as forbidding children to work long hours in sweatshops and uninteresting jobs only as a result of the technology that has sprung from science. Far from enslaving man, the machine increasingly gives him a choice as to what he shall do." [4] The achievements of science-technology result not only in new products, but also new and high-paying jobs which make high levels of consumption possible. (There is an old story of an offer by a supernatural apparition to give people a secret that would make life more convenient and more free and permit new experiences. In payment for the secret, the apparition demanded a sacrifice of 50,000 human lives every year. With outrageous indignation, the people, to the individual, rejected the offer. In the mysterious and mischievous ways of the supernatural, the secret, nonetheless, was made known. The chosen individuals set about developing the automobile—and fulfilled the apparition's sacrificial demand.) Science affirms, confirms, and reaffirms a humane universe in a perpetual state of progress.[5]

Scientific-technological attainments rest in no small part on the ability to predict, conquer, and control nature and the ability to transform practical considerations into power applications. The mutual reinforcement of science and technology results in a merger in which theoretical considerations, based on the logic of domination and the rationality of control, can be applied to nature with much of the force that the historical practice can provide—organization, funds, libraries, time, energy, expensive equipment, and inexpensive graduate-student manpower. Many comforts and conveniences can be made possible even in areas where science-technology cannot yet control but can predict, such as the weather.

The great scientific-technological achievements (partially resulting from the logic of domination and the rationality of control, great social upheavals, the unstable nature of the economy, the developing large-scale organizations, and the humanistic heritage) served as spurs for social theorists to develop a *social* science which would, hopefully, in turn create similar accomplishments in the social sphere. One of the first to recognize the impending promises of a social science was Lester Frank Ward, the "father of American sociology," the "American Aristotle," and the "Prophet of the New Deal." [6]

Social Science and the Humanistic Heritage

Ward wanted to develop a social science that would be consistent with the humanistic heritage as well as with scientific canons. Social science, like physical science, was to be a humanistic endeavor, and, like science-technology, it was to be based on the logic of domination and the rationality of control. Just as the physical sciences sought to control the physical sphere, so too must social science (and especially sociology which by Ward's reckoning was the highest science of all) "plunge boldly into the field of *social* control." [7] *"Voir prevoir; prevoyance, d'ou action":* sociology should "predict in order to control." [8] Ward felt that because predicting in order to control was the logical history and process of all science that sociology, as a science, must fulfill destiny in the social affairs of mankind.

As far as Ward was concerned, *the* major problem confronting social science—overcoming stubborn and resistant moral forces—was almost achieved, at least theoretically. Recognizing that there is a vast difference between the theoretical and practical solution to the problem of resisting moral forces, Ward contended that "the statement of the problem is its theoretical solution, which can be nothing less than *the conquest by science of the domain of the social as it conquered that of the physical forces."* [9]

Ward illustrates many views expounded by other social theorists of his time. For example, William Graham Sumner wrote that "Sociology is a science which deals with one range of phenomena produced by the struggle for existence"; it is "still in its infancy," and being infantile, it is still "in a tentative state"—yet it was mature enough to "affirm with certainty" that "social phenomena are subject to law, and that the laws of the social order are in their entire character like the laws of physics." [10] For Sumner, scientific sociology was also integrated into other established American traditions, since scientific sociology was to be utilitarian and practical; its "practicality consists in deriving [rules of right living] from the facts and laws which prevail by nature in the constitution and functions of society." [11] Consequently, sociology, which is "as full of promise for the welfare of mankind" as any other science, "must come into collision with all other theories of right living which are founded upon authority, tradition, arbitrary invention, or poetic imagination." [12]

Franklin Giddings, another early U.S. sociologist, found sociology to be the "scientific description of society." He also discovered that customs and institutions have no "sacredness in themselves, that there is no other warrant for their existence than their power to contribute to the safe and comfortable maintenance of human life, or to further progress of the human mind in knowledge, power, reason, and moral perfection." [13]

These men felt that scientific conquest of the social domain would be guided by the same humanistic heritage that directed the scientific conquest of the physical domain. At the base of Ward's scientific sociology was the conquest of human desires—social forces —in order to improve and better society.[14] Freedom was a necessity if the "good society" was to be developed, but so were other preconditions. For example, hunger is a deprivation of food needed for energy and life: "Abundant nourishment for the body is therefore the first condition to liberty." [15] And one of the major problems confronting sociology as a science was how to secure "to the members of society the maximum power of exercising their natural faculties." [16]

Scientific sociology itself "aims at the organization of happiness" which rests "upon the science of sociology": if the individual is to exercise his natural faculties to reach his self-realization, then the social forces—human desires—must be controlled and dominated to the extent that they can be guided into channels through which they can flow in harmony with the safety of society, a society based upon the freedom necessary for self-realization, upon the liberty required for the development of substantive rationality, upon the democratic principles required for equal participation of all individuals. Social science and scientific sociology were, like the physical sciences, integrated into the established humanistic heritage of North America.

From the humanistic perspective, Ward's sociology designated the malignant minority—the pampered, the idle, the favored, the shrewd distributors of wealth, the wizards of finance, the legal parasites, and the lazy inheritors of wealth who abused their wealth by using business shrewdness, mental force, legal fictions, business diplomacy, and other forms of deception to maintain their privileged positions—which sought its happiness at the expense of the majority as the major "social problem."

The key cause of this problem was, Ward discovered, the inequality of education which not only created a chasm between the rich and the poor but also created a government founded upon plutocracy and paternalism toward the marketeering interests, a government that granted the marketeers monopolies, franchises, and control over most of the natural resources, especially petroleum under Rockefeller. The inequality of knowledge also created the masses who had to bear the brunt of evolution and the existing market society, and who had to live in squalor, groveling in a prolonged drudgery which sapped their strength and made them diseased and dead very early.

Physical Science and the Marketeering Mentality

Men knew how to make beer and the pottery from which to drink it long before they understood the "scientific explanations" of the processes involved. This is also true of certain agricultural techniques, metalworking, the windmill, the waterwheel, and chemical techniques such as those concerning dyes and gunpowder.

Science was able to explain these techniques only recently—for example, Pasteur's studies of yeast, about the time of the Civil War, yielded important insights into the technique of brewing—but it was not until science could prove its *practical* worth to the marketeers that it gained acceptance and became integrated into the *power* structure. Historically, scientists have had to explain and justify themselves and their work to the nonscientific elites of power that have dominated privilege and prestige.

Gaining acceptance into the ranks of the high and mighty in North America was not easy for the scientists; significant advances were made only after much hard work—hard accommodating work —and as a result of events, including war and other crises, extraneous to science itself. The Coast Survey as early as 1832 assisted the marketeers by supplying accurate charts and maps which led to new frontiers. And later the West was surveyed by, among others, West Point-trained engineers who thereby contributed to the elimination and control of Indians and the domination of the West for the manifest destiny of marketeers. Botanists and chemists as well as soldiers accompanied the expeditions toward the new frontiers. Following the first seven-year depression, 1840–46, scientists founded the American Association for the Advancement of Science at which time they announced they were trying to make science more useful. At the time of the Civil War, academic and governmental scientists obtained a charter from Congress for the National Academy of Science which was to mobilize scientists on behalf of the northern war effort. The impact of World War I on industrial research was significant as wartime shortages of optical glass and many chemicals dramatized the U.S. dependence on German research. Scientists such as Karl Compton suggested in the 1930s that government-sponsored research could invent new devices and techniques which would bolster the economy.[17]

This, however, is not to suggest that crises affecting the marketeers can explain the rise and development of (their) science, but rather that science cannot be fully understood without realizing the impact of sociohistorical events such as crises. Scientists at the turn of the century were beginning to convince marketeers that science could be a useful aid in marketeering. General Electric established its Research Laboratory in 1902 which was quickly emulated by Du Pont, Eastman Kodak, and American Telephone and Telegraph. By the 1930s less than 20,000 people were employed in marketeering laboratories, but by the end of World War II, the war that provided science with its major opportunity to prove its subservience and usefulness to the marketeers, there were over 130,000. Both "hot" and "cold" wars have been greatly advantageous and profitable for scientists. They have been extremely instrumental in science-technology's adaptation to the marketeers, and as the cold war developed over 300,000 people were employed in the labs. It has been noted, even by conservative liberals and/or liberal conservatives, that "the prospect of peace breaking out . . . posed a real threat to the continuation of governmental subvention on such a high scale." [18]

Proximity fuses and herbicides, radar and fungicides, atomic energy and pesticides, as well as sulfa drugs and computers, plastics and polyvinyl films, automation and synthetic rubber, antibiotics and fertilizers, cybernation and vaccinations, have helped scientists prove to the marketeers and the militarists what they have known for so long, namely, that scientists could (and would) contribute to the functioning of the "good society." The partnership between the militarists and the scientists had advanced from the days of establishing reliable charts and the instruments for calculating the correct time; and now the "good life" was deeply fused with military metaphysics and scientific theorizing. "Better living through chemistry" was more than a Madison Avenue advertising technique. It was now a reflection of reality.

John A. Hannah, then president of Michigan State University, at a Parents' Convocation in 1961, said that "our colleges and universities must be regarded as bastions of our defense, as essential to the preservation of our country and our way of life as supersonic bombers, nuclear-powered submarines, and intercontinental ballistic missiles." [19] He was, of course, correct, because many universities became intricately involved with the creation of those very supersonic bombers, nuclear-powered submarines, intercontinental ballistic missiles, as well as other tools which the professional killers use.

Further evidence for President Hannah's argument can be found in the fact that almost 70 percent of all university research funds in the United States comes from the Department of Defense. Ten of the 2,000-odd universities—the University of California, Stanford, Cornell, MIT, Columbia, Harvard, Chicago, University of Illinois, University of Minnesota, and the University of Michigan— received 38 percent of the funds for research and development. Over a billion dollars (i.e., $1,000,000,000.00) are poured into forty-seven research centers which are managed by universities. Johns Hopkins University, for example, receives over a million dollars a year for "administering" the fifty-million-dollar-a-year budget of the Applied Physics Laboratory.[20]

The University of California, for example, operates both the Lawrence Radiation Laboratory and the Los Alamos Scientific Laboratory which have a combined staff of over 11,000 scientist-technicians and administrators with an annual budget of over $250 million. Professors, deans, university presidents, and other university personnel have been able not only to supplement their salaries by working part-time, and in some cases full-time, for these centers, but they have been able to set up "spin-off" industries, establishing small but essential corporations of their own. The money used by the professors to create these corporations is usually borrowed from the bank upon whose board their own university president serves. The university president then becomes a director for the new corporation.[21]

While Senator William Fulbright was considering the failure of the universities to develop "an effective counterweight to the military-industrial complex by strengthening their emphasis of the traditional values of our democracy," and arguing that they have "joined the monolith, adding greatly to its power and influence," Hubert H. Humphrey was declaring that "I don't know whether I ought to say this or not, but . . . I sort of feel that if the university wants to exclude itself from the life of the nation, then it will most likely find itself living a rather barren life. . . . I hope that there will not be a breach [between the university and the government] because if there is it will not be the government that suffers, because the government can set up its own laboratories." [22]

While Senator Fulbright of Arkansas contemplates the lack of democratic concern in the universities, the Pentagon itself maintains a strain of death-producing microbes in Pine Bluffs, Arkansas, which, with the rest of the stockpile of chemical and biological weapons, can destroy about 100 billion people; somewhere around 30 times the world's population. The UCLA Medical School, Texas University, Baylor University, Cornell Aeronautical Laboratory, Johns Hopkins, Maryland, Yale, the Illinois Institute of Technology, and the Stanford Research Institute (among others) have all contributed quite mightily to the death-producing potential of the military forces, the professional warriors. Of the $8 billion research and development budget of the Defense Department, about $450 million annually goes to universities and nearly $700 million to university-related contract centers. These figures gain added significance in view of the fact that the universities, over 2,000 of them, themselves spend only $8 billion a year on education.[23] Nevertheless, military research and development funds are only one means by which the military metaphysics and marketeering mentality have come to dominate the universities and science.

Science in North America was once primarily an avocation of a few university-located scholars who were somewhat autonomous from the marketeering realm. From this inauspicious beginning it developed into a complex organization which bestows prestige and power. Science today is supported by the power, prestige, and bureaucratic organizations of the marketeers; by the university structure which supplies a pool of undergraduates from which fresh recruits can be drawn; by resources from big government, universities, and directly from the marketeers themselves; by an all-out cold-war effort; by a military that has found new, complex machines a necessity; by a general public that believes the myths and folklore of science automatically being in the service of humanity; and by social theorists who covet, crave, and court the privileges, power, and prestige of an organized and powerful science.

Social Science and the Market Mentality

Ward wanted to disassociate sociology from the stigma already placed upon the discipline of economics—the reputation of being a spokesman for the high-and-mighty marketeers. Sociology, he argued, would become a spokesman for all the classes, i.e., mankind. The father of sociology in the United States wrote articles on the abuse of wealth and attacked other scientists for giving legitimacy to the older marketeering.[24] He established a science giving aid and comfort to neomarketeering, and it was this achievement which, posthumously in 1950, earned him the title, Prophet of the New Deal.[25] Ward's science discovered the basic desires—those for property and wealth—which pushed men to produce an excess of goods for generating the basis of a humane civilization, that is, the creation of an artificial world no longer subject to the law of the "survival of the fittest." [26]

The Prophet of the New Deal invented a science justifying great accumulations of wealth, more and active governmental participation, and an increasing role for sociologists. Other sociologists, such as Albion Small, closely aligned themselves with Ward's sociology. The wealthy marketeers were discovered as "necessary" for industrial and social advancement, and Ward pleaded with them to take their already proven talents to the governmental arena where they could, by using sociological principles, bring the many new social reforms needed to maintain slow and steady progress. If the wealthy marketeers and their heirs would help to maintain evolution, then they would avoid the impending revolution anticipated by Ward in the absence of social change.[27] Through a primary social reform—increased education—and several secondary reforms, all based on social science principles, the poor would gain their share of the world's excess production and, accordingly, appreciate the rightful position of the wealthy marketeers. Thus the market society would be salvaged, and it in turn would come to appreciate and understand the need and necessity for sociologists to play key roles in the government.

From his marketeering perspective, Ward viewed those who questioned the soundness of marketeering—socialists, communists, anarchists, misguided workers—as dangerous and their activities as social problems. He discovered that all the existing problems connected with marketeering were remnants of the older economic order, of laissez faire which had to be relegated to history. As the older structures gave way to the newer form of marketeering, the beliefs and notions supporting the old order would change. The United States would then be on its way to permanent and progressive evolution, forming a society which he called Sociocracy, a society in which all the various and sundry interests would be balanced.

Social-Physical Science and Humanistic Marketeering

Ward argued that if government were in the hands of social scientists it might be elevated to the rank of an applied science, and if sociological laws were followed it would be discovered that "Man is as easily managed by intelligence as . . . nature was shown to be." [28] Social control has been and remains one of the most basic concerns on the part of most sociologists and is one of the best-selling concepts in the discipline. The attempt to make sociology more scientific, especially in mocking or imitating the physical science model, is of utmost importance to the "discipline." As one contemporary true believer, May Brodbeck, has suggested, the "possibility of a social science in principle as perfect as physics remains the unexamined premise of the vast majority of present-day social scientists." [29]

The 1967 president of the American Association for the Advancement of Science and dean of the John Fitzgerald Kennedy School of Government at Harvard, Don K. Price, recently pointed out that the hope of social scientists has been that a more exacting discipline could provide not only more reliable guides to those who have to make policy decisions, but they might also provide the "answers to the main policy problems." [30] He discovered that as the social sciences do in fact rely more on the physical science model, on the quantitative techniques, they *are* beginning to furnish "the politician or administrator who must decide policy questions with an increasing quantity of data and of methods that can be useful to him. There is every reason to believe that, as they become more exact and reliable, they will continue to do so." [31] One need only turn to the U.S. war against Vietnam for a multitude of living examples.[32]

The ascendancy of science in the twentieth century has been partially based upon the ability to turn *theoretical* considerations into *power* applications. Ward realized this before the turn of the century, before aeronautics and space programs became a reality, before science proved its ability to conquer nature. And he realized, too, that power application, i.e., social control, was essential to the scientific conquest of men.

In helping to conquer nature, scientists fused their theoretical discoveries and inventions into an already existing technology and power base dominated by the marketeers. Following this lead, Ward and other founding fathers of sociology fused their theoretical discoveries and inventions into the same power base, a tactic eventually rewarded. Just as Ward realized the potentiality of science, he also realized the potentiality of large-scale organizations, and he supported this potentiality. This tactic also gained rewards. The Prophet of the New Deal deserved his title! Ward's sophisticated analysis set the temper and mood of sociology for the next hundred years, and contemporary social science owes much of what it is to the following statement by a contemporary social scientist. It is an example of scientific arrogance, but it may also be considered as a logical extension of Ward's achievements: "One of the most general functions of social structure is to provide a basis for predictability and regularity of social behavior. . . ." [33]

Like Ward, many contemporary social scientists have made their theoretical conceptions confluent with prevailing power applications. As Ward integrated his basic conceptions into the basic assumptions of a marketeering society in transformation, many contemporary social scientists accommodate their conceptual frameworks and theoretical schemas to the prevailing market society, a society in a constant state of flux. Just as the marketeers made their march on Washington when they finally realized, after the Great Depression, that small-town lawyers and merchants acting as congressmen could not be trusted to manage the political economy, scientists, after proving their capabilities to bolster the market society and having invented new theoretical justifications for the maintenance of the marketeers' positions of power and privilege, made their march on Washington.

No longer, for example, do sociologists have to sit with depressing social workers in dingy and ill-lit offices, but now enter the various and sundry outposts and inposts of the marketeering power domain. Far from the spinster social workers' teacups, petty criminals, and unwed mothers, the contemporary social scientist drinks Scotch and martinis in air-conditioned offices with, among others, generals, corporate chieftains, CIA directors, admirals, and RAND personnel. The scientists' march on Washington has raised social theory to one of the major administrative adjuncts of the welfare-warfare state. Partially because of its proven ability to help the marketeers in their times of need to meet their numerous crises, science has become one of the major political pressure groups in the United States.

When George Lundberg quickly replied "Yes" to his question, "Can Science Save Us?" he failed to explain fully many of the implications involved, not the least of which is the "Us" who are to be saved. The science he advocated was a science not merely compatible but one intricately interrelated with the administrative problems of bureaucratic marketeering.

Other contemporary social scientists, such as Lewis Coser, William Kornhauser, Jessie Bernard, William Gamson, James S. Coleman, S. N. Eisenstadt, W. J. Goode, Jiri Nehnevajsa, Rex Hopper, and Neil Smelser, all sociologists, participated in one degree or another in Project Camelot, one of the military's attempts to bring university professors and researchers into closer harmony with the marketeering mentality and the military metaphysics. Other value-free sociologists, e.g., Seymour Martin Lipset, take money from the air force to practice their sociology.[34] These as well as many other sociologists have elaborated Lundberg's potential concerns and endeavored to apply them in highly practical ways.

Harry Alpert, for example, argues that social science focuses on "man and his problems" with the "same objectivity and the same passion for truth which have in the past given us some understanding and control of the physical world." [35] He found that defense mobilization and World War II were catalytic events leading to an expansion of funds by the government for social science programs. Social science proved its intrinsic worth to administrators by, for example, assisting the militarists with, among other things, orientation programs, morale problems, command problems (particularly among Negro troops), and recruit adjustment. Social scientists interested in basic research have received support from the Office of Naval Research in order to discover how to bring about conformity.[36]

As these examples suggest, the scientific blending and identification of *man's* problems with the administrator's problems becomes complete; social science becomes an adjunct of administrative decision making, an important aspect of a bureaucratic organization supporting "scientific" marketeering.

Scientific sociology can be divided into several schools and approaches, and one that seems to be gaining in popularity can be referred to as the *mod squad* approach. This "set" sees itself as "action oriented." One of the leading swingers of this approach is Marvin Sussman who, in his article "The Sociologist as a Tool of Social Action," [37] argues that the sociologist should permit himself to be used as a tool.[38] The sociologist as tool, the action sociologist, is no longer satisfied with being confined to teaching and research. He wishes to be "in" on the action—especially to be admitted to the inner chambers of the large bureaucracies where "things" are accomplished, where "big" decisions are made.

One way for the sociologist to become action-involved is by means of his consultant role which is, of course, "his most professional one"—as a consulting expert, the sociologist "places at the disposal of his client his total repertoire of knowledge and skills, as well as the time necessary to diagnose, treat, and solve a given problem." [39] As a consultant it can be assumed that "the agency or institution seeking assistance has one or more problems begging for solution and is therefore engaging a person with an apparently high degree of expertise to help solve them." [40] Today, Sussman continues, the social scientist has "a responsibility equal in value to that of his colleagues in the natural and physical sciences and their professions." [41]

The mod university, realizing its responsibilities, wishes to "direct" knowledge toward curing a "malignant disease" or solving a "critical social problem" by urging social science research "to find solutions to health, military, industrial, economic, and family problems." [42] The responsible scientist takes his wares to the bureaucratic leaders, makes his talents and skills disposable to those in the commanding positions of power and privilege. The aims and goals of sociology convolute and merge with the administrative needs of the market society.

A popular variation on the action sociologists are the "little helpers" who try to develop "helping theories" as well as a "helping methodology." [43] These men are engrossed in "milieu therapy" whereby, it is hoped, many of the problems confronting major bureaucracies can be eliminated or at least brought under control. A good example of applying the approach is related to the forced eviction of poor tenants when the power structure decides a particular urban area is to be demolished. In one article, "Controlled Intervention—the Helping Professions and Directed Social Change," a little helper, William Key, explained how he went about assisting the bureaucratic decision to "relocate" people. Armed with a sociological theory which assumed that these poor people would be upset by the fact they had to move, it was soon discovered, after some contact with this "target population," that permanency was not a luxury the poor could afford. The little helper discovered that the poor had become accustomed to moving, that it was part of their life styles. The need for "cooling" the "relocated" was all but nonexistent. Not to be daunted or dismayed, the little helper focused his attentions and theories on another aspect of poverty, namely, on worker dissatisfaction, and assumed that the displaced people needed "vocational rehabilitation." [44]

On a different level of abstraction, many contemporary "heroes" or "stars" of sociology integrate their social theories and the "needs" of the marketeering society, presenting conceptual schemes and discovering (inventing?) data which provide legitimating symbols to established power groups. The ideological implications and nuance of, say, Robert Merton, Seymour Martin Lipset, and Talcott Parsons are notorious and have been examined on various occasions.[45]

On almost all levels of abstraction and on almost all levels of data-discovery or invention, many sociologists have fairly well integrated their sociologies with the ongoing market society. As the market society shifts because of national and international imperatives, as old symbols of legitimation lose their strength, new symbols are needed.[46]

No longer solely relying on gods to be on their side, no longer claiming a monopoly on defining natural rights, no longer able simply to rely on tradition, the marketeers have found science to be quite an adequate defender, a new and useful provider of symbols. Whether the present rejection of science-technology is but a passing fad or whether it is a phenomenon that will evoke a thoroughgoing change is still open to question. The social sciences, united primarily around the physical science model, have been quite successful for a number of decades in helping to forestall any kind of serious threat to the marketeers.

Not only have the social sciences been able to contrive and concoct successful symbols of legitimation, but the physical sciences have been able to devise and construct enough consumer goodies and voyages into new frontiers to restrain consequential considerations of viable alternatives to the market society. Science-technology has been elevated to such an important and near-sacred position that its achievements serve as a great distractive force. Sociologists have been at the forefront of this distraction. For example, onward-and-upward technology (under the control of the marketeers) has been given theoretical significance as an almost autonomous entity. Marketeering technology was viewed, especially since the early 1920s in the sociological scheme of William F. Ogburn, as that behind which "culture" lagged. This "cultural lag" theory quite readily gained great popularity among marketeering sociologists.

Ogburn discovered that culture required necessary changes if it were to keep abreast of science-technology, that "progressive" social changes were needed if the market society was to prevail. Many changes he advocated were accepted, forestalling or eliminating the threats he felt were facing the marketeering enterprise, while allowing marketeering to "advance" to a "higher" stage. Science-technology, as the model by which social sciences were to be judged, served, in its sociological manifestation, as one means by which the marketeering society could be salvaged.

From Ward to Ogburn to Merton and Lipset, there has been a massive theoretical drive to bring men's behavior under control, to make men more predictable. Given the nature of grand and abstract theorizing, given the nature of scientific rationality, sociological concepts can be discussed as neutral, value-free, objective. When removed from their celestial tranquility, when brought down from their abstract perch where their pristine pureness is stained by concrete situations of men participating in their historical practice, then abstract neutrality is no longer indifference, value-freeness is no longer cool unconcern, and objectivity is no longer apathy. Neutrality becomes commitment, value-freeness changes to predilection, and objectivity transforms into inclination. Sociology in the hands of, say, the Wards, Ogburns, Mertons, and Lipsets, becomes committed, predilected, and inclined toward marketeering; sociological concepts coalesce objectivity, absorb neutrality, and merge value-freeness, fasten analysis, entangle inquiry, and imprison explanation into the historical practice of marketeering.

When functionalism is removed from its heavenly sanctum by, for example, Merton, *its* historical practice becomes, indeed, functioning marketeering. Functions, dysfunctions, manifest functions, and latent functions, when deprived of their lofty, contemplative status, derive their content from a sociohistorically located form of human practice, the practice of an ongoing marketeering. Function is as function does, and functionalism is as marketeering does. Mertonianism is an increment of marketeering; the basic concepts are imprisoned within the confines (the means and end) of the market "system," the analysis is operationalized to make the "system" smoother and more functional. Abstract analysis becomes, in practice, theoretical reinforcement. As marketeering becomes smoother, behavior becomes more predictable, and functionalism becomes a predictive science. The vested interest of predictive science is apparent. The interests of the marketeers and social science become synonymous at this point.[47]

Sociologists, mocking and imitating the quantitative and rigorous methods of natural science, are leading toward a scientific unification. Sociology has, since its inception in the United States, endeavored to make physical science concepts viable to the social realm, borrowing such terms as functions, equilibrium, system, organism, mechanism, forces, processes, law, and homeostasis, and using such concepts within, of course, "responsible" reason.[48]

"Responsible" reason is related to the logic of domination contained in the physical science model, a model which not only permits but also encourages an attempt to mobilize and pacify nature. Social science, using the same model, permits and encourages the attempt to mobilize and pacify man. As the physical science model is used to work nature over, it is also used to work men over; it treats men as calculable social units, mere extensions of the technological reason applied to nature. As rigorously quantified units, men are defined as extensions of the technological apparatus whose success is defined by its achievements in mobilizing nature for, of course, human welfare. Men are defined by their ability to acquire skills and attitudes "geared" to the technological apparatus, and are defined by their abilities to perform preconceived roles. "Responsible" reason coincides with the rationality of the technological apparatus, with its bureaucratic structure. The technological apparatus, not individuals, forms the seat of reason.

Rationalization becomes regimentation, part of the means whereby men are mobilized and coordinated in unison with good management principles. Men become "geared" to the technological apparatus not only by becoming extensions of the machine, but also by identifying with the "goodies" it produces. The identification is partially revealed in the question of "Where are you parked?" and in the reply "I am parked in lot 1-A" when the referent is actually an automobile. Men, rational men, sleep, drink, eat, and make love when it does not interfere with the technological apparatus. The logic of domination in the physical science model reinforces this rationalization, this mobilization, this coordination, and this predictable state of affairs. As men become more and more predictable, they become less and less free.

Preconceived performances, rationally attuned to the technological apparatus, are also consistent with the division of men into units whereby they coordinate their "time" (another rationally calculated entity to which rational men regiment their behavior) in rhythm with the productive process. Free time is a portion of time allotted to resting up for reparticipation, a time allotted for consuming the technological goodies. The ritual of denying one's identity with and assimilation into the technological apparatus is belied by the daily practice of participating "freely" in these preconceived performances.

The physical science model which helps make nature produce the technological goodies—the best evidence of its efficacy—also serves, when it is switched to the social domain and aimed at a "target population," to coordinate behavior into a high standard of living and an increasingly "gross" national product. That this gross national product (as well as the gross standard of living) is dominated by technological aspects reflects the success and integration of the sciences that use the physical science model. That human needs are made synonymous to the needs of a social "system" supporting and merged with technological rationality partially attests to the power of the scientific method. The unification of individual interests with the interests of those dominating and receiving the greatest privileges and prestige reflects, in part, the ascendancy of scientific unification.

Science has helped to precondition men to accept their own mobilization, their own coordination, their own participation as voluntary "gears" in the apparatus. It has helped men to adjust to the "demands" of the machines which are producing goodies designed to become obsolete, and which are oriented toward status and prestige, and which can best be described as junk. Science, in almost all of its aspects, helps to make men more predictable, to make human behavior more attuned to the scientific model. The application of the scientific method to men and nature as objects to be manipulated according to the prevailing technological rationality is helping produce "cheerful robots" with "happy consciences" loyal to the "system." [49]

While science-technology has prompted the marketeers to

strengthen their own privilege and power positions, scientist-technologists have gained more and more power and privileges of their own. Science-technological discoveries and inventions facilitate not only existing power structures within the market society by providing goodies and ideologies which serve to paralyze criticism within the nation-state of the "mother" country, but simultaneously serve as a very important means by which inroads have been made into other nation-states. Science-technology in the name of neutrality and value-freeness has been very instrumental in maintaining and promoting marketeering imperialism on a worldwide scale.

The claim for neutrality and objectivity might have served as a means to retain "autonomy" in the early stages of scientific-technological development, and this may have been one of the reasons the scientists were not accepted as useful employees by the marketeering elite, but as soon as scientific practice rather than ideology became the criterion for the marketeers' evaluation, then the scientists were permitted to join the technologists who already had been accepted by the marketeers.

The claim for neutrality, objectivity, value-freeness also rationalizes the scientist-technologists' inclinations to escape responsibility.[50] Historically, elites have tried to avoid claims of responsibility by invoking legitimating symbols—divine rights, natural laws, human nature, the majority opinion, and the like. As science-technology gained ascendancy, scientist-technologists created new symbols of justifiable unaccountability. For example, if scientists were objective, value-free, and neutral, then it stands to reason they should not be accountable for their discoveries and inventions. After all, as scientists they (merely!) search for truth, letting the chips fall where they may. It is not *their* fault that truth comes forth more favorably to the marketeers and that the chips fall upon the heads of the poor and the oppressed.

Also, it was more than apparent that scientific-technological truths would be compatible with the welfare of *all* men. Nylons, golf balls, pesticides, nuclear bombs, biochemical warfare, were not only helping to bring civilization but also making "life" more generally tolerable and enjoyable for all. Discoveries in the social sciences, like those of Giddings and Sumner, proved that marketeering coincided with human betterment as well as democracy. Giddings discovered that marketeering forays into foreign countries were necessary for the spread of civilization.[51] Sumner opposed the use of the military to perpetuate marketeering interests in general, but he favored military intervention in specific cases, that is, where the natives interfered with the "atmosphere" needed for private marketeering. Contemporary social science has many spokesmen generating social theories justifying marketeering expansion and development. For example, in sociology, the social theories of men such as Talcott Parsons, Edward Shils, Wilbert Moore, and Marion Levy, Jr., among others, are used to defend or promote marketeering expansion in other countries. All these objective, value-free, neutral theories are, of course, consistent with the humanistic heritage of the United States as interpreted by official sociology.

The convergence of marketeering interests and the humanist heritage has not been established exclusively by scientist-technologists but they have made important contributions. In one sense, this convergence can be partially understood as one of the major science-technological achievements of the market society. The worth and dignity of the individual has been partially made synonymous with the worth and dignity of the marketeering society where the individual's potential ability to influence his life fate is confined to the survival of the marketplace. The emphasis upon the development of a social situation where a high degree of self-autonomy can be realized has been successfully linked to the development of a social situation where a high degree of self-autonomy has been established for the corporate enterprises which dominate a meaningful proportion of the individual's life.[52]

The aspect of the humanistic heritage which has emphasized self-realization has been made not only compatible with but also dependent upon the self-realization of the military-industrial-governmental coterie. The anticipation of a day-to-day life in which the individual personality is of priceless value has been successfully reconciled to the anticipation of private gain in which profits are of priceless value. The search for a public sensitivity in which rational men are to have an equal voice in the determination of public policy has been integrated into the private interests of the marketeers where public insensitivity provides the foundation for a bureaucratic rationality for determining public policy. The seat of reason which, in the humanistic heritage, resides in the individual is now located in the inner workings of countless committees where the public interest is equated with public relations. Science-technology, far from being a negative force for critical assessment of events and governmental policies, has been a positive instrument in assessing the positive role of corporations and government to influence events in the directions favorable to the interests of the marketeers.

The merging of marketeering interests with the humanist heritage has been accomplished to such a high degree that the humanistic heritage cannot provide, except in a very weak and ineffectual sense, a critical force by which events and policies can be judged. The humanistic heritage provides a framework by which marketeering intervention into foreign countries can be accomplished, where villages (foreign people?) can be destroyed for their own good, where terror at home and abroad can be spread with the minimum of public protest, where human destruction can be judged as moral, where human potentiality can be denied with righteous indignation, where poverty can be maintained without guilt.

The destruction and terror generated by the marketeering mentality is a destruction of compassion and a terror of sympathy. The high infant-mortality rates of blacks and Indians in the Americas and the more rapid marketeering elimination of human life abroad are examples of compassionate destruction. The fear and anxiety of being hungry and without the means by which life can be enjoyed and appreciated, generated on both sides of the U.S. nation-state boundaries by the market mentality, are systematically encouraged by sympathetic terror; they result from the merging of the marketeering mentality with the humanistic heritage which enables an individual to highly differentiate between political murder and bank robbery by those opposed to the market society and the (legalized?) robbery and deaths inflicted by the marketeers. The moralizing over the kidnaping-death of a marketeer is quite empty and forceless in view of the deaths necessary to maintain the market society.

The United States and its accomplices in its "sphere of influence" have been constructed upon the blood and backs of blacks, reds, and yellows, and they are being maintained by spilling the same blood and breaking the same backs; the United States is also constructed on the graves of many white human beings prematurely laid in their graves. The moralizing over the deaths caused by those refusing to cooperate with, and by those fighting against, the marketeering society must be evaluated alongside those direct and indirect deaths caused by maintaining these market societies. In short, the denial of human potential as well as the denial of life itself can be historically located in and specifically related to the form of marketeering practices in day-to-day life. One important reason why these deaths, and the denial of men's potentiality, are not being historically and socially located in and related to existing marketeering is the scientific-technological achievement of merging the humanistic heritage with the marketeering mentality.

The scientific-technological elite which forms an intricate part of the marketeering elite must take responsibility and be held accountable for its achievements. The claim for unaccountability under the guise of objectivity, neutrality, value-freeness must be seen as an ideology—an elite ideology—which justifies the crimes of marketeering—including terror and human destruction—as humanitarian crimes, as crimes *for* humanity. To the degree that scientist-technologists have given aid and comfort to the marketeers in their march toward physical and social conquest, they are to that degree guilty of the crimes committed. That scientist-technologists suffer little or no guilt attests to the power of their own positive thinking.[53]

NOTES

1. See George Sarton, *The History of Science and the New Humanism* (Bloomington: Indiana University Press, 1962).

2. George Russell Harrison, *The Role of Science in Our Modern World* (New York: William Morrow, 1956), p. 225.

3. Ibid., p. 20.

4. Ibid., p. 202.

5. Those who would be quick to dismiss these statements as not representative of value-free scientists should bear in mind that the author is none other than George Russell Harrison who has served not only as dean of the School of Science at MIT, but has also received the highest civilian award the United States confers, the Presidential Medal of Merit.

6. See Dusky Lee Smith, "Some Socio-Economic Influences upon the Founding Fathers of Sociology in the United States" (Ph.D. dissertation, State University of New York at Buffalo, 1970).

7. Ibid., p. 317; emphasis supplied.

8. Ibid., p. 318.

9. Ibid.

10. Ibid., p. 37.

11. Ibid., p. 36.

12. Ibid.

13. Ibid., p. 124.

14. Ibid., p. 315.

15. Ibid., p. 316.

16. Ibid.

17. David D. Van Tassel and Michael G. Hall, *Science and Society in the United States* (Homewood, Ill.: Dorsey Press, 1966), p. 238.

18. Ibid., p. 246.

19. *The University-Military Complex* (New York: North American Congress on Latin America, March 1969), p. 4.

20. James Ridgeway, *The Closed Corporation* (New York: Ballantine, 1969), pp. 4, 5.

21. Ibid.

22. Immanuel Wallerstein and Paul Starr, *The University Crisis Reader*, vol. 1 (New York: Random House, 1971), p. 240.

23. Sidney Lens, *The Military Industrial Complex* (Philadelphia: Pilgrim Press, 1970), pp. 123–27.

24. Smith, "Socio-Economic Influences," chap. 5.

25. Ibid.

26. Ibid.

27. Ibid.

28. Ibid., p. 314.

29. May Brodbeck, *Readings in the Philosophy of the Social Sciences* (New York: Macmillan, 1968), p. 1.

30. Don K. Price, *The Scientific Estate* (Cambridge, Mass.: Belknap Press, 1965), p. 109.

31. Ibid., p. 100.

32. See Noam Chomsky, *American Power and the New Mandarins* (New York: Vintage, 1969), esp. pp. 23–158.

33. Dusky Lee Smith, "Robert King Merton: From Middle Range to Middle Road," *Catalyst* 2 (Summer 1966): 34.

34. *Subliminal Warfare* (New York: North American Congress on Latin America, 1970), p. 19.

35. Donald M. Valdes and Dwight G. Dean, *Sociology in Use* (New York: Macmillan, 1967), p. 487.

36. See the "small group" studies of men like Theodore M. Mills, Robert Hamblin, and A. Paul Hare. See, especially, A. Paul Hare, Edgar F. Borgatta, and Robert F. Bales, eds., *Small Groups: Studies in Social Interaction* (New York: Alfred Knopf, 1955) for a small group of studies which are almost all conducive to the development of behavior consistent with the desires of the Office of Naval Research.

37. In A. B. Shostak, *Sociology in Action* (Homewood, Ill.: Dorsey Press, 1966), p. 3.

38. For an interesting and more revealing definition of "tool" than is found in *Webster's Dictionary* one can consult Eric Partridge's *A Dictionary of Slang and Unconventional English* (New York: Macmillan, 1961), p. 898.

39. Valdes and Dean, *Sociology in Use*, p. 6.

40. Ibid., pp. 6–7.

41. Ibid., p. 4.

42. Shostak, *Sociology in Action*, pp. 3–4.

43. Ibid., pp. 115–22.

44. Ibid.

45. See Alvin Gouldner, *The Coming Crises of Western Sociology* (New York: Basic Books, 1970); Smith, "Robert King Merton"; Dusky Lee Smith, "The Sunshine Boys: Toward a Sociology of Happiness," *The Activist* 14 (Spring 1964): 166–77.

46. Hans Gerth and C. Wright Mills, *Character and Social Structure* (New York: Harcourt, 1953), pp. 274 ff.

47. Sussman's appeal for making social science available to the highest bidder is only a variation of Merton's technical approach to sociology. Merton has argued that the sociological technician should accept "alternative proposal for policy as a basis for research, providing *only* that these alternatives be technically amenable to research." If marketeers, for example, desire to improve the Negroes' morale without giving up segregation, "the technician finds this definition of the problem adequate and confines himself accordingly." See Smith, "Robert King Merton."

48. See May Brodbeck's use of "system" and "law" in her *Readings in the Philosophy of the Social Sciences* (New York: Macmillan, 1968), esp. pp. 372, 375. Also, look for the teleological implications in her use of "imperfect laws." A law is imperfect when "it does not permit us to compute (predict or postdict) the state of the system, either an individual or a group, at *any* given moment from its state at one moment" (p. 375). Compute, predict, postdict, system, law are all so "sciency" and so involved with the very nature of individual freedom. Democracy, at least for C. Wright Mills, is related to the power and freedom of individuals to change laws according to agreement upon rules, rules which may also be changed, and to some kind of collective control over the structural mechanics of sociohistorical change. He believed that in so far as men are free to some degree, they are not readily predictable. See C. Wright Mills, *Sociological Imagination* (New York: Oxford University Press, 1959), pp. 116 ff.

49. See Mills, *Sociological Imagination*, and Herbert Marcuse, *One-Dimensional Man* (Boston: Beacon Press, 1964).

50. Sidney Willhelm, "Elites, Scholars, and Sociologists," *Catalyst* 2 (Summer 1966): 10.

51. Franklin Giddings, *Democracy and Empire* (London: Macmillan, 1900).

52. As one outstanding marketeer stated, "What is good for General Motors is good for the country." This philosophy finds substantiation in official sociology.

53. I would like to thank McMaster University for providing me with the time necessary to think through some of the implications of the present organization of science.

5

THE RELIGIOUS INSTITUTION

The Opium-producing Appendage

David Bartelt

"Religious distress is at the same time the expression of real distress and the protest against real distress. Religion is the sign of the oppressed creature, the beast of a beastless world, just as it is the spirit of a spiritless situation. It is the opium of the people." [1]

Several points are being asserted simultaneously by Marx in the above passage. First and foremost is that the religious institution is dependent upon the presence of inequity, oppression, and human misery for its continued existence. A second major thrust of his argument is that religion does not cause these problems, but for many it is the sole response they make to these conditions. It is an attempt to ease the pain, at least for the moment, of living in an alienating, oppressive, and exploitative society. A third implicit point is that religion, to the extent that it commands the attention of the people, serves to deflect them from the actions necessary to eliminate the social forces giving rise to their oppressed condition. Since religion is a post hoc response to a problem, an attempt to succor and solve an already existing pain, it can in no way be directed at the source of the problem. Thus, poverty is met with the promise of a rich afterlife, powerlessness with the idea that there is one more powerful than any here on earth, injustice and oppression with the promise of a Final Judgment Day, exploitation with the idea that "God helps those who help themselves!" In short, religion argues in the face of the most widespread structurally produced problems that "God's in his Heaven, all's right with the world."

Placing these general comments in historical perspective, then, Marx was arguing that at the same time that the religion of his time was a perfectly logical and necessary adjunct of laissez faire capitalism and its structural problems, specifically widespread poverty and alienation from the means of production (and the consequent powerlessness of the proletariat), it was a barrier to the development of revolutionary action that would eliminate these problems. In the case of mid-nineteenth-century Germany, the political disenfranchisement of certain groups added a further dimension to religion's opiate characteristic, as the class conflict that accompanied the development of capitalism was translated into religious conflict by the vehicle of officially sanctioned anti-Semitism.[2] Marx was able to locate the source of the religious conflict in the economic-political processes of the time, and was further able to use the occasion to develop a theoretical argument for the analysis of religion and society based on the social organization of capitalist society.

As might be expected, this analysis of religion has received short shrift in American sociology; indeed, the closest one gets to even an attempted explicit rejoinder is in Lenski's *The Religious Factor*, when he attacks the rather general and unspecified theory of "economic determinism." [3] Lenski's work is representative of Zeitlin's comment that much of sociology is largely a debate with Marx's ghost.[4] Most authors in the sociology of religion are content merely to cite Weber and Durkheim as twin originators of the field.[5] One is compelled to note, however, that while much research has been done which is anti-Marxist in origin and purpose, the major conclusions support a

Marxian analysis rather than either the Weberian or Durkheimian models. The statement is made here that, indeed, all the evidence necessary is in (regarding the religious establishment in America) to support such an analysis, given the changes that have occurred in the shift from laissez faire, colonial capitalism to the corporate, imperialistic variety experienced today.

As one example of the inherent anti-Marxist sentiments of the sociology of religion, let us consider that masterpiece of reassurance to the petit bourgeoisie, Max Weber's *The Protestant Ethic and the Spirit of Capitalism*.[6] Apart from his rooting the causes of social behavior in personal attitudes (that were reflections of cultural themes),[7] there is an aspect of Weber's work that supports the Marxian analysis, yet is conveniently ignored by contemporary sociologists. The main thesis of Weber's work was that the development of Protestantism, especially of the Calvinist variety, was necessary to provide a social psychological "set" conducive to capitalist behavior. Specifically, the attitudes associated with "this worldly asceticism" were seen to be essential for the rational planning activity seen by Weber as essential for a capitalistic system. Several points come to mind. First, in no way does Weber's argument account for the manner in which capital develops from merely a momentary exchange to the real basis of capitalism.[8] Second, as Yinger notes,[9] Geneva (scene of most of John Calvin's activities) was a well-established center of capitalist market activity before Calvinist theology developed, thus giving rise to the interpretation that religion was simply altering its ideology to fit and justify a changed social order. Finally, Weber and his followers have missed a crucial aspect of the ascetic ideology: it applauds success (by equating it with salvation), but it also tells the failure (its view of the poverty-stricken) that they simply have not "tried" hard enough. They thereby legitimate the very social structure that produced their "failure." In short, Weber's position in the bourgeois community of pre-World War I Germany encouraged in him a merchants' interpretation of Protestantism that has been part and parcel of standardized sociology ever since.

The point of the above has been to help demonstrate that the lack in American sociology of Marxian interpretations of the religious institution as opiate producer is not a function of overwhelming counterevidence, but is part of a studied avoidance of any form of radical analysis by the sociologists of the sunshine state—celebrators of consensus, pluralism, value-integration, interest group democracy, nonegalitarian classlessness, and all the other liberal ideologies of corporate capitalism.[10] In so doing, as we shall see below, they have mistaken both the nature of modern society and the place of religion in it. Instead of religious irrelevance, à la Peter Berger, we will deal with its commitment to and support of the corporate state; instead of motivational qualities regarding "ultimate" questions, à la Parsons and Nottingham, we will deal with its deflecting of real problems into ultimate ones; instead of congratulating the activists in the religious community, we will deal with the inherent inadequacy of their approach to human problems; instead of reducing all problems to those of the soul, we will deal with the extent of man's alienation from himself, his fellow man, and his social circumstances that gives rise to soulful problems. In brief, we shall turn religion on its head in order to better see it right side up.

Contemporary Capitalist Society

When the name of Karl Marx is brought into a sociological argument, the typical establishment response is that he was (1) a utopian; (2) a social philosopher, not a sociologist; or (3) wrong, because his predictions did not come true. It is, of course, only the latter objection that concerns us here, as the remainder are merely attempts at slander via the genetic fallacy. In noting that we have not arrived at the final crisis of capitalism, much less the development of a socialist society, most anti-Marxists seem convinced that history has ceased its movement with their arrival on the intellectual scene. The celebration of the "end of ideology" seems premature, at best.[11] We still live in a capitalist society, none of its contradictions having been removed. What has happened is that both laissez faire and robber baron capitalism have been replaced by the more impersonal corporate variety. Chief among its characteristics are the presence of large-scale bureaucratic organization, oligopoly, international economic expansion with its consequent attempts at American ecopolitical hegemony, and an extensive diversification of production ("synergistic" companies)—all of which are aimed at satisfying the goal held by large corporate bodies that in the end *all* consumers *must* interact with them when they (the consumers) enter the market.[12] The consequences of such an economic organization in the United States, with its particular historical development are as follows: a power elite whose long-run interests coincide with one another as domestic "law and order," military expenditures and logic, and a protected multinational factory and marketplace become allies in the "great American Dream";[13] and continuation of institutionalized racism, as blacks become economically irrelevant, save in the perpetuation of this racism;[14] a politics of sham and ritual, which induces the voter to pull the lever of the machine that screws them;[15] a status split in the proletariat, which to this point has barred effective class-conscious economic and political actions on their part;[16] an entrenched poverty class, which seems to shrink and grow more with the lag between census statistics and accurate cost of living indices;[17] and a generalized ethical ideology of "tolerance" and "reason," which serve to protect the wielders of power and disarm radical movements.[18]

This cataloging of the major structural issues in American society is a backdrop against which the discussion of religion as opiate producer may proceed. It should be noted here, however, that religion itself is a different institution in contemporary American society than in Marx's Europe. The major difference is between monopoly organization and oligopoly. In the European case, there was a tendency toward a "national religion"—a single, all-encompassing belief structure that was dominant in a given nation-state, and officially or unofficially sanctioned by it.[19] In American society, we observe the phenomenon of "denominational pluralism," which Berger asserts illustrates the "free market" approach to religion.[20] In point of fact, this is a self-limited market, with all the characteristics of oligopoly noted by Baran and Sweezy.[21] Eleven denominational bodies split up 94 percent of the church membership population;[22] they exist in friendly, "fair" competition with one another;[23] and as shall be seen below, they are quick to pick up the successful aspects of the smaller religious businesses—the sects that make up the remaining 6 percent of the churchgoing population.

The phenomenon of "controlled competition" in a marketplace, while undoubtedly a way of regulating the war of all vs. all that was seen by Marx as the hallmark of capitalist society, is also the chief characteristic of oligopoly—a means of achieving monopoly capital by splitting up the market and agreeing not to put the other producers out of business.[24] This analysis seems fruitful when applied to the organization of American religion. The voluntary and privatized nature of this religion is essential as it cannot be marketed without being oriented to individual consumers.[25] The celebration of Americanism noted by Herberg[26] is likewise vital, as it provides the unifying force necessary to make the product needed. To be American is to be religious is the equation offered—it does not matter what denomination one adheres to. Thus, just as someone is regarded as eccentric, nay un-American, if he can afford a television set, or a telephone, and does not have one, the same is felt toward someone who does not (1) have a religious affiliation or (2) have a well-developed and defensible position regarding it—e.g., an agnostic. What is not tolerated is the treatment of religion as irrelevant, harmful, and a waste of time.

The "need" for religion that has been advanced by sociology to account for religion's persistence is that it somehow answers "ultimate questions" that confront people in times of crisis and stress. As one example of this, consider the statement made by Elizabeth Nottingham regarding the fictional example of Brubacher in *The Bridges of Toko-ri*. Brubacher died while leading a bombing raid on strategic Korean bridges, and Nottingham notes that while his wife could intellectually understand the situation, she could not deal with it emotionally.[27] At this point religion's stress-relieving function enters by dealing with the "ultimate questions" of meaning. Parsons,[28] in another vein, cites Paul Tillich, Protestant theologian, in noting that these questions of "ultimate concern" must be accounted for in any society—hence the presence of religion in every society. What is vital to note here is the manner in which personal alienation is accepted as a normal and inevitable circumstance in society. In the first case, all the rhetoric of "heroic" American intervention is seen to be not sufficient as a explanation of death—and when it fails, religion is there to call it an ultimate question. In the second, and more general case, the assumption that man is forever saddled with ultimate questions, is a reflection of that very split in society mentioned earlier—for there is the rational side of man, corresponding to the market and political spheres of life, and the emotional side, revealing itself in his day-to-day civil relationships. To assert that man will never construct a society in which this form of alienation (called "role separation" by the social-psychological apologists of this aberration) ceases, is to be an ideologist of the first order. Further, we would argue that these "ultimate questions" are not so much natural to man as they are an indication of the success of religion and its handmaiden, bourgeois academic philosophy, in propagandizing its own case for social acceptance. We have here the equivalent of Ma Bell arguing that everyone needs a telephone and then turning around and selling you the very product it has convinced you that you need.

The height of the trend toward religious oligopoly is reached in the ecumenical movement. Whether it is through the National Conference of Christians and Jews, the National Council of Churches, intrachurch mergers, the Grand Alliance of Eugene Carson Blake,[29] or the Vatican Councils, the impact is the same—formal recognition is given to corporate religion's first concern: it's not *what* you buy, as long as you buy *something*.

As in the case of drugs themselves, where a whole gamut of new synthetics has served to replace the more "distasteful" and déclassé aspects of opium, religion has been supplanted by other institutions in certain areas demanding sedation and control in modern society. We refer here to the opiate properties of education and social science. Instead of having to wait until a later life to alleviate poverty, for instance, one is urged to achieve social mobility via education. The fact that this mobility seems to be from one *type* of job to another, rather than primarily "upward" mobility, is rarely mentioned.[30] An additional opium producer, especially in its effects on cognition, is contemporary social science. It achieves this dubious distinction by explaining away structural problems—e.g., war, poverty, racism—as the result of aberrant or undersocialized personalities (an example of individualistic idealism) or subcultural nonintegration (simply a collective form of that same idealism).[31] But to argue that religion does not now continue to be a major opiate producer is to ignore the popularity of religion among selected sectors of the population as well as the ways in which it has altered its theology, organization, and appeals to fit the requirements of corporate capitalism.

Religions in America

Key to this analysis of American religion is the argument that it has declined in power and influence with the development of the nation-state form of social organization which was itself a characteristic of the shift from feudalism to capitalism. The Reformation of Protestantism and the Counter-Reformation of the Roman Catholic church were both commitments to the egoism of capitalist consciousness, as well as confirmations of the power of the state. The pattern of a priestly overseeing of the activities of man, and the rooting of the political order in divine rights (e.g., England, France, Spain) was altered so that the new religion became one of the individual's own personal and private relationship with his God, and the nation-state became legitimated by "human rights" in a constitutional form. In particular, the former fact is of crucial importance for our analysis here; it is precisely this characteristic of contemporary religion that links Marx to establishment sociology. For virtually all modern sociologists of religion—Parsons, Berger, Yinger, Herberg, Wilson, and O'Dea, to name a few—single out this feature as the chief characteristic of modern religion. Where Marx and established sociology diverge is on the social sources of this privatized religion.

If one looks to sociology for the answer, it turns out to be some variation on the sacred-secular theme—the proposition that Western European civilization is becoming increasingly secular in its approach to problem solving ("rational" and "scientific" are two other terms often used in place of "secular"). Religion is thereby seen as increasingly irrelevant to macroscopic social problems, and only relevant for the more personal troubles—death, family friction, etc.[32] What is ignored is the source of this secular trend; usually it is either left to be explained by someone else or considered a historical force in its own right.[33]

Parsons has a suggestive solution to the issue, albeit it is located in the world of value-determinism and functional requirements. He notes that the family and religion are very close in their functions, the first being charged with the development of personability according to the values of the society (see chapter 8, this volume), and the second with "the regulation of the balance of the motivational commitment of the individual to the values of his society, and through these values to his role in it." [34] Important for our purposes is Parsons' linking of the family and religious institutions. It is much more important than his explanation of this linkage—which is that these institutions help preserve a balance between sacred and secular forces in the society.

Jurgen Habermas also tries to indicate the source of the sacred-secular movement by arguing that both are present at the same time in the society, represented by two styles of social conduct in everyday life, work, and interaction.[35] The first of these is seen as taking place in a problem-solving atmosphere, with externally applied technical rules, and a commitment to purposive rational behavior (from Weber). This is viewed as part and parcel of the organization of the secular society, particularly politics, economics, and the military. Interaction, on the other hand, is the hallmark of negotiated day-to-day behavior (especially of the type examined by the ethnomethodologists, it would appear). According to Habermas, "the older mythic, religious, and metaphysical world views follow the logic of interaction contexts" and hence they must fall prey as legitimators of power processes to the inevitable expansion of capitalist economy—which justifies itself by the "justice" of the marketplace, rather than salvation or damnation.[36] Once again, it is the division into two societies that is vital here—the secular "work" arena and the ethical, or sacred, interaction arena.[37]

What both explanations fail to recognize is that the split between two arenas of life should not be the end of their analysis, but the beginning. Essentially they miss a point that Marx remarked on a century and a quarter ago, namely, that the organization of "democratic," capitalist nation-states demanded this separation between political economic activities and a so-called civil realm.[38] The economic organization of capital demands an egotistic population—one ready to celebrate its own individuality. The personal differentiation demanded by the market is accomplished by revolutions of democracy that abolish state religious and ethnic discrimination in order to make this personal differentiation possible. The separation of a civil realm of society, apart from the economic-political realm, is a paean to individualism: it is the establishment of a realm of life wherein choice is everything, and egoism rules supreme. The very fact of this division, this alienation of men's work activities from their other activities, only serves to mask the lack of personal control that he has in these work activities, as he reflects only on the many choices he has in that netherworld of civil society.

The denominational pluralism that is the most commonly noted structural feature of American religion (with its private-zeal nature merely a selling point) has its roots in the same process. Since capitalism demands for its success the alienation of each individual from all others in the society, particularly in the case of the proletariat, the differentiation into a wide variety of social groupings with differing social identities attached to them is a handy way to achieve this. This argument thus differs from Niebuhr's in that he saw only the end product of this differentiation, i.e., denominationalism, in its specific historical format, without its social causes.[39] Indeed, without understanding the nature of the economic organization of capitalism in the United States, one is forced (providing he is not totally ahistorical in orientation) into such phrases as "nationalism," "the ethnic church," "churches of the disinherited," etc. It was not a figurative melting pot that brought all these religious organizations to America; it was the operation of colonial capitalism and later of American capital's own labor needs. Instead of tracing out the parameters of denominationalism, the issue becomes why pluralism arose in the first place, rather than following the European example of a state religion, or why it did not simply die out. The answer lies in the role of political rights in the expansion of egoistic civil society and its role in the support of capitalist economy.[40]

We can gather from the above that the location of religion as an integral aspect of "civil" life would indicate that it operates largely to opiate the problems of that world, and not so much to deal with the problems of the political-economic world (see chapter 1, this volume). In general, we find this to be so, and the manner in which this occurs will constitute the major part of the remainder of this chapter. It would be false to argue that this is completely the case, however. The church has not been totally uninvolved with the areas of economics and politics, and we shall also examine the manner in which it seeks to hide the nature of the political and economic world behind the sweet smoke of incense and the invocation of spiritual blessings.

Religion and the Political-Economic World

Endemic to the organization of corporate capitalism are its political-economic problems of international hegemony, racism, and poverty. The class conflicts that are a part of capitalist economy and produce the stratification system, of which poverty is but one aspect, serve as the bridge to the civil branch of society—a point to which we shall return below. One might assume that the decline in power of the religious institution would mean that it could no longer address itself to the major structural problems of the society. To do so would ignore one basic fact: the structural difficulties of a society bring about personal problems as well. The pursuit of hegemony means death, institutional racism a constant form of oppression and potential genocide, and poverty the constant psychological debasement and physical pain of being hungry in the "land of plenty." While these are defined largely as political problems, and hence are accompanied by political ideologies ("democracy," "integration," and "retraining") as the major illusions regarding their solution, religion plays its part as well—albeit a supporting one. Its role is in its primary devotion to society as such, as it adds both its explicit and implicit blessings to the status quo of the American social order—thereby perpetuating the myth that all of these problems are resolvable within the current institutional sphere. (Thus, Durkheim's theory of religion, namely, that it celebrated the unity of society, was largely accurate. It was his image of the consensual society that was inaccurate, as nowhere in the entire evolution of modern society do we find a discussion of inequity, misery, ruling-class ideologies, class interests—in short, his analysis of religion was that it held together an unreal society in a nonexisting time.) It would be remiss if we did not consider some of the ways in which this occurs.

INTERNATIONAL HEGEMONY

Robert Bellah has written of the new American civic religion that it generalizes the concept of God in order to legitimate political activities and celebrations.[41] The theology of Americanism underlying all religion, i.e., that cited by Herberg,[42] is thus reciprocated by the American political elite as it invokes the blessing of America's God on its actions. In its own right, this may seem to be a trivial case of political expediency—to fit into the slogan of Mom, the Flag, and Apple Pie. Yet Bellah's argument gains more weight when one realizes that it is exactly this generalized commitment to religion that is instrumental to the success of religious oligopoly. In the case of American attempts at international hegemony, the implication that one must christianize the remainder of the world before "Godless atheism" (i.e., communism) takes over, has become part of the day-to-day justification of corporate imperialism. Note, for instance, the statement of William McLoughlin, writing in the liberal journal *Daedalus*:

> Ultimately, then, the third force in christendom [is] the pietistic spirit of American culture itself—not only the American sense of mission which leads it into world leadership for the containment of Communist expansion in the name of democratic freedom for all men, and not only the sense of charity or stewardship which leads it into giving economic assistance in billions of dollars each year to help others help themselves, but the sense of religious commitment and ideals that Americans inscribe to democracy and their way of life.[43]

For those of us who are slightly more cynical than Mr. McLoughlin, this is a blatant commitment to political hegemony, economic exploitation, and false consciousness. In a sense, however, McLoughlin puts his finger on the role of the church vis-à-vis the international scene. It is to serve as part of a shotgun theory of ideology—if a government gives enough false reasons for its actions, then it will keep the people pacified. Thus, we intervene in Southeast Asia to save the Catholic population there (despite or because of its solid support for a blatantly fascist government); we help out in the Middle East, because of our Judeo-Christian heritage (more Christian than Jewish, so not as much involvement); and we send troops and supplies to the Congo, because white missionaries are being slaughtered by "ungrateful" black recipients of Western European culture. It is no coincidence that the church sent in missionaries as the shock troops of colonial capitalism—it sends them to pacify and subjugate (*read:* convert). As it does so, it becomes a small part of American overseas investments and one that is invoked at the proper moment.

RACISM AND RELIGION

There are two faces to the role of religion in American racism: the white face and the black face. One deals with the justification of oppression, the other with deflecting reactions to it away from whites—legitimating racism from the standpoint of the oppressed. The racism of the white churches has been a constant factor virtually from the time of the first slave shipments. Washington's analysis of the black church is excellent in its historical treatment of the role of the white churches in perpetuating racism.[44] We can isolate several major phases, corresponding to the gradual shift from economic necessity to pure racism that Willhelm has noted in his work.[45] In the beginning of the slave shipments, the white churches defined the slaves as heathen. When the plantation economy became more entrenched, maintained, the church took an active role in justifying this system, both to whites and blacks. When the "freedmen," slaves who had purchased their freedom, especially in the North, started joining previously all-white congregations, they were expelled when their numbers became too many, or when they sat in "white" pews. The black denominations formed as a result of these expulsions, while nominally sharing a title with major denominations, were not until recently even recognized as part of those same traditions. Finally, the granting of "equality" to black religion by "integrating" its major denominational bodies into the conference on church unity seems to be a rather subtle way of perpetuating the separation of black from white religion: the denomination is integrated into a larger collectivity, but is still recognized as the black segment of the religion. Oligopoly has been served, not the end of racism.

The inherent racism of the white churches, however, is perhaps not so relevant here as the manner in which black religions serve as opiate-producing arms of that same racism. There are two major ways in which this opium is marketed: via fraternalism and the myth of parallel institutions. Fraternalism, especially as anlyzed by Washington, refers to the celebrating of community, or brotherhood, in the face of adverse situations, namely, being black in America. Within the context of black religion, freedom is achieved to express a life style and a community that is impossible outside the religious context.[46] This celebration of "community" is a common factor in both white and black religions, but the structures against which they react are wholly different, so that the "community" in black religion seems much more real than that of white religion (see below). What is most vital here for understanding the opiate character of black religion is to recognize that this "community" is merely a reflection of the society that gave it birth. It is the celebration of ghetto existence without the day-to-day misery of that existence.[47]

This brings us to the second major way in which black religion serves as an opiate—through its myth of the parallel institution as a solution to racism. Succinctly put, this argues that if black people act more white than whites, they will be accepted by them. It has other manifestations, black capitalism being the best known. As Frazier points out, it is the major point used by the black middle class to separate itself from the label of black.[48] In the case of religion, it results in trying to establish religion as an even more important force in the black community than in the white. In terms of criticism of that religion coming from within the black community, it is usually directed as much toward the "weaknesses" of that religion, e.g., its lack of theologians, money, propriety, as it is toward its hyprocrisy and irrelevance.[49] In short, the black church as parallel institution argues that imitation of whites will bring acceptance by whites, while serving as a celebration of the necessary separation of the races.[50]

RELIGION AND POVERTY

Chief among the effects of the class structure that concern us at this point is its reaction to poverty situations. Two items of interest pertain here, one related to the structural fact of oligopoly and one to the historical stage of colonial capitalism. It is generally agreed that sect development and sectlike aspects of established denominations reach their height as one descends the social-class ladder.[51] In part this may be accounted for by the ecstatic nature of sects and their requirement of deep involvement with the religious life as being opiates to the brute facts of poverty. Given this, it does not explain the nature of the relationship between church and sect. Reducing it to a mere continuum obfuscates the effects of oligopoly on religion.

What seems clear when one applies the Baran and Sweezy argument here is that sects bear the same relationship to churches as small businesses do to the large corporations. The large businesses, the denominational churches, spend most of their time and energy marketing their established product. When it comes to innovation, or to a market they consider unprofitable, large businesses permit, and indeed encourage, smaller businesses to enter the market, secure in the knowledge that they will be able to either buy out the innovation or incorporate any dramatic successes into their own productive processes.[52] Particularly regarding urban poverty, the church as oligopoly has followed exactly this model: it is leaving the city as an untenable market, establishing itself firmly in suburbia, watching the development of storefront churches, and finally resorting to the missionary approach of colonial capitalism as its method of reentering the urban market.[53]

Harrington's work on *The Other America* is at least partially instructive here.[54] When one considers the social groups related to the phenomenon of poverty, particularly people of color, the aged, the rural poor, the "misfits" (e.g., the mentally ill, alcoholics, criminals), and the student, the approach of religion reinforces their separation from the rest of society, thereby helping to construct and perpetuate the structure of domestic poverty. The means used is the transformation of the poverty populations into mission areas. The Episcopal Diocese of Philadelphia is the most blatant in labeling its special forces "urban missionaries." In the same city there is a walk-in office of referral services, mostly to official agencies, called the Center City Lutheran Parish, which is in the forefront of the "urban mission" (their terms, not mine). The forgotten aged are reassured in a half-hour session that they really are not forgotten, that God remembers them. Students are met with "hip" ministers on the campus, who are really misfits being farmed out to the colonies. The pattern remains the same: a missionary is sent to deal with the results of poverty and to assure the poor that they really do not have it so bad. This combination of oligopoly and colonial mission serves to comfort the poor, in exchange for their commitment to the alienated religious world view and its implicit rejection of drastic social change to end that poverty.[55]

Religion and Civil Society

The major work of religion, however, comes not in its response to the particular structural problems of corporate capitalism, but in its response to the universal problem of capitalist society: human alienation. The egoism so necessary to capitalism carries with it the eclipse of community, the end of *Gemeinschaft*, and the isolation of every man from every other. Only the contractual relationship remains as the bond that relates man to man, with its impersonal requirements sundered when the interests of both parties are served. Religion's chief opiate is its maintenance of the illusion that participation in its activities will be either the source of relief from this alienation, or the means of establishing a nonalienating social order. The established church clings to the former approach, and the fringe groups and "radical" theologians to the latter. We shall examine them in turn.

The explicit selling point by which religion accomplishes its task is the celebration of and attempt at achieving *koinonia*. A Greek word meaning "communion" or "community," it has become the legitimation for religion's presence in the marketplace for man's alienation. Religion thereby gains an advantage of advertising an addition to one's life that no other organization can fulfill. It thereby reaffirms the dual realms of society, while offering a solution to the problems of living in that society. Religion's voluntary nature and its privatization never eliminate the egoistic alienation of capitalist man, but instead reinforce it. Bryan Wilson argues as follows:

> American churches seem almost casual—affirming a vague ideological orientation, rather than a deep spirtuality, and affirming it largely through social activities which have little specifically to do with spiritual values as such. Thus, there are literally dozens of different social activities in the church program. . . . The churches become surrogate communities, based on the will for togetherness (the essence of voluntaryism). . . . The demand for togetherness is evident throughout American society, but in churches and church-promoted enterprises it sometimes even appears as a goal in its own right. . . . In America the very general nature of religious activities implies only segmental participation, the operation of interest groups, and that form of togetherness which theologians do not hesitate to deny the status of *koinonia*.[56]

While an apt reporter on the religious scene, Wilson's analysis of the causes of the huckstering of "community" on behalf of religion are the same tendentious and hackneyed phrases common to established sociological analysis: urbanism and mobility are seen as the chief factors lying behind this appeal of "community" for church members. What we have here, masquerading under the need for community, is the failure to recognize the nature of man in a capitalist society—the isolated, atomistic, egoistic individual who is separated from his fellow man. If religion is the heart of a heartless society, then it should certainly qualify as the community of a community-less land.[57] What Wilson does not develop is the dependence of urbanism on the marketplace and its expansion and the requirements of mobility on behalf of a capitalist labor force.[58] Religious *koinonia* is thus first and foremost dependent upon the lack of community in the nonreligious world—it is a pseudo-*Gemeinschaft* reaction to a *Gesellschaft* world. The pseudo community of religious communities is but the extension of the same status hierarchies into religion that have effectively split the proletariat into many divisions: it is the extension of status conflict in order to prevent open class warfare.

It is, after all, the special interests that Wilson speaks of, but does not analyze further, that interest us now. Social class and religion have quite often been examined in sociological research, but seldom analyzed from our perspective here.[59] Most findings are of the correlation variety, although they too are suggestive in their own way.[60] Also included in this general area are the more speculative types of inquiries that impinge upon the relationship between class structure and religious practice.[61] Virtually all these studies suffer from the limitation noted by Milton Gordon as true of most research on social stratification: they study subjective status dimensions rather than objective social classes.[62] Once it is recognized that these status groups are in fact being examined, however, certain of the findings become relevant for the case being made here—that the *koinonia* of the churches is in fact merely a reflection of status communities. Its opiate character lies in the claim that it brings alienated men together and transcends their alienation. In point of fact, the churches are continuing the role of isolating as many different groups of men as are possible, according to the demands of the market.

As an example of a status split which acts to isolate men rather than bring them together along class-interest lines, let us consider the common division between white-collar and blue-collar classes. What is essentially a status split within the proletariat—established in the context of corporate bureaucratic management of the productive process—becomes reified (in sociological research, for one) to the level of a class distinction. Thus, what is a status distinction (as apart from a power distinction) within production becomes the core for the *party* politics of irrelevance (an integral part of the educational process) is extended via the mass media into the area of consumption, and forms a basis for neighborhood organization. If as a professional sociologist one is concerned with demonstrating the lack of revolutionary potential in American society, he would naturally interpret the white-collar/blue-collar distinction as a class one, not a status one. Recent articles and events that challenge this interpretation are Wilensky's article on "The Professionalization of Just About Everyone" (an analysis of the way in which sociology cooperates in spreading an ideology of the white-collar worker); Mills' analysis of the essential powerlessness of the white-collar group; Habermas' interpretation of the modern university (along with Vaughan's, chapter 7 in this volume); indeed, student revolts against the channeling functions of the draft and the university; the anti-Uncle Tomism of black liberation movements that resists cooptation into "gray"-collar jobs and positions; and the growing deprofessionalization of the teaching "profession" and the shift in recognitions of their employee position in the organization of labor in society.[63]

Religion, then, also plays on these status splits by establishing activities that screen out voluntary participants according to their status groupings. Attendance at church services is never the total goal of a church; it hopes to include members in as many "activities" as possible. One suspects that in addition to the sermon being the technique of limiting church attendance to broad status groupings, the type of interest group isolates smaller status groupings within the church. Men's groups that are the gatherings of the petit bourgeoisie, athletic teams that mimic the industrial league, young couples groups that are geared to the rising young executive, ladies groups oriented to the nonworking wife, coffeehouses for the affluent young, summer camps for the even younger—all of these and more become the arena whereby one's membership in the community of the church becomes a reality—as long as you already fit into the status community that the congregation already appeals to.[64] The church then argues for its contribution to the end of alienation via "community"—which ostensibly transcends class boundaries through "brotherhood"—all the while perpetuating the very status and class conflicts it pretends to solve.

Further evidence for this is found when we recognize the very localized nature of religious activity.[65] This virtually ensures the legitimation of local power structures, along with the careful division of denominational choice along status-group lines.[66] When one includes the matchup of individual preference along church-sect lines with the practices of churches in emphasizing their "churchness" or "sectness," then the formula allows little variation.[67]

Certainly it would be an exaggeration of the most grievous kind if we were to assume that all denominations and church spokesmen practice, much less favor, such an approach to religion—a basically passive one which seeks no change in individuals or society. Just as certainly, however, is the fact that this is the dominant approach in contemporary America. The minority approach is a disparate one, including active ministers as well as their ideologist, professional theologians. It ranges from Fundamentalism to Catholic radicalism, from Carl McIntire to the Berrigan brothers. It includes such heavies as Dietrich Bonhoeffer, and such lightweights as Harvey Cox and Peter Berger. What each of these movements and persons has is an assertion that religion can and should be the basis for an end to basic social problems in society, including alienation. Each is a call for an end to mere ritualism, hypocrisy, the theology of irrelevance and a consequent beginning of a return to a true religious life for the whole society. It is a call for the reestablishment of the religious institution as the central one in society.

The Berrigan brothers are perhaps the most straightforward in their advocacy of one such alternative world.[68] It is one that may have to occur through "revolution," but a revolution based on love and brotherhood. It is a preeminently "Christian" revolution that will ostensibly ease poverty, the abuse of power, international empire, and human alienation. Scarcely as radical as the Berrigans, and self-admittedly "only a layman," is Peter Berger. His aims are the same, however different his methods. He prescribes a healthy dose of religion "practicing what it preaches" to help change the modern world.[69] These are the "radlibs" of American religion. They base their arguments largely on the analysis of the role of the sacred in a secular society provided by such theologians as Dietrich Bonhoeffer and Harvey Cox.[70] These argue with a greater or lesser effectiveness for the end of illusion about the nature of the modern world (the fascist state for the former and the secular city for the latter) and for an ethical Christianity that will lead men to make that world a better one. These leaders in the "radical" religion movement correspond directly to the role played by Charles Fourier, Auguste Comte, and Ludwig Feuerbach in nineteenth-century philosophical-ethical thought proposing a new religion to lead to a new society.[71]

In the more conservative vein we find the approach of Fundamentalism[72] and Orthodox Judaism.[73] Theirs is an end to social alienation via the route of the religion of the forefathers. It is the Bible and the Talmud that have the answers to all problems of living, or at least can give you the "strength" needed to deal with your problems. It is still a call for the establishment of religion as the center of social life. They correspond, in part, to the political solutions offered by American conservatism, namely the reestablishment of laissez faire capitalism. Just as much as the more radical approach, these religious orientations are utopian in nature, as they ask for a religion that cannot exist under corporate capitalism. If one wished to descend to the level of individualistic analysis, these constitute the "true believers" of the religious world, those for whom the opium of religion has resulted in full-scale addiction.

Religion and Social Change

By this point all those clergy and faithful laymen who marched and were arrested—for civil rights, against poverty, and against the war—must be livid that I have not discussed how religion can be a moral basis for social change movements. Let us now consider those examples of modern morality. The first of these asserts that the religious lobby, especially the activities of the National Conference of Christians and Jews and the National Council of Churches, was in part responsible for the passage of the 1964 Civil Rights Bill. Further, several clergy died and many, including "some of my best friends," went to jail as part of the "movement"—motivated by their religious beliefs. Here, as with the rest of this discussion, it would be good to recall the words of friend Marx: "The road to Hell is paved with good intentions." Morality simply cannot replace the realities of social structure. Dick Gregory comes closer than morality does when, in the course of his campus appearances, he notes that while white men have constitutional rights, black men get a separate bill of civil rights. Deeper in his analysis is Sidney Willhelm, who argues that the legalistic approach to race relations at this point in the history of white supremacy only serves to perpetuate institutionalized racism.[74] In essence, the Civil Rights Bill of 1964 made it mandatory for black men to join in a competitive system in which it was predetermined they would lose. Indeed, the church must take partial credit for contributing to the constitutional approach to racial genocide.

With respect to poverty, less of a success has been achieved, so that churchmen participating in the domestic war on poverty, or in international areas for that matter, have little to applaud themselves for except good intentions. Again, a major problem with the religious approach is its analytical framework, namely, that poverty is an issue of morality in a country as rich as the United States.[75] *Solution:* provide food and housing for all those who need it. *Barrier:* politically unfeasible. *Strategy:* appeal to the consciences of political decision makers. What these morally committed men do not perceive is that the structural sources of starvation and inadequate housing are their commodity natures. As long as this form of organization of the necessities of life exists, i.e., the marketplace approach, then someone will be hungry and without housing. Such is the justice of the market, and pleading for another justice from those who serve the market is as futile as spitting into the wind.

Finally then, let us consider the war. We will overlook the role of the church in support of that war but consider the "moral" response of the churches to that war, its attempt to bring it to a close. Considered here are the activities of such organizations as the Episcopal Peace Fellowship, Clergy-Laymen Concerned, and the various Quaker action groups. In the first place, virtually all of these antiwar groups are limited to that one area—the war. Few have been able to see the connection between the Vietnam war and attempts at international hegemony. It seems that churchmen would consider it all right if the United States did control large areas of the world, as long as they did not kill anyone to do it. If this is their logic, even Max Weber could help them out, for it is for Weber the monopoly of the means of force that determines the legitimate state—and this implies their use. Further, a reading of the Pentagon Papers[76] reveals that intervention in Southeast Asia, particularly in the Kennedy years, was designed to prove this point: that the United States would use force to achieve hegemony. Finally, religious protests against the war are self-defeating, as they appeal to the consciences of political decision makers. The constant thread of moral justification of the war seen in the Pentagon Papers reminds one of Marc Antony's speech at Caesar's death: "So are they all, all honorable men."

Herein lies the ultimate opiate of religion—that it appeals to the consciences of men whose consciences have little if anything to say about the activities that govern their lives. In the end it is the corporate capitalist form of economic organization that produces the situations that men live in and must react to. To adopt a religious base for actions against these situations is to practice the art of self-alienation—to deny that the society must be radically restructured in order for any sort of nonbourgeois morality to exist.

Conclusion

The analysis here has focused on religion as an opiate producer in modern corporate capitalist society. Specifically, the argument has been that it celebrates the image of egoistic, marketplace man, as well as helping to make that image a reality through its privatized and voluntary nature. Further, it enhances and supports the alienation in men's lives between their political-economic activities and their "civil" ones, to use Marx's term. It further masks the alienation between man and his fellow man by creating a false community under the rubric of *koinonia,* which serves as only a temporary remedy for a condition endemic to a stratified market society—the lack of human community that is not linked to status conditions and inequity. Finally, the nature of religious movements for reform have been dealt with as essentially inadequate efforts, as prisoners of the conditions that gave them birth.

The purpose of this analysis is not to call for atheism as a mechanism for social change. This would be irrelevant. Nor is there the possibility that religion can somehow change itself and thereby change the world. The separation between the church and the world is a separation rooted in the nature of that world, not of the church. The purpose of this analysis, and it ends with this, is that stated by Marx in 1844: "The basis of irreligious criticism is: Man makes religion, religion does not make man. . . . The demand to give up the illusions about its condition is the demand to give up a condition which needs illusions. The criticism of religion is therefore in embryo the criticism of the vale of woe, the halo of which is religion." [77]

NOTES

1. Howard Selsam and Harry Martel, *Reader in Marxist Philosophy* (New York: International Publishers, 1963), p. 227.

2. T. B. Bottomore, ed., *Karl Marx: Early Writings* (New York: McGraw-Hill, 1963), pp. 3–40.

3. Gerhard Lenski, *The Religious Factor* (New York: Doubleday Anchor, 1963), chaps. 1 and 8.

4. Irving Zeitlin, *Ideology and The Development of Sociological Theory* (Englewood Cliffs, N.J.: Prentice-Hall, 1968), pp. vii–viii.

5. See especially J. Milton Yinger, *Religion, Society and the Individual* (New York: Macmillan, 1957); Thomas F. O'Dea, *The Sociology of Religion* (Englewood Cliffs, N.J.: Prentice-Hall, 1966); Elizabeth Nottingham, *Religion and Society* (New York: Random House, 1954); Talcott Parsons, *Structure and Process in Modern Society* (New York: Free Press, 1960), pp. 295–321. For the nonfunctionalists, see Peter Berger, *The Noise of Solemn Assemblies* (New York: Doubleday, 1961); idem, "Religious Institutions," in *Sociology*, ed. Neil Smelser (New York: Wiley, 1967), pp. 329–80; Bryan Wilson, "Religion and the Churches in Contemporary America" in *Religion in America*, ed. William McLoughlin and Robert N. Bellah (Boston: Houghton-Mifflin, 1968), pp. 73–110; and Lenski, *The Religious Factor*.

6. Max Weber, *The Protestant Ethic and the Spirit of Capitalism* (New York: Scribner's, 1958).

7. See Reynolds' Introduction to the present work.

8. Karl Marx, *Capital* (New York: International Publishers, 1967), esp. pp. 146–230. One should also note Weber's failure to distinguish between hoarding behavior and active capitalist behavior in the marketplace.

9. J. Milton Yinger, "A Critique of Weber's Thesis," in Yinger, *Religion*, pp. 529–42.

10. Dusky Lee Smith, "The Sunshine Boys," *Activist* 14 (Spring 1964): 166–77. I have taken the liberty of adding some additional catch words of the sociologists of happiness.

11. See Daniel Bell, *The End of Ideology* (New York: Free Press, 1960) for the substance of the argument. A better counterargument is made by Noam Chomsky, *American Power and the New Mandarins* (New York: Vintage, 1969), pp. 23–258.

12. Paul Baran and Paul Sweezy, *Monopoly Capital* (New York: Monthly Review Press, 1966), esp. pp. 1–51.

13. C. Wright Mills, *The Power Elite* (New York: Oxford University Press, 1956); Seymour Melman, *Pentagon Capitalism* (New York: McGraw-Hill, 1970); David Horowitz, *Empire and Revolution* (New York: Random House, 1970).

14. Sidney Willhelm, *Who Needs the Negro?* (Cambridge, Mass.: Schenkman Press, 1970). One should add that the economic necessity of blacks still remains in at least one area—that of policing and servicing the black ghetto.

15. C. Wright Mills, *Power, Politics and People* (New York: Oxford University Press, 1963).

16. C. Wright Mills, *White Collar* (New York: Oxford University Press, 1951); see also Daniel Cohn-Bendit and Gabriel Cohn-Bendit, *Obsolete Communism: The Left-Wing Alternative* (New York: McGraw-Hill, 1968).

17. Michael Harrington, *The Other America* (New York: Macmillan, 1962); David Caplovitz, *The Poor Pay More* (New York: Free Press, 1963).

18. Herbert Marcuse, *One-Dimensional Man* (Boston: Beacon Press, 1964); Robert Paul Wolff et al., *A Critique of Pure Tolerance* (Boston: Beacon Press, 1967).

19. Berger, "Religious Institutions."

20. Ibid., pp. 364 ff.

21. Baran and Sweezy, *Monopoly Capital*.

22. Edwin Gaustad, "America's Institutions of Faith: A Statistical Postscript, in McLoughlin and Bellah, *Religion in America*, pp. 111–33.

23. Parsons, *Modern Society*.

24. Baran and Sweezy, *Monopoly Capital*.

25. Ibid.; see also Wilson, "Religion and the Churches."

26. Will Herberg, *Protestant, Catholic, Jew* (Garden City, N.Y.: Doubleday, 1955); see also Robert Bellah, "Civil Religion," in McLoughlin & Bellah, *Religion in America*, pp. 3–23.

27. Nottingham, *Religion and Society*, pp. 30–31.

28. Parsons, *Modern Society*, pp. 317–18.

29. The Consultation on Church Union, including the United Presbyterian church in the U.S.A., Presbyterian church in the U.S., Episcopal church, United Church of Christ, Christian Churches, Methodist church, African Methodist Episcopal Zion church, Christian Methodist Episcopal church, and the Evangelical United Brethren.

30. Jurgen Habermas, *Toward a Rational Society* (Boston: Beacon Press, 1970), esp. pp. 1–30.

31. See Reynolds Introduction; C. Wright Mills, *The Sociological Imagination* (New York: Oxford University Press, 1959).

32. Berger, *Noise of Solemn Assemblies.*

33. In its positive sense, it is the idea of progress, slightly rehashed. See George Sorel, *The Illusion of Progress* (Berkeley and Los Angeles: University of California Press, 1969). In its negative interpretation, it is the decline of civilization; e.g., Oswald Spengler, *The Decline of the West* (New York: Knopf, 1926). See also Howard Becker and Alvin Boskoff, eds., *Modern Sociological Theory in Continuity and Change* (New York: Dryden, 1957), pp. 133–85.

34. Parsons, *Modern Society*, pp. 302–3.

35. Habermas, *Rational Society*, pp. 81–122.

36. Ibid., p. 96.

37. Erving Goffman, *The Presentation of Self in Everyday Life* (New York: Doubleday Anchor, 1961).

38. Bottomore, *Karl Marx.*

39. H. Richard Niebuhr, *The Social Sources of Denominationalism* (Cleveland: Meridian, 1957). This might be more aptly titled "The Historical Sources of Denominationalism."

40. It should be noted that the ideologists of the American Revolution used predominantly arguments of the egoistic contract philosophies of John Locke. For a penetrating discussion of his role in the development of capitalist ideology, see Maurice Cornforth, *Science and Idealism* (New York: International Publishers, 1943).

41. Bellah, "Civil Religion"; see also W. Lloyd Warner, *American Life: Dream or Reality* (Chicago: University of Chicago Press, 1963).

42. Herberg, *Protestant, Catholic, Jew.*

43. William McLoughlin, "Is There a Third Force in Christendom," in McLoughlin and Bellah, *Religion in America*, p. 66.

44. See Joseph Washington, *Black Religion* (Boston: Beacon Press, 1964); see also Benjamin Mays and Joseph Nicholson, *The Negro's Church* (New York: Institute of Social and Religious Research, 1933).

45. Willhelm, *Who Needs the Negro?*

46. Washington, *Black Religion*, esp. chaps. 2 and 3; Lenski also comments, without analyzing, that Negro Protestantism seems to be a major religious orientation in its own right.

47. Only Malcolm X tried to use that religious base for radical political action, and he was eliminated by either the elements of false conscious religion or a threatened government.

48. E. Franklin Frazier, *Black Bourgeosie* (Glencoe, Ill.: Free Press, 1957).

49. Washington, *Black Religion*, esp. chap. 2.

50. Nothing could be further from my thoughts at this point than arguing for a truly integrated religion. Besides its irrelevance to the argument here, it is impossible to achieve, given the extent of institutionalized racism in contemporary American society.

51. See the following: Ernst Troeltsch, *The Social Teachings of the Christian Churches* (New York: Macmillan, 1932); Russell Dynes, "Church-Sect Typology and Socio-Economic Status," in Yinger, *Religion*, pp. 471–80; and Nicholas J. Demerath, III, *Social Class and American Protestantism* (Chicago: Rand McNally, 1965).

52. Baran and Sweezy, *Monopoly Capital.*

53. Wilson, "Religion and the Churches"; Gibson Winter, *The Surburban Captivity of the Churches* (New York: Macmillan, 1962).

54. Harrington, *Other America.*

55. For a discussion of similar problems on an international scale, see Andre Gunder Frank, "The Sociology of Development and the Underdevelopment of Sociology," *Catalyst* 3 (1967): 20–73.

56. Wilson, "Religion and the Churches," p. 79.

57. See especially Maurice Stein, *The Eclipse of Community* (Princeton, N.J.: Princeton University Press, 1960).

58. Karl Polyani, *The Great Transformation* (New York: Farrar & Rinehart, 1944); see also Richard Lichtman, *Toward Community* (Santa Barbara: Center for the Study of Democratic Institutions, 1966).

59. Liston Pope, *Millhands and Preachers* (New Haven: Yale University Press, 1962); See also Robert S. Lynd and Helen M. Lynd, *Middletown* (New York: Harcourt, 1937).

60. See Dynes, "Church-Sect Typology"; Demerath, *Social Class*; and Lenski, *Religious Factor.*

61. For instance, John Seeley et al., *Crestwood Heights* (Toronto: University of Toronto Press, 1956); and Arthur Vidich and Joseph Bensman, *Small Town in Mass Society* (rev. ed.; Princeton, N.J.: Princeton University Press, 1968).

62. Milton Gordon, *Social Class and American Sociology* (Durham: Duke University Press, 1958).

63. Harold Wilensky, "The Professionalization of Just About Everyone," *American Journal of Sociology* 70 (1964): 37; Mills, *White Collar*; and Habermas, *Rational Society*, pp. 13–30.

64. Joseph Fichter, *Social Relations in the Urban Parish* (Chicago: University of Chicago Press, 1954). This outlines quite well the nature of the parish as a geographical–social status unit.

65. Wilson, "Religion and the Churches."

66. See especially the Lynds, *Middletown*; Seeley et al., *Crestwood Heights*; and Winter, *Suburban Captivity*.

67. Dynes, "Church-Sect Typology"; Demerath, *Social Class*.

68. Philip Berrigan, *Prison Journals of a Priest Revolutionary* (New York: Ballantine, 1971); Daniel Berrigan, *Night Flight to Hanoi* (New York: Macmillan, 1968).

69. Berger, *Noise of Solemn Assemblies*. After castigating the churches for their failure, he spends the latter half of the book showing religion how to get itself back in shape.

70. Dietrich Bonhoeffer, *Letters and Papers from Prison* (New York: Macmillan, 1967); Harvey Cox, *The Secular City* (New York: Macmillan, 1965).

71. The "death of God" movement has been left out here, largely due to its transitory nature and lack of impact (apart from the sensationalism created by newsweeklies) upon the religious establishment. It is of course, simply another way of setting up an ethical system and letting this decide your actions for you. As such, it is merely a ritual-less approach to religion.

72. McLoughlin, "Third Force."

73. Nathan Glazer, *American Judaism* (Chicago: University of Chicago Press, 1957).

74. Willhelm, *Who Needs the Negro?*

75. This is the general tone of most liberal establishmentarians, and reflected in the CBS treatment of *Hunger in America*.

76. *New York Times, The Pentagon Papers* (New York: Bantam, 1971).

77. Selsam and Martel, *Marxist Reader*, pp. 226–27.

6

THE
MEDICAL
INSTITUTION

The Death and
Disease-producing
Appendage

Janice M. Reynolds

Marketing in Death and Disease

The production and distribution of medical knowledge and care in the United States exemplify the basic contradictions and issues present in the structure of human relationships in that nation. Ostensibly organized to care for human health needs, the medical helping professions form a privileged and autonomous cartel operating within a context of political and moral neutrality that isolates them from the responsibility of evaluating the consequences of their actions for their clientele and releases them from accountability to their patients. Wielding a monopoly on technical medical expertise —a monopoly guaranteed by the state—medical practitioners have made health care an increasingly expensive and scarce commodity. In a period of unprecedented progress in the development of daring and radical surgical procedures, "miracle cures," and expansion of the scientific basis for treatment, the death rate of the benefited population remains at a near standstill or, as with the infant mortality rate among certain segments of the population, is actually rising.

Politicians concerned about reelection and trading on the anti-doctor sympathies of their constituents sense a problem, an ailment in the distribution of health care. Accordingly they prescribe a Band-Aid, subsidies of one form or another for medical consumers. The physicians' organization, the American Medical Association, imbued with the spirit of free enterprise and anxious to maintain their autonomy, resist such subsidies with less success than in times past.

In order to lay bare the bases of present conditions, the nature of patient-practitioner relationships must be examined concretely; the ideology of medical knowledge, including the concept of disease itself, must be critically questioned in order to understand the inherent limits of the present administration of health. Then the question of possible alternatives can be addressed, so that we may perceive what is to be done.

The Fee-for-service Relationship in Solo Practice

The prevailing type of patient-practitioner relationship, the type in which most medical treatment takes place, is the fee-for-service relationship between the solo practitioner and his patients. Although there is an increasing use of hospitals for diagnosis and treatment, the majority of these activities still take place in an outpatient setting, usually in a physician's office.

Recent popular literature often gives the impression that solo physicians treating private patients are becoming a thing of the past. While it is true that a smaller and smaller proportion of physicians are going into this type of practice, it is not true that the other MDs are developing new types of relationships for treating patients. These MDs are simply not adopting specialties directly related to patient care. They are not practicing at all.[1]

Thus the majority of physicians involved in the care of patients

are still solo practitioners, and the largest proportion of the patients'
medical expenditures is for physicians' fees for treatment outside the
hospital. These facts give a more accurate sense of proportion in
viewing medicine from the usual patient's experience.

The fee-for-service relationship is basically entrepreneurial, the
quantity and quality of the service controlled by the physician who
takes into account the patient's desires and ability to pay. Relationships between physicians are uncoordinated and relationships between patients nonexistent.

It is precisely this type of entrepreneurial relationship that severely limits the range of results that medical men and their clients
can obtain. This organization of practitioners and patients, if one
can call it organized, is the one within which those seeking to reform
medical care have had to work, often with disheartening results.
Hence this model has often received the harshest criticism from those
seeking change. And rightly so, for fee-for-service relationships produce scarcity, are inefficient in the use of resources, wasteful and irrational in terms of implementing a goal of maintaining health. In
short, the present web of entrepreneurial medicine is enough to give
a technocratic mind nightmares. All of these negative characteristics
are hotly denied by the ideologues of the American Medical Association—chief apologists for the entrepreneurial practice of medicine.
The close detailing of the characteristics of the fee-for-service relationship that follows reveals some of the inherent limitations this relationship places on the possibility of maintaining and improving the
health of the people with a semblance of economy.

Like other relationships in a market society, the patient-practitioner relationship is based on a short-term, specific contract. The
patient's entry into the contract hinges upon an isolated illness episode with which he contracts the physician to deal. The physician
specifies his fee for treatment based on the kind of service, rather
than time spent, results, etc. In addition, the relationship is specifically focused on illness and measures taken to ameliorate the illness. The contract can be renewed for each illness episode with the
same practitioner or with a variety of practitioners. The consequences of this contractual basis are that flexibility in terms of what
may be required to maintain health—as opposed to treating specific
illnesses—is made difficult.

The practice of charging on the basis of specific procedures[2] creates constraints upon the physician to give the patient something visible that only a physician can give—e.g., a shot of penicillin or a prescription—in this way legitimating his fee to the patient. However, sound medical opinion may at times dictate that these actions are unwarranted and ineffective.

The patient-practitioner relationship I am now describing involves one patient and one physician. This individualistic relationship precludes a preventive approach. Prophylactic measures often have no easily identifiable beneficiary to whom the fee can be charged. When a physician secures safety measures in a factory or alerts public health officials of an undesirable condition, to whom does he present the bill? Yet, preventive action may be more economical to the community than treating sick individuals, even if one excludes working time lost, misery, and death in the calculation.

Present organization reflects the fact that preventive medicine cannot be incorporated into fee-for-service practice. Public health departments have been established to fill the void. However, these departments are greatly dependent upon the cooperation of solo practitioners and are not related to them or to patients in any direct and systematic way.

It is not only that physicians deal with patients as isolated diseases, but that patients are related to physicians on a one-to-one basis. Given that physicians are increasingly preparing themselves for specialized pursuits, this means there is little or no coordination between and among the physicians themselves. And since physicians are in potential competition with one another, referral of patients involves the risk of losing the patient. In times of short supply of practitioners this risk may be slight, but coordination of treatment activities vis-à-vis a given patient is outside the scope of the relationship among practitioners and is usually left to the patient.

To bemoan the increased specialization and speak of the good old days of the general practitioner is in vain and actually defeats the goal of utilizing advanced knowledge and training. But existence of specialized practice makes the need for coordination of efforts among practitioners more imperative than before. Patients who are kept totally ignorant or are left to glean their knowledge from popular magazines can hardly be expected suddenly to become medical traffic engineers, taking care to avoid duplication, conflicting treatments, and confusion, and initiate a smooth flow of bodies by themselves.

As coordination is left entirely in the hands of the individual patient so too is the task of making the physician accountable for his actions. Because of his lack of knowledge and his almost total lack of recourse to alternatives, the possibility of even a minimum level of accountability is not there. There is the threat of a malpractice suit, of course, but the effect of this type of action is dubious. For one thing, only extreme violations are covered. There is also the difficulty of producing evidence since medical professionals are hesitant to testify against a peer in a court of law. Skolnick shows that even in those cases where there is a malpractice judgment, the penalties are minor. Indeed physicians often attempt to diminish the penalty by referring patients to the convicted physician when he returns to practice.[3]

In solo practice, the control of treatment is entirely in the hands of a single practitioner because he is isolated from his colleagues and, with a few exceptions in hospital procedures, operates with no surveillance by peers. The organization of physicians, the AMA, claims that the profession is self-regulating, and through this self-regulation maintains the highest standards. But such claims literally mean no regulation of performance aside from that received by the physician in training. Indeed, the AMA has resisted group practice which would make collegial surveillance possible and has idealized the virtually unregulatable solo practice.

The lack of coordination among physicians and the inability of individual patients to hold physicians accountable show in the tremendous inefficiency and resultant high cost of medical care. Solo practice involves the procurement by each physician of expensive equipment which is seldom used to even half-capacity. Much of the equipment, office space, and auxiliary personnel is duplicated by other practitioners, each one utilizing them only periodically. Nevertheless, this duplication need not be costly to the established practitioner; he can merely pass on these costs to his patients in the form of higher fees. Because this is so, the physician has no real reason for reorganizing personnel and equipment in a more efficient way.

It has become popular among politicians to speak of medical care as a right due to citizens of all conditions. In reality, a direct link exists between ability to pay and use of specialized medical skills. Health care is a commodity that is bought and sold, and if one has the money, one can get the Mayo Clinic to treat a case of the sniffles. Indeed, those who have sufficient means can suffer from medical overkill with regular checkups utilizing every conceivable diagnostic test, sometimes leading to iatrogenic illnesses. As to medical care as a right of the citizenry, it ranks far, far below the right to police protection. Governments have addressed much more effort to the protection of property from fire and theft than they have to protecting persons from illness.

The class interests served by the present organization of medicine have seldom been questioned. The morbidity (illness) and mortality (death) rates for nearly every disease favor the higher classes. Although most Americans suffer from the inefficiency of American medicine, it is clear that the poor suffer most. Indicative of this situation is the widening gap between the infant mortality rates of white and nonwhites.[4] Those who argue on ideological grounds for the preservation of the market in medicine do so in an extremely one-sided manner. It is only the medical consumer who is in a market situation, not the medical practitioner. For the state, though, its maintenance of licensing regulations excludes chiropractors, nurses, and other healers from the practice of medicine. These restrictions have been favored and extended by the medical profession as they enhance the profession's monopoly. This example reveals the true principle on which the profession operates: restriction of enterprise is favored only when it benefits the physicians.

The prevalence of solo practice indirectly accounts for the inequitable distribution of physicians geographically in the United States. Some areas, particularly rural areas remote from urban centers, suffer from an acute shortage of physicians. In many areas the number of patients is sufficient to provide a high income for practitioners, but the unattractiveness of solo practice in these areas is realistically perceived by young MDs. Inevitably, taking such a practice would mean becoming the only physician for thousands of people and would require being on call nearly all the time. No "free" periods, no vacations, and little time and less opportunity to develop professional knowledge and skills are all conditions that keep physicians away from such areas.

This section has focused exclusively on solo practice and the fee-for-service relationship because it is the most prevalent type of medical care relationship in the United States. The characteristics of this type of practice yield an explanation of the more blatant deficiencies of health care in the United States today. There are other modes of practice: public health administration, medical research, military practice, and full-time hospital practice in mental hospitals as well as in federal, state, and local hospitals and sanatoriums. None of these practices involve a fee-for-service relationship with clients and the relationship between practitioners also differs from that of solo practice. These differences raise issues that are somewhat different from those produced by entrepreneurial medicine and will be dealt with later in this chapter.

Blood, Drugs, and Other Commodities

No analysis of the health market would be complete without some attention to those industries that deal in life-preserving pharmaceuticals and other supplies and equipment used in health care. Here the dictates of profit operate without the overlay of ethics and service that mystifies the patient-practitioner relationship. Thus one can perceive more readily how accidental it is that any health needs of the populace are served at all by these industries.

In the United States, blood flows from the bottom of the class structure to the top. So it is quite literally true that the privileged classes draw the very blood of the poor. Only a small portion of the blood supply in the United States is contributed by voluntary donors, even if we include various types of inmates who are volunteers only in the minimum sense of the word.[5]

Some 50 percent of the total supply of this precious fluid is obtained from private profit-making banks. The standards affecting such enterprises are minimal and seldom enforced. The banks flourish in skid rows and poor sections of urban areas, buying from people who need a quick five dollars. When profit is the primary value, checking the medical history of the blood supplier can go by the wayside. The result is a high rate of serum hepatitis which can be lethal to patients recovering from surgery. Although this may be seen as a sort of poetic justice—the rich can leech the blood of the poor only with a high risk of disease—these deaths are entirely unnecessary. The voluntary system in Great Britain has an exceedingly low mortality rate.

Another result of free enterprise in the blood market is a great deal of waste. Whole blood even under optimum storage conditions deteriorates rapidly. The short supply, poor quality, etc. lead hospitals to order more blood than they need, thus contributing to the wastage already high from poor storage methods used by the banks.

One cannot say that the network of private banks doesn't work. It does, after a fashion, creating scarcities in some areas, oversupplies in others, poor quality in all. What is needed, of course, is a coordinated network of community blood banks, using donors, and answering to the needs of the community. Titmuss records a thwarted attempt to do precisely this. Unfortunately the courts ruled that the hospitals could not rely exclusively on such a source for they would then be infringing upon the rights of the private banks.[6]

Information on the drug industries came to public attention in the late 1950s during investigations of price-fixing by the Kefauver Committee. The hearings revealed how exorbitant the prices of drugs were when considered in relation to the actual costs of manufacturing the drugs. Representatives of the industry blandly told of a drug that cost about a penny a tablet, sold to the retailer for 8 cents and for 14 cents to the patient.[7] They said they did not think such a markup excessive since it meant only a few pennies a day for the patient. But for diabetic patients the costs were actually over $150 a year—hardly a trivial amount.

A policy of cooperative self-protection among drug firms was revealed by the testimony. Prices seemed to be determined by what the market would bear and competition in price or anything having to do with the usefulness of the drug was strictly avoided.

The industry justifies its prices on the grounds that the costliness of drugs is due not to manufacturing costs but to research expenses, expenses that the industry argued were necessary if continued progress and excellence were to be forthcoming. Closer inspection gives no indication that the research will be used for the patient's interests. As one of the industries' spokesmen put it: "If we, in the field, introduce a new product that is ten times as effective, and which costs us one-tenth of the amount per dose, and if we reduce our selling price to one-tenth of the price for the product already on the market, we have just reduced our market and cut it to one-tenth of its previous volume.. This is not a businesslike way of doing things, when you have a natural monopoly going now, in a captive market." [8]

Taking every advantage of the misery of others for profit's sake is merely good business. Much of the research done by companies has no possibility of yielding meaningful improvements upon existing products. The so-called research is aimed at useless duplication in order to have a larger number of products. The result is often a combination of old drugs of no specific use and which make sound medical practice difficult. The combinations of antibiotics, each minutely different from the other, make it difficult to prescribe correct dosages, encourage "shotgun therapy," impede proper diagnosis, and are without advantages compared to each drug taken separately. Most of the progress in drug research has come from European researchers. American research is designed to modify the original drug only enough to get a patentable derivative, a practice that has no effect on the quality of drugs available to the patient.[9]

The real cost in drugs comes from advertising expenses which are four times as large as the expenditure on research, other than market research. Some of this advertising effort serves to inform physicians, but when the products are the same, indeed manufactured by the same firm and differing only in brand name, such efforts are sheer waste.[10] In addition to the waste, numerous cases of deception in advertising have been documented, involving such major drug companies as Upjohn,[11] Parke-Davis, Pfizer, Merck,[12] Merrell.[13]

All the practices discussed above demonstrate the contradiction between the blood marketeer's and the pharmaceutical corporation's interest in maximizing income and the provision of safe, effective and fairly priced health products. What the American public gets is proprietary products that are ineffective, blood that is deadly, and prescription drugs that are exorbitantly expensive in terms of both price and waste.

Reforms in Medical Care: Third-party Payment, Public Subsidies, and Private Comprehensive Health Care

In considering several reforms in medical care that have taken place in the postwar era, it can be seen that by and large these reforms have not been able to transcend the problems in health care because they have not altered the fee-for-service model.

The most widespread of these changes has been the introduction of private health insurance. At present, about 72 percent of the civilian population is covered by some type of health insurance plan.[14] The objective in these types of plans is to pool risks and substitute known small costs for uncertain, but possibly large ones.[15] The individual consumers payments are calculated on the basis of the average for the group of subscribers for specified types of services. In no way does private health insurance represent a saving for the consumer in the long run; in fact, the service costs increase his expenditure.

While nearly three-quarters of the population subscribe to a private health plan, the benefits from these plans amounted to only about 30 percent of medical care expenditures.[16] Discounting the 19 percent that is public payment for private care, this means that over 50 percent of medical expenses are still paid directly.

People in low-income brackets, the aged included, were never covered by private insurance. Those who spend a larger proportion of their income on medical expenses do not subscribe. They clearly cannot afford to, since the annual premium cost for a minimal coverage plan would be more than is directly paid for health care by low-income families now.[17]

In effect, private health insurance changes nothing. The corporation that forms the third party in the relationship has no interest in what passes between the other two, since if costs go up, premiums are raised or coverage curtailed. From 1950–64 the cost of health insurance increased by 241 percent, the rate of increase being second only to nursing home care and comparing with the 206 percent increase in hospital care cost that finished third.[18]

Private hospitalization insurance has perhaps changed one aspect of the content of health care: it has stimulated the already increasing use of hospitals as the focus of treatment.

All the private health insurance plans are closely geared to the deficiencies of the fee-for-service model. In reality, it is sickness insurance, not health insurance. Benefits are itemized for specific services which are strictly limited by the corporation instead of being determined by the needs of the subscriber and his community. Little or no attempt is made to check quality of services covered, and increased costs do not have to be justified by the servicing agency, hospital, or physician.

Recognition of one failure of private insurance plans, their failure to provide for high-risk and/or low-income people, has brought about the establishment of health insurance plans similar in all other respects to the private plans but subsidized by public funds rather than private premiums. With Medicare and Medicaid we see more interest in quality and costs, presumably since public funds are expended. Analysis of testimony and investigation of primarily Medicare benefits reveals how closely these plans are designed to maintain the free hand of hospitals and physicians and how little accountability is built into them.

The prime reason for investigation of Medicare and Medicaid expenditures was the unexpected costs of the program. Part of these were explicitly built into the laws and mock horror over the yearly increases by conservative congressmen must be dismissed as anti-Medicare propaganda, assuming they read the bill. The other increases revealed a curious inflation of costs far exceeding the increases in other consumer items. In only a few of the most blatant cases was this noted. In others, increasing costs were merely assumed to be the result of the insatiable demands of old and poor people for more medical care. If any party was insatiable, it was the hospitals and their medical staffs. But again, this inflationary aspect must be assigned to the opportunity provided in the bill itself.

Hospitals were allowed to calculate their charges to the government by taking the proportion of Medicare-Medicaid beds of the total beds used for the year as the proportion of total operating costs of the hospital. Thus the cost to the government could be increased without any corresponding increase in direct services to the patients. Research costs, salary increases, instruction costs, and elaborate equipment for use primarily on other patients could be written off to the government. And so it went. Such an accounting procedure puts corporate medicine on near-equal footing with defense industries with their cost-plus contracts. It makes solo practitioners scrounging for their part of the medical dollar look like pushcart peddlers.[19]

The Medicare-Medicaid experience should not be considered a

unique miscalculation on the part of its proponents for it is a logical consequence of the way in which "the crisis in health care" has been conceived since at least the Kennedy Administration. In the view of government officials, the health care problem was and is seen as one of the distribution of care. The organization of the production of medicine is said to be in glowing health, but the distribution system breaks down because some consumers cannot afford even minimum care. These "consumers," the poor and the aged (since they are often poor), needed to be given a subsidy for their care out of public funds.

The end result, the government program resembled in crucial ways other such subsidies. Provisions for modest health care for the aged were secured; opportunities for states to provide similar care for the poor were encouraged. Hospitals and physicians remained in control of the content and terms of the relationship except for the requirement that minimum accreditation and licensing standards be met and the admonition that their fees be reasonable. The government could hardly be said to have acted neutrally, for its subsidies were allocated in proportion to the power positions of the parties participating, and for the aged and the poor something was better than nothing.

In discussing professional medicine and the federal government, the enigmatic position of the AMA, particularly its political wing, the American Medical Political Action Committee, requires some analysis. Here it has been argued that the medical profession benefits substantially by government regulation and subsidy. Yet, without doubt, the AMA opposes vociferously any governmental participation in medical matters.[20] It would be easy to dismiss this opposition as irrational adherence to a laissez faire economic ideology. There are some indications that this is an inadequate explanation.

Heretofore, we have been analyzing the medical profession as if the position of all physicians was the same, yet the profession itself is divided by differences akin to those between big and small businesses. Medicine contains two establishments, the AMA and what are sometimes called "hospital doctors" by AMA. This second establishment has been gaining in power as evidenced by the resounding defeat of the AMA in the Medicare fight and the fizzle of the AMA boycott proposal.[21]

Hospital doctors are not entrepreneurs by and large; they are employees in the high-prestige teaching hospitals, university hospitals, and research centers. Yet they are more independent than would be inferred by the fact of their employee position. Their clientele is often their national and international colleagues, and their salaries are often higher than the average for solo practitioners. In addition, they need not rely on the personal loyalty of their patients but are oriented toward a status hierarchy dependent upon their contribution to knowledge and new applications of knowledge. The foundation, the federal grant, the university or hospital position, all fairly scarce, are what they must compete for. Their successful acquisition of these resources has greatly enhanced their power position in the postwar era.

The physicians represented by the AMA are simply unable to compete, having neither the capital resources nor the requisite efficient organization to provide top-quality care in a highly technological business. For them, most government programs mean reducing their position relative to that of corporate medicine.[22] Opposition deriving from such a basis must be couched in terms of maintaining the doctor-patient relationship, free-enterprise ideology, etc. by the AMA, since naked self-interest supposedly conflicts with their service ethic.

This situation within medicine does not mean that the private practitioner in business by himself will disappear. Like other skilled crafts, these MDs could continue indefinitely, performing services deemed either unique or too simple to benefit from incorporation within a mass corporate service.

Prepaid comprehensive medical care plans organized by or as private corporations illustrates the potential of corporate capitalism in medical care. The comprehensive care plan is unlike health insurance plans in that it provides prepaid medical care covering nearly all health needs. In addition, it alters the patient-physician relationship: the physician becomes an employee of the corporation either receiving a salary or being paid on a per capita basis. The relationship between physicians is altered also, since the doctor works with a number of general practitioners and an array of specialists. Friedson describes this as a collegially controlled group practice. The corporation typically owns the equipment, offices, and also either owns its own hospital or contracts with a hospital to provide for its patients and physicians.

The Kaiser-Permanente[23] group, which started as a plan for Kaiser employees and has expanded mainly on the West Coast, is a good example of the benefits and limitations of comprehensive health care organized by corporate enterprise. The waste and inefficiencies of solo practice are eliminated, which makes for a saving of an estimated 30 to 40 percent for the medical consumer. The profitability to the corporation is unknown but it pays physicians well and to help the profit motive offers "partner" physicians a profit-sharing plan. Physicians do not control the corporation, however; the Kaiser Family Foundation does. And members or employees of the plan do not participate on the board of directors.

Kaiser-Permanente demonstrates how easily corporate profit priorities decide the kind of care the community is going to get. Kaiser patients wait hours to see a doctor, but Kaiser Industries is busy constructing more Kaiser hospitals to expand the plan. Construction, steel, aluminum, and cement are the firm's real business and fortunately a good customer, the Kaiser Health Plan, is right there.

Although there are no studies of Kaiser, one study of a New York group shows that group plans are comparable in effectiveness of medical care to other types of care.

What is imperative in the comprehensive health plans is member participation in determining what their health needs are and the conditions under which they will be met. When the plan is privately owned, this is impossible. As Henry J. Kaiser said, "You don't ask your corner grocer to share his ownership with people who buy at the store." [24] Given private ownership, the profit prerogatives of the owner cannot be limited by the clients or the employees.

This leads to the alternative type of comprehensive medical care, a health service, organized by the federal government along the lines of the British or Soviet health service. Such a service would go beyond the present subsidization of private medical care to the actual reorganization of care. Without such reorganization, all the waste and inefficiency would be incorporated into the structure of the health service.

Since it would be an agency of the government it would seem

possible to incorporate a maximum of community participation in decision making. Yet, given the experiences of other countries, such participation does not seem likely. Instead, design and administration of the total program would be placed in the hands of health experts and professionals.

Governmental administration of the nation's health needs raises the specter of monolothic political control of bodies through the physician acting as a government agent. In actuality, the near-opposite seems more likely; that is, the government will merely extend further the autonomy of the experts. Physicians of the National Health Service in Great Britain and Ministry of Health in the Soviet Union[25] show no more evidence of political domination than do physicians now in the United States. The National Health Service in England operates with no lay influence over the content of medical care, although the quantity of expenditure is limited by political agencies. Within its budget, it has considerably more discretion than the Pentagon. Hence, it seems likely that, rather than limiting the autonomy of the medical profession, a national health service in the United States would greatly enhance its autonomy. Physician performance would be regulated by professional standards somewhat more than is possible under the conditions of solo practice, but clients would have as little to say about their health care as they do now.

The present situation in medical institutions has been criticized mainly because in the United States these institutions fail to provide efficient and effective care comparable with that available in other heavily industrialized nations. For the highest per capita expenditure on medical care, the United States male receives a shorter life expectancy than males in at least eighteen other nations.[26] A reorganization of the administration of health care designed and carried out by the health professions without participation by laymen would be accepted virtually without question because a consensus exists that technical solutions, based upon objective, scientific knowledge, administered by professional experts, are the only "real" solutions. In medicine, as well as in many other fields, there is a pervasive belief that 99.44 percent of our problems have been solved in this way and that the remaining difficulties will yield to such solutions. Aside from a powerless, "ignorant" minority who still value politico-moral solutions, most Americans—particularly the more affluent, the college-educated, and the powerful—value neutral, supposedly disinterested scientific solutions.

Nowhere is this more apparent than in the writings of sociologists. Social scientists have done critical work on institutions which label and produce moral deviants but have been curiously silent [27] or abjectly boot-licking[28] toward those institutions and professions that wield the power to decree that certain types of deviance stem from deviation from a biological norm. The consequence of their so doing is that the middle ranges of power, the AMA (which has already lost much), the police, psychiatric, and penal institutions and other agencies of social control (who hardly have a mandate for action anyway) are critically examined, but the most powerful groups—whose authority is based on a clear consensus—are analyzed uncritically, often taken at their own word.[29] Such a hierarchy of analysis in the long run solidifies and extends the credibility and power of the very highest elite as it undercuts the authority of their closest competition.

The following section examines the dubious benefits of granting nearly unlimited autonomy to certified experts in medicine. The analysis could easily be applied to a host of other expert professionals who, although not as successful as those in medicine in their efforts, seek to expand their prerogatives in administering the lives of others. The purpose of the analysis is to demonstrate that active participation in medical institutions by patients and laymen of various perspectives is essential if the medical profession is to serve rather than determine the public's interests.[30]

The Ideology of Illness

At the root of the physician's present authority is his exclusive right to define illness and health and to determine the mode of prevention or intervention to control the one and maximize the other. The healer has not always been in a position to transform and create the substance of his own work; he often has had to work within the definitions of laymen. But in modern societies this exclusivity is in large part maintained by the belief that modern man owes his longevity to the advances in medical science brought about by scientists and scientific practitioners unencumbered by the morality and ideologies of ordinary men. Thus the validity of medical practitioner's knowledge and actions is based upon what is taken to be a consequence of it—the fact that life is no longer brutal and short where medical science prevails. And given such a past record of success, great achievements in controlling cancer and heart disease seem imminent. Who can seriously doubt that a "magic bullet" will be discovered to cure cancer, as penicillin was discovered to cure the microbial diseases. Only antediluvians contend otherwise!

Perhaps so, but a look at the past history of disease and disease control reveals how historically unique such an occurrence would be. For although the average life expectancy has doubled within the last two hundred years, little if any of these increased years can be attributed to specific medical treatments for disease. Long before effective drugs were developed for the treatment of tuberculosis (the "white death" of the nineteenth century), its often fatal consequences were virtually eliminated—the most significant influence probably being an improved diet.[31]

And so it goes with all the great killers of the eighteenth and nineteenth centuries—typhus, typhoid and continued fever, cholera, and dysentery were controlled by hygienic measures such as control of water, sewage disposal, etc. Scarlet fever and some of the above diseases also reduced their contribution to the death rate because of a more favorable relationship between the infection's agent and the human host; that is, the diseases themselves for a number of not fully understood reasons simply became less lethal.

As strange as it may seem to those who have a profound belief in the efficacy of science and technology, all the killer microbial diseases were virtually wiped out in England, Wales, and Western Europe by the combined effects of a higher standard of living which made possible better diets and the efforts of sanitary reformers who promoted the values of cleanliness, fresh air, sunshine, and moderate habits—reformers who often had not heard of, or if they had, did not believe in the germ theory of disease.[32]

In the twentieth century, further declines in the overall death rate were due largely to the decline in the infant mortality rate (rate of deaths in the first year of life).[33] Because of many complicating factors it is not entirely clear what caused this decline, but it is possible that higher standards of living produced it. Anderson, in a study of infant mortality in noble families, showed that the infant mortality rate was lower in these families in 1850 than it is in the United States today.[34] However, Stolnitz has argued that after 1875 standards of living were of secondary importance and environmental sanitation and public health programs were primary.[35] Nonetheless, surgical intervention, pharmacology, and chemotherapy were of minimal importance. And these are the basics of modern medical technology.

The point here is that we have tended to overrate the importance of specific intervention therapies in the history of disease control. Changes in social patterns have more drastically altered relationships between man and nature that result in the particular incidence and types of disease in man's historical experience.[36] Awareness of these facts is crucial if one wishes to evaluate the lofty claims of science more realistically.

We tend to think of disease as a relatively constant factor in the social life of man and, to the extent that there may be few "new" or "extinct" diseases, this may be accurate. However, the existence of an identifiable clinical disease entity may have little or no undesirable effects on a population. The history of diseases shows remarkable fluctuations in the incidence and gravity of many diseases. Changes in patterns of social existence can turn a rare annoyance such as the plague into a deadly killer of epidemic proportions. The same with leprosy, that dread debilitating disease of the Middle Ages that had all but disappeared from Western Europe by the twelfth century. In our own time industrial life with its attendant air pollution has made chronic bronchitis a major disease. Thus, patterns of life can provide the conditions that make certain diseases common and lethal while controlling and minimizing the effects of others.

Social definitions of what bodily conditions or human behavior require medical treatment also vary historically and cross-culturally. In American society we have redefined many everyday experiences as conditions requiring drug therapy.[37] We take pills to think, pills to feel elated, or if we feel elated, pills to tranquilize. We take pills to go to sleep, to wake up, to defecate, micturate, and copulate; pills to play games or simply get through the day. Indeed, nearly every life experience comes to be defined as a medical problem requiring some kind of pharmacological solution.

The above definitions of experience have no scientific basis but rely upon evaluative judgments of what is normal or abnormal, desirable or undesirable for a given situation in a given society. Since in present society medical professionals and those in allied businesses are the chief authenticators and producers of the definitions of situations as medical problems, there is a decided tendency for them to define the sources of "problems" in everyday experiences in a way that renders them amenable to solutions over which the profession and industry have exclusive control. The legitimacy for such definition stems from its implied scientific basis. But in its attempts to persuade the public and the medical profession that such a common experience as anxiety before exams is a medical problem, the pharmaceutical manufacturers have no more competence than the ordinary man and considerably more self-interest in a particular solution.

Particularly in the area of mental illness it is easy to recognize the political and moral components of the definition of health. Kingsley Davis,[38] in an ingenious analysis of the ideology of the mental hygiene movement, describes the parallels between the definition of mental health and the ideology of competitiveness, acquisitiveness, adjustment, and individualism. In short, mental health is a synonym for WASP virtues.

The etiological theory or what is said to cause mental illness is based upon unsupported assumptions. As Thomas Szasz[39] has pointed out, the prevailing view that the "cause" of mental illness (and hence the use of the term "illness" and the concomitant medical treatment) lies within the individual's skin is based on the presumption that human relationships prevailing in our society are inherently harmonious. If the individual is miserable it must be because of some defect in his character or physiology. Hence he is labeled ill and treated by medical methods.

The autonomy of medical scientists and practitioners, although ultimately backed by the police power of the state, is dependent on its claim that the knowledge content and skills of medical practice are too specialized and complex to allow for participation and evaluation on the part of laymen. If this claim is unfounded in fact, then it becomes a mask for privilege. A critical examination of experts who invoke scientifically verified knowledge as the basis of their power and privilege all too often reveals feet of clay.

In American society—particularly but not only in the area of health—expertise has led to a type of ideological imperialism whereby medical experts have encroached upon areas previously defined as political, legal, or moral issues or no issue at all. The danger in this encroachment by experts medical and otherwise is that as the areas of discussion allocated to experts expands, the role of the ordinary citizen contracts. Political and moral judgments, in which every citizen has some recognized rights to participate, diminish, restricting further control over one's life. For this reason the point cannot be made too strongly that the basic substantive health issues are political in nature and consequence.

It seems worthwhile here to make a distinction between the body of knowledge upon which medicine is based and medical practice, which is the application of that knowledge.[40] They are not the same thing, and in the United States the organizations that produce the basic knowledge are different in structure and separate from the organization of practitioners that applies the knowledge.

The perspective which orients the thinking and practice concerning health we will call the "disease paradigm." In using this term we include the etiological theory of disease which includes substantive "facts" and statements of relationships between them as well as assumptions and rules of evidence that direct the path of inquiry.[41] Implicit and explicit beliefs concerning disease that are supported by some evidence are part of a paradigm. The theory of disease rests upon a moral premise, an evaluative statement, concerning what health is and ought to be. Thus health is defined as what is average or acceptable under present conditions or as an ideal optimum condition to be worked toward. In any case, the definition chosen reflects the values of the defining agency.[42]

It is one thing to chart the cause, course, and consequences of a bodily process and another to label the consequences undesirable. But it cannot be assumed that the latter process is evaluative and moral while the former in medical science is neutral and disinterested.

Dubos argues that the present tendency for medical researchers to define as fundamental those problems "that are reducible to simple laboratory models and preferably to molecular biology," [43] is preventing a natural science directly concerned with human welfare. He documents the parochial vision that leads physiochemical biology and its specialists to be accorded the privilege of performing any activity no matter how trivial while the study of more complex living systems is considered unsophisticated, marginally scientific. The institutional structure of medical schools and research institutes fosters disinterest among students in the study of whole organisms in the environment in which they live.

Prestige and access to facilities are controlled by people who have demonstrated success in an already well-defined and accepted field, causing young investigators to shy away from less safe topics, however important they may be for human welfare. Of course, the experts constructing the definition of "important" research owe their positions of power to their own success in the experimental research area.[44]

Hence, it is obvious that selectivity, interest, and ultimately evaluative statements of political consequence are basic components of the paradigm which directs the research of natural scientists who produce the knowledge on which some medical practices are based. Medical science is not ideologically neutral. Its claim to special privileges such as autonomy, self-regulation, and nonaccountability to the community that supports it on the basis of its self-proclaimed neutrality is naive at best.

Another component of the medical paradigm that has its basis in the way in which most medical knowledge is produced is what Freidson refers to as the "clinical mentality." [45] The knowledge produced in any discipline is shaped and limited by the methods used in producing it. In medical practice much of the knowledge-orienting action is based on clinical observation. The whole field is organized from the medical school, the consulting room, and the medical research center to produce evidence based on clinical observation. Such evidence is likely to be biased by the sampling procedure, that is, the type of clients who select the practitioner, the type of patient he elects to treat, and what symptoms they elect to present to him. Thus knowledge gained from clinical practice is likely to be inapplicable outside that highly selective situation. Descriptions of diseases and of effective treatments intended as universal all too often reflect only the particular characteristics of a population shaped by the biases of a few patients and their practitioners.

When standards and nosology developed in a clinical situation are applied to a representative population the results are often astounding. Conditions supposed to be seriously debilitating are found to be widespread and apparently causing little or no difficulty to many persons.[46] In the case of mental illness, nosology developed from private mental patients in a clinical practice is neither meaningful nor serviceable in other situations, e.g., a practice in a mental hospital or the military.[47]

The question here is not so much to demonstrate the lack of scientific validity of the knowledge produced but to show the limitations inherent on medical knowledge produced by the structure of the organizations in which the knowledge arises. To transcend the institutionalized limits of medical experts' experiences would require that the institutional basis itself be transcended.

We have been dealing up until now largely with the basic knowledge aspects of medicine that we have called the disease paradigm, noting the limitations produced by the assumptions' selectivity and mode of producing evidence contained in the paradigm. But medical practice is an applied science also. The physician learns only that which is necessary about the disease to enable him to treat it effectively. The administration of treatments is subject to wide variability in the degree to which these activities are based upon any systematic, objective knowledge. Given knowledge about a disease, the question of how to apply this knowledge—whether to adopt a collective, preventive approach or an individualized treatment approach, whether or not to hospitalize the patient, what to tell the patient, whether to sedate or otherwise restrain the patient, whether to restrict his civil rights, at whose convenience will the treatment take place—all of these and a host of other alternatives are considered legitimate prerogatives of the physician alone, yet his choices are based on personal opinion and biased experience. These bases are the ones on which laymen's choices are also based, but he is given no special privilege in effecting his choices in the relationship. Accumulated wisdom, custom, and arbitrary rulings come to have a credibility they do not deserve when mouthed by experts of all types in our society. But in medicine, more than in other areas, a purely humanitarian purpose is widely assumed to underlie the actions and prescriptions, often leading to uncritical acceptance of statements that in reality reflect a doubtful conception of what is the general good. A benevolent despotism administered under an ostensibly humanitarian guise is a tyranny nonetheless. Its benevolence is accidental and all too often entirely superficial.

The present problems in health care stem directly from the limitations of the relationships in which the knowledge and practice of medicine are produced. The fee-for-service relationship between the solo practitioner and the patient produces waste, inefficiency, and above all makes of life itself an expensive commodity reserved for those who can purchase it. The autonomy of medical expertise based upon the assumed ethicality and humanitarianism of the medical profession and purportedly scientific basis of their applied knowledge must be altered if the populace is to prevent the profession from creating the patients it needs out of the human beings it is supposed to serve.

Examination of the paradigm that orients the process of inquiry with its designation of certain selective human states as "pathological," and its current theories of disease causality and emphasis upon experimental methods in laboratory settings, reveals how exceedingly narrow and limited the resultant body of knowledge is. For while its selective focus enables one to control some phenomena, it produces "new" phenomena which cannot be dealt with within its own limited framework. The particular type of knowledge produced is not accidental but emerges from the way in which the experiences of researchers are organized, which in medicine has been largely clinical and encompassed within the laboratory framework. Thus, for the limitations of the present knowledge to be transcended, the present institutional structure of its production must be transcended.

The increasing acceptance, especially among the more educated segments of the populace, of technical solutions—solutions administered by disinterested, politically and morally neutral experts—results in the withdrawal of more and more areas of human experience from the realm of public discussion. For when drunkenness, juvenile delinquency, subpar performance, and extreme political beliefs are seen as symptoms of underlying illness or biological defect, the merits or drawbacks of such behavior and beliefs need not be evaluated.

The conception of the patient as irrational and unable to help himself leads easily to the position that the medical recipient's role in the health market should be that of supplying a continuous supply of illnesses. Given such an asymmetrical relationship both on a one-to-one level and between the medical profession and its clientele, there is no way of preventing that profession from imposing its own ideology, which is biased by its own limited experience and secured by the state from external accountability to the client public. Only with mutual participation in both the production and distribution of medical knowledge and services by patients and other laymen can the limitations of the present system be avoided.

NOTES

1. U.S. Department of Health, Education, and Welfare, *Health Manpower Source Book, Manpower in the 1960's* (Washington, D.C.: Government Printing Office, 1964), p. 29.

2. Paul Revere, DDS, in his *Dentistry and Its Victims* (New York: St. Martin's, 1970) analyzes this practice's effect upon dentistry.

3. Richard Schwartz and Jerome Skolnick, "Two Studies of Legal Stigma," *Social Problems* 10 (Fall 1962): 133–42.

4. Robert B. Semple, Jr., "Negroes' Health is Found Lagging," *New York Times*, 14 March 1967.

5. Richard M. Titmuss, *The Gift Relationship* (New York: Pantheon, 1971).

6. Ibid., pp. 147–52.

7. Estes Kefauver, *In a Few Hands* (New York: Pantheon 1965), p. 33.

8. Ibid., pp. 16–17.

9. Richard Harris, "The Real Voice," *New Yorker*, 21 April 1964, pp. 102–3.

10. Kefauver, *In a Few Hands*, pp. 17, 50.

11. Ibid., p. 53.

12. Harris, "Real Voice," 14 April 1964, p. 102; and 21 April 1964, p. 124.

13. Kefauver, *In a Few Hands*, p. 60.

14. David Robbins, "The Measurement of Voluntary Insurance Coverage in the United States," *American Journal of Public Health* 49 (July 1959): 874–80.

15. Herman M. Somers and Anne R. Somers, *Doctors' Patients*, and *Health Insurance* (Washington, D.C.: Brookings, 1961).

16. Louis S. Reed and Dorothy P. Rice, "Private Medical Case Expenditures and Voluntary Health Insurance, 1948–1961," *Social Security Bulletin* 25 (December 1962): 5.

17. Odin Anderson, Patricia Collette, and Jacob J. Feldman, *Family Expenditure Patterns for Personal Health Services* (Health Information Foundation, Research Series 14, 1960), pp. 7–8.

18. L. S. Reed and Ruth S. Hunft, "National Health Expenditures, 1950–1964," *Social Security Bulletin* 29 (January 1966): 15.

19. Barbara and Jon Ehrenreich, *The American Health Empire* (New York: Vintage, 1971).

20. Similar issues are raised in the attitudes of businessmen toward governmental economic action—actions which are usually beneficial to businessmen. See G. William Domhoff, *Who Rules America?* (Englewood Cliffs: Prentice-Hall, 1967), for his answer.

21. The American Medical Association is still formidable opposition, as can be seen by its success in influencing Richard M. Nixon to withdraw his nomination of John Knowles whom the AMA opposed because he was a "hospital doctor."

22. One saw a similar split in the response to the British National Health Service between the general practioners and staff physicians of hospitals. The Health Service put an end to the already limited professional mobility of the general practitioners.

23. Judith M. Carnoy, "Kaiser: You Pay Your Money and You Take Your Chances," *Ramparts* 9, no. 5 (November 1970): 28–31.

24. Ibid., p. 31.

25. Eliot Freidson, *Profession of Medicine* (New York: Dodd, Mead, 1970), p. 43.

26. Brian Abel-Smith, *An International Study of Health Expenditure* (Geneva: World Health Organization, 1967), p. 41. Eighteen is an approximation. Nearly every time the comparative life expectancies are calculated, the U.S. position has slipped downward.

27. Howard S. Becker, *Outsiders* (New York: Free Press, 1963), p. 5.

28. Samuel Bloom, *The Doctor and His Patient* (New York: Free Press, 1965).

29. See Talcott Parsons, *The Social System* (New York: Free Press, 1951), chap. 10, for an excellent example of medical practice "explained" by citing medical ideals and ethics as they seem to apply.

30. Thomas Mckeown, *Medicine and Society* (London: Allen & Unwin, 1965), p. 57.

31. René Dubos, *Man Adapting* (New Haven: Yale University Press, 1965).

32. McKeown, *Medicine and Society*, p. 58.

33. Odin W. Anderson, "Infant Mortality and Social and Cultural Factors: Historical Trends and Current Patterns," in *Patients, Physicians and Illness*, ed. E. Gartley Jaco (Glencoe, Ill.: Free Press, 1958), p. 16.

34. Anderson, ibid.

35. B. N. Benjamin, *Social and Economic Factors Affecting Mortality* (The Hague: Mouton, 1965).

36. René Dubos, *The Mirage of Health* (New York: Harper & Row, 1959), passim.

37. Henry L. Lennard, Leon J. Epstein, et al., *Mystification and Drug Use* (San Francisco: Jossey-Bass, 1971).

38. Kingsley Davis, "Mental Hygiene and the Class Structure," *Psychiatry* 1, no. 1 (February 1938): 55–65.

39. Thomas Szasz, "The Myth of Mental Illness," *American Psychologist* 15 (February 1960): 113–18.

40. Freidson, *Profession of Medicine*, p. 339, makes a similar distinction. He treats four dimensions, two aspects of which are basic and two applied.

41. This usage is adapted from T. S. Kuhn's development in *The Structure of Scientific Revolutions* (Chicago: University of Chicago Press, 1962).

42. To see the difference one has only to compare the definition of the World Health Organization, a United Nations agency, health is a "state of complete physical, mental and social well-being" with that of Talcott Parsons: "Illness is the inability to perform normal social roles." See Talcott Parsons, *The Social System* (New York: Free Press, 1951), chap. 10.

43. Dubos, *Man Adapting*, p. 445.

44. Ibid.

45. Freidson, *Profession of Medicine*, chap. 8.

46. Ibid., p. 271, speculates that the picture of general "unfitness" that emerged from the mass medical examinations of World War II draftees was the result of labeling diseases on the basis of the select population seeking treatment, labels that were inapplicable to the non help-seeking population.

47. Thomas Szasz, *Law, Liberty, and Psychiatry* (New York: Macmillan, 1963), pp. 24–36.

7

THE EDUCATIONAL INSTITUTION

The Indoctrinating Appendage

Ted R. Vaughan

The central contention of this essay is that the much-discussed crisis in American education has been seriously misconceived. Rather than deriving from conditions that restrict the educational system from accomplishing what it is organized to do, the thesis argued herein is that the fundamental educational crisis arises in the context of the system's success, not its failure.

Almost everyone seems to agree that contemporary American education is in a state of crisis. But the crisis is typically conceived, albeit by persons with decidedly different orientations, in such terms as the school system's inadequate financing, outmoded curriculum, reticence to experiment, de facto segregation, inability to keep many lower-class youth in school beyond the minimal legal age requirements, poorly trained and qualified teachers and administrators, or the impossibility of educating so many students with such divergent interests and motivation. Despite the vast differences in educational philosophy and political ideologies contained in these varying conceptions of the educational crisis, they share in common the assessment that these kinds of problems impede the normal operations of the system. These conceptions assume and accept the normalcy of the system to the extent that it functions as it is designed and organized to operate.[1] Such concerns focus upon internal means as problematic while the broad educational goals and outcomes are implicitly accepted. This centers attention on the problems of the educational system, not on contemporary education as a human problem.

Such a conceptualization of the crisis is consonant with the traditional image of the role of education within American society. Throughout much of its history, the American educational system has enjoyed widespread support in its role as a provider of solutions in various forms to the problems of society. Even as other institutional spheres have come increasingly under attack, a high degree of public confidence has been maintained that, given proper time and adequate resources, problems in other institutional sectors could be solved through education. This faith in education is predicated on the belief that society's problems are basically intellectual in nature and, if we have the correct information and if it is correctly applied, problems can be solved to the satisfaction of all. Education has thus come to be counted on to resolve such problems as racism, poverty, alienation, and a host of others. In short, education is regarded as a problem-solving agency, not as a possible problem itself.

This conception of the problem-solving nature of education has had profound implications for responses to its malfunctioning and failure. Whenever the educational system was believed to be failing in its role, the failure customarily has been attributed to defects in the procedural apparatus. It was not what was being done, but how it was being done that was at fault. Consequently, it was the procedure that had to be altered. Such a diagnosis resulted in the continuous modification, usually labeled "innovations," of the procedural system. In the course of these changes, the schools developed a relatively effective process for producing a product competent to deal with many of the technical problems for which solutions were desired and needed in a complex urban-industrial society.

Yet, despite the steady refinements in educational procedures, the malaise persists. Evidently, the attention to procedures has been at least partly misdirected. The continuous implementation of educational changes and the debates they engender have served to divert attention from the fundamental crisis, the crisis of pervasive contradiction within the system. At the same time that the educational system has been conceived in terms of problem-solving service to state and nation, it was also expected to discover and teach objective truth and knowledge. There was and is the assumption that the two demands imposed on education were mutually compatible and simultaneously attainable. The pursuit of objective knowledge and informed action in its terms were taken to be coextensive with the needs of the ongoing social order.

But the pursuit of objective knowledge requires the cultivation of independent, creative, and discriminating thought and thinkers. The a priori necessity that objective knowledge correspond with the ongoing society's instrumental demands violates the requisite autonomy of the former. Thus, the educational contradiction results from the constraints placed on objective knowledge by the imperative of service.

As the simultaneous demands were made on the educational system, something had to give. And that "something" in the American system could be assumed. If the schools were responding well to society's instrumental needs, the unrestricted pursuit of knowledge could be assumed. Although it is legitimated in terms of the development of independent thinking, the educational system is organizationally structured to attend its service role. And success in terms of the latter imperative does not imply, logically or otherwise, success with respect to the former. In fact, the organizational structure occasions a vast discrepancy between the school's stated intentions and its actual performance in this regard. As a number of critics have suggested, it is not just that the school fails in this respect, but that the inquiring, creative, and independent mind is systematically stultified.[2]

Despite the claims of some critics, this systematic stultification of intellect clearly is not a conspiratorially intended, or even necessarily recognized, outcome. It is simply not conceived as possible that the good of the community and nation in their present forms and the discovery and dissemination of objective truth and knowledge are not necessarily the same things. In directing primary attention to the former and assuming the latter, the educational system has been so organized that stultification of the intellect is the normal, although unintended, outcome.

To address the fundamental educational crisis requires the investigation of the very organizational structure responsible for the successes of American education. The success emanates from an organizational arrangement capable of producing and disseminating certain kinds of highly valued knowledge, knowledge congruent with and instrumental to the dynamics of the present social system. Conversely, the educational system is not organized to accomplish its avowed purpose.

In the balance of this chapter, I want to illustrate and analyze the organizational process by which the systematic inversion of educational.claims occurs. Although this contradiction pervades all levels of American education, both public and private, it seems currently to exist in its most exaggerated form in public universities and colleges. Institutions of higher education have routinely made the claim that their primary purpose is the development of the sensitive intellect. Yet, as students themselves have made abundantly clear, the university participates actively in constraining that which it purports to develop and defend. Paradoxically, but not surprisingly, it is the students' protests against the university's participation in and perpetuation of the contradiction that have come to be identified in the public mind as the major crisis in contemporary education.

The Crisis in Higher Education

The crisis manifests itself in attacks on and disruptions of the traditional educational framework by university and college students. So pronounced had the trend become that in the spring of 1970 the system of higher education seemed for a time to border on collapse. A presidential advisory group reported, in fact, that as centers of intellectual activity certain major institutions were dead and others were dying. The threatened demise of one of America's most prized institutions has produced voluminous commentary and concern, including the attention of a number of social scientists.

One important dimension of the crisis has involved the debate among the commentators over the real locus of the crisis. Differing conceptions of the problem have produced a variety of assessments of the causes and correctives of the controversy.

The predominant assessment has located the source of the problem in the personality traits and needs of the student dissenters. That is, those students who have viewed the university itself in problematic terms have been defined as having characteristics that constitute the real problem in higher education. Theories ranging from excessive parental permissiveness in childhood to meaningless existence occasioned by an affluent society have been offered as explanations of student unrest. Adherents of this persuasion reject, explicitly or implicitly, the validity of student charges against the universities. It is the students, the argument goes, who are attempting to force universities from dispassionate search for knowledge to partisan political activity. Consequently, it is the students—and not that to which they direct their protest—that must be changed if the universities are to return to their "rightful mission of dispassionate, disinterested, objective pursuit of knowledge."

While many social scientists would not likely share the political implications attendant in this argument, a number of sociological studies have contributed, albeit selectively, to the notion that students constitute the proper focus of problematic attention. These studies, concentrating as they have on the identification of personality and social background characteristics of student dissenters, reinforce this popular conception of the problem.[3]

To be sure, this conception of the problem has not been uncontested even among nonstudents. A segment of educational opinion, both within and outside the academy, has traced the causes of student disorders to certain weaknesses in higher education. Directing attention to some of the same problems emphasized by students, such as poor teaching, an irrelevant curriculum, and inadequate educational opportunities for minority group members, these commentators charge that the educational system has been unable to keep up with the demands placed upon it. But these weaknesss tend to be interpreted as administrative anomalies which would be corrected if priorities were revised and more resources were allocated.

A partial overlap exists between this assessment and the argument that attributes student unrest to conditions in the broader society over which higher education exerts little control. These commentators point to the Vietnam war, the draft, and a complex assortment of social ills as targets to which students have directed their protests. Acknowledging that universities may have contributed in varying ways and degrees to these troublesome conditions, universities are not, it is contended, primarily responsible and are in no position to alter such conditions. Since the source of student protest places it beyond the purview of universities to control it, campus disorders will persist, it is argued, until problematic conditions in the broader society are changed.

Although each of these generalized assessments of the educational crisis is expressed in a variety of modifications, these and similar arguments misconstrue the nature of the problem. On the one hand, these explanatory efforts focus attention on particular segments of the crisis situation and attempt to account for the total phenomenon in these partial terms. More importantly, in tacitly accepting student protest actions as the problem to be explained, these efforts have subscribed to the definition of the problem provided by the system that is the object of student protest. They have thus diverted attention from that which is common to the myriad forms and concerns of student protest—the university itself. In order to understand the crisis, it must be approached in terms of the serious concerns students confront and voice.

Student protests have been directed toward many different targets and have assumed a variety of forms. Issues central to a specific protest have ranged, for example, from San Francisco State where protests, eventuating in a strike closing the school, were aimed primarily at increasing the number of black students, to a protest at the University of Texas, which ultimately reverberated throughout the entire administration, that was intended to prevent university authorities from cutting down trees in order to expand the football stadium. With the great variety in issues, few campuses have been totally immune to student protest and disruption. Student demonstrations have occurred on virtually every campus—from the large, state-supported multiversity to the small, religiously oriented liberal arts college, although the proclivity for disruption has been greater among the former. Additionally, demonstrations have erupted on campuses largely independently of the administrative and faculty stance on particular issues. Demonstrations have occurred where faculties and administrators have taken hard lines, but they have also occurred where faculty and administrators have been generally sympathetic to student articulated problems and their protests.

This multifaceted character of student protests has been variously explained. Some commentators, seizing upon the international dimension of student demonstrations, are convinced that a vast conspiracy exists, that the same sinister force lies behind all disruption. Others account for it in terms akin to contagion. But the strongest implication seems to be that there is something common to the student experience in higher education that produces the student reaction.

Although students have directed their protests to such social ills as the war, draft, racism, poverty, and exploitation and to such internal matters as poor teaching, discriminatory practices, and impersonalization, they do more than register disapproval of these problems. A common factor in their multifaceted protests has been their contention that education, both institutionally and individually, should act in the service of mankind's enhancement. In so doing, they are, in effect, reaffirming education's description of itself. Pointing to such facts as the universities' crucial role in weapons research and their failure to work publicly and forcefully against racism and poverty, student activists have concluded that in many important respects universities have failed in their primary mission.

Taking universities at their own word that the college experience should produce minimally the ability to think independently, critically, and discriminatingly and to act in terms of the knowledge this process produces, students have attempted to move the process from where it is to where it claims to be. But when this procedure has led them to conclusions differing from traditional rationality, they have discovered limitations placed on the knowledge process. And when they have resorted to unconventional procedures to insist upon the examination of these limitations, the issue has been joined.

Fundamental to the crisis, then, is the inability and unwillingness of the university to act in terms of its own injunctions. The problem to be accounted for is this pervasive discrepancy within higher education. To understand why the university fails to act in terms of its self-description and frequently acts in opposition to these ideals, it is necessary to view the present system as fundamentally problematic. The "taken-for-granted" dimensions of higher education must be examined. In the course of challenging the existing structure on other grounds, student action and the system's reaction have pointed to the very structural arrangements by which the routine activities of higher education are conducted as systematically producing the basic problematic condition. Education in the sense of its professed ideals is impossible, for the discrepancy itself is the normal, inevitable product of present organizational arrangements. These arrangements systematically work against the accomplishment of expressed goals. Only in the process of crisis have these organizational characteristics become visible. And this process has pointed to the problematic nature of the normal.

The Structure of American Education

The elementary fact of American education is that it has adopted the organizational pattern of the broader society—bureaucracy. Selection of this organizational form from the available alternatives is not, of course, fortuitous. It is a product both of certain unique conditions of mass education and higher education's servicing role vis-à-vis the bureaucratically organized political and economic sectors. Although some important advantages in terms of efficiency criteria accrue from bureaucratic organization, it must be recognized that all such hierarchical organizations are predicated on the principle of dominance. Because of the special nature of education, the principle of dominance has profound influence in shaping the character of education and knowledge.

As a principle of organization, dominance implies that organizational positions, and consequently the persons who occupy them, are ultimately bound together as a series of coercive relationships. The educational system is thus a hierarchy of dominant-dependent relations. Consequently, the dynamics of educational activity occur within a context of differential power, a context by definition incompatible with the principle of unrestricted inquiry and action informed by such inquiry. But predication on the principle of dominance does not dictate that the process of education and its outcomes are the typical results of undisguised force exerted by superordinates over subordinates. Occasion for the overt exercise of power is lessened in part by the legitimate authority principle in which agreement assigns prerogatives to certain offices that are denied to others. More important, perhaps, in conjunction with their structural principles, bureaucratic organizations are human enterprises in which social actors interact with one another. The educational process and educational outcomes are to a certain extent the product of negotiations among the various participants.

But what is typically ignored or minimized in discussions of negotiated order is the impact potential power has on such negotiations. Social order is rarely negotiated or constructed in toto. Such negotiations occur within the context of existing norms and structures, and these constitute the raw materials from which negotiated order is constructed. That is, certain elements present in the relationship must be taken into account in the construction of joint social action, and these have powerful implications for its outcome. Thus, for example, in order for someone to participate in negotiating educational order, he must be accepted into the organization. Even the tacit acceptance of legitimate authority necessary for entrance into the organization places one in an initial position of dependence, for he has not participated in negotiating the assignment of prerogatives. This initial power imbalance establishes the structural basis for extending differential power beyond the prerogatives of legitimate authority.

Differential power derives from several interrelated properties of dominant-dependent relations. In hierarchical organizations, subordinant positions are directly responsible to only one superior. Conversely, the same superordinative position is connected directly with multiple subordinative positions. This means that all such relations are asymmetrical, because the superordinate diffuses his dependency over several relations, thereby reducing the reciprocity in any given one. This diffusion of dependency occurs in connection with a virtual monopoly on communication and information. Certain offices are legitimately the caretaker of the files. This affords access to information on subordinates that they in turn do not have on their organizational superiors. Perhaps most importantly, the legitimate right to formulate rules and regulations is accompanied not only by the prerogatives to enforce rigidly, to enforce selectively, or to ignore the enforcement of the rules, but also to make rules contrary to existing ones. Collectively, these structural conditions establish the dominance-dependence relation as the basic structural bond in educational systems.

In education, as in other hierarchical systems, this relationship is serial in nature. Consequently, occupants are simultaneously in positions of dominance over some positions and dependent with respect to others. Only the extreme positions in the hierarchy escape this duality. The implications of this serial dimension are portentous for the educational process. The position of faculty member, for example, is at the same time dominant over students, but dependent with respect to administrators. Consequences of dependency are thus translated into imperatives in the dominance relationship.

In sum, the educational system is so organized that differential power is a normal part of the operating system. Power can be invoked at any point in opposition to the principle of unrestricted inquiry and action. This state of affairs is obviously incompatible with ideals of the knowledge process, for, if it does not mean that truth can be determined by fiat, it does mean that knowledge contrary to the prevailing climate of opinion can be ruled outside the existing realm of discourse. Thus, the educational power imbalance not only permits establishing the rules, it also enables criteria for acceptable knowledge to be determined by location in the hierarchy.

The power differential is of vast importance in education because it becomes the root decision-making criterion when there is conflict over the nature of education and knowledge. That is, when definitional categories of superordinates are challenged by subordinates, power becomes a crucial factor. And conflict of interest is inherent in dominance-based systems.

Inasmuch as the dominance-dependence relationship is essentially a contractural relationship structurally similar to the employer-employee relationship, some features of this more general relationship are present in educational relationships. Included among these is an inherent conflict of interest between the participants in the relationship. As contractural relations normally operate, each participant is oriented toward a different goal and the other party is a means to that end. In education, the participants use the relationship as a means to achieve their respective educational goals. Although the simultaneous accomplishment of conflicting goals is not impossible, when this situation is combined with exchange between unequals the divergent ends are unlikely to be attainable simultaneously.

In American education, the inherent conflict of interest is activated and extended through the simultaneous commitment and responsibility to multiple sectors, particularly such traditionally incompatible ones as intellectual and political spheres. Partisans of varied positions are present in the existing organization. Such pluralistic representation is not, of course, educationally deleterious in itself. But, instead of permitting and encouraging differing positions to challenge one another in order that intellectual judgments could be applied to the respective arguments, institutional arrangements bequeath unequal power to differing positions. And this power can be invoked at any time to avert confrontation.

The deep contradiction within the educational system may be illustrated by the following excerpts from a speech by a United States senator delivered shortly after the great campus upheavals of May 1970:

> The University should be a sanctuary . . . for the greatest diversity of thought, the freest exchange of ideas, and the most painstaking search for facts. . . . "Go home and work in this year's Congressional elections. Learn how to use the system, and do not be taken in by those few charlatans who would write it off as hopeless." [4]

At the same time that this spokesman portrays the university as encouraging the greatest diversity of thought, the freest exchange of ideas, and the painstaking search for facts, he also admonishes students not to listen to those who think differently about the nature of the system and the organizations within it, whose ideas are critical of these, and whose painstaking search for facts have led inexorably to the conclusion that the system may well indeed be hopeless.

Such spokesmen are neither intentionally hypocritical nor insincere. They simply do not recognize the contradiction between the description and the admonition.

From the perspective of the categories of rationality of the existing system, fundamental opposition to it is patently irrational. Thus, for one who accepts the logic of the system, the exclusion of "irrationality" is intellectually justified. Rationality triumphs over irrationality. What is not permitted in the free exchange of ideas is the examination of the character and premises of the "rational." So self-evident, so natural are our categories of rationality that conceiving of them as irrational is virtually impossible for one who accepts the system as workable, needing only modifications now and then.

It is not just the acceptance of the viability of the social system; its inherent logic mitigates against according intellectual legitimacy to negative categories. The principles of maximum diversity, free exchange, and unlimited inquiry are logically circumscribed by the internal rationality of the present system. There is thus no contradiction in not permitting a hearing for those ideas that are by the definitions of the system irrational. The logical givens of the present system simultaneously exclude examination of both the "rational" and "irrational."

Because the boundaries of rationality are established and only those questions and discussions that can meaningfully be carried on within these confines are possible, students either deal with the questions that emanate from the ongoing system, or their failure to do so is interpreted as evidence of their immaturity and irresponsibility and used as grounds for their exclusion from education's substantive discussions. The system cannot tolerate what in its terms are meaningless discussions.

It is the acceptance of rather than reflection upon the system's own categories of understanding that, from the perspective of historical alternatives, occasions the university's contradictions. These permit, for example, university directors to define their own political acts as intellectual and the intellectual opposition to this process as political. It is this same closed system that intellectually justifies the suppression of "irrational" ideas and dissent in the name of protecting the high place of reason within the university.

What is not always understood about these contradictions by those who oppose this state of affairs is that they are not necessarily, or even probably, deliberately conspired efforts to restrict knowledge on behalf of selfish interests. They are, rather, the natural consequences of accepting the categories of the system in terms of their own claims of objectivity and rationality.

The Dynamics of Contradiction

The conflict of interest is present in its most direct and exaggerated form in the positions of governing board members and students. Across the country, board members of the large state-supported institutions are appointed by and indirectly responsible to political authorities. They function, theoretically at least, as representatives of the general public. Yet these board members are rarely chosen because of any long-term interest in education, and even more rarely are they selected because of special knowledge or expertise with respect to education. Appointments are, rather, typically political rewards. Since white, upper-middle-class attorneys play such a prominent role in American politics, it is hardly surprising to find that on many university controlling boards they are predominant. Successful white businessmen with ties to the corporate elite are also overrepresented. There is, in fact, a rather sizable overlap between these two categories. Since these categories are so vastly overrepresented, other categories—occupational and otherwise—are perforce underrepresented. Persons with direct educational ties or unattached intellectuals are almost never appointed to these boards.[5]

Whatever the specific composition of these boards, members are at least indirectly responsible to the broader populace. As part of its function, the university is expected to operate in behalf of the general interests that members represent. Education's proper role comes to be defined and defended in terms of its contribution to the larger social system. From the perspective of the board members representing the system, the unrestricted inquiry they espouse naturally leads to knowledge instrumental to the operation of the system and the resolution of its problems. While intellectual endeavors that seem to be irrelevant to the maintenance of the system are permitted and even encouraged, inquiries that question the fundamental categories of the system are not within the purview of meaning dictated by the directors' responsibilities.

Students, on the other hand, have no constituency to represent. They are responsible primarily to themselves. They can afford to be interested in knowledge independently of its instrumental effect upon the existing social system or special interests. As Yale psychologist Kenneth Keniston has expressed it, their university years afford them the opportunity to reflect upon the failings of their society and to measure those failings against the "traditional creedal American values like free speech, citizen's participation in decision-making, equal opportunity and justice."

Between these positions in educational organizations are faculty members and administrators. Theoretically, faculty members are responsible only to the world of scholarly intellect, a responsibility that would seemingly orient them in the direction of student commitments. But faculty members develop stakes in institutional survival and success, and these depend in part upon support from outside the university. This encourages a commitment to the educational goals of those outside the academy. Administrators, frequently drawn from faculty ranks, are even more likely to have altered their primary commitment from the world of the intellect to those concerns calculated to ensure institutional survival and success. The location of these positions in the educational structure produces an ambiguous image of the nature of education, although the images incline toward the instrumental conception. But, whereas administrators are almost certain to defend the instrumental conception in times of controversy, faculty members are more likely to act in terms of their ambiguous images by urging compromise through their mediation.

These differing commitments, responsibilities, and opportunities lead educational participants to conflicting images of what education is and should be. As indicated above, governing board members tend to conceive education's proper function in instrumental terms— not necessarily in the crass sense that it is solely committed to preparation for the occupational structure, but in the sense that it serves the basic needs of the existing society. Many students, conversely, view education not as a means for making a living nor even as a means of acquiring knowledge for its own sake, but as a vantage point for reflecting on the nature and quality of life. In short, genuine education is viewed as providing a transcendental perspective on human existence, including the role of instrumental education within the present system. This more comprehensive view is threatening to those who run the universities, for it converts education from a provider of services in the form of information and trained personnel into an evaluator of the actions these services maintain. This transformation is adjudged to be outside the scope of education because, it is said, it confuses moral judgment with intellectual analysis. In separating moral and intellectual, university authorities assume that life and knowledge about it are segmental, and education is properly concerned with only certain segments of it. Consequently, the attempt to treat social life in wholistic terms is rejected as grievously threatening the existence of the university, because it represents invasion of other institutional spheres.

The conflicting images of the nature of education and knowledge are joined most dramatically in the controversy over political neutrality in the university.[6] The gist of the argument, on the part of university authorities, is that students are attempting to politicize the university, and the university would sacrifice its proper mission if it were politicized. Students claim, on the contrary, that the university is already heavily politicized and that it must begin to evaluate its complicity with the broader society.

University board members, administrators, and a sizable segment of the faculty argue that the university is and must remain aloof from political struggles. They describe the university as a forum for free and unfettered inquiry, probing and discussion of ideas. It is, they claim, the center of intellect, the repository of reason, and the generator of new knowledge, and must be the site of unassailable responsibility and unimpeachable integrity. If a university is to serve its destiny, freedom of inquiry must prevail. The scholar must be allowed to investigate any idea, to be exposed to any ideology, to reason by the standards of his discipline, and to report the conclusions of his inquiries in an open forum. In order that freedom of inquiry obtain, the university must be free from political constraints. If the university becomes a political advocate, academic freedom will be destroyed by direct political intervention.

This argument, opponents charge, is based on an extremely narrow conception of the political sector. From this perspective, political action is viewed almost entirely as political party activity: supporting a political candidate for office; taking a public position with respect to a political issue; publicly aligning oneself with a political party or partisan organization. These are the kinds of acts university authorities believe should be proscribed from university life.

Activist students argue that this conception of political activity ignores a wide spectrum of politically relevant actions which have already bound universities inextricably to political processes. The modern university is, for example, heavily dependent upon political processes for financial support. Further, it provides a vast array of services demanded and encouraged by the larger society, particularly the military. With little self-awareness, universities directly support a wide assortment of goals and programs that are politically established and maintained.

In the face of such vast political involvement, students argue, the neutrality argument permits the university to be drawn further and further into the orbit of the political sector. Far from supporting the independence of the university from politics, it facilitates the incorporation of the university into the political apparatus and the erosion of the boundary between educational and political institutions. It permits the voice of the university to become an echo of the voice of the state. It is only by abandoning its claim to neutrality that the university can begin to establish the possibility of an independent intellectual stance.

These students, and an increasing number of professors as well, contend that in the face of political complicity the university must begin to accept moral responsibility for the eventual consequences of its action. To accept responsibility is to refuse to be simply a means in the pursuit of ends over which the university has little control.

Opponents of the neutrality model argue that it has become an ideology. We are now being told that academic freedom includes freedom of inquiry but not freedom of advocacy, a position entirely incompatible with the realities of political entanglements. It now appears possible that free expression will be allowed only for those ideas and programs that do not challenge the established order or threaten the university's political position. Others will be defined as violations of the neutrality principle and banished from the scene.

The protracted controversy over the politics of the university surfaced in the spring of 1970 when President Nixon precipitously expanded the Vietnam war into Cambodia. In far greater numbers than on any previous occasion, students demonstrated against governmental policy and the university's complicity in this and interrelated political matters. During the course of the demonstrations, students were killed in confrontations with authorities. These killings convinced many students that universities now function merely as appendages of the political and economic systems. In the widespread and forceful demonstrations that followed, students insisted more fervently than ever before that complicity must end, priorities be reassigned, and that they as integral parts of the educational process must be permitted to participate in the formulation of the university's general public and educational policies.

This effort to reshape the educational structure produced the same general response as previous attempts.[7] Whenever students have attempted to move this process from where it is now to where it should be according to its own description, the massive force of institutional power has been used against them.

The first line of institutional defense is the declaration that students cannot legitimately participate in policy formulation because they are not actually members of educational organizations. On matters of policy, particularly those policy concerns relating the university to the larger society, students are defined as clients. And transitory clients have no rights to participate in the formulation of policy that will still be in effect long after they are gone. This power to treat them as clients reaffirms the students' contention that education is not a process of discovery but rather a system in which all important decisions are made for them to accept—an indoctrinating system. Being defined outside the system in terms of anything important has convinced many of the most capable, sensitive students that if education is to be made viable, arbitrary power will have to be contested.[8]

As long as students contented themselves with challenging internal policies, university authorities were often willing to make some concessions. To be sure, even these concessions were not gained without confrontations. But these concessions have amounted to administrative alteration of rules, rather than a fundamental shift in power relations whereby students would henceforth have a place in the formulation of rules. Although it has become a general practice to admit student representatives to university, college, and departmental committees, their participation is at the procedural, not policy, level.

It is when students have exceeded what is defined as their legitimate sector of involvement (i.e., matters involving them as students, such as housing regulations) and have insisted, despite their defined status as clients, on participating in externally related policy formulations that overt power has been exercised.

The overt exercise of power has routinely taken the form of invoking disciplinary punishment against student leaders without benefit of due process. This administrative move has had an important consequence, perhaps unintended. But whether authorities do this intentionally or not, severe and arbitrary punishment almost always has had the effect of diverting students from their original goals to considerations of protecting themselves against university discipline. Thus, student demands that the university terminate its complicity with the government are shifted to such immediately important concerns as amnesty and procedures for future disciplinary cases.

It has usually been the administration's unwillingness to lessen its authority in these matters that has led to escalation of the controversy. Interpreting amnesty, for example, in any form as capitulation to student power, administrators have developed a confrontation mentality. In response to administrative provocation, demonstrations have become more massive and militant. The university has countered by declaring a state of emergency permitting the call for massive police power. The campus has been transformed into a battleground.

When the battle has been joined between administrators and students, faculties have discovered that they have little power to influence the situation. Their retreat from issues central to the conduct of the university has often prevented them from taking any position. Even when they have resorted to compromise attempts, as they frequently have done, administrators have been at liberty to ignore their efforts, and they frequently have done so. And the readiness of faculties to compromise rather than assume an intellectual position and defend it has further alienated students.[9]

The inability of faculty members collectively to influence the situation has left university directors in a position not only to oppose successfully demands for redirection of the university but also to punish participating students and faculty. In the case of faculty, the punishment is often subtle and protracted. Nevertheless, even tenured faculty who have opposed the orientation of universities have been dismissed in some cases. The protection of tenure is minimal in such cases, for in American jurisprudence tenured faculty are defined as employees. Employees have rights specified in the contract, but American courts have not yet recognized the right to be employed.

In other respects, too, universities can impose their will with impunity. If students attempt to strike the university, they are accused of being antiintellectual and of acting irrationally. But in the spring of 1968, authorities at Columbia University canceled all formal classes and examinations for the remainder of the semester on the pretext that it was educationally necessary.

These examples illustrate the use of power in the settlement of academic differences. Rather than contest such differences in intellectual terms, that sector of education with the most restricted image of the nature of intellectual processes can impose its will on the other participants in the enterprise. The exercise of power is not necessarily self-serving in the narrow sense, but is exercised to preserve rationality as those in power understand it.

Summary and Conclusions

I have attempted in this chapter to demonstrate that student activists are confronted with an objective problem in contemporary American education. We minimize or ignore the reality of the objective problem and its intellectual seriousness when we accept campus unrest as the problem to be explained and then account for it in terms of the characteristics of the participants, particularly the student protestors. The objective problem is the university's inability and unwillingness to act in terms of intellectual criteria. A corollary of this is the failure of the university's directorate to understand that they do not conduct the affairs of the institution in the terms they avow. This objective condition is not a pathological condition; it is the normal consequence of educational organization.

Education is so organized that differential images of the knowledge process are built into its routine operation. Conflicting images of what education is and should be occur within a context of unequal power distribution. The present arrangements in which educational outcomes are shaped are predicated upon the principle of dominance. This asymmetrical distribution does not permit the unrestricted exchange of ideas or the advocacy of certain actions derived from the knowledge process. It does permit to a considerable extent the exchange of ideas, but these occur within a predetermined context that is itself not subject to discussion. Because of the nature of the existing framework, only certain kinds of questions make sense.

It is this structural restriction of ideas, the unseen privations, the absence of negative categories that represent the contradiction in modern education. It is to these contradictions that student protests have ultimately been directed. Admittedly, student dissenters rarely articulate problematic concerns and priorities in these analytic terms. But the patterns of their actions clearly show that the university itself in its failure to provide intellectual leadership is a central problem.

This essay also attempts to illustrate what happens when the inherent contradictions are challenged. The very characteristics that systematically produce the contradictions are called into play to resist the challenge. Instead of responding in intellectual terms to the challenge, power is used to suppress it. And this exercise of power is expressed in a clearly defined pattern.

If American education, particularly higher education, is to be a viable force in the liberation of men's minds, it must be fundamentally restructured. Educational planning must be alert to the organizational sources of current problems lest they be transmitted as givens into new structures. While it is not the purpose of this essay to detail an alternative structure, we must consciously plan for the minimization of power, even in its most covert and subtle forms, as an instrument in the knowledge process. Although it often seems that students are seeking to replace those presently in power, students have generally conceded that in a reordered system faculty and administrators would generally be in authority. But this authority would result from knowledge and professional competence, not from position in the system. Behind what seem to be violations of civility, students seek a situation in which knowledge and informed action cannot be determined by power. As long as education is based upon the dominance principle, it cannot accomplish this potential. The thesis argued here does not imply that higher education should attempt to establish a community reminiscent of the medieval university.[10] The informed mind must recognize that we cannot dismiss the world. But an educational system based on confrontation with minimal and offsetting power is an objective possibility.

NOTES

1. The assumption of the school system's normalcy is not restricted to the layman's analysis of American education. It is institutionalized as a scientific canon by social scientists in their commitment to the study of "what is." For examples of this orientation in the study of education, see Ronald Corwin, *A Sociology of Education* (New York: Appleton-Century-Crofts, 1965), and Wilbur Brookover and David Gottlieb, *A Sociology of Education* (New York: American Book, 1964), perhaps the leading textbooks in the sociology of education.

2. For an elaboration of this point, see the collection of essays edited by Beatrice and Ronald Gross, *Radical School Reform* (New York: Simon & Schuster, 1969).

3. See, for example, Richard Flacks, "The Liberated Generation," *Journal of Social Issues* 23 (1967): 52–75; David Westby and Richard Braungart, "Class and Politics in the Family Backgrounds of Student Political Activists," *American Sociological Review* 31 (1966): 690–92; and S. M. Lipset and Sheldon Wolin, eds., *The Berkeley Student Revolt* (Garden City, N.Y.: Doubleday, 1965). Richard Peterson, "The Student Left," *Daedalus* 97 (1968): 293–317, provides a useful summary of the research on personal and background characteristics of student activists. Even in studies concentrating on the organizational context, such as Roger Kahn and W. J. Bowers, "The Social Context of the Rank-and-File Student Activist," *Sociology of Education* 43 (1970), the emphasis has been on the relation between personality characteristics and the protest-promoting institutions. For illustrative studies by psychologists, see Fredric Solomon and Jacob Fishman, "Youth and Peace," *Journal of Social Issues* 20 (1964): 54–73, and Kenneth Keniston, "The Sources of Student Dissent," *Journal of Social Issues* 23 (1967): 108–37. David Whittaker and William Watts, "Personality Characteristics of a Nonconformist Youth Subculture: A Study of the Berkeley Non-Student," *Journal of Social Issues* 24 (1969): 65–90, provide one of the few studies on the personality characteristics of nonstudents engaged in campus protests.

4. Senator Thomas Eagleton, in a 1970 address to the Scholarship

Foundation of St. Louis. The President's Commission on Campus Unrest (1970) voiced a quite similar view. The report consistently alludes to "America's shortcomings" and to "university defects" suggesting the limits within which criticisms of either are legitimate.

5. For illustrative discussions of board members, see "The Regents" by Marvin Garson in Hal Draper, *Berkeley: The New Student Revolt* (New York: Grove, 1965).

6. The discussion of political neutrality in the university borrows heavily from J. Kenneth Benson, "The Political University: An Essay on Neutrality and Engagement" (unpublished ms., 1970).

7. A fairly extensive body of case materials suggesting confrontational patterns has been developed. The situation at Berkeley has been extensively documented: Draper, *Berkeley*; Lipset and Wolin, *Berkeley Student Revolt*; Michael Miller and Susan Gilmore, *Revolution at Berkeley* (New York: Dell, 1965); the 1968 Report on the Select Committee on Education in *Education at Berkeley*; and a lengthy monographic analysis by Max Heirich, *The Spiral of Conflict: Berkeley, 1964* (New York: Columbia University Press, 1971). The 1968 unrest at Columbia is reported in *Crisis at Columbia* (New York: Vintage, 1968). San Francisco State is covered in William Orrick, *College in Crisis* (Nashville: Aurora, 1970). A chapter is devoted to each of these universities in addition to one on the campus upheaval at Cornell in Howard S. Becker, ed., *Campus Power Struggle* (Chicago: Aldine, 1970).

8. Studies have consistently shown that student activists are disproportionately drawn from the clearly outstanding students. For a summary of research findings, see Charles Hampden-Turner, *Radical Man* (Boston: Schenkman, 1970), esp. chap. 12, pp. 349–95. See also Kenneth Keniston and M. Lerner, "The Unholy Alliance Against the Campus," *New York Times Magazine*, 8 November 1970.

9. On faculty responses, see Steven Cole and H. Adamson, "Determinants of Faculty Support for Student Demonstrations," *Sociology of Education* 42 (1969): 315–29, and William Morgan, "Faculty Mediation of Student War Protest" (Paper presented at the Midwest Sociological Society meetings, 1969).

10. One of the weaknesses of conventional radical proposals for reconstructing education is the easy acceptance of historical models as guides for alternative educational systems. This occurs in conjunction with a limited awareness of the nature of the educational structure which they have insightfully described, but have not analyzed. Failure to address systematically and seriously the problems to be encountered in transforming the schools is reflected in their astructural experimentation. Whatever success can be attributed to these endeavors derives largely from the fact that they are experimental. There has been at best limited success in translating in any substantive way principles derived from such experimentation to the education of

the total populace. Weaknesses of this nature abound in the sort of literature represented in the collection edited by Gross and Gross, *Radical School Reform*. For an important exception to this kind of criticism, see Robert Paul Wolff, *The Ideal of the University* (Boston: Beacon Press, 1969).

8

THE
FAMILIAL
INSTITUTION

The Alienated
Labor-producing
Appendage

Erik Grønseth

Value-laden Misconceptions in Family Sociology

In scientific pursuits, as in other areas, what you see depends upon what you are looking for. After some thirty years of "value-neutralist" hegemony in American social science,[1] it is now increasingly accepted that the scientific works of those who pose as declared "value neutralists" have been "value-biased," [2] as the latter would have called it. Their unadmitted value commitments have been largely conservative, at times with a kind of liberal conservatism and at other times more reactionary. Their value commitments have thus been almost identical with those largely taken for granted in their own society. For this reason most people, scientists and laymen alike, have failed to take much notice of this massive value commitment until recently. Only when value conflict and dissent emerged on a large scale in the society did many American social scientists recognize the value commitments inherent in their analyses.

In the specific field of family sociology, because of this pervasive but hidden conservative/liberal value bias, aspects of family life have been described, analyzed, and interpreted as if today's most "developed" nations represented the best of all societies. Problems are recognized, of course, but they are seen as solvable by mere superficial improvements upon the existing family and social order. The facts of overwhelming human repression and of perverted social relations at the marrow of families in all social classes[3] are seen as peripheral when seen at all; while their anchoring in the economic and political macrostructure and in the psychological structures among the masses of the populations has hardly been discussed from any critical point of view.[4]

Of course, the family has been studied in relation to class structure and mobility, to economic conditions and industrialization; but seldom from the point of view that there was anything basically wrong, unjust and repressive, or destructive and dangerous about these relationships.

Family sociology, like its parent discipline, has thus generally been purged of any vital and basic perspective that would include as a focus of orientation those dangerous aspects of contemporary social reality that are inimical to life and that come to their tremendous fore in hot or cold wars, and in the precarious "terror balance."

At the base of a series of value-laden factual omissions and misconceptions in family sociology lies the ethnocentric taking for granted of the American and "modern" family and its goodness, along with the wish to evade those vital issues that would smother these cherished ideas. Five of these pervasive misconceptions shall be pointed out here by way of introduction; others will be brought up in discussing the alienated labor-producing function of the family and its husband-provider mechanism.

1. Much textbook family sociology tends to give the impression that *the* nuclear family, as essentially portrayed in the image of the idealized American middle-class family, is a phenomenon that exists universally. Family forms not fitting this impression are regarded as

abnormal, deviant, nonsuccessful, or as special cases.[5] This perspective on other family types serves to legitimate the "normal" (*read:* idealized) modern middle-class nuclear family. For if this particular family type is not simply peculiar to the American or "modern" middle class, but rather is basically common to all known societies, then surely there can be nothing seriously wrong with this middle-class family.

While it is probably true enough that most societies exhibit an overriding tendency for the mother-child dyad to establish itself as a relatively stable relationship, at least during the child's first years of life, and for a *pater* to be designated as a reference point for the child's social placement, family arrangements beyond these bare essentials vary enormously,[6] both in life-repressive and life-affirmative directions (the celebrated Trobrianders being one example of the latter).[7]

A few vital facts need to be recapitulated in this context. In those "primitive" societies organized on an extended family and clan or lineage basis, the nuclear family is clearly subordinated to, and to a large extent absorbed into, the wider family and kinship units. In most matrilineal and matrilocal societies, the main male socializing agent is not the child's father, but the mother's brother, who is also principally responsible for the economic provision of his sister and her children. There may be no essential economic cooperation between the spouses, as the husband-father works within the economic unit of his mother's family, while the wife-mother works within *her* family of orientation.

The kibbutzim also have no economic cooperation or dependence between family members as such. Parent-child relations are free of disciplinarian elements and of most practical tasks; these are taken care of by the personnel of the children's house.[8]

Such different forms of family organization tend to leave women in a relatively strong and free position to avoid economic dependence on marriage as well as the consequent repressive sexual regulation in childhood, youth, and adulthood.[9]

When one is interested in showing that it is possible to have family structures that avoid essential repression and neurotic conflict, it is, of course, of great importance to emphasize such forms of nuclear and extended family organization as are vitally different from the repressive forms that exist in market and state capitalist societies. Only in the service of repressive, conservative interests is it important to force all family forms into an artificially constructed idea of "the universal nuclear family."

2. We here come to two other related, value-biased misconceptions in family sociology. One is that "The nuclear family is maintained universally to be that form of social relationship which provides sexual gratification." [10] In several societies, however, sexual gratification is sought both in and out of marriage, or even mainly outside it,[11] while the marriage principally serves economic or political functions along with legitimization of the children. To the extent that sexual gratification is sought in marriage, it is in some societies (as in our Victorian past) sought mainly by the men, while it is *avoided* by the sexually subjugated and inhibited women. Furthermore, it can be inferred that the primary result even for men in many societies, our own included, is nongratification of full genitality, and satisfaction merely of a neurotically disturbed sexuality.[12] To speak, without major qualifications, of the family of modern or past male-dominated societies as simply "providing sexual gratification" hides the fact that our family system actually is basically repressive of the sexuality of its population from infancy on.[13]

Another intimately related misconception is the one that the modern family especially provides "emotional satisfaction." [14] Here again the neurotic and symbiotic, and thus basically stunted, shallow, or conflict-laden nature of these emotional satisfactions is often overlooked, a theme to which we shall later return.

3. (a) A doing away with the idea of the universality of the nuclear family in its more or less modern middle-class form immediately shakes a further cherished misconception: that "the universal nuclear family" generally, and that of modern society particularly, is "*the* basic social institution" upon which other institutions depend and by which they are influenced.

If in a life-affirmative perspective the important thing to note is that basic family forms are not the same but vary drastically from one society to another, then other aspects of these societies than their family forms must be decisive. Actually, we hardly know what factors are basically responsible for the extreme variations along that vital societal dimension of accepting or repressing primary biopsychic need gratification. Maybe the basic factors and events lie in the realm of climatic and ecological factors or in prehistoric anxiety-creating natural catastrophes? We do know, however, that economic resources, technology, and consequent basic forms of economic and class structure are more decisive for kinship and family forms than vice versa.[15] Subsequent and secondary important influences and limitations from the family upon the economic and class and political structure are of course not precluded. Also not precluded is the truth that in modern market and state capitalist societies repressive family forms are necessary for the continued maintenance of the prevailing exploitative, alienated, and hierarchically centralist social structure. But this is far from saying that the family is *the* basic institutional structure, or that if present-day family forms were radically changed, the basis for an inhumane social order would be removed!

In market and state capitalist societies, the family is actually of *less* directive influence than was the family in preindustrial societies. Those kinds of economic organization that had given rise to varying family and kinship forms were in turn incorporated into the very family and kinship forms of their own "creation." From then on, economic, as well as political and religious, life was organized in terms of ascribed family and kinship relationships. In industrialized societies, however, the family has come to share traditional family or kinship activities with the new occupational, political, and religious institutions. And it has lost control over the decisive aspects of its activities.[16] As for the independence and autonomy of the majority of the family units, they had been subjugated to a minority of upper-class extended families long before industrial capitalism.[17]

Far from being the basic institution in modern society, the family is more apt to be an increasingly weak and defenseless prey, molded by capitalist industry and its state apparatus,[18] and thus essential to it.

(b) We can now also see how misleading is the widespread idea that the modern nuclear family, as distinct from the traditional family, is an *autonomous* social unit. From the fact of the nuclear family's relatively new autonomy vis-à-vis extended family and kinship ties, one sociologist has leaped to the value-laden and misleading generalization that the modern nuclear family is "autonomous," period! [19]

The subjugation of the modern nuclear family to the economic-political institutions is strategically mediated, not simply by "the long arm of the job," but more specifically by the husband-economic-provider-role.

This mechanism operates directly on the social organizational level in the following way: through the absorption of the husband-father's time, energies, and the surplus values of his work into the elitist national and international economies, and through the consequent mother-child isolation, most men and women are sociopolitically immobilized. For this reason, among others,[20] they have to adjust their family life to the demands of the economic-political system of the market or state capitalist class societies.

The above should not, however, push us into the ditch of the orthodox Marxist who thinks that any important and radical change in family, sex roles, and sexual love must come about only after a revolution in the political and economic structure. On the contrary, as pointed out by Reich, and in different ways also by Horkheimer and Fromm,[21] when repressive family forms have become the factories of repressive and neurotic personalities and of their conservative, liberal, or fascist ideologies, radical change in family and child-rearing practices and institutions has to take place hand in hand with (and, if possible, in part even prior to) the radical political-economic changes. Otherwise, radical political-economic changes may easily be perverted into yet another form of authoritarian, and repressive regime, such as in the Soviet Union.[22]

4. The prevalent idea that "today's family" is a sovereign child-socializing agent is undermined when we realize how, in modern society, families are far from being either sovereign or equal partners in their exchange with other institutions and structures. The ways in which parents rear their children are largely in the interest of the surrounding economic, political, and class structure, and they are caused by these as well as by the repressive mass psychological structure in which the parents also share. Thus, the children of the upper and white-collar classes typically turn out to be ambitiously compensating, competitive, anxiety-propelled "achievers." They dominate or ignore those left behind; admire and apple-polish those ahead. The bulk of the blue-collar children turn out as obedient submitters,

law-and-order-abiding, oriented to external rules and authorities, barking at the system and taking their fun whenever and wherever they find it.

Obviously, the kind of socialization parents can give their children is determined by conditions and forces that in market or state capitalist societies are to a large extent out of their hands. This is especially so in lower white-collar and blue-collar classes. The relative isolation of the nuclear family and the peripheral position of the father in its structure is forced upon families by the basic organization of occupational life and by the husband's provider role. Buttressed by sex-role identifications and defense mechanisms these factors operate so as to leave the main early socialization of children to a consequently smothering or rejecting mother.

The neighborhood of the upper and high-income white-collar classes, structured as it is in terms of family privacy, with housing and standards of living completely beyond the reach of working-class families,[23] makes for different familial and extrafamilial socialization practices.[24] All kinds of other factors beyond family control, from the influence of the school and the mass media to road constructions and traffic patterns, lack of free and secure play facilities, etc., also seriously influence that limited socializing activity in which parents themselves engage.

5. A fifth source of misconception in the sociology of the family is the omission of the family's labor-producing function. This function simply does not appear on the standard lists of functions for either the "universal" or the "modern" family.

Is this because such an item would not quite fit the idealized image of the "modern" family held by most sociologists (and by nonsociologists)? For mention of the family's labor-producing function must necessarily lead to the question: for whom does the family produce labor? And the answer would be: for the companies, for the industries, for the educational apparatus, for the government offices, for their increment of the GNP, the major share of which goes to the powerful minority and to their middle-class supporters and beneficiaries.

There would be nothing critical or provocative in talking about the family's labor-producing function if its labor "product" was used primarily in harmony with the good of the families themselves, and if they had control over that "product" and received a just return from it. But in private and state capitalist societies (indeed in societies throughout the history of Western civilization) this basic labor-producing function of the family is perverted through exploitation by the power elite. Furthermore, the work for which the family-produced labor force is used is socially and psychologically alienated work—work over which the worker has no control, in which he has little pride and no joy.[25]

While the perversion of the labor-producing function of the family is against the *real* interests of the working population and against the vital and natural family functions, the development of alternative ways of work and family life, or at least attempts to do this, is absent. Thus it seems that *perceived* interests, which may be false and neurotically perverted, are served. In terms of our false consciousness and armored biopsychic structure, we receive enough compensatory satisfaction, enough anxiety relieving solace from succumbing to the alienation and exploitation, and from consuming the poisoned food, the numbing TV shows, and the desublimated repressive sexuality as to find things as they are in our best (if false) interest.[26]

By letting ourselves, our family life, and our labor be exploited and perverted, we are spared the burdens of responsibility, self-determination, and freedom and spared the breakthrough of that deep-seated anxiety that would emerge, should we let come to the fore the presently repressed potent life energies and primary needs. Taking on these liberating burdens and bearing these breakthroughs would be the psychological precondition of taking control in freedom, responsibility, and cooperation with our fellow men.

Let us see how the alienated labor-producing function of today's families, along with their repressive socialization and sexual control functions, draws the vitality out of other family functions and thus mesh with the resulting perverted forms of the latter.

The labor-producing function is a derivative of other family functions. But it is nonetheless an essential and dominant function. It is a composite function, overlapping with a series of other, more widely recognized functions that under market and state capitalist conditions are bent to its alienated services. It builds on the half-repressed sexual activity and on the resulting reproductory function over the generational cycle. It builds on the half-repressive and armored nursing[27] and child rearing, as well as on the family's economic provider function. Also, over the generational cycle, it is based on that educational function which takes place outside families but is financed by them, directly or through taxes.

Over the daily to yearly cycles the labor-producing function builds on the adult level upon in-the-family and family-sponsored leisure and labor "recreational" activities including the more or less neurotically "expressive" and emotional "gratification" function.

The direct and indirect repressive sexual control of the modern family, from the individual's infancy on, contributes sociopsychologically in a fundamental way to the labor-producing function. The libidinal and bioenergetic bodily contact deprivations through maternity ward and infancy separations of mother and child, through scheduled and bottle feeding, through the parents' emotional rejection of the child's spontaneous pleasure activities, all lead to a basic clogging and blocking of the individual's creative life forces, of its love for the other person, of its solidarity, of its sense of vital needs and interests, and of its capacity for self-regulation.[28]

The individual becomes neurotically and moralistically controlled in his core energy and consciousness functions. The biopsychically sick foundation is thus laid for subordination to continued repressive regulations at hands of self or others in work contexts also, so that the individual willingly puts his and his children's labor at the disposal of the exploitative and alienated occupational and economic order.

In addition, the family's consumption function, directed by neurotic, compensatory needs, manipulated by subliminal sales techniques, contributes indirectly to the labor-producing function. Through its consumption at high prices of the partly useless and nonsensical, the partly poisonous, and partly self-destroying products of the market society, the family contributes to the expansion and prosperity of business and industry, of their owners and managerial echelons. Thus, possibilities exist for the employment of more alienated and exploited labor. This helps motivate adults to produce more children for the labor market, and to sell their own labor as well.

The "sexual function," the reproductive function, the socialization function, the personality-forming function, the economic-provider function, the consumptive function, the expressive or emotional functions, etc., all feed into the overriding labor-producing function.

The same holds true for other family functions. Thus, the status-placement function along with the transmission of ascribed elements of social position, of property, of power and of culture and life styles, all serve to channel the labor force into work, class, economic, and power structures advantageous to the material well-being and compensatory, life-inimical, polluting achievement and thus in the long run really false interests of the upper classes and power elites.

There would of course be nothing wrong, in and by itself, about the other family functions being influenced and in some measure regulated by a natural, vital, labor-producing function of the family. In any society, even in a classless and sane society, the family undoubtedly must have labor-producing functions, and this also by way of its other functions. What is wrong today is that this interplay is out of balance, to the *perversion* of all other functions. The power elite has expropriated work life and thus the natural labor-producing function of the family. And the rest of us have correspondingly abdicated from our freedom, responsibility, and self-determination in our work as well as in our family and love life.

In what more specific sense, then, can the labor-producing function of the family be said to operate to the detriment of the family? It is dramatically seen in periods of unemployment, or in cases of forced migration of labor to peripheral areas, or in industrial relocations and factory closedowns. Also detrimental are rationalizations undertaken without securing new jobs for the workers. Profit-oriented regional planning and localization of industry dislocates and uproots families, or forces breadwinners to endure several hours of daily commuting between home and workplace.

The frequent breakups of modified extended family bonds and of neighborhood and friendship relations are the result of the competitive labor-selection mechanisms, the desire to get the "right" man in the "right" place. Such is the reality behind the celebrated "highly mobile" (and therefore "democratic!"), industrially well-developed nations.

Witness also the general lack of consideration for happy and healthy family, love, and sex role relations in most of the occupational structure[29] (except when it wants to accommodate the "right" men of the upper- or upper-middle-class echelons).[30] Think also of the big-city slums all over the industrialized and industrializing world, and of the dreary monotony of working-class housing areas, be they old or of the new "functional" design—functional mainly with respect to their functions of stirring and producing alienated labor.

Think of the counted and uncounted numbers of occupationally caused accidents and diseases, somatic as well as psychic. They occur also among mothers overburdened from house and child care *plus* employment for extra money, or from being more or less socially isolated with children who are deprived of secure and stimulating play facilities. This does not exclude the well-to-do families from being victims of their own powers and exploitation. Nervous and psychosomatic illnesses and family unhappiness flourish among the materially prosperous and powerful as well.

From an ordinary middle-class point of view, most of the massive and depressing facts about the nature of the labor-producing function of the families in our "affluent" societies are screened from sight and negative impact by selective information and "education" systems and by barriers to true communication across class and national boundaries. Such facts are also not widely recognized because, especially in the United States, sizable proportions of the white-collar class and the skilled blue-collar class enjoy a materially high living standard, leaving "only" about 40 million people in outright slums. The segregated material well-being of a majority of Americans and of a smaller majority of Europeans is, of course, also based upon the monopoly capital exploitation of the millions of poor laborers and their families in the neocolonial "developing" countries. This is but one example of how Western seductive prosperity and affluence and the labor-producing function of the family must be seen, not in a limited national perspective, but in the global perspective of neocolonialism and economic imperialism.[31]

From what has been indicated about the mass psychological and ideological, as well as about the economic and power-political anchorings of the continued alienated labor-producing function of the family, solutions to family enigmas and perversions in market and state capitalist societies must be sought as much in the mass psychological structure of the population at large as in the power elites. It must be sought in the microsocial, repressively adaptive webs of social relations within families and neighborhoods, and within occupational, economic, and political structures as cherished by those who are suffocated by them. Radical solutions must be developed as much on these mass psychological and microsocial levels as on the macro level. Drastic and sudden change in the macrostructural economic and power relations, without simultaneous liberating changes in the microsocial and mass psychological contexts (so as solidly to ground new, truly democratic, macrostructures) may not help much.

The microsocial radical restructuring must, on the other hand, be guided by an insight, a consciousness, and a direction that include the macro-sociopolitical-economic as well as the individual and mass psychological structure. One can only hope that people in top-level positions can also be moved to start radical actions in their upper-class milieus.

The ability of the masses of the population to find ways of cooperatively and democratically sharing economic and political powers must be combined with a sense of direction deeply rooted in a contact with the basic bodily and psychic needs and joys of life.[32] And it must become the task of "interdisciplinary" social and life sciences to contribute to a deepening of such experience and consciousness and to the simultaneous restructuring of life-affirmative social relations.

Child Care in Market and State Capitalist Societies: The Husband-Economic-Provider Role

The remainder of this chapter focuses on one key mechanism in family structure through which the labor-producing function of the family in private as well as state capitalist societies is perverted: the Husband-Economic-Provider Role. This particular role has a series of negative consequences for the individual, for the family unit, and for the total social structure.

All societies have some pattern for allocating the economic responsibility for child care. While the patterns this concept refers to have long been recognized, they have not been sociologically conceptualized and analyzed as such.[33] It should be noted that this economic responsibility includes not only the material costs of children's direct needs, but also the economic support or pay of persons who care for the children. Traditionally this economic responsibility has been allocated to *all* working members of a society by virtue of their contribution to household units that are simultaneously economically productive and engaged in rearing children. In these societies a mechanism of allocating the economic responsibility for child care has existed which we call a Total-Society-Economic-Provider Role.

Especially after the first phase of industrialization (with its employment in factories of entire families, children included) the economic responsibility for child care was shifted to the husband and father almost exclusively. The institution of this role for the husband-father signaled the emergence of a historically new pattern of allocating the economic responsibility for child care, and simultaneously this role formed the basis of a new type of nuclear family structure.[34]

This role of the husband as economic provider refers, on the institutional level, to that complex of institutionalized ideals and operative norms and to those typical behavioral patterns according to which husbands have the chief responsibility for the economic provision of their children and their main carers, usually their mothers.

In societies where the husband as sole economic provider is the basic pattern, other patterns of economic provision for child care may exist as partial supplements to the husband's role or as more or less adequate substitutes for it. A widow's pension may be an example of a substitute method of economic provision for child care. Still another substitute exists to the extent that a divorced husband-father is required to provide for his children and also his former wife.

Partial alternatives to the basic husband-provider role exist in the obligation of unmarried or divorced fathers to provide some economic support for their children but not for their children's mothers. Thus, as a deceased or divorced husband and father, the male may provide economic support for his children and their mothers, or as an unmarried or divorced father he may partially supplement child-care costs.

The main alternative to the husband-provider role, especially in the case of unmarried mothers, is still the inadequate economic-provider role of the mother. It may be supplemented somewhat by the minimally developed role of the total society as an economic provider for children and their carers. Examples of this are various publically financed programs such as Aid to Dependent Children in the United States. Children's allowances in some countries are another way in which the total society supplements the husband's role, and the gainful employment of the mother may represent a supplementary economic-provider role of the mother to the husband's basic role. When, as feminists and Scandinavian social democrats advocate, both parents provide economically for their children, the now-prevailing role of the husband as economic provider with an economic-provider role for the mother would be equal parts of a new Parent-Economic-Provider Role. This pattern is now more or less approached in the behavior of dual-work and dual-career families.[35] Such a new role, however, would not solve the economic predicament of single mothers, nor would it lift the present economic discrimination against two-parent families with dependent children.

While the husband-provider concept has long been recognized (under different terms, say, "the breadwinner"), it has not been specifically analyzed as one *specific* type of the more *general* phenomenon of the pattern of allocating economic responsibility for child care. While the husband-economic-provider role as a concept is closely related to, for instance, Talcott Parsons' "husband occupational role," [36] the husband-economic-provider role refers to a more limited phenomenon, but has wider applicability. It may be seen as a specific key *aspect* of today's particular type of husband's occupational role. However, there is nothing in our definition which implies that the husband-provider role is a *necessary* consequence of the husband's participation in an occupational role generally. The abolition of the husband-provider role would thus not prevent a type of occupational role from being developed for both husband and wife. Also, compared with the more general concept of the economic-provider role of *males,* the husband-economic-provider role is more limited and has wider applicability. This general role of males refers to the idea that *all* working males are actually or potentially providers for their wives and children, and consequently shall be paid somewhat more than female workers and have the prerogative on scarce and well-paid jobs. As we shall see, this has as one of its consequences the institution of a "living wage" for the *male* earners, one large enough to reproduce the labor force adequately. *With both private capitalist and state capitalist* [37] *processes of industrialization a historically new family structure was institutionalized in which one person, the husband-father, on the basis of his work alone, became chiefly responsible for the economic provision of his children and of their caretakers.*

While we emphasize that the husband-economic-provider role is a historically new role we must note its elements of continuity with the past in that it is an extension of the preexisting Husband-Father-Status-Provider Role.[38] The *economic*-provider role of the husband adapts the four- to six-thousand-year-old patriarchal principle to industrialized circumstances of today's civilization, East and West.

The apparently universal function of the family, that of placement of the children of a society in their "full" social position (ascribing them a status) is substantially limited in industrialized societies to the role of the husband-father of providing *economic* support.[39] Thus, the husband-*status*-provider role of preindustrial societies is combined with his *economic*-provider role in industrial society through the comprehensive occupational role of the husband. The role of providing status placement for children is made possible only by the husband's full-time position in a bureaucratically authoritarian and alienated private or state capitalist occupational life. *No adequate or fully recognized source of alternative provision exists for a child whose mother does not have a husband, nor for that husbandless mother herself.* Even in their present welfare-state phase, the private capitalist societies have not been able to allot more than meager supplements and inadequate alternatives to the dominant pattern of assigning economic responsibility to the husband.[40]

In spite of important partial progressive changes in the position of women, their economic and social status dependency upon a husband in their capacity as *mothers* still remains. This is the most serious consequence of the institutionalization of the husband-economic-provider role. Women remain in a position of subjugation in the realms of economic production *and child care* because these realms are structured by the husband-economic-provider role. This leads to their partial subjugation in the spheres of reproduction and sexuality,[41] as well as in education and political life. The transfer of the economic burden of raising children from all members of the society to the father (and to *some* extent the mother) of their children has occurred at the same time as parents are getting not more but less economic *return* than others from their children or their work in adult life. For all but those with very high incomes, this means a heavy economic discrimination against families with children.

As long as this husband-economic-provider role prevails, however modified by supplements from public funds or by movement toward a *parent*-provider role (as when employed mothers also share in economic responsibility), the family will be virtually forced to continue its alienated labor-producing function.

Alternatives to the Husband-Economic-Provider Role

In order to see more easily the possibilities for alternatives to today's husband-economic-provider role, it is important to recognize that in a comparative sociological perspective, making the husband economically responsible for child care is only *one* specific mechanism of allocating economic responsibility for child care. To emphasize the singularity of our social mechanism, let us briefly note that the distribution of economic responsibility for children and for the carers of children can also be arranged as follows:

• As a more or less equal concern of the total society, implemented through all working individuals in their capacity as members of extended families (to which nearly the total population belongs, at least by way of household membership, much as in former European peasant societies). All extended family and domestic household members are here mutually dependent economically upon one another.

• As the concern mainly of the total society, implemented through child-care institutions (as in kibbutzim where all family members are totally independent of one another economically)—or implemented through the mother's brother and his extended family (as in some tribal matrilineal societies, where all extended family members are initially dependent economically on one another).

• As the concern mainly of *both* parents of the children (as among peasant nuclear families and in many lower-class complete families, or in middle- or upper-class double-career families). Father and mother are here mutually dependent economically.

• As the concern of the father-husband (as in U.S. middle-class families today) supplemented by public policies, tax reductions, children's allowances, wife's part-time work, etc. Here the parents are mutually economically dependent with primacy on the wife's dependence on the husband. As the concern mainly of the children's mother, supplemented more or less by contributions from their father and/or from public welfare children's allowances, single mother's benefits, etc. (as in the case of single-parent families and of unemployed fathers).

• In future industrial societies, the function of providing economically for children, for the mothers and other caretakers, may be taken out of the family by transforming the present husband-provider type of allocating economic responsibility for child care into a Total-Society-Economic-Provider Role, distributing the economic provision responsibilities among all working (or otherwise income-earning) members of the society, more or less according to their income.[42]

• The private family costs of providing materially for children as well as the necessary and desirable in-the-family child-care work could be covered through a change from the present inadequate family or children's allowances into a children's pension that would include a child-care wage.

The Family's Gratis Labor-producing Function

By means of the economic-provider role of the husband, market and state capitalist societies have developed an ingenious social structural squeeze upon one of the most powerfully motivating forces in the population, its love for mate and children, however neurotically disturbed that love may be. The husband-economic-provider role exploits this wish to help one's mate and offspring in their state of economic dependence. This situation of economic dependence is itself created by the husband-economic-provider-role structure of the society. Through this exploitation, the power elites of market and state capitalist societies have a virtually guaranteed, nearly free-of-charge family production of labor power. Due to the economic pressure on family emotional bonds, the husband-father exerts himself in occupational life even on exploited and alienated terms—provided a minimally sufficient income can thus be obtained.

Mainly through the wife's exploited domestic labor and "expressive" activities in the home, the family is the group in which the worker's energies and motivation are recharged, enabling him to return to his alienated labor.

For her services in thus resupplying the husband's labor energies, the wife is paid only in kind, and by a little share from the one-man income earned by the husband-provider. Her labor-producing services are given free of charge to the employer. The same is true of her domestic services for the children which, among other things, ensure that children are appropriately socialized for their "proper" adult roles as housewives and workers from whom business and government may harvest economic returns. By her husband-tending and child-care services the housewife helps produce *their* labor force, a labor force serving the interests of profit collecting owner and bureaucratic state managers.

Over the generational cycle, the role of the husband as economic provider and family structure based on this role contributes gratis production of labor for the well-to-do, by fostering and financing the next generation of husband-providers and child carers on the basis largely of a one-man income—supplemented or not by the income of an employed mother.

The tiny contribution to the in-the-family material and child-care costs of children from those who harvest the surplus value of the labor output of these children as adults is limited to a fraction of the real costs. It consists mainly in the average higher wages paid to men as opposed to women workers, in recognition of the fact that women are not generally expected to be economic providers for children. Add to this the pocket-money-size children's allowances, tax exemptions, and a few other economic aids to families with dependent children. However, such aids are in the main given also to well-to-do families.

In the reasoning above, the care of infants and children is regarded as *work*, even when it is carried out on an ordinary family basis whether by the mother, father, siblings, relatives, or others. And this essential work consists not only in changing diapers and washing clothes, but also in nursing, cuddling, playing, talking, and the necessary "just being there." That this work at its best, even under present family conditions, may be joyful and satisfying, is no argument against recognizing its work qualities. To some extent, the motivation for rearing children is based on satisfaction received, but this is also the motivation for work which is monetarily rewarding. In-the-home work, although done (too much) in the private confines of the family, is of as great a public and collective interest as any other work. How otherwise would societies (and old people) survive to the extent they do?

Further Negative Consequences of the Husband-Economic-Provider Role

Theoretical considerations. The remaining part of this chapter fo-cuses on the husband-economic-provider role (for which the abbre-viation HEPR will hereinafter be used) of family structure in market and state capitalist societies and shows how this institutionalized role serves not only the family's labor-producing function, but also has a series of other detrimental consequences for the population at large.[43]

The HEPR institution is strategic from a perspective of future possibilities for social, family, sex role, and sexual *policy action.* For it seems that the abolition of the HEPR is within reach; it can be abol-ished if we wish. Such a course of action will open further possibili-ties for still other measures that may unleash considerable amounts of creative energies and joy-of-life.

Certainly a lot of theorizing, hypothesizing and some empirical research has been addressed to the consequences, and sometimes to the dysfunctions, not of the HEPR, but of today's sex differentiation and sex roles generally.[44] We propose to show that some of these themes, analyzed earlier in the literature as related to aspects of sex differentiation, may fruitfully and strategically be seen as conse-quences[45]—in the present, although perhaps not historically—of a common, underlying HEPR phenomenon.[46]

The phenomena herein regarded as consequences of the HEPR are not determined by the HEPR alone but also as consequences of other converging aspects of the present-day social structure. The HEPR is itself rooted in a series of social circumstances. For instance, as it appears in Parsons' analysis of the husband's occupational role, the HEPR is highly functional for capitalist industrial societies as well as for the present authoritarian and repressive forms of charac-ter structures that prevail in them. But it is not, I think, functional for a further development toward democratic social structure and a creative, self-regulating character structure.

In this sense, the HEPR is rooted in the authoritarian, alienated, and exploitive aspects of today's economic, political, and psychological structures of capitalist class societies.[47] Attempts at the abolition of the HEPR will therefore require change also in the structures in which it is embedded. Nevertheless, if the HEPR were removed, one essential underpinning of the unfortunate phenomena upheld by it would also be removed.

Without the abolition of the HEPR it is impossible to abolish other dysfunctional sex role aspects and HEPR's dysfunctional consequences for family, economic, and political structures or the individual's primary need gratification, mental health, and social fulfillment.

It seems reasonable within social and family policy potentials to remove the HEPR institution by introducing a composite alternative pattern of economic responsibility for child care, through the simultaneous building of emotionally adequate day-care centers, part-time occupational employment of fathers as well as mothers of small children, and a publicly financed children's pension, covering not only the cost of their material provision but also a child-care wage for those persons who take part in the emotional and physical care of the child.

It should be noted that the abolition of the husband-provider role and the other main effects obtainable through a children's pension, including a child-care wage, will *not* be obtained through current proposals of a "guaranteed minimum wage" or a "negative income tax" unless the latter are designed specifically to incorporate the former measures. While a children's pension should perhaps not be given to children of families with well-above-average per capita incomes, it certainly should be given to children of families with incomes far above the minimum levels now being debated.[48]

HEPR-rooted elements of the nuclear family and sex roles in industrial societies. A good many consequences of the HEPR are mediated through its family and family sex role structural consequences.[49] Given the competitive occupational structure, the HEPR encourages economic and social [50] isolation of the neolocal nuclear family, as well as its privatization[51] and egotism.[52]

The husband-provider role is what directly establishes the essentially instrumental family role of the husband-father,[53] which by Parsons' definition is virtually identical with his income-earning activities. As a structural corollary the husband-father's social and emotional position in the nuclear family becomes extremely peripheral.[54] The combination of these two HEPR consequences leads to a relative isolation of the mother-child as well as to the wife-mother's role as a predominantly "expressive" leadership role, and, at least under specifically North American conditions, to its momism quality.[55] The children's source of authority as well as love and comfort becomes predominantly maternal. The husband-father's overall family authority seems generally not to have been abolished, although it has changed.[56]

Despite reports about joint conjugal role relations in middle-class and upwardly mobile families,[57] Parsons finds that because of the husband's occupational role, the amount of sex differentiation is basically as great—or greater—both within the family and outside it.[58] In lower-class families in stable, traditional communities, the HEPR contributes to the conservation of an especially high degree of role segregation,[59] and in poor families to mother-focal and mother-headed families.[60]

Not only sex roles within the family are seen by Parsons as resulting from the husband's occupational role.[61] The total sex-role structure in industrial society also rests on this role,[62] and Parsons is well aware of some of the personality strain and role conflict it produces,[63] although he has lately come to see these difficulties as less drastic. Among several consequences ignored in Parsons' discussion are discriminatory wage practices against women, economic discrimination against families with dependent children, political passivity, authoritarianism, etc.

Double role of the gainfully employed mother. The HEPR leads to the fact that, with some social-class variation, the wife does by far the major part of direct child-care and household chores. And this is largely the case even when the wife herself is employed.[64] A mother's gainful employment thus leads to the "double role" of the working mother. This is probably true because of a common recognition that it is the husband's job or career which counts in the long run, since under HEPR conditions, his job pays better and contains the best promotional possibilities.

As the occupational structure is now gradually able to absorb an increasing number of subordinate, low-paid women, the number of "double-role" women is increasing. The pattern of dual roles no longer means different roles at different periods in the life cycle[65] but the combination of two roles during the mothering period when children are most dependent upon their mother's care.

This increasing burden on the mother is a consequence also of HEPR-based economic discrimination against families with dependent children. New socioeconomic developments, the increasing costs of rearing children, plus a general rise in material aspirations and the increased frequency of the housewife's isolation, make more women ready to avail themselves of the opportunities for gainful employment. For much the same reasons, the husband does not see fit to reduce his occupational absorption and do his share of housework and child care.

The new burden of masculinity. One might conclude that there is now also a "double role" for men.[66] One aspect of this "new burden" is that the husband-father's role is no longer as exclusively concentrated on his instrumental-provider duties, but comprises expectations that he also be a nurturant carer for infants, a kind and playful fatherly comrade, and a skillful lover.

These new, potentially liberating expectations conflict with the still-dominant HEPR expectations and may lead to conflicts and guilt feelings in men when they sense that they are not living up to the new expectations.[67] However, the actual "burden" for men has hardly "doubled" to the extent that it has for the gainfully employed mother.

The consequences of the HEPR discussed above receive some recognition in family sociology. We turn now to other consequences that are largely neglected by academic sociologists.[68]

Economic discrimination against gainfully employed women. The HEPR still, at least under private capitalist conditions, is the basis for the exclusion or discouragement of a majority of married women from occupational careers and from higher education. They are generally relegated to subordinate, low-paid work, and experience wage discrimination as well.[69] Such fundamental facts about sex roles within the occupational structure have important repercussions on sex roles in the family.

> If it is always assumed that the husbands have a duty, from which their wives are exempted, *of providing for their families, women only needing to provide for themselves,* one might be able to understand the special privileges accorded to men in the form of higher pay for the same work, tax relief, better educational opportunities, better promotion prospects and superior influences in local government, etc.[70]

This discrimination hits women who are actually providers especially hard: the mothers with unemployed husbands, unmarried mothers, many divorcees, deserted wives, and widows.

> Perhaps a more serious and troublesome consequence of the "bread-winner concept ethos" is the discrimination that exists regarding *access to the labour market as a whole.* Married women are not treated on the same level as men. Women who have been at home for some time looking after the children and then want to start working again *find it very difficult to get work,* but they are not counted as unemployed. If they are lucky enough to get a job at all, it will generally be on very unfavourable terms. Only during the last few years have the makers of labour market policy come to devote any particular attention to this state of affairs. Even today in this year of grace, 1969, the right of the married woman to work is still not self-evident in Sweden, although emancipation has made more progress there than in most other countries of the world.[71]

Because it is the result of partial and inconsistent attempts to repair injustices caused by discrimination,[72] the current taxation and social security systems in Scandinavia contribute to the economic discrimination against gainfully employed women as compared with the nonemployed married women without dependent children.[73] Regardless of whether they are engaged in child-care work or not, nonemployed married women are exempt from paying social security premiums. The husband gets income tax deductions, since the childless wife is in this context legally defined [74] as economically dependent upon him. She is also exempt from paying taxes, either for the actual economic value of her service work for her husband or for the returns from her husband that she receives.

Whether the employed woman has dependent children or not, she nevertheless has all the duties in terms of taxes and social security payments, but none of the privileges.[75] Thus, the married woman who wants her own income is economically discriminated against, while the married woman who remains fully dependent upon her husband is economically rewarded. Similarly, marriage and not parenthood is rewarded. All this results from HEPR-rooted legal, familial, educational, and labor-market policy definitions of the married woman as one who is economically dependent.

Economic discrimination against in-the-family child-care workers. Another kind of economic discrimination against women which is rooted in the HEPR institution concerns those women who do the child-care work in the subsistence economy enclaves of families. In-the-family child-care work, except in families with very high-income husbands, is grossly underpaid. This is the case even when the husband-provider's income is supplemented from public sources or from the gainfully employed mother's wages. As long as economic support for in-the-family child-care work is mainly limited to the husband's income, it cannot be economically remunerated to the extent ordinary occupational work is, nor can it be an economic basis of living independent of a husband or a marriage.

At present this discrimination mainly affects women and mothers, but it can also affect fathers or other in-the-family child carers to the extent that they engage in such work.[76] But as long as fathers are better paid than mothers in their occupational life, they cannot afford much participation in child care. Mothers are therefore not expected to work outside the home. Such HEPR expectations create obstacles against the development of alternative child-care facilities.

This economic discrimination against in-the-family child-care work is as fundamental and as consequential as the straight occupational discrimination against women. Yet it has been largely neglected, not only by sociologists but also by feminists.

Economic discrimination against families with dependent children. This in its turn results from two types of economic discrimination discussed earlier. When a provider for one or more children earns the same as a childless employee doing comparable work, it is clear that the former's family has a much lower living standard than the latter's. This difference in living standards increases with the number of dependents.[77] This economic discrimination is counteracted only slightly by children's allowances, tax reductions (which favor high incomes and discriminate against working women), or other minimal family relief measures.[78]

Economic discrimination, especially against the single-mother family, consists primarily of the lack of any adequate alternative pattern of assuming economic responsibility for child care in cases where HEPR expectations cannot be met. Therefore, unmarried mothers are often forced to take full-time employment in order to support a child [79]—even when the child is very young. The only alternative is to have the child adopted.[80] In their employment, these mothers meet not only the same "one-man, one-wage" principle as do the male providers, but also wage discrimination against women. In either case, it is generally necessary to leave the child too long in what may be inadequate day-care institutions, or in other poor circumstances.

The incomplete families for whom alternatives to the HEPR are least developed are the families of unwed mothers. This results in part from the fact that the unwed mother has blatantly broken the rule that each child shall have a husband-father to provide for it and to avoid becoming a burden to the rest of society.

Economic dependency[81] *of children and mothers upon the husband-father.* The economic dependency of mothers and children upon the husband, and thus upon marriage, follows HEPR's near monopoly as an economic basis for child care, for instance via the HEPR consequences of occupational and educational discrimination against in-the-family child-care work. Although a mother's economic *dependence* upon a husband may be implicit in the HEPR, an economic *dependency* of mothers and children upon a husband-father is an explicit implication of HEPR's near-monopoly on economic bases for in-the-family child care.[82]

It should be noted that the recent, somewhat increased occupational and educational opportunities of women have generally eliminated the economic dependency (although often not the dependence) of married women.

Women's subjugation and sex-role inequality. Women generally find themselves in a basically subordinate position in the family, as a result of economic discrimination and economic dependency inherent to the HEPR.

Contrary to the interpretation of several American family sociologists, and also to a widespread egalitarian ideology, equality between the sexes generally exists neither in America nor in any other industrial society—not in childhood or in adult life and not inside or outside the family. The wife-mother's expressive, socioemotional leadership or even "momism" does not change this, as long as the husband-father's instrumental leadership actually sets the basic conditions and boundaries. The wife is subjugated in the family, because the basic family structure and activities (if not many day-by-day details) are geared to the demands of the fundamental HEPR and the husband's occupational role, as these are interpreted by the husband, and by the demands of the occupational structure. The basic frame for the wife's decisions is laid down by the husband, based on *his* occupational conditions, upon which the mother and the children are economically dependent. The HEPR is the basis for the legitimacy of the husband's superior authority and for his superior status.

Relative to the alienated economic and political forces, husband and wife are in the same boat. But the husband is the captain who directs the boat's course, while the wife is the crew who may be left to make all the decisions on keeping the boat going but only in the direction in which she has been instructed. Variations in terms of autocratic-syncratic, patri/matri-central, "egalitarian," etc. conjugal relationships seem generally to represent mere variations of, and possibly deviance from, this basically institutionalized, dominant structure.

Also, the persons in the positions of power in the working world, in local, national, or international finance and politics where the conditions for the family's and the women's life are set, are *male* elites—not female. And the basis for their male monopoly on these power positions is their HEPR-based privileged footing in the occupational and economic life.

Economic ties on marriage. Under present conditions the economic dependency of children and the mother-wife remains even after divorce. Because of the surviving humanist values, the divorced husband-father is held legally and morally responsible for their economic provision on the basis of his one-man income. Of course, the costs of financing a family is considerably higher once the family is split into two households.[83] Even when the moral, legal, and symbiotic emotional obstacles against dissolving a marriage have been overcome, many loveless marriages remain legally and practically intact for financial reasons.[84]

It is too costly to establish a new household. The HEPR duties of a divorced husband-father mean that the economic tie on marriage applies also to the husband. Neither he nor the wife is economically free to separate as long as they have dependent children.[85] These circumstances are the chief economic and social reasons underlying the prevailing ideals of lifelong monogamy and "marital duty."

Considering the inverse proportion between frequency of divorce and socioeconomic status, it seems, however, that the economic tie on marriage rests on relative, not absolute, economic deprivation of families with dependent children.[86] The reference group for the relative deprivation is the family's actual or aspired socioeconomic status group. It also seems that the economic circumstances referred to become an obstacle to divorce only when the marriage offers a certain amount of economic advantage through the husband's relatively good income, i.e., when a divorce means economic loss.

Conversely, when the divorce rate increases as the husband's income decreases, it does not necessarily mean that the husband's provision is so little that there is "nothing to lose." Rather, it indicates that the economic difficulties resulting from a minimal-provider income increase the emotional conflicts to such an extent that they become intolerable and outweigh the further increased economic difficulties following a divorce.

Marriage and parent-child relationships. Through economic discrimination, economic dependency, and the economic tie on marriage, the sentimental, sex-oppressive romantic-love ideal as well as symbiotic dependencies are reinforced. Neurotic emotional gratifications are obtained, and neurotically weak personality structures are stabilized.[87]

In Parsons' analysis, one can see some of the repressive and neurotic aspects of the momentary functionality of the HEPR-based family. At one point, he shows how the husband's absorption in his occupational role "narrows the range in which the sharing of common human interests can play a large part" in the marital relationship; and how it thus hampers the development of companionship,[88] even in the otherwise emotionally overburdened middle-class marriage. The marital sexual relationship is described in one sense as a *ritual* of marital solidarity. It is characterized as a mother-child, pre-Oedipal relationship, balanced by the provider demands on the husband and by the housewife demands on the wife.[89] In a way, Parsons is aware of a conflict between the economic and, at least, the regressive sexual-love aspects of today's marriage. But he does not go into the deeper conflict between, on the one hand, both these mutually conflicting elements and, on the other hand, the underlying, repressed striving for full primary and genital love gratification.

Moreover, the parent-child relationship is seen by Parsons as basically repressive, balanced by external realities.[90] His awareness of the directly repressive character found in the early mother-child relationship comes out in his analysis of the place of frustrated sexuality in today's typical socialization process. There the mother's manipulation of the child's mother-fixated, frustrated sexuality (which Parsons called "eroticism") is realistically seen as "the rope" by which the dependent child is "pulled" into adult independence.[91]

Enforced marriages and single-parent families; abortions and adoptions. A considerable number of marriages, especially among the very young, are not engendered by love. Rather, they take place in order for the mother and child to ascertain at least a minimum of economic and social status. The HEPR-buttressed sanctions against premarital intercourse are probably an essential reason for the nonuse or inefficient use of contraceptives. This leads to unwanted pregnancies, which under HEPR conditions result in enforced marriages.[92] These marriages are in fact formed through a fear of the socioeconomic consequences for mother and child if they do not have a husband-father.

Another type of marriage formed in this way is probably that entered into by unmarried mothers to escape very difficult economical and practical situations. We have already mentioned how the HEPR tends to contribute to the divorce rate among the lower classes by its severe impact of economic discrimination against families with children. Similarly it contributes to the especially high divorce rate of early marriages, since many of these have an exceptionally weak economic basis. Probably not only enforced marriages, but also many emotionally well-founded early marriages, break down for these reasons.

Of course, a corresponding number of HEPR-rooted, single-parent families occur because of these HEPR-stimulated divorces. As a result of the divorcing father's HEPR duties, the mother is usually given custody of the children; consequently, divorced single-parent families are mainly single-mother families.

When the institutionalized prescriptions of the HEPR are coupled with a nineteenth-century individualistic ideology and with a competitive, profit-oriented economic system, as in the United States, the HEPR also contributes to the public refusal of adequate economic welfare assistance to families wherever an earning male is present in the family household—regardless of the adequacy of his contribution to the family's income. This in turn stimulates the male's real and fake *desertions* from the family and his avoidance of inadequately paid jobs.

The HEPR contributes also to the direct formation of single-mother families at a scale somewhat corresponding to the number of illegitimate children. This happens when unwed expectant fathers break up the relationship fearing the provider responsibilities resulting from marriage, perhaps often despite a love or liking for the woman that might otherwise have been sufficient motivation for marriage.

Especially in America, the insistence on the full operation of the HEPR among the lower class is probably another mechanism by which their poverty is perpetuated. A large number of adult males, in the face of their failure as adequate providers, withdraw from both their provider role and from the occupational and family system as well. In the resulting "matri-focal" families, the father's peripheralness then becomes so extensive that even the compensatory achievement motivation in the boys, necessary for their "adequate" occupational performance, does not seem to be established.

In the United States the remarriage rate for single mothers with children is at least as high as that for the never-married childless women, and usually the period of singleness does not last more than one or two years.[93] Nevertheless, one may ask to what extent these marriages are based on love and to what extent on considerations of economic and practical convenience. One may also ask under what circumstances widowed and divorced mothers remain unmarried because of otherwise eligible men's reluctance to take on the economic burden of providing for the children in question.

Instability of premarital love relations. The direct HEPR demand that a man be economically able to provide for a wife and children before he marries, combined with the HEPR-buttressed ideal of life-long marriage, seem powerful obstacles against the full sexual love development of many youthful relationships, the increasing frequency of early, often wife-supported marriages notwithstanding. In part, youth may fear full emotional and sexual involvement because of the present economic implications of parenthood, and they also may fear disturbing their education or careers. In part, young people are also emotionally disturbed by the immediate social sanctions against premarital sexual relations—chief sanction being the lack of regular privacy and housing facilities for unmarried couples.

To these difficulties is added the confusing and further sex-oppressive ideology of romantic love, which perfectly fits the HEPR necessity of discouraging premarital sex by invoking an individualistic, internalized sexual discipline. During the difficult premarital period of relative sexual renunciation, the romantic-love ideal maintains the sublimated dream and false promise of a future marital "dance on roses."

In addition to such direct social, organizational, and normative obstacles in the way of premarital love relations are all the indirect psychological obstacles. Thus the HEPR-buttressed sex-oppressive childhood family climate and socialization practices typically lead to a basic and severe sexual repression in both sexes, and to a splitting up of the originally unitary sexual and love emotion.[94]

Because of the boy's feminine identification and compensatory masculinity (caused by HEPR-rooted father peripheralness), he experiences discontinuity in his socialization and in his role-taking process.[95] Under modern "mom" family conditions, this probably loosens his early, femininely derived superego formation. Also, the boy's sexual vitality and aggressiveness must not be curbed too effectively, or he might lose even that compensatory aggressive "achievement" drive upon which depends his occupational capacity and his provider ability. These constellations allow him to give vent to an aggressive, compensatory sexuality, but then demand that he repress the tender components of sexual love. Typically he is hereby instilled with an anxiety and an aggressive tendency toward women in general—to the extent of usually avoiding motherly, dominant, or simply healthy self-reliant women. Also typically, this characterological constellation makes him both expect and be attracted to a superficial and compensatory type of sex appeal and glamour in the girl.

The girl's greater vulnerability (under HEPR conditions) to the socioeconomic risk of premarital pregnancy results in her being subjected to a stricter upbringing than the boy, especially in sexual matters. Her unbroken and one-sided same-sex identification with an often frustrated and socially isolated mother (under the conditions of HEPR father peripheralness) probably results in an overdeveloped superego formation. This further accentuates her sexual repressions. The thus isolated, sentimentally developed, tender and loving aspects of her sexual love and emotionality come to the fore. This represents the exact opposite constellation of the boy's separation between love and sex. When encountering the boy's desire for "sex" and glamour, however, it seems that the girl typically develops a shallow, compensatory glamour and sex appeal alongside her sexless sentimental "love."

The insecure, femininely identified young man thus often resorts to the arena of more or less loveless sexuality. This is not only a result of sexual need, but is also due to the necessity to feel "masculine" in order to combat his underlying feelings of anxiety, inferiority, and femininity. This occurs especially prior to his obtaining a full male-dominant position over his wife and children, in the capacity of an adequate and successful provider.

An additional and directly corresponding social organizational and HEPR-rooted difficulty is the difference in the role expectations presented to the boy and girl in the premarital relationship. These appear partly to emanate from the still widely practiced, if not ideal, double standard. The general expectation, especially from adult sources, is that it is the girl's primary responsibility to "draw the line," to refuse the boy's desire for full intercourse. Keeping up the "morality" is squarely placed on her shoulders. Correspondingly, it is the general expectation, especially from his peers, that the boy tries as hard as he can to obtain "the forbidden fruit." Thus, premaritally *she* is the one given the instrumental role, oriented to adaptation and long-term goal attainment; *he* is ascribed the expressive role of pressing for immediate emotional gratification.

Personality constellations and role expectations such as these lead to the heterosexual social constellation, where the boy typically wants "sex," while the girl avoids it. She wants marriage and HEPR-committed "love," which the boy fears as much as he would her natural self-assertiveness.

How frequently such constellations occur, rather than the more traditional alternative of the boy having sex with one set of "bad" girls, and feeling relatively sexless love and respect for his potential marital partner, would be interesting to know. The continued flourishing of prostitution indicates that the last type of HEPR-rooted constellation is still somewhat prevalent. On the female side, prostitution has, as one of its characterological bases, the extreme developments of the HEPR-rooted feminine character traits such as sexual submissiveness and being pseudo-sexual, frigid sex objects. Prostitution has its roots in the HEPR-based educational and economic discrimination against women.

Undoubtedly, these HEPR-rooted constellations are important and more specific elements in the conflicts, frustrations, and break-ups of premarital love relations, as well as of marital ones. Thus, the much celebrated romantic love—and seemingly "participant-ruled" [96] field of eligibles in the marketplace for marriage contracts —becomes the first decisive field for the battle between the sexes, where the frustrating love dyads of youth are destroyed on a mass scale in the name of sexless romantic love—or loveless sex—until the third, fourth or twentieth eventually ends in marriage. Even with the spreading standards of "permissiveness with affection" [97] the traditional HEPR-based double standard and its social relational and psychological structure still live on.

Sexual oppression and repression. The strategic relationships between sexual freedom and regulation, on the one hand, and HEPR-aspects of the family and sex-role structure, on the other, have been analyzed only minimally in academic sociology.[98] The central consequences of the HEPR consist here, first, in the noted drastic economic, social, and consequently psychological danger in which a household headed by a mother and her child are left. For parents with social status to lose, the premarital pregnancy of their daughter becomes a danger to the parents also.[99] Such circumstances make for a widespread and realistic fear of premarital sexual intercourse. They motivate parents, educators, and other authorities to discourage premarital sexual intercourse. They also probably stimulate oppression of *childhood* sexuality.

Second, the economic tie on marriage leads in part, by way of the consequent ideals of compulsively "faithful" and lifelong marriages, to sexually ungratifying marriages and to difficulties in establishing new sexual relations.[100]

The resultant repression of the parents' own sexuality aggravates their anxiety over the emotional and sexual vitality of their children. When it does not lead them openly to threaten or punish the children's sexuality, it will generally prevent parents from giving them that warmth and acceptance upon which these aspects of the children's growth potential depend for maturation and gratification. Lasting marital sexual frustration may also lead parents to tie the children sexually to themselves.

These sources of childhood sex repression are decisively supplemented by the HEPR-based, relative social isolation of the nuclear family. The parents now become the near-exclusive objects of their children's unconscious sexual attachments and fixations, while open sex play and love in relation to children of other families is prohibited.[101]

Furthermore, the HEPR-type of sex-oppressive, father-peripheral family and sex-role structure helps to shape a frustrated and neurotic mother, who cannot satisfy her baby's early oral needs, and who consequently stultifies the baby's spontaneous and slow growth to independence.

In industrialized societies, this situation is dramatically represented at the moment of the baby's birth, and immediately thereafter. In line with the whole HEPR-based family structure, mother and baby are at first left alone in alien hospital surroundings, as the husband-father is forcefully placed in the literal periphery. For the baby, the ensuing consequences are probably mediated mainly through the mother's sense of loneliness and anxiety. This is in itself likely to reduce her ability to give her baby full love and care. The separation from her husband—and from friends and relatives—probably also contributes to her defenselessness against the time-scheduled hospital routine, which is decisively out of touch with the basic rhythm and needs of both infant and mother. The periodically enforced isolation of the mother from the baby also disturbs the mother's spontaneous contact with her child. It is probably at this point that the first basic distrust and life anxiety begin to grow in the baby.[102]

No doubt, the above type of libidinally repressive HEPR consequences are dysfunctional to the love relationships in marriages and families regarding sexual-love gratification "goal attainment," gratifying "tension management," and a love-based "integration,"— to put it in Parsonian functional requisite vocabulary.

Sociopolitical conformity and nonparticipation. The HEPR contributes, by way of the husband's occupational absorption and the wife's preoccupation with the children, to a lack of sociopolitical participation. Further, the dependent position of women, along with their generally stronger superego and related political conservatism,[103] may lead them to encourage men's family egoism and their absorption in their occupational-provider role, as well as discourage their nonconformist activities in work and politics.[104] Because of male domination in public and political life, important issues are defined and acted upon from the man's point of view.

Equally as important as the direct social organizational causes is the type of authoritarian and repressive character structure formed by the HEPR-based family structure, which causes adults to desire either to be irresponsible and subjugated, or to be dominant.[105] Repressed energies, as well as the energies mobilized to effect the repression,[106] devitalize the individual organism and deprive it of energies needed for independent and efficient sociopolitical participation.

Elitist authoritarianism and fascist political tendencies. The above-mentioned sociopolitically relevant personality constellations clearly contribute to the upholding—and under certain conditions to the intensification—of the elitist authoritarian, exploitative, and alienated aspects of the work, economic, and political structures in market and state capitalist societies. The HEPR-rooted sex-role and family structures become important mechanisms for maintaining the authoritarian power structure.

As described by Reich, a sexually and otherwise repressed personality resulting from an oppressive family structure, in some essential respects still characteristic of the modern "democratic," "companionship," "permissive" family, has a high potential of destructive aggression (besides anxiety, guilt, shame, dependency longings, etc.). Under anomic social conditions and crisis (found, for instance, in Germany in the 1920s and '30s, and to some extent in the United States today), the ordinary oppressive socialization and social control—as well as the support and reward of conventional conformity—become so weak that the secondary perversions and destructive rage break through the moral and conventional outer layer of the character structure. To a considerable extent the primary, sociable life forces of the individual exist then only as repressed beneath the layers of outward conventionality and secondary, usually repressed rage, infantilism, and emotional conflicts.[107] Under anomic conditions such a character structure may become easy prey for political leaders who appeal to its repressed destructive impulses, to its helpless longing for freedom and security without responsibility.

Societal dysfunctionality in market and state capitalist societies. It is most significant that Parsons' conclusion about the basic and net-sum functionality for industrialized societies of the husband-occupation-based family structure rests on the short-term functionality it undoubtedly has for the occupational and economic system—*as that system now functions and develops on the manifest level.*

This is the limited-system reference for Parsons' imputation of what he thinks is a basic functionality of the husband's occupational role. And he seems to think that this limited functionality applies also to society as a whole.[108] The justification for this generalization seems to be the observation that of the four systems requisites, that of *goal attainment* is the one that American (as well as other industrial) society generally gives highest priority in the name of what Parsons—in a sense correctly—thinks is its highest value: "achievement." [109]

This "achievement" value seems, however, to be of a very special and limited sort. It is an individualistic, compensatory,[110] competitive achievement which, on the societal level, leads to and can be measured in terms of increased GNP and private or national profit or income, in which costly waste is counted as positive. This kind of dominant "achievement" value thus seems actually in conflict with that of creative and rational productivity—for which the HEPR is hardly functional at all.[111]

While Parsons is right in his characterization of the dominant value in industrial societies, he is probably wrong in seeing no basic American or capitalist *dilemma* between the compensatory achievement orientation and the "American creed." Parsons places this real dilemma between what he considers a unitary *occupational* vs. a unitary *family* value system. Parsons sees this conflict being solved by the victory of *the occupational "achievement"* value—precisely by means of the husband's occupational role.

Parsons also avoids the question of who shall decide, and on what grounds, which of the conflicting social and value systems within an authoritarian societal system shall represent the comprehensive system. Actually Parsons, like other traditional "objective" sociologists, equates the presently dominating subsystem with its coalition of competing elites, and *that order* of the inclusive system, which the power elite and the authoritarian elements of the masses keep going to the great dysfunctionality of the constructive and democratically working elements, with the concept "society." In other words, that which is functional turns out to be basically that which serves the status quo. In today's market (and in state capitalist societies in general) this means that which serves the hegemony of the oppressive elements of the ruling elites, as well as of the submissive elements of the masses. The value implications are massive and fundamental to the whole analysis—and they have to be. The same holds true if the functional analysis is done according to a paramount value, such as "achievement," or to a paramount functional requisite, such as "goal attainment." The paramount value or requisite has become defined as paramount by the definition of the most authoritarian elements in the power groups and among the masses.

Now, in a limited and short-term perspective, the private or state capitalist achievement "good" may be good or functional for the economic-political elites and for the privileged middle class—and even for the oppressed and exploited masses—to the extent that they may not be capable of any creatively productive, democratic order. But *basically* the compensatory, repression-based achievement "good" is hardly functional or good for these societies *in their totality*, since it is precisely *this alleged good which seems to be one of the chief disinte-*

grative, conflict-generating forces that may lead, and do lead, to national and international fascism and imperialism, to civil and national wars. These seem to be some of the likely consequences of ignoring the more basic and specific *work democratic*[112] "integration" requisite, and of likewise ignoring the specifically *primary need-gratifying* "tension management" requisite of social systems.

In this situation (admitting the biopsychically rooted value implication of any functional analysis) one has, of course, the choice to pick as a final reference point for one's analysis one that does not mirror the exploitative and authoritarian interests within the present hegemonic and submissive groups. *One may choose as one's reference point the more or less suppressed primary needs, biopsychic health, and the genuinely democratic interests and elements that exist presently within all population groups and social classes.*[113] This presupposes, however, a consciousness of these constructive life forces.

And insofar as Parsons is right in his analysis that the HEPR-based family structure is the producer of that type of male compensatory achievement-motivated personality structure adequately socialized to function in the present, widely exploitative, repression- and alienation-generating occupational and economic life, then not only this type of occupational and economic system, but also this family structure and its HEPR basis, are in the long run not functional. Rather, they are dangerously dysfunctional for the comprehensive society—defined in terms of its primary creative, biopsychosocially rooted life forces.

The HEPR and its sex-role and family structure are *secondarily* and at *present* functional, only to the (unknown) extent that neither men nor women, neither capitalists nor workers, are capable of living by any other, more freedom- and responsibility-demanding economic responsibility for child-care, family, sex-role, and work structure.

NOTES

1. Robert W. Friedrichs, *A Sociology of Sociology* (New York: Free Press, 1970); and Larry T. Reynolds and Janice M. Reynolds, eds., *The Sociology of*

Sociology: Analysis and Criticism of the Thought Research and Ethical Folkways of Sociology and Its Practitioners (New York: McKay, 1970).

2. Alvin W. Gouldner, "Anti-Minotaur: The Myth of a Value-Free Sociology," *Social Problems* 9 (Winter 1962): 199–213. Gunnar Myrdal, *Value in Social Theory* (London: Routledge & Kegan Paul, 1958). See also chapter 4 in the present volume.

3. R. D. Laing, *The Politics of Experience* (London: Ballantine, 1967); Jules Henry, *Culture Against Man* (New York: Random House, 1963); John Mogey, "The Formation of Images and Counter-Images of the Family," in *Images and Counter-Images of Young Families*, ed. J. Preslevou and B. de Bie (Louvain: ICOFA, 1970).

4. Exceptions are Wilhelm Reich, *The Mass Psychology of Fascism* (New York: Albion, 1970); Erich Fromm, *Escape from Freedom* (New York: Farrar & Rinehart, 1941); Herbert Marcuse, *Eros and Civilization* (Boston: Beacon Press, 1955).

5. Gerald Leslie, *The Family in Social Context* (New York: Oxford University Press, 1967), p. 13.

6. Ira L. Reiss, "The Universality of the Family," *Journal of Marriage and the Family* 27 (1965): 443–53.

7. Bronislaw Malinowski, *Sex and Repression in Savage Society* (New York: Meridian Books, 1955); and Malinowski, "Parenthood, The Basis of Social Structure," in *The Family: Its Structure and Functions*, ed. Rose L. Coser (New York: St. Martins Press, 1964), pp. 3–19; see also J. K. Folsom, *The Family and Democratic Society* (New York: Wiley, 1948).

8. Melford Spiro, "Is the Family Universal?: The Israeli Case," in *A Modern Introduction to the Family*, ed. Wendel Bell and Ezra Vogel (Glencoe, Ill.: Free Press, 1968).

9. Wilhelm Reich, *Der Einbruch der Sexualmoral* (Copenhagen: Verlag, 1936).

10. Leslie, *The Family*, p. 15.

11. Clellan S. Ford and F. A. Beach, *Pattern of Sexual Behavior* (New York: Harper & Row, 1951).

12. Wilhelm Reich, *The Function of the Orgasm* (New York: Farrar, Strauss, Giroux, 1961); Talcott Parsons and Robert F. Bales, *Family, Socialization and Interaction Process* (New York: Free Press, 1955), pp. 20–22; and Albert Ellis, *The American Sexual Tragedy* (New York: Twayne Publishers, 1954).

13. Talcott Parsons, "The Incest Taboo," *British Journal of Sociology* (1954): 101–17; and Erik Grønseth, "Some Remarks on Parsons' Conception of Sexuality and Socialization," *Organomic Functionalism* 5 (1958).

14. Laing, *Politics of Experience*, and Mogey, "Formation of Images."

15. Meyer F. Nimkoff, *Comparative Family Systems* (Boston: Houghton Mifflin, 1965), chap. 3.

16. Eugene Litwak, "Extended Kin Relations in an Industrial Democratic Society," in *Social Structure and the Family*, ed. Ethel Shanas and G. F. Streib (London: Prentice-Hall, 1965).

17. In the case of Norway, see Erik Grønseth, "Notes on the Historical Development of the Relation Between Nuclear Family, Kinship System and Wider Social Structure in Norway," in *Families East and West*, ed. R. Hiland and Karl Kønig (Paris: International Family Research Seminar, 1970).

18. Jurgen Habermas, *Strukturwandel der Offentlichkeit* (Berlin, 1965).

19. See William N. Stephens, "Family and Kinship," in *Sociology: An Introduction*, ed. Neil J. Smelser (New York: Wiley, 1967), pp. 508–43.

20. See pp. 266–84 for a discussion of how this subjugation mechanism on the social organizational level is reinforced by way of the repressive characterological consequences of a family structure based on the husband provider role.

21. T. W. Adorno et al., *Autoritat und Familie* (Paris, 1936).

22. Wilhelm Reich, *The Sexual Revolution* (New York: Farrar, Strauss, Giroux, 1962), part 2.

23. John Mogey, "Family and Community in Urban, Industrialized Societies," in *Handbook of Marriage and the Family*, ed. Harold T. Christensen (Chicago: Rand McNally, 1964), pp. 501–34.

24. Melvin L. Kohn, *Class and Conformity* (Homewood, Ill.: Dorsey Press, 1969).

25. Erich Fromm, *The Sane Society* (New York: Holt, Rinehart, Winston, 1955); and Robert Blauner, *Alienation and Freedom* (Chicago: University of Chicago Press, 1964).

26. Wilhelm Reich, *Listen Little Man* (New York: Orgone Press, 1948); and J. H. Goldthorpe, "Attitudes and Behavior of Car Assembly Workers," *British Journal of Sociology* 17 (1966): 227–44.

27. Elsworth F. Baker, *Man in the Trap* (New York: Macmillan, 1967), part 4.

28. Reich, *The Sexual Revolution*.

29. See the discussion of the husband-economic-provider role in this chapter.

30. Marvin B. Sussman and Betty E. Cogswell, "Family Influences on Job Movement," *Human Relations* 24 (1971): 477–88.

31. Harry Magdoff, *The Age of Imperialism* (New York: Monthly Review Press, 1969); Gunnar Myrdal, *The Challenge of World Poverty* (London: Pen-

guin, 1971), and Andre Gunder Frank, "Sociology of Development and Underdevelopment of Sociology," *Catalyst* 3 (1967): 20–73.

32. See Dennis Wrong, "The Oversocialized Conception of Man in Modern Sociology," *American Sociological Review* 26, no. 2 (April 1961): 183–92; and Alexander Lowen, *The Betrayal of the Body* (New York: Macmillan, 1967).

33. For further development of some of the concepts outlined here, see Erik Grønseth, "Economic Family Policies in Norway and Its Guiding Images: Inconsistencies and Consequences," in *National Family Guiding Images and Policies*, ed. B. de Bie and J. Preslevou (Belgium: Louvain University, 1967), pp. 55 ff.

34. As basically described in Parsons and Bales, *Family, Socialization and Interaction Process*, chap. 1. See also C. C. Harris, *The Family* (London: Allen, 1969).

35. See Michael P. Fogarty, *Sex, Family and Career* (London: Sage Publications, 1970); and Margret Polomas' chapter in *Family Issues of Employed Women in Europe and America*, ed. Andree Michel (Leyden: Brill, 1971). It would not solve the economic predicament of single mothers, however, nor the present economic discrimination against complete families with dependent children.

36. See Talcott Parsons, "The Kinship System of Contemporary United States," in Parsons, *Essays in Sociological Theory, Pure and Applied* (New York: Free Press, 1954).

37. There is nothing to indicate that the husband-economic-provider role is not also the basic economic responsibility for child-care pattern in the Eastern state capitalist countries, although it seems more extensively modified in the direction of a parent-economic-provider role, in that the percent of working married mothers is considerably higher than in the private capitalist countries (except Finland). In the kibbutzim the husband-economic-provider role has, of course, been abolished, but these communities are not industrialized societies. Also in some "people's communes" in China, a total-societal-economic-provider role may have been realized. Dysfunctional consequences of kibbutz and Chinese communal child rearing should probably not be attributed to the total-societal-economic-provider role, but to the specific *child-care* pattern with which it has been combined—and specifically to the extremely early and extensive mother-deprivation of infants, at least in the kibbutzim.

38. See Malinowski, "Principle of Parenthood."

39. For an argument that holds this function to be derivative of a more basic reproductory function see Robert F. Winch, *The Modern Family* (New York: Holt, Rinehart, Winston, 1963).

40. See previous section in this chapter dealing with partial supplements to the husband-economic-provider role.

41. For an analysis of women's position in terms of these four realms, see Juliet Mitchell, *The Longest Revolution* (London: New Left Review, 1964). Only when the sum of supplementary sources of provision has grown so large that the husband's share is no greater than that of most other working people, and when fully adequate alternatives are regularly available in cases where a husband's provision is not available, could the husband-economic-provider role be abolished. Only then could a total-society-economic-provider role be said to be instituted.

42. This would be one essential way of meeting Juliet Mitchell's call for a continuation of the family differentiation described by Parsons. See Parsons and Bales, *Family, Socialization and Interaction Process*. The specifically future economic-provider patterns (as well as child-care patterns) may be differentiated from the family. See Mitchell, *Longest Revolution*.

43. The following pages represent (apart from a few minor adaptations and some deletions) a reprinting of most of the author's article "The Husband Provider Role: A Critical Appraisal," in *Family Issues of Employed Women in Europe and America*, ed. Andree Michel (Leyden: Brill, 1971). Reprinted with the kind permission of the publisher.

44. For a survey and theoretical analysis of a substantial part of this literature, see Harriet Holter, *Sex Roles and Social Structure* (Oslo: Universitetsforlaget, 1969), chap. 10.

45. It must be noted that here and elsewhere "consequence" is used in a wide and tentative sense. The effects attributed to the husband-economic-provider role are often highly indirect or conditioned by one or more intervening as well as ramifying variables. Also, the consequences will often by rather general ones, in need of much further specification and qualification.

46. To the extent that some of these consequences already have been related to the similar phenomena of the "husband occupational role" (Parsons), or the "male provider role" (Bonnevie) or to modern "patriarchy" (Reich), my contribution consists in trying to bring previously established, disparate findings and conjectures into one integrated, more specific husband-economic-provider-role point of view, and into a corresponding, more comprehensive husband-economic-provider-role interpretation. More specifically, my proposition is that *more than any other* sex-differentiating phenomenon—given the private or state capitalist industrial societies—the husband-economic-provider role is at present at the social structural *root* of most of the *other* main sex-differentiating phenomena, and of their functional and dysfunctional consequences, as well as at the root of some additional dysfunctional phenomena not usually attributed to any kind of sex differentiation at all (such as today's elitist, authoritarian political structures).

47. That the husband-economic-provider role historically has its roots in similar, but other circumstances, is another question.

48. For a general discussion of economic family policy measures, see Alva Myrdal, *Nation and Family* (Cambridge, Mass.: MIT Press, 1968); and James Vadakin, *Children, Poverty and Family Allowances* (New York: Basic Books, 1968).

49. The husband-economic-provider-role consequences for other sex-role aspects, located primarily outside the family, will be considered in later sections.

50. Marvin B. Sussman and Lee Burchinal, "Kin Family Network," *Marriage and Family Living* 24 (1962): 231–39.

51. G. Palm, *Indoktrineringen i Sverige* (Stockholm, 1968).

52. H. Schelsky, *Wandlungen der Deutschen Familie in der Gegenwart* (Stuttgart, 1955).

53. Parsons and Bales, *Family, Socialization and Interaction Process*, p. 13.

54. Erik Grønseth, "Research on Socialization in Norway," *Family Process* 3 (1964).

55. Erik H. Erikson, *Childhood and Society* (New York: Norton, 1950).

56. Parsons, *Essays in Sociological Theory*.

57. Elizabeth Bott, *Family and Social Network* (London: Tavistock, 1957).

58. Parsons and Bales, *Family, Socialization and Interaction Process*, p. 24. The same conclusion is reached by Holmberg, *Kon Elder Kynne* (Stockholm, 1965).

59. Mogey, "Family and Community in Urban, Industrial Societies," pp. 501–34.

60. Lee Rainwater et al., *And the Poor Get Children* (New York: Quadrangle Books, 1960).

61. Parsons, *Essays in Sociological Theory*, and H. Rodman, *Marriage, Family and Society* (New York: Random House, 1965), p. 274.

62. Parsons, *Essays in Sociological Theory*, pp. 90 and 95.

63. Talcott Parsons, "The Social Structure of the Family," in *The Family: Its Function and Destiny*, ed. Ruth N. Anshen (New York: Harper & Row, 1949).

64. See Fogarty, *Sex, Family and Career*.

65. Alva Myrdal and Viola Klein, *Women's Two Roles* (London: Routledge & Kegan Paul, 1956).

66. Helen Hacker, "The New Burden of Masculinity," *Marriage and Family Living* 19 (1957): 227–33.

67. Holter, *Sex Roles and Social Structure.*

68. The consequences of a husband-economic-provider-role pattern will be greatly affected by the degree to which it has *monopoly* on the economic provision. This obviously depends on the degree to which it is supplemented by economic provisions from sources other than the husband and, more important, upon the existence of alternative patterns of economic responsibility for child care for families that cannot live up to husband-economic-provider-role expectations. Furthermore, the husband-economic-provider role will have different *consequences* for individual families, depending upon the socioeconomic and cultural context in which it occurs. It is generally worse, for instance, for poor or single-mother families in a society like the United States with its "underdeveloped" collective social and welfare responsibilities. It is generally better for such families in welfare states. See Dorothy R. Blitsten, *The World of the Family* (New York: Random House, 1963), chap. 8. We do not, however, have occasion to go much into such distinctions in the following generalizing, partly hypothesizing and conjectural presentation, based most closely on the United States and Scandinavian situations.

69. See Margrete Bonnevie, *Patriarkatets Siste Skanse* (Oslo, 1948).

70. Astrid Schonberg, *The Concept of the Breadwinner* (Stockholm: Hertha, 1969), p. 12.

71. Ibid.

72. This discrimination does not occur with employed women as it does with married women *with children* who do all or most of the child-care work, since there is much more economic discrimination against this child-care work.

73. See Grønseth, "Economic Family Policies in Norway and Its Guiding Images."

74. For an analysis of the varying legal conceptions of the provider role and of economic dependency in European countries (especially Denmark), see Inger Marie Pedersen, *Forsorgerbegrebet Betaenknins* (Copenhagen, 1966), and Grønseth, "Economic Family Policies in Norway and Its Guiding Images."

75. Only recently in Scandinavia a parent's expenses for child care have become deductible from taxable income—as are other such expenses.

76. This discrimination also affects the father (and children) when the mother is doing the main child care, because the lack of pay for child-care work from other than the husband-provider source is an essential aspect of the total discrimination against families with dependent children.

77. One exception to the general sociological neglect of this phenomenon is Edmund Dahlstrom, ed., *The Changing Roles of Men and Women* (London: Duckworth, 1967).

78. Vadakin, *Children, Poverty and Family Allowances*.

79. In Norway in 1960 about 60 percent of the unmarried mothers were gainfully employed, as opposed to 10 percent of the married women.

80. In Norway about one-third of the women giving birth outside marriage place the child for adoption. See Else Oyen, *Ugifte Mødre* (Oslo, 1967).

81. In discussing these interrelationships, a distinction should be drawn between an enforced dependency on the one hand and a voluntary dependence on the other.

82. Such general economic dependency of children and mothers *upon having a husband-father* may also exist *independently* of the husband-economic-provider role. Furthermore, social conditions other than the husband-economic-provider role may mean that a husband-father and a marriage is necessary in order to get a solid basis for economic provision. This seems to have been the case in the patriarchal Europe prior to industrialization and prior to the introduction of the husband-economic-provider role.

83. The often prohibitive cost of additional housing alone may be decisive.

84. Peter C. Pines, "Disenchantment in the Later Years of Marriage," *Marriage and Family Living* 23 (1961): 3–11. See also Reich, *The Sexual Revolution*, chap. 7.

85. Parsons has pointed out that this type of solidarity is functional for the occupational and societal order *as it now is*, since it is a precondition for "adequate" socialization to this order. See Parsons and Bales, *Family, Socialization and Interaction Process*. However, Reich has shown the basic bio-psycho-social "dysfunctions" of these compulsive elements in marriage. See Reich, *The Sexual Revolution*.

86. This reasoning rests on the assumption that class differences in divorce frequencies also exist among families with economically dependent children—a question in need of further research.

87. Parsons and Bales, *Family, Socialization and Interaction Process*, chap. 1.

88. Parsons, *Essays in Sociological Theory*, p. 100.

89. Parsons and Bales, *Family, Socialization and Interaction Process*,, p. 22.

90. Ibid., p. 21.

91. Parsons, "Incest Taboo."

92. G. Kooy, *Enforced Marriages* (Wageningen, 1969). Mimeographed.

93. William J. Goode, *After Divorce* (New York: Free Press, 1956); and Robert O. Blood, *Marriage* (New York: Collier-Macmillan, 1969).

94. See Reich, *The Sexual Revolution*, and Alexander Lowen, *Love and Orgasm* (New York: Macmillan, 1965).

95. Parsons, *Essays in Sociological Theory*.

96. Ira L. Reiss, *The Social Context of Premarital Sexual Permissiveness* (New York: Holt, Rinehart, Winston, 1967), p. 172.

97. Ira L. Reiss, *Premarital Sexual Standards in America* (New York: Free Press, 1964).

98. One notable exception is Hallowell Pope and Dean Knudsen, "Premarital Sexual Norms, the Family and Social Change," *Journal of Marriage and the Family* 27 (1965): 314–23; and "Letters to the Editor," *Journal of Marriage and the Family* 28 (1966): 5–6.

99. Ibid., pp. 314–20.

100. Whenever divorces occur, the emotionally destructive upheavals, fights over children, and economic arrangements seem considerably sharpened by the husband-economic-provider-role circumstances. The turmoil is partly motivated in neurotic emotional attachments, based in the partners' own childhood family husband-economic-provider-role constellations.

101. It should be noted that an essential aspect of Parsons', as well as Freud's, direct argument for the unavoidability of a severe childhood sexual repression due to the incest taboo rests on their ignoring exactly this possibility of the children's sexual love attachment with each other. Parsons' other argument here really rests on the unnecessary assumption of an unavoidable tendency to a neurotically fixated and repressive dependency of the infant upon the mother. See Parsons, "The Incest Taboo," and Grønseth, "Some Remarks on Parsons' Conception of Sexuality and Socialization."

102. Baker, *Man in the Trap*; and Paul and Jean Ritter, *The Free Family* (London: Gollancz, 1956).

103. M. Duverger, *The Political Role of Women* (Paris: UNESCO, 1956); and G. Palm, *Indoktrineringen* (Stockholm, 1968).

104. Palm, *Indoktrineringen*.

105. A chief psychological mechanism is the formation of sexual and authority-fixations to the oppressive parent(s), fixations that in adult life become generalized and transferred to the authorities in family, work and political life. See Reich, *The Sexual Revolution*. Another mechanism is the increased suggestibility and consequent openness to authoritarian and mass media manipulation to which sexual repression gives rise. See Ingjald Nissen, *Seksualitet og Disiplin* (Oslo, 1934).

106. This by means of direct chronic muscular tension—the muscular armoring being functionally identical with the psychic defense mechanisms. See Wilhelm Reich, *Character Analysis* (London: Orgone Press, 1945).

107. See Reich, *The Function of the Orgasm*, pp. 148–63.

108. Parsons might have also added the function of keeping the married women as a flexible labor force reserve for employment and unemployment according to fluctuations in the economy and in the labor market.

109. See Parsons, *The Social System* (New York: Free Press, 1951), pp. 133–43.

110. On the one hand the *compensatory* masculinity which Parsons thinks is the motivational basis for the male's occupational performance, and on the other hand the more basic and general sex repression already common at the oral stage in both sexes, as implied in Parsons', "Incest Taboo."

111. With regard to America in particular, Parsons' assessment is very different, for instance, from Gunnar Myrdal's in his account of "The American Creed," where not only "individualism" but *rationality*, the classic *humanitarian* values, and the Golden Rule are the dominant elements. See Gunnar Myrdal, *An American Dilemma* (New York: Harper, 1947), pp. xlvii–xlviii.

112. Reich, *The Mass Psychology of Fascism.*

113. See Reich, *The Function of the Organism*, and Grønseth, "Some Remarks on Parsons' Conception of Sexuality and Socialization."

9

THE LEGAL INSTITUTION

The Legitimizing Appendage

Leon Shaskolsky

All modern industrial societies possess an intricate network of written laws and an intertwining framework of institutions created for the purpose of formulating, interpreting, and implementing those laws. In practical terms, few would challenge the need and desirability of law and legal institutions. Philosophically and ideologically, however, diverse approaches have been adopted with respect to the meaning of law in society, the source of its authority, and its ultimate purpose.

For some, law is an inviolable precept to be implicitly and automatically obeyed; for others, a set of rules to be examined and, if necessary, challenged or even deliberately flouted. For some, law is the embodiment of the highest aspirations of morality shared by all members of a society; for others, it is the means by which the privileges of the few are preserved while control over the many is assured. For some, law is a quest for justice; for others, a search for order. For some, law is an expression of the will of the people; for others, a manifestation of the will of the authorities. For some, law is a lodestar guiding men in their everyday actions; for others, it is a coercive instrument inhibiting the natural propensity of men to do good. Some see law as a means of ensuring freedom; others see it is an instrument of repression.

Any analysis of the legal institutions of a particular country must thus be predicated on certain assumptions about law, both in its general intent as a universal aspect of all societies and in its specific implementation in any one society.

Diverse as the various approaches to law are, four distinct orientations may be delineated:

1. Law is a striving after some greater good, e.g., justice, order, or approximation to divine command.

2. Law is a given, to be accepted on its own terms without reference to any larger goals or normative values.

3. Law is closely bound to the values of the society, seeking to implement the everyday needs of the citizens by expressing, at any particular time, the fluctuating will of the people.

4. Law is an instrument for furthering the interests of certain groups within society, thus lacking those noble ideals attributed to it by the first approach, lacking the basic legitimacy assumed for it by the second approach, and lacking the practical advantages suggested by the third approach.

Differing Philosophical Approaches to Law

The original basis for many of the approaches in the first, or natural law, group may be traced back to the historical roots of Western civilization. For the Hebrew prophets, law was inextricably linked to the idea of morality as part of a divine plan; for the Greek philosophers, it was an attempt to seek out absolute justice; for the Roman jurists, it was the means by which order in human relations was achieved. For many Christian philosophers, the task of law was the incorporation of natural law principles into human legal systems; human laws should be aimed at enacting the eternal moral verities contained in natural law, and in the event of a flagrant disparity between the two, the secular law could be called into question. Thus, Augustine contended that an unjust law is no law at all, and no better than the activities of a robber band.[1] The continuation of this approach underlies most modern arguments for civil disobedience, such as the syllogism put forth by Martin Luther King, Jr.: "Any law that uplifts human personality is just. Any law that degrades human personality is unjust. All segregation statutes are unjust because segregation distorts the soul and damages the personality. . . . So I can urge men to disobey segregation ordinances because they are morally wrong." [2]

In contrast to this approach is one which presents law at its face value, devoid of any basis in morality or justice or any other absolute principle. In the words of Thomas Hobbes, "Law properly is the word of him that by right hath command over others." [3] For Hobbes law *is* morality; without the law there is no morality, only the self-seeking desires of egoistic individuals. This attitude laid the foundation for the positivist school of jurisprudence, whose foremost exponent, John Austin, believed that "law, properly so called, is the command of the sovereign." [4] Later Hans Kelsen developed the Pure Theory of Law, with its search for a *Grundnorm*, the basic foundation upon which a whole legal system is built.[5] A similar analysis may be noted in the work of Max Weber, who was concerned not with the goals of law but with the basis of its authority, and who pointed out that legal power may rest on one of three bases: traditional, rational, or charismatic.[6]

A third view, represented by the European school of historical jurisprudence and the American school of sociological jurisprudence, sees law as an expression of the will of the people. Savigny, an exponent of the former school, spoke of the law as an expression of the *Volksgeist*—the will of the people—constantly changing according to their moods, beliefs, and sentiments.[7] American jurisprudence has developed its own theories, stressing the sociological considerations involved in understanding law, and ignoring some of the more romantic aspects of European theory.[8]

Emile Durkheim adopted this third approach when attempting to show the close relationship that exists between the nature of a society and the type of law it gives rise to. He drew a correlation between the increasing division of labor and the development of legal relationships from repressive to restitutive in nature. As men, because of the division of labor, become more dependent on each other, and as society changes from one of mechanical solidarity, based on the similarities among its members, to organic solidarity, based on the differences among them, the emphasis in legal relationships is shifted from criminal law, with its repressive tendencies, to restitutive civil law.[9]

The Radical Approach

The fourth approach to law agrees that law does indeed have a clear-cut purpose but contends that this purpose is not the attainment of absolute ideals, nor the satisfaction of practical needs, nor the expression of a social spirit, but the enhancement of the interests of those dominant groups in society that have access to the power structure, including the institutions where law is legislated, adjudicated, and enforced.

Two major schools of thought fall under this heading: anarchism, with its contempt for all formalized rules, and Marxism, which condemns all the institutional paraphernalia of bourgeois society. These two philosophies will be examined in some detail, since they will serve as the basis for analyzing the manner in which legal institutions in the United States have carried out the mandate entrusted to them.

Philosophical anarchists believe that the state and its myriad institutions are an affront to the dignity of man and an assault upon his liberty, his individuality, his creativity, and his spontaneity. Man cannot fulfill himself when he is constantly encumbered by institutions that attempt, at the least, to guide him and, at the worst, to control him. Law and legal institutions are examples par excellence of the manner in which the state imposes its values on its citizens and forces their compliance. Law is a rigid set of rules whose initial intent and ultimate achievement is to ensure conformity and to undermine the uniqueness of each individual. Such intent and achievement are, of course, never spelled out specifically, as the law subtly coopts many of the prevailing norms and mores of society. By expressing and enforcing some of society's widely held values, the law arrogates to itself the right to express and enforce *all* values; gaining sufficient allegiance from the populace for it to delve into other areas, it finally claims precedence over individual conscience. Says Kropotkin:

> All laws have a *double origin*, and it is precisely this double origin which distinguishes them from customs established by usage and representing the principles of morality existing in a particular society at a particular epoch. Law confirms these customs; it crystallizes them; but at the same time it takes advantage of these generally approved customs, in order to introduce in disguise, under their sanction, some new institution that is entirely to the advantage of the military and governing minorities. For instance, Law introduces, or gives sanction to, slavery, caste, paternal, priestly, and military authority; or else it smuggles in serfdom and, later on, subjection to the State. By this means, Law has always succeeded in imposing a yoke on man without his perceiving it, a yoke that he has never been able to throw off save by means of revolution.[10]

In rejecting the validity of laws, anarchism does not deny the need for justice and morality. On the contrary, it holds that true justice can be attained only when there is complete equality, not the inequality so often engendered by stratification patterns of industrial states as sanctioned by the law. True morality is that which flows from the free operation of the conscience, guided by the individual's own search for what is good and right, not determined by artificial ethical standards laid down by those in authority. Indeed, as Hocking has suggested, "so far as the state requires good of men it *deprives that good of moral value.*" [11]

An act, then, can be considered good in its own right only when it flows from the inner conviction of the actor, not from the external imposition of the state. The more the law attempts to intervene in the sphere of morality, the more it is likely to undermine the moral climate of society. For the anarchist, "it would be true to say, as many have who have addressed themselves to the nature of human morality, that making certain behavior illegitimate is the very cause of its performance." [12] Modern criminologists have taken this "forbidden fruits" argument even further. Criticizing the overlegislation that is characteristic of today's society, Schur and Morris and

Hawkins contend that the best way to reduce the crime rate would be to abolish those laws which, in their effort to enforce so-called moral standards, actually interfere with the private behavior of individuals.[13]

Although anarchism professes a revulsion against all institutional controls, much of its criticism is reserved specifically for the institutions set up by capitalist society. A typical example is Kropotkin's analysis of the laws of nineteenth-century industrial nations:

> The major portion have but one object—to protect private property, i.e., wealth acquired by the exploitation of man by man. Their aim is to open out to capital fresh fields for exploitation, and to sanction the new forms which that exploitation continually assumes, as capital swallows up another branch of human activity, railways, telegraphs, electric lights, chemical industries, the expression of man's thought in literature and science, etc. The object of the rest of these laws is fundamentally the same. They exist to keep up the machinery of government which serves to secure to capital the exploitation and monopoly of the wealth produced. Magistrature, police, army, public instruction, finance, all serve one God—capital; all have but one object—to facilitate the exploitation of the worker by the capitalist. Analyze all the laws passed and you will find nothing but this.[14]

Even those laws that seem ostensibly to provide an extension of man's freedom are no more than a restoration of liberties possessed by man before the ruthless onslaught of broad legislative enactments by powerful nation-states. And such laws actually provide no more than a modicum of the freedom possessed by men who once lived in small communities and city-states.[15]

Formidable though Kropotkin's argument may have been, it was Karl Marx who gave the economic theory of law its most thorough exposition. Marx contended that a full understanding of any society could be gained only when one realized that the basis of social life was embedded in the economic structure of that society. The economic infrastructure is generally not discernible to the masses of people, since it is hidden by an extensive, all-embracing, and attractive superstructure created for the purpose of both furthering the interests of the dominant economic classes and camouflaging the nature and extent of their domination. Marx's attitude is stated succinctly: "I was led by my studies to the conclusion that legal relations as well as forms of state could neither be understood by themselves, nor explained by the so-called general progress of the human mind, but that they are rooted in the material conditions of life." Thus, "the totality of these relations of production constitutes the economic structure of society—the real foundation on which legal and political superstructures arise and to which definite forms of social consciousness correspond." [16]

Few aspects of the superstructure have such significance as the legal institutions. Other aspects—philosophy, art, religion, literature—have undoubted persuasive capacities, both enticing and cajoling the masses to respect and preserve existing institutions and standards. But law not only presents an attractive portrayal of the status quo; it also has the power to enforce obedience, particularly upon those individuals who do not succumb to the blandishments of the superstructure. *Law thus becomes the ultimate means of ensuring adherence to the prevailing values when all other approaches have failed to achieve this objective.*

Laws are regarded as a means of buttressing the interests of the economically dominant factions within a society, and at the same time possessing sufficient attractiveness to gain and hold the allegiance of the lesser privileged classes. In order to appreciate the significance of a law, the motivation for passing it, and the pressures for enforcing it, one must analyze the structure of the society to determine where the economic power resides.

This approach has been used by Rusche and Kirshheimer to show the close relationship that has existed throughout history between the economic needs of society and the types of punishment meted out to criminals. Banishment and transportation, for example, were used to dispose of surplus population; convicted criminals were put to work manning galleys until the advent of the sailing ship rendered such labor superfluous; the idea of prison labor gained credence and currency in the early stages of industrialization, since it contributed to increased production.[17]

Barrington Moore, Jr., has used a similar Marxist perspective in explaining the manner in which the English aristocracy in the seventeenth and eighteenth centuries implemented the policy of enclosures, thereby totally and finally destroying the underprivileged peasant class. Superficially acknowledging the force of the law and abiding by legal precepts, the aristocracy nevertheless derived the maximum benefit from such legality and deprived the peasants of their few remaining rights:

> It was Parliament that ultimately controlled the process of enclosure. Formally the procedures by which a landlord put through an enclosure by act of Parliament were public and democratic. Actually the big property owners dominated the proceedings from start to finish. Thus the consent of "three-fourths to four-fifths" was required on the spot before Parliament would approve a proposal to enclose. But consent of what? The answer turns out to be property, not people. Suffrages were not counted, but weighed. One large proprietor could swamp an entire community of smaller proprietors and cottagers.[18]

Moore notes that there has been some disputation among historians as to the manner in which the legislation relating to enclosures was enacted. Some thinkers argue that this revolutionary change in English social and economic life was instituted only after strict compliance with the principles of democracy, as understood at that time; other, more radical theorists hold that the deliberations and decisions of Parliament showed clear bias and even corruption. However, as Moore neatly suggests, the best case for the radical approach is to be found in the kind of arguments advanced by those who claim that the change was induced through democratic means. Moore quotes an article by Tate, who presents his support of the democratic point of view in the following manner: "There seems no reason to suppose that injustice was done on account of the private self-interest of the members concerned, *except insofar as injustice must necessarily occur to some extent when, in a class society, members of one class legislate concerning the livelihoods and properties of those occupying a very different position in the social order.*" [19]

The Marxist school is not concerned exclusively with civil law; indeed, some of Marx's most trenchant criticisms of the legal system were reserved for his analysis of criminal law. According to this view, not only is the law in general oriented toward the needs of the upper classes and toward the preservation of the rights of property and the free operation of a contractual market system, but criminal law itself fulfills a very real economic need in modern society. The status of criminal becomes necessary for society, not only because of the harm that has been caused to society, but also because of the benefits that society derives from this status. The whole administration of justice parasitically feasts off the criminal while it sanctimoniously sits in judgment upon him. Even those in areas far removed from direct involvement in the administration of justice are often gratuitous, and even unknown, beneficiaries of the criminal act. Although this thesis is not the central theme of Marx's analysis of the law, it bears quoting in detail because of the unusual, yet consistent, approach he has adopted:

> A philosopher produces ideas, a poet verses, a parson sermons, a professor text-books, etc. A criminal produces crime. But if the relationship between this latter branch of production and the whole productive activity of society is examined a little more closely one is forced to abandon a number of prejudices. The criminal produces not only crime but also the criminal law; he produces the professor who delivers lectures on this criminal law, and even the inevitable text-book in which the professor presents his lectures as a commodity for sale in the market. There results an increase in material wealth. . . .
>
> Further, the criminal produces the whole apparatus of the police and criminal justice, detectives, judges, executioners, juries, etc., and all these different professions, which constitute so many categories of the social division of labour, develop diverse abilities of the human spirit, create new needs and new ways of satisfying them. Torture itself has provided occasions for the most ingenious mechanical inventions, employing a host of honest workers in the production of these instruments.
>
> The criminal produces an impression now moral, now tragic, and renders a "service" by arousing the moral and aesthetic sentiments of the public. He produces not only text-books on criminal law, the criminal law itself, and thus legislators, but also art, literature, novels and the tragic drama, as *Oedipus* and *Richard III*, as well as Mullner's *Schuld* and Schiller's *Rauber*, testify. The criminal interrupts the monotony and security of bourgeois life. Thus he protects it from stagnation and brings forth that restless tension, that mobility of spirit without which the stimulus of competition would itself become blunted. He

therefore gives a new impulse to the productive forces. Crime takes off the labour market a portion of the excess population, diminishes competition among workers, and to a certain extent stops wages from falling below the minimum, while the war against crime absorbs another part of the same population. The criminal therefore appears as one of those natural "equilibrating forces" which establish a just balance and open up a whole perspective of "useful" occupations. The influence of the criminal upon the development of the productive forces can be shown in detail. Would the locksmith's trade have attained its present perfection if there had been no thieves? Would the manufacture of banknotes have arrived at its present excellence if there had been no counterfeiters? Would the microscope have entered ordinary commercial life . . . had there been no forgers? Is not the development of applied chemistry as much due to the adulteration of wares, and to the attempts to discover it, as to honest productive effort? Crime, by its ceaseless development of new means of attacking property calls into existence new measures of defence, and its productive effects are as great as those of strikes in stimulating the invention of machines.[20]

While not as extreme as Marx, a number of recent theorists have given support for his basic contentions. Writers such as George Herbert Mead, Karl Menninger, and Kai T. Erikson have argued cogently that society senses this need for criminals and, therefore, unconsciously or deliberately creates the conditions for the existence of a criminal class.[21] In its treatment of criminals, society often seems to adopt policies calculated to ensure the perpetuation of this behavior. Mead and Erikson ask very pertinently whether society is actually attempting to ensure that its need for criminals will be fulfilled. More specifically, Becker's probing of the operations of laws such as the Marihuana Tax Act of 1937 indicates that this law not only created a new type of crime, but gave extra power and authority to the Federal Bureau of Narcotics, provided work for thousands of agents, and, in the course of time, became a self-serving institutional structure. Becker tends to support Marx's thesis when he suggests that some law enforcers "may not be interested in the content of the rule as such, but only in the fact that the existence of the rule provides [them] with a job, a profession and a raison d'être." [22]

The theoretical perspectives of Kropotkin and Marx are unequivocal in their assessment that laws are used primarily as an exploitative device by the dominant groups in society. The masses, however, are not only exploited by the laws, but are also manipulated into accepting them as the embodiment of the highest ideals of their society—a guarantor of law and order and the means by which equality is ensured for all, since the law ostensibly treats all, rich and poor, haughty and humble, with objective consistency.

It is now necessary to examine to what extent the approach adopted by Kropotkin, Marx, and their respective followers may be vindicated and substantiated by the empirical operation of the legal system in the United States.

Legal Institutions in the United States

The basic thesis to be explored will be that, inasmuch as the laws are open to interpretation, the legal institutions in the United States have consistently favored the interests of the economically powerful; have stressed the superior nature of private rights over the public welfare; have elevated the concept of property to a status akin to sacred; have provided the legal basis for the smooth operation of a free enterprise economy (while simultaneously permitting the surreptitious development of large monopolistic corporations and burgeoning conglomerates); have hindered the legitimate aspirations of deprived groups such as workers, blacks, and various classes of deviants; have tolerated an inequitable enforcement of the criminal law; and have responded more to the pressures for conservative retention of the status quo than to the pleadings of those who wished to effect peaceful and progressive change.

It is quite true that during the period when Earl Warren was chief justice, a host of far-reaching transformations in the realm of civil rights was induced by liberal decisions in which the Supreme Court acted as a catalytic agent for progressive advances. Yet it should not be forgotten that many of these decisions basically redressed wrongs perpetrated and perpetuated by government agencies, including the courts themselves. Thus, the key decisions in criminal law of *Gideon*, *Escobedo*, and *Miranda* were direct responses to long-standing abuses by various police forces throughout the country, while *Brown* v. *Board of Education* made amends for a fifty-eight-year-old decision that had provided the legal basis for the continued practice of segregation, with all its deleterious effects. Indeed, until the Warren Court, the constitutional requirement of "due process of law" had been applied with far more diligence to the protection of property than to the protection of life and liberty.

Henry Steele Commager, a "consensus" historian, sums up the Court's role with a calm appraisal that is also a devastating indictment: "That the sanctity of private property was ordained by natural law was assumed by economists in Europe and America alike; in America alone that assumption was transfigured into a doctrine of constitutional law." [23] The end effect of the due process clause was, to paraphrase Justice Holmes, the enactment of Spencer's *Social Statics* (a treatise extolling ruthless individualism) into constitutional dogma.[24]

The Economic Basis of the Constitution

Before looking at the actual workings of the Courts in the United States, it is advisable to examine briefly the document in which judicial authority is grounded and which has materially affected judicial decision-making.

In his 1913 study, *An Economic Interpretation of the Constitution of the United States*, Charles A. Beard, one of America's leading historians, attempted to posit the personal and group advantages that accrued to the sponsors and supporters of the Constitution. His analysis, influenced, as he concedes in his preface, by Marx's theories, and stimulated by the academic aspiration to search for truth, touched off an ongoing debate in the ranks of historians and constitutional lawyers.

The thesis of Beard's book is succinctly stated in its concluding pages:

> The movement for the Constitution of the United States was originated and carried through principally by four groups of personal interests which had been adversely affected under the Articles of Confederation: money, public securities, manufactures, and trade and shipping. . . .
>
> A large propertyless mass was, under the prevailing suffrage qualifications, excluded at the outset from participation (through representatives) in the work of framing the Constitution.

The members of the Philadelphia Convention which drafted the Constitution were, with a few exceptions, immediately, directly, and personally interested in, and derived economic advantage from, the establishment of the new system.

The Constitution was essentially an economic document based upon the concept that the fundamental private rights of property are anterior to government and morally beyond the reach of popular majorities.

The major portion of the members of the Convention are on record as recognizing the claim of property to a special and defensive position in the Constitution.[25]

Beard's thesis is predicated on the idea that in industrial societies the basic needs of citizens lie in the protection of their property interests, and that protection from personal danger and bodily harm become of only secondary significance. (Interestingly, Beard makes no mention of the need for law to provide guarantees of free speech, freedom of movement and assembly, etc.) Thus, "inasmuch as the primary object of a government, beyond the mere repression of physical violence, is the making of rules which determine the property relations of members of a society, the dominant classes whose rights are thus to be determined must perforce obtain from the government such rules as are consonant with the larger interests necessary to the continuance of their economic processes." [26] Since power was to be shared among the populace at large through elections, it became necessary for the dominant classes to ensure their control over the organs of government by writing into the Constitution adequate protection of their interests.

Beard finds philosophical substantiation for his pioneering study in the writings of James Madison, a participant at the Philadelphia Convention. In *The Federalist Papers* Madison stated clearly that part of the task of a state was to protect the inequalities arising from property rights. Noting the problems involved in assuring an identity of interests among all citizens, he argued that

the diversity in the faculties of men, from which the rights of property originate, is not less an insuperable obstacle to a uniformity of interests. The protection of these faculties is the first object of government. From the protection of different and unequal faculties of acquiring property, the possession of different degrees and kinds of property immediately results; and from the influence of these on the sentiments and views of the respective proprietors, ensues a division of society into different interests and parties. . . . The regulation of these various and interfering interests forms the principal task of modern legislation.[27]

Those who opposed the ideology of the Federalists and fought the adoption of the Constitution were no more idealistic, according to Beard, than were its proponents. The conflict over the Constitution was not between high-minded visionaries and hard-headed realists, nor between larger national and narrow sectional interests, but between opposing economic groups represented by "a popular party based on paper money and agrarian interests, and a conservative party centered in the towns and resting on financial, mercantile and personal property interests generally." [28]

Beard's provocative analysis has come under attack, perhaps most notably by Forrest McDonald, who in his book *We the People* attempts to refute Beard's thesis by an examination of the social and economic backgrounds of the framers of the Constitution. McDonald claims that the framers were a far more heterogeneous group than Beard had depicted them to be, that their attitudes lacked any of the kind of consistency necessary to sustain Beard's thesis, and that many of them were adversely affected by the final provisions incorporated into the Constitution.[29]

Another opponent of the Beard thesis is Robert E. Brown, who, unlike McDonald, asserts that there was indeed a great deal of homogeneity in the framers' backgrounds. This he attributes to the fact that the United States was at that time almost a classless society, with little differentiation between the various strata. Therefore, the delegates, in serving their own interests, would automatically be serving the interests of all citizens. "For good or bad," Brown writes, "America in 1787 was a country in which most men were middle class property owners, especially the owners of real estate. . . . Having fought the Revolution to preserve a society based on the natural rights of life, liberty and property, it is not at all surprising that they would adopt a Constitution which provided for the protection of property. In fact, had the people suspected that the Constitution would not protect property, I doubt that it would have had the slightest chance of adoption." [30] Here is another example—like the quotation cited earlier with reference to the enclosure system in England—of a kind of argumentation aimed at downgrading the economic forces at work in molding the law which, in fact, only serves to buttress the economic thesis. One does not know, for instance, whether the disenfranchised members of early America—the propertyless whites and the enslaved blacks—would have shown the same enthusiasm for the constitutional provisions as did those whose votes ratified (in some states, only by narrow margins) the Constitution.

The importance of property and of economic considerations continued to play a role in the adoption of additions to the Constitution. Many historians have argued that some of the amendments, ostensibly enlarging the liberties of individuals, were designed primarily for the protection of property rights. The most blatant example of such dual functions was the Fourteenth Amendment which, in the wake of the Civil War, was supposed to provide the black community in the southern states with adequate safeguards against oppressive acts of local authorities. Howard Smith, author of *Economic History of the United States*, maintains that the true reason behind the adoption of the Fourteenth Amendment was not to protect the newly won rights of Negroes, but to defend growing industry against any future governmental controls: "When it is recalled that the amendment was presented as a 'package' to be accepted or rejected as a whole, the intent of the procedure becomes . . . suspect. The attention of everyone was to be centered on the problem of the poor unfortunate Negro while at the same time a special protection for the vigorous and not at all unfortunate corporation was to be given constitutional sanction." [31]

New economic developments, increasing utilization of technology, and accumulation of capital were rendering ever more important the protection of large corporations against interference, not only from the federal government (such protection had already been given in the Bill of Rights) but also against any inroads that covetous local governments might wish to make in the form of taxation and regulatory enactments. Hence Smith's claim that, far from providing a basis for racial equality, "the passage of the Fourteenth Amendment can be referred to as the definitive beginnings of American laissez-faire." [32]

The debate between the Beardians and their opponents has not been resolved. Nevertheless, it would seem that Beard's thesis has supplied an important perspective for looking at the Constitution and at the manner in which it has been used as a basis for day-to-day judicial reasoning. Indeed, the real test of a radical analysis of American legal institutions must be based not so much on the motivations of the nation's founders and the framers of its Constitution as on the way subsequent generations have utilized those institutions. What interpretations have been given to some of the ennobling phraseology of the Constitution? What pattern of responses emerges from the decrees of judges? What interests have been served by the accumulation of judicial precedents? What kind of protection and advantages have been provided for the property and personal rights of citizens? In the final analysis, it is the decisions of judges that give tangible import to the abstract and amorphous intent of legislation.

The Judiciary in the United States

The impact of judge-made law is more marked in the United States than in most other Western industrial states because of a number of factors unique to the American judicial experience: the existence of a written constitution guaranteeing certain rights, the concept of checks and balances among the three major branches of government, the principle of judicial review, and the importance of political philosophy in the appointment of judges. Political battles lost in the electoral and legislative arena may often be pursued in the more refined atmosphere of judicial confrontation. The role of judges in the United States was exemplified in the candid admission of one of America's greatest jurists, Justice Holmes, who said, "When socialism first began to be talked about, the comfortable classes of the community were a great deal frightened. I suspect that this fear has influenced judicial action . . . has led people who no longer hope to control the legislatures to look to the courts." [33]

Ever since the principle of judicial review was laid down in *Marbury* v. *Madison*, the U.S. Supreme Court has had tremendous power as the third arm of government to guide and lead the nation, and to help formulate and articulate the moral and social values by which the citizens would conduct their lives. The Court has an almost unique power to nullify legislation and to overrule the executive and legislative branches of government. It has the capacity to protect the ordinary citizen against arbitrary and inequitable government actions, to actively create new norms and standards, to ponder and expound on the larger issues involved in specific litigation, and to serve the overall interests of the nation.

In determining the facts of a case, the meaning of a law, and the deeper considerations of justice, the Court is perforce obliged to involve itself in the critical issues of the day. In so doing, it is confronted with the basic dilemma facing all intellectual theorists honestly attempting to relate to the real problems of society. In the view of Karl Mannheim, intellectuals may choose to give ideological support to an extant situation or to challenge society to move on to new utopian vistas.[34] The Warren Court was an example of visionary possibilities applied to the realm of reality, for it gave legal encouragement to the incipient civil rights struggle and intervened to eliminate many long-standing abuses within the system of law enforcement and administration of justice. In fact, by showing what could be done, the Warren Court has thrown into relief the sorry records of earlier courts. Their inequities have become all the more blatant— and all the more tragic in their ultimate consequences. For not only has the end result of the accumulation of Supreme Court decisions been to dispense a host of injustices, but at least one decision, the *Dred Scott* case, is believed to have played a major role in creating the conditions that led to the Civil War.

In recent years the Supreme Court has been inundated with civil rights cases and has given liberal interpretations to constitutional provisions, so as to protect underprivileged individuals and minority groups. Yet in former years those same provisions were used to thwart the needs of the underprivileged and to advance the interests of the powerful. One of the strongest indictments of the Supreme Court's insensitivity to civil rights was made by a law professor who subsequently became a federal judge. Writing in 1937, Edgerton claimed that no federal action had ever been voided merely to protect an individual's civil liberties.

> There is not a case . . . which protected the "civil liberties" of
> freedom of press, speech and assembly. . . . There is not one

which protected the right to vote; on the contrary, congressional attempts to protect the voting rights of Negroes were de-
feated by the Court. There is not one which protected the vital
interests of the working majority of the population in organizing or in wages; on the contrary, congressional efforts to protect
those interests were frustrated by the Court.

In contrast to these examples was a series of acts which *were* nullified
by the Supreme Court:

> One group [of decisions] protected mistreatment of colored peo-
> ple; another group protected business or business methods hurt-
> ful to the majority; another . . . protected owners of business at
> the direct expense of labor; another protected owners of busi-
> ness against taxation; another protected the recipients of sub-
> stantial incomes, gifts, and inheritances against taxation; and
> other cases protected the interests of property owners in other
> ways. Not many cases of any importance fall outside these cate-
> gories.[35]

Despite the significant gains made by the Supreme Court in the
last two decades, there can be little doubt that the overall and cumu-
lative effect of judicial decisions has been to subvert progressive legislation, to hinder moves toward social reform, and to negate the rights
of lesser-privileged sections of society while, conversely, ensuring that
the freedoms enshrined in the Constitution would be interpreted so
as to allow unfettered individualism to pursue its self-seeking ends, to
provide legal justification for the philosophical mystique of property,
and to sanction the free and full enjoyment of the gains of capitalist
profit, unmitigated by social responsibility. An almost random pe-
rusal of court decisions, particularly those of the Supreme Court, reveals the strength of the judges' commitment toward bolstering the
economic position of the rich and the powerful. Time and again one
meets decisions masquerading as high-minded idealism, yet in actuality biased in favor of the privileged classes. The lesser-privileged
have been denied their rights while receiving eloquent assurance of
the consideration afforded their problems and of the benefits that
will accrue to them.

Social Reform and the Courts

The history of social reform in the United States may almost be
written in the form of a struggle between progressive legislation and

conservative judicial interpretation. Numerous legislative measures, hesitantly answering to the needs of the people, were declared null and void, or were rendered impotent, by court decisions. There are countless instances of tense social confrontations which were exacerbated by insensitive judicial decisions. The struggle of the labor movement for recognition was just such a confrontation.

In its initial struggles, the labor movement faced constant frustration as it tried to "work within the system" and to use legislation and peaceful protest to improve the welfare of the working class. Certain gains were made as the agonies of industrialization became increasingly manifest, and the need for government intervention to protect the needy, the poor, and the powerless became more urgent. Yet the courts would generally allow such legislation to stand only when it benefited society at large; where the "beneficiary of the legislation seemed to be labor as a class rather than society as a whole, the courts were apt to register a veto." [36]

The very right of the workers to organize in furtherance of their own interests was continually called into question as detrimental to free trade. In the early part of the nineteenth century, when trade unionism was in its incipient stages, the early pioneers were threatened not only with civil restraining actions, but with criminal indictments generally accusing them of such acts as "conspiracy to increase and augment the prices and rates usually paid and allowed to them" for their labor, or of conspiracy to keep nonorganized workers from employment. One important case during this period was the *Philadelphia Cordwainers'* case, in which the judge relied on traditional laissez faire economic principles to convict a number of workers on charges of criminal conspiracy for trying to organize a union. The reaction of workers to these and other such convictions was fierce: "Mobs of laborers held mock trials of judges and hung them in effigy to show their resentment at being treated as common criminals for having done what they believed they had a perfect right to do. Juries were refusing to convict in some of these prosecutions." [37] The general antagonism reached such a level that by the second half of the century, use of the antiquated doctrine of criminal conspiracy was allowed to lapse (only to be resuscitated in the late 1960s for use in such trials as that of the Chicago Seven).

Criminal conspiracy was replaced by other laws and legal principles designed to destroy the fledgling labor movement. One of the most potent legal weapons was the injunction. Trade unions were constantly embroiled in litigation concerning the right to strike. From the original efforts of Eugene V. Debs to the latter-day militancy of John L. Lewis, trade-union leaders were often the victims of punitive measures taken through the medium of the criminal courts. In the late 1890s a federal judge issued an injunction against Debs, ordering him to call off a strike or face a criminal charge of contempt of court. The case was appealed to the Supreme Court, which dismissed the contention of the defense that Debs had been imprisoned without benefit of a jury trial, and accepted the prosecution's argument that the contempt citation was valid, since Deb's action in calling a strike had interfered with interstate commerce. This case established a precedent for the wholesale use of injunctions in the legal fight against the young trade-union movement, until the Norris-La Guardia Act of 1932 finally put a stop to them. Even so, similar procedures have been widely used in recent years to incarcerate leaders of strikes involving government workers, as such strikes are still not regarded as a legitimate part of the workers' bargaining power.

An example of such legal action against government employees was the 1947 coal miners' strike involving Lewis, who was sent to prison for violating a court injunction. On appeal to the Supreme Court, Lewis claimed that he was immune from contempt of court proceedings under the Norris-La Guardia Act; the Court, however, accepted the government's argument that this Act did not apply, since at the time of the strike the coal mines, which had been seized, were under government control. It is not possible to elaborate on all the legal technicalities involved in this case, but Gregory's comment in summing up the reaction to it is worth noting: "Many lawyers who were completely out of sympathy with the course taken by Lewis and his union nevertheless believed that the Supreme Court had perverted the law of the land by honoring an injunction issued to prevent the continuance of a labor dispute, contrary to the terms of the Norris-La Guardia anti-injunction act." [38]

Further judicial sabotage of social reform measures created to benefit the working class can be seen in the way in which the Supreme Court has used the due process clause to extend rights associated with liberty and, particularly, property to a degree probably never hoped for, perhaps never even envisaged by the property-conscious authors of the Constitution. Liberty and property have consistently been interpreted in as broad a manner as possible, so as to give the Court maximum power to intervene under the due process clause, and then applied empirically in as narrow a manner as possible, so as to favor the dominant economic classes. For example, the right freely to contract for a wage has been called an integral part of an individual's liberty and property. This right to contract has then been used to prevent legislatures from "depriving" workers—including women and children—of the "right" to work long hours at substandard wages. Under this formula state and federal laws designed to achieve shorter working hours were for many years declared unconstitutional. Thus, despite the desire of many legislatures to eliminate sweatshop conditions, the courts provided legal and moral justification for these conditions.

One such decision, handed down in 1895 by the Illinois Supreme Court, and annulling an act providing for an eight-hour day limitation for working women, was severely attacked by a contemporary Chicago newspaper:

> There is a ghastly sort of irony in the attempt of the Supreme
> Court to explain or excuse its decision upon the plea that it is
> protecting the rights of weak individuals with labor to sell. Of
> course, a judicial tribunal cannot be expected to take cogni-
> zance of the facts that working people, in so far as they are rep-
> resented by labor organizations and earnest but unofficial
> friends of the laboring classes, urged the enactment of the law,
> and that millionaire firms attacked its constitutionality. . . .
> What a mockery it is to read that the Supreme Court has de-
> molished this humane, this civilizing law on the plea that it
> robs the poor of their right to sell their labor at will.[39]

Discussing this same case, Ely suggests that "especially irritating is the claim of the judges that they were carrying out the wishes and desires of the wage-earning class when they were really carrying out the schemes of the big firms behind them who had put up their money to defeat the law." [40]

An even more blatant example of the way in which the courts rallied to the aid of conservative business interests is the 1918 Supreme Court decision of *Hammer* v. *Dagenhart*, in which a federal child labor law aimed at eliminating the abuses to which children were subjected in many factories and business corporations was struck down. The bill prohibited work by children under the age of fourteen, and limited the employment of fourteen-to-sixteen-year-olds to an eight-hour day and a six-day week. Clearly beneficial in its social implications, and relatively innocuous in its threat to business interests, the bill nevertheless aroused a great deal of opposition in some sections of the business community. By a narrow 5-4 majority the Supreme Court declared it unconstitutional. It took nearly two decades before this decision was overruled and the United States joined other industrial countries in providing minimum and basic protection to children against unprincipled exploitation.

The evil effects of *Hammer* v. *Dagenhart* upon two whole generations of children are reflected in the anguished cry of Edith Abbott, whose sister had headed the federal Children's Bureau at the time when the original child labor law was invalidated: "Hammer v. Dagenhart is overruled! But what of the army of children who have come and gone from the mills and factories and lumber yards, the millions of weary days of work, and the lost vision of an education to do a proper share of the world's work? These children, many of them now living as unemployed workers, should indict the Supreme Court of these United States for their stunted minds and broken lives." [41]

In other areas as well, the protection of property was constantly interpreted in such a way as to ensure the economic interests of the individual property owner over the larger interests of the public. As long ago as 1914, Ely was bemoaning the manner in which basic control over building patterns in cities was denied to local authorities because of the sacrosanct rights of private property. Much-needed prior planning was neglected, general public needs were ignored, and implications for the future were considered irrelevant. At a time when public opinion is awakening to the ever-increasing problems of urbanization caused by rampant business interests acting in pursuit of the profit motive, Ely's words, written sixty years ago, sound tragic and mocking:

> Why should we struggle so long to secure the recognition of beauty as a public concern? And how arbitrary are the distinctions between what can and what cannot be done, due to the

failure to grasp the full import of the true nature of property as a social institution. German and Dutch cities regulate the height and width of buildings and make the regulations different for various sections of the city in accordance with their character and destinations as residential quarters, factory districts, etc. Thereby they are made beautiful and attractive in the interest of rich and poor alike and their legislatures and courts do not intervene. *Our courts call such regulations invasions of property rights.*[42]

While tightening the reins on the government's power to legislate for the public welfare, the courts were simultaneously giving big business its head, even when their decisions ran counter to popular opinion. Thus, the spirit of the people in the late nineteenth century was clearly antagonistic to the growth of large monopolistic corporations. Not only did these corporations have harmful social consequences, but they actually struck at the very heart of the individualistic ethos so dominant in American life. They belied the principle, and nullified the practice, of an Adam Smith-type free market, and aroused both revulsion and fear on the part of the populace. Legislative expression was given to these widely held sentiments through the Sherman Antitrust Act, under which the federal government could declare illegal any combination of business interests acting in restraint of interstate commerce. Yet "one of the most conservative groups of justices who have ever sat on the [Supreme] Court"[43] interpreted the act in such a confining fashion as to emasculate its power to control large corporations. Although not declaring the act to be illegal, judicial decision effectively nullified it, "and kept it nullified during the most critical period in our industrial history, when most of the great trusts were formed."[44] The large corporations were thus enabled to pay intellectual homage to Adam Smith's laissez faire principles, and to exploit them to the full as part of America's vital ideology, at the same time making a mockery of his ideas through judicially sanctioned monopolistic practices.

The courts exercised a similarly constraining influence on legislation designed to control price fixing in essential areas involving the public interest. While, as in the case of the Sherman Act, laws were often allowed to stand, their application was limited as narrowly as possible, in keeping with the courts' underlying rationale of encouraging the free play of supply and demand in a laissez faire economy.

An outstanding example of Court intervention that held up progressive legislation was the 1895 *Pollock* decision. By a 5–4 margin, the Supreme Court invalidated large sections of the federal income tax laws because, according to a lawyer in the case, they were part of a communist march and, according to one of the judges, were an assault on capital.[45] It took twenty years before a constitutional amendment, overruling *Pollock*, enabled the government to proceed with the vital task of collecting sufficient revenues to help it cope with the increasing social problems attendant upon urbanization and industrialization.

At no time was the power of the courts to serve the interests of certain powerful groups in society at the expense of the public at large more clearly revealed than in its efforts to frustrate New Deal legislation set up as a counterweight to the economic catastrophe of the early 1930s. Much of the controversy in which the Supreme Court was embroiled revolved around a very real and legitimate debate as to the extent of the authority accorded to the federal government to control interstate commerce. There can be little doubt, however, that the conservatism of the judges, and their distaste for any suggestion of "creeping socialism," played a more weighty role in their deliberations and decisions than did the strictly legal questions.

The Court invalidated a number of acts designed to ameliorate the overall economic situation and to alleviate the suffering of groups most adversely affected by the depression. One of these, the National Industrial Recovery Act, had provided codes of fair competition and regulations relating to business practices and labor relations. A later act, the Guffey Coal Act, attempted to introduce similar provisions specifically into the coal industry. It, too, failed to survive the judicial scrutiny and philosophical biases of the justices. Other decisions were threatening to undermine the entire New Deal program, and the likelihood of a constitutional crisis loomed larger as President Roosevelt threatened to pack the Court if it continued to thwart the will of the electorate.

The impasse between the warring branches of government was finally resolved in 1937, when the National Labor Relations Act (the Wagner Act), with provisions and intent similar to those of the ill-fated NIRA, was found to be acceptable by the Supreme Court.

The reason for this volte-face can only be understood against the backdrop of the constitutional crisis engendered by the Court's prior decisions and the President's threats to pack the Court. It was not a new philosophical approach or legal interpretation nor a more refined and sensitive social consciousness that led the justices to change their minds, but the political pressures in the wake of Roosevelt's 1936 landslide victory and the potential damage to the Court's prestige. As Powell cruelly, succinctly, and probably accurately summed up the confrontation, "A switch in time saves nine." [46] The government was finally able to implement its policy of saving the country from some of the most horrendous effects of its laissez faire economic principles, without fear of further intervention from the conservatively inclined judiciary.

A final example of judicial favoritism enjoyed by the business community is a legalism invented by the Supreme Court in connection with its interpretation of the Fourteenth Amendment, already alluded to in another context. Originally intended to benefit emancipated slaves, the amendment provided that no person should be deprived of life, liberty, or property without due process of law. With the growth of joint-stock companies, the major goal of commercial interests became the recognition of corporations as "persons." This legal fiction was obligingly provided by the Court in its 1886 *Santa Clara County* v. *Southern Pacific Railroad Company* decision. "With this decision," writes Carr, "it was clear that [the] assertion that the Amendment was designed primarily to protect Negroes no longer carried weight." [47] Large corporations were now entitled to seek the sanctuary of the courts whenever the government tried, in the public interest, to exert any control over trade and commerce.

The impact of that decision goes beyond the specific purview of the Fourteenth Amendment. The legal fiction devised by the Court also created an apparent equality between corporations and individuals, as if they were possessed of equal rights and of equal capacity to defend themselves. The penniless widow is, within the august atmosphere of an impartial court, the judicial equal of a Rockefeller; the unemployed laborer has the same legal right to sell his labor at its best price in the free marketplace as the corporate employer has to seek the lowest price.

The patent fallacies of this viewpoint have been exposed by many, including one of America's leading jurists, Roscoe Pound:

> Why . . . do the courts persist in the fallacy? Why do so many of them force upon legislation an academic theory of equality in the face of practical inequality? Why do we find a great and learned court in 1908 taking a long step into the past of dealing with the relations between employer and employee in railway transportation, as if the parties were individuals, as if they were farmers haggling over the sale of a horse? Why is the legal conception of the relation of employer and employee so at variance with the common knowledge of mankind? [48]

From the standpoint of sociological jurisprudence, the answer to such a line of questioning is to be found in the inability of the courts to assess accurately the fluctuations in social circumstances and to adapt their interpretation to new social realities. From a radical perspective, however, the answer lies in the way in which the legal superstructure is exploited so as to provide an ideological justification —the legal fiction of "equal rights"—for deep-seated economic inequality, which, of necessity, must lead to inequities in the law courts. The fictional equality of the law provides a cover for the factual inequality of the economic system—but it is often a threadbare covering, unable to hide its shabby injustices.

Criminal Law: White-collar Crime

It has been suggested thus far that a philosophically biased interpretation of the Constitution has been of constant assistance to the powerful and wealthy classes in the United States. These classes, however, have not contented themselves with a legalistic manipulation of constitutional provisions to further their economic interests. They have also insisted upon legislative enactments favoring their position, even to the extent of establishing special and unique legal procedures to deal with such of their acts as violate the law.

In the early 1940s, Edwin H. Sutherland drew attention to an ignored aspect of criminal behavior, "white collar crime," which he defined as a crime "committed by a person of respectability and high social status in the course of his occupation." [49] By intensive and careful fact gathering, he exposed the hidden record of criminal and quasi-criminal behavior indulged in by major corporations. In so doing he was acting very much in the muckraking tradition of early American journalism. Yet his study goes much further in that it raises the basic questions of what exactly is a criminal act, who is a criminal, what sort of decision is necessary to confirm the commission of a criminal act, and who is to make that decision.

Whereas Myers, Josephson, and others had documented the violations of the law that often formed the basis for wealth in nineteenth-century America,[50] Sutherland pointed out that the law itself had been enacted in such a way as to allow its violation with impunity. Through their use of power and their corruption of public officials, the robber barons avoided being called to account for their actions; modern white-collar criminals exploit special provisions of the law in order to avoid, *within the terms of the law,* criminal sanctions.[51]

White-collar criminals use subtle means to achieve their ends. For example, instead of being subjected to the hazards and indignities of court proceedings, corporations have persuaded the government to create special administrative tribunals to deal with violations committed by business. Thus, in Sutherland's words,

> persons who violate laws regarding restraint of trade, advertising, pure food and drugs are not arrested by uniformed policemen, are not often tried in criminal courts, and are not committed to prisons; their illegal behavior generally receives the attention of administrative commissions and of courts operating under civil or equity jurisdiction . . . [P]ersons of the upper socioeconomic class engage in much criminal behavior . . . [T]his criminal behavior differs from the criminal behavior of the lower socio-economic class principally in the administrative procedures which are used in dealing with the offenders.[52]

Basically the contention underlying the concept of white-collar crime is that the legislature, acting in the overall interests of society, has deemed certain acts performed in the business world to be undesirable, and has, therefore, prohibited them; yet, despite the fact that these acts cause serious harm to the public, their perpetrators are not considered criminals and are generally not brought before a criminal court. This contradiction is reflected in the fact that special *noncriminal* institutions and procedures have been established to determine whether or not a business corporation has committed a criminal act.

Where there has been a violation of legislation relating to trade and commerce, the government may forego prosecution of the corporation and its top executives, choosing instead one of several other options. It may ask the Court for an injunction or a cease-and-desist order against the company, as a warning to the company that it is acting in violation of the law and that further violations may lead to criminal prosecution. Some laws provide for a stipulation on the part of the company wherein the company admits that it has committed a violation and promises not to do so in the future. A third alternative gives any party harmed by the illegal act the right to sue the offending company for treble damages; this device encourages private companies to share the responsibility of controlling illegal actions of other companies, thereby further avoiding direct government action.

The effect of these provisions, of course, is to provide unique means for acting against the most powerful groups in society; they enable the government to exercise minimum control over these sectors while concealing from the public the fact that the acts complained of are criminal in nature. The harm caused by the corporation is thereby only partly minimized, while the full power of the law is not invoked. The end result is that corporations can take risks on the periphery of the legally permissible, often with harmful consequences to the rest of society, without fear of calling down the wrath of society when the limits of legality are exceeded.

Sutherland based his thesis on an extensive survey of the actions of the top seventy corporations in the United States, up to the mid-1940s. He found that altogether these companies had committed a total of 980 violations of laws relating to restraint of trade, misrepresentation in advertising, infringement of patents, trademarks and copyrights, unfair labor practices, financial fraud, and violations of war regulations. Only 158 of these violations had been tried in criminal courts; the rest were adjudicated by administrative tribunals. Sutherland contends that these remaining 822 cases also constituted criminal action, since in nearly all of them the government, had it so desired, could have sued in criminal court.

This notion has been attacked by other criminologists, who assert that an act is not a crime unless it is punished in criminal court.[53] Sutherland's reasoning, however, is that the key to an understanding of criminality is not whether an act is actually punished, but whether it is *punishable*. A theft does not become a theft only after the thief is convicted; the statistics of crimes known to the police are not based on convictions in criminal court but on legitimate complaints filed. Accordingly, it should not be necessary for a corporation to be actually tried in a criminal court for society to realize that the act committed is, in reality, a crime.

In his introduction to the 1961 edition of Sutherland's book, Cressey poses the question: "Explanations of why such a pattern should remain for so long outside both popular and scientific purview is a sociological question of first-rate importance . . . [T]he next important step in research on white collar crime is determination of the society's structured conditions which create differentials in the degree of the *public character* of various types of criminal offenses. . . . Why does a society report the crimes it reports, why does it overlook what it overlooks, and how does it go about deciding that it has, in fact, overlooked something?" [54] Newman, too, has suggested that any analysis of upper-class crime must take account not only of theories of crime, but also of theories of stratification, and must deal not only with "those who *break* the laws, but . . . those who *make* laws as well." [55]

It is suggested that the perspective adopted in this chapter will indicate a fruitful basis for such research. Indeed, Sutherland himself has provided the theoretical framework for Cressey's ruminations by pointing out the cultural homogeneity of legislators, judges, and administrators with businessmen, and the respect the former have for the latter as respectable and successful executives. Basically the businessmen are accorded the same privileges that all dominant groups in society secure for themselves:

> The most powerful group in medieval society secured relative immunity from punishment by "benefit of clergy," and now our most powerful group secures relative immunity by "benefit of business," or more generally by "high social status." The statement of Daniel Drew, a pious old fraud, describes the working of the criminal law with accuracy: "Law is like a cobweb; it's made for flies and the smaller kind of insects, so to speak, but lets the big bumblebees break through." [56]

Having seen, in part, how the criminal law deals with the "bumblebees," it now remains to see how it treats the lesser breeds.

Criminal Law and Social Class

For the poor, no special privileged institutions or procedures are available. They must run the full gauntlet of police apprehension, court adjudication, and correctional control. For them the final result of this process is often to end up discarded in society's wastebasket, the prison. It seems almost redundant to point out that the prisons do not contain a fair sampling of the criminal population of a society. Becoming a convicted criminal and being incarcerated is not only a consequence of personal variables relating to the crime committed and to the character of the criminal, but a result of an intervening process of selection, in which a host of social variables materially affect the outcome. The poorer the person, the more likely he is to be arrested, charged, convicted, and imprisoned. This is a simple statement of fact, which few would attempt to dispute or refute. Yet society embellishes its concept of justice with earnest explanations that the courts are equally accessible to all; that the constitutional protections serve to ensure that the indigent and the illiterate will receive the munificent benefits of the law; that justice is impartial, knowing no differences of race, religion, education, or economics; that trained, hand-picked judges and honest, randomly chosen jurors will without prejudice seek the truth. The fact remains, however, that members of the middle and upper classes can commit with impunity acts which, if performed by lower-class persons, would bring harsh societal retribution.

This contention is substantiated by numerous research findings dealing with "hidden" crime and delinquency—crimes that are not prosecuted and form no part of the official crime statistics. The fundamental conclusion that emerges from such studies is that criminal acts are far more equally spread out among the different classes than laymen's thinking, official statistics, and criminological theorizing would indicate.

A number of factors contribute to this discrepancy. Selective police practices which increase patrols in poor areas (particularly those inhabited by ethnic minority groups), and which show less tolerance and flexibility toward poor people, will obviously contribute to the disparity between upper- and lower-class prisoners. Such selective and often biased procedures for determining criminality are continued in the prosecutor's office and culminate in equally biased proceedings in the courts, where impecunious defendants are, in the words of Justice Hugo Black, subject to "increased dangers of conviction merely because of their poverty." [57] These dangers result not so much from willful policies or unbridled prejudices (though these may play a part), as from the regular, orderly, smooth, and accepted operation of the courts.

Indeed, the courts' role in discriminatory practices precedes the actual trial; the court is an active partner in the operation of the bail system which, though desirable in theory, has proved pernicious in practice. Despite the much-needed reform that it has undergone recently, the bail system as practiced in the United States is still based on a rather narrow, perhaps perverted, view of human nature: that financial inducements are a better way of ensuring a defendant's attendance at his trial than his sense of honor, his desire to prove his innocence or, conversely, to pay his debt to society, or even his desire not to be a fugitive from justice. Actually, bail is hardly a financial inducement, since the defendant generally puts up only 5 or 10 percent of the total. The rest is provided by a bondsman, who—untrained, responsible to no public authority, and often himself of marginal status in society—becomes the kingpin of the judicial system, determining, solely on the basis of financial considerations, which persons shall be jailed prior to trial and which shall go free.

A large proportion of defendants is unable to meet the financial requirements of bail or is unable to persuade a bondsman to stand surety for them. Hence they are obliged to spend their pretrial period in detention, even though some are subsequently found to be innocent, others have the charges against them dropped, and still others spend more time in detention than the time prescribed by their final sentence. With few exceptions, it is only the poor who cannot afford to post bail.[58]

It should be noted that detention before trial always involves a denial of basic rights to a person presumed by law to be innocent. Pretrial detention not only deprives a defendant of his liberty, but may also cause irreparable damage to the preparation of his defense, such as meeting with counsel and contacting witnesses. Furthermore, he is subjected to the stigmatizing effects, often irreversible, of detention: "A detained defendant often comes into the courtroom pallid, unshaven, dishevelled, demoralized, a victim of the jailhouse blues. He comes and goes through a special door that the jury soon learns leads to the detention pen beyond. He is always closely accompanied by a police escort or marshal." [59]

Although the authors of the Bill of Rights tried to protect citizens against arbitrary arrest by decreeing that no man shall be detained without bail, blatant injustices are inevitable in a system that measures the right to freedom not in human terms, according to some value system, but as a business transaction based on financial considerations. For many years even government commissions have railed against the system. A 1963 report stated that "the bail system administered in the federal courts, relying primarily on financial inducements to secure the presence of the accused at the trial, results in serious problems for defendants of limited means." [60] Four years later the President's Commission on Law Enforcement and Administration of Justice openly admitted that "By and large money bail is an unfair and ineffective device. Its glaring weakness is that it discriminates against poor defendants, thus running directly counter to the law's avowed purpose of treating all defendants equally." [61] It was only with the pioneering work done in New York by the privately funded Vera Foundation during the 1960s that the first real inroads into the bail system were made. Meanwhile, generations of judges have blandly forced thousands of impoverished accused (many of them innocent of any crime) to spend lengthy periods in pretrial detention.

Thus bail, in principle an essential guarantee of freedom, becomes in reality a meaningful protection only for those with money. "In a system which grants pre-trial liberty for money, those who can afford a bondsman go free; those who cannot stay in jail." [62] Indeed, an objective appraisal of the bail system as practiced in the United States would justify an embellishment on Marx's original explanation of the function of criminal law: Bail exists primarily to provide work for the bail bondsman. There can be little doubt that other, more efficient, more equitable, less expensive, and less dehumanizing methods could be used to assure a defendant's attendance at his trial.

A second constitutional guarantee central to the administration of criminal justice is the right to counsel. Recent Supreme Court decisions have extended this right, and today the courts provide fairly wide protection for indigent defendants. Yet it took more than 160 years for the courts to make this Sixth Amendment guarantee more than mere pious exhortation. In the 1942 *Betts* v. *Brady* case, the Supreme Court held that in a noncapital state felony, the right to counsel was not essential. Carefully analyzing historical precedents in the various states, the Court concluded that "in the great majority of the states, it has been the considered judgment of the people, their representatives and their courts that appointment of counsel is not a fundamental right, essential to a fair trial." [63]

Betts v. *Brady* was overruled twenty years later by *Gideon* v. *Wainwright*. Although *Gideon* is widely admired as a milestone in American jurisprudence, it also emphasizes the weakness of the judicial system. Prior to this case, defendants were not automatically provided with counsel in noncapital state offenses. The Supreme Court, by declaring such a denial to be an infringement of fundamental rights, has thereby tacitly criticized the administration of justice in pre-*Gideon* days. *Gideon* has also not been made applicable to nonfelonies, the category in which the poor predominate. Each lower court has its assembly line of drunks and drug addicts, hoboes and petty thieves, who parade before the judge—alone, without legal advice—in a never-ending procession, to have justice meted out to them. The denial of basic rights in these courts is probably immeasurable; yet it is here that most injustices to poor defendants are perpetrated. The principle of the right to counsel for all will be fully effective only when that right is extended to misdemeanors.

Even the right to counsel, however, is no guarantee that the rights of the accused will be fully safeguarded. The presence of a lawyer in the courtroom ensures that in the full glare of the public eye, a trained jurist is at the side of the accused, guiding and advising him. But it provides no guarantee against what can happen in the nooks and crannies that make up the rest of the judicial system. The automatic provision of a lawyer does not assure the accused of necessary prior preparation and planning for the trial; of the capacity to call in expensive, but often vital, expert witnesses, or to utilize the services of trained investigators; nor of the financial resources to appeal a ruling and to manage the expenses of such an appeal, including payment for the trial transcript and the posting of bail.

Judges in Their Social Milieu

The problem of equal justice in American courts is not limited to the provision of lawyers for poor defendants. In a country where racial tensions underlie human relationships, where prejudice may be inculcated in the schools and discrimination enacted in the legislatures, Baldwin's question penetrates to the heart of the judicial system: "What Negro can be assured that he will get equal justice with a white man for the same offense? What Mexican-American in the Southwest? What Puerto Rican in our eastern cities? Is justice as equal in any court for the non-conformist and unpopular as for the regulars?" [64] These questions were asked in the early 1960s. Even the advances registered by the Warren Court did not provide assurances that members of minority groups, particularly those accused of misdemeanors, would be vouchsafed the full protection of the law.

Conversely, the political polarization of the past decade has once again subjected members of militant and radical movements to all the prejudices and passions of "respectable" jurors and judges. The trials and tribulations of Dr. Benjamin Spock and his co-defendants, the Chicago Seven, and of many Black Panthers are still too vivid to require retelling. In many respects, however, they are only cyclical repetitions of judicial response to tense social confrontations. People whose ideas fall outside the mainstream of standard American ideology have frequently found it as difficult to gain protection and a fair hearing in the courts as to gain popular support outside. William Kunstler, defense lawyer for the Chicago Seven, has documented ten of the more significant of these trials.[65] The harassment of trade-union leaders has already been referred to; World War I also brought a harvest of vindictive punishments against pacifists and draft dodgers; the troublesome 1930s saw radical thinkers facing judicial retribution for their views and activities. One, Angelo Hendon, a black communist, was tried for disseminating communist literature and was sentenced to twenty years in prison under the provisions of a pre-Civil War Georgia statute aimed at coping with slave revolts! In this latter case the injustice to the accused was so flagrant, and the embarrassment to the judicial system so acute, that the Supreme Court overruled the decision—albeit by a narrow 5–4 margin.[66]

In times of social stress, the courts are inevitably exposed to tremendous pressures as they try to preserve an air of judicial calm amid the turbulence around them. Trials of radical thinkers in particular expose the weaknesses of any judicial system. The courts are called upon to show both tolerance and firmness, and the façade of judicial respectability can easily be destroyed when the accused shows no respect for the judge or for the institutions and values that he represents. In such confrontations the more subtle weaknesses of the courts, unnoticed in less volatile trials, are ruthlessly revealed. The conduct of Judge Julius Hoffman in the Chicago Seven trial[67] was only partly a manifestation of his own cantankerous personality; it was also, to a large degree, symptomatic of his background and profession.

With few exceptions, judges represent a very narrow spectrum of the total population. Their backgrounds, education, personal and professional connections, and their values are oriented to the upper classes of society; their commitment is to a maintenance of the status quo. These biases they bring to bear in their decisions, whether consciously or unconsciously. The elaborate precautions taken to guarantee that no judge will sit in a case in which he has a direct interest only serve to obfuscate those myriad cases in which judges have an interest based on their class and other affiliations.

The Supreme Court crisis of 1969 focused attention on the personal qualities and the social milieu of judges. One candidate for the Court, Clement Haynsworth, was rejected by the Senate because he had participated in cases in which his own financial interests were affected; the other, G. Harrold Carswell, was found unworthy because he had made virulent racist statements as a candidate for political office in the South. Although both were rejected as unsuitable for the highest court in the land, it is often forgotten that both continued to function as judges in courts only slightly inferior to the Supreme Court. As such they continued to make decisions crucial to the well-being of individual citizens, to serve the larger interests with which they identified, to propound the philosophies in which they believed, and to base their decisions on their overall *Weltanschauung*.

The influence of a judge's social background on his decisions is not a new phenomenon. In 1912 Gustavus Myers studied the personal histories of all the Supreme Court justices and concluded that most of them came from a similar type of background and tended to serve the needs and interests of the class with which they identified. Starting with the first justices appointed by Washington, Myers shows how inextricably many of the "nine men" have been linked to wealthy and powerful business interests. The very first chief justice, John Jay, when given the choice of any federal position, picked that of chief justice because of its potential power to further the interests with which he was connected. "His appointment was hailed with unconcealed delight and gratification by the powerful landholders; among the mass of people a corresponding sense of deep dismay was not slow in expressing itself." [68]

Rodell claims that the original six justices appointed to the Supreme Court were "wealth-conscious and conservative in the extreme," [69] and not at all deserving of the high position to which they were elevated. The two most prominent justices, Wilson and Rutledge, were both "wealthy and belligerently tough-minded about the protection of wealth by government." [70] Wilson, who had a "penchant for land speculation," [71] subsequently became embroiled in the Yazoo land fraud scandal, while Rutledge, as a delegate to the Constitutional Convention, had been "the chief mouthpiece of the Southern slave-holders [and] perhaps more than any other delegate, was instrumental in defeating in that convention the proposition to prevent the importation of slaves." [72] A third justice, Cushing, had "served the creditor class well as Chief Justice of Massachusetts," [73] while making himself "extremely obnoxious to the laboring and yeoman class by his decisions and attitudes." [74] The two remaining justices were Blair, "who was later to get rich by gambling heavily in government securities," [75] and Iredell, who prior to his appointment had been an attorney for large North Carolina landholders.

This pattern is consistently maintained, reaching its peak at the end of the nineteenth century, when appointment as an attorney for one of the large corporations, especially the railroads, became, if not a sine qua non for appointment to the bench, at least a useful credential. Myers suggests that

> the fact that nearly all of the men ascending to the Supreme
> Court of the United States had, as attorneys, served powerful

individuals or corporations need occasion no undue comment. Understanding the development of modern society, and its evolutionary transitions, we can clearly perceive that certain men skilled in law had to do the indispensable legal work of capitalist interests. . . . Able servitors of the ruling economic forces, it naturally followed that those forces, controlling Government, should select certain of those lawyers to go on the Supreme Court Bench." [76]

Commager, assessing the work of the judges from a nonradical standpoint, has attempted to explain the more reprehensible of their decisions as flowing from the philosophical perspective of natural and historical law which had molded their thinking. His language is more moderate, his criticism more restrained, his explanation based on a different philosophical rationale, yet the end result remains the same: a long line of judicial decisions that bring no honor to the court or to the people in whose name they were made.

> By a resort to the principles of natural and historical law, judges could, and did evade responsibility; and when they voided acts of which they disapproved, they generally accompanied the nullification with the confession that they had no choice in the matter. Thus the most humane judges could strike down laws providing compensation for the victims of industry or prohibiting child labor or a sixty-hour week for women in factories with a clear conscience, reassuring themselves that they were but impersonal agents of an impersonal mechanism. [77]

Conclusion

The courts of the United States, taking a lead from the Supreme Court, have been able abettors of the interests of the dominant groups in society. They have provided a legal framework amenable to the interests of landowners, capitalists, and corporations, and conducive to the amassing of large fortunes. That framework has been created through a series of decisions inimical to the interests of the lower classes and detrimental to the overall needs of the total society. These decisions have arisen only partly from the personal idiosyncrasies of the judges and from their personal corruption, weakness, or prejudices. Their decisions are fundamentally a consequence of the society in which they function. *In a stratified society there can be no equal justice.* It is futile to think of the courts as a possible haven or refuge, an idyllic island equitably dispensing justice in a society which lacks a strong commitment to justice and equality at all times, in all circumstances, for all men. The courts are a microcosm of society; they mirror its ugliness and its beauty, they reveal its errors and defects, they echo its values and ideals.

A society that sanctifies property will find its courts denying human rights; a society that allows large disparities of wealth and poverty will find its poorer citizens deprived of necessary legal protection; a society that praises its robber barons will find its trade-union officials and radical thinkers harassed in the courts; a society that tolerates discrimination will find its ethnic minorities suffering differential penal punishments; a society that fails to control burgeoning wealth will find the wealthy influencing its judiciary. Where there is no equality and justice in the cities and towns and villages, in the streets and schools, and on the farms, there can be no equal justice in the courts.

This last point becomes all the more striking when one realizes that the courts are the one institution in stratified capitalist societies that are presented as providing equal treatment for all. Capitalist ideologues never presume to argue that both rich and poor are entitled to the same kind of education, the same kind of medical care, the same kind of housing, the same kind of burial. Differential treatment in all these and other areas is looked upon as an inevitable, and even desirable, consequence of the play of market forces in a free society. No apologist for the system would, however, have the audacity to assert that similar differential treatment should be tolerated in the courts of law. This is the one oasis from which all presumably drink in equal portions. Thus, the ideological superstructure creates a constitution ostensibly guaranteeing equal protection for all, and sets up a court system that is supposedly blind to external differences. For no other part of the superstructure is so much energy devoted to prove that the needs of all the people are being met in equal measure. Conversely, respect for law and order, and reverence for judges, is demanded of every citizen.

A radical approach to legal institutions, as set out in this chapter, shows up the shallow fallacies of this contention. The courts are not immune to the weaknesses of the society in which they operate. They cannot rectify its defects and evils. At the very most, with the necessary goodwill on the part of judges, they may redress some grievances and mitigate some of the defects—but they cannot eradicate them.

More often, particularly when popular pressures build up for social change, it is the courts that stand firm as the ultimate bulwark guarding the powerful economic forces underlying the social structure. Even a series of progressive judicial decisions will do no more than bring immediate relief to certain underprivileged individuals and groups; they will not threaten the long-term interests of the propertied and commercial classes. In this sense, the court more truly reveals a society's nature than do most other institutions. It acts not only as a mirror reflecting the outer image, but also as a microscope probing into the infrastructure usually hidden from view.

If this is true, then one might well argue that in the decisions of its courts a society may be judged. In the words and deeds of its courts, the United States stands indicted.

NOTES

1. Augustine, *City of God.*

2. Martin Luther King, Jr., "Letter from Birmingham Jail," in *Civil Disobedience: Theory and Practice*, ed. Hugo Adam Bedau (New York: Pegasus, 1969).

3. Thomas Hobbes, *Leviathan*, chap. 15.

4. John Austin, *The Province of Jurisprudence Defined* (1832).

5. Hans Kelsen, "The Pure Theory of Law: Its Methods and Fundamental Concepts," *Law Quarterly Review* 50 (October 1934): 474–535.

6. Max Weber, *The Theory of Social and Economic Organization*, ed. A. R. Henderson and T. Parsons (London: W. Hodge, 1947).

7. Friedrich Karl von Savigny, *Of the Vocation of Our Age for Legislation and Jurisprudence* (1814).

8. The leading exponent of sociological jurisprudence is Roscoe Pound. See his *An Introduction to the Philosophy of Law* (1922).

9. Emile Durkheim, *The Division of Labor in Society*, ed. G. Simpson (New York: Macmillan, 1933).

10. Peter Kropotkin, *Modern Science and Anarchism (1912)*, in *The Anarchists*, ed. Irving Louis Horowitz (New York: Dell, 1964), p. 151.

11. William E. Hocking, *Man and the State* (1926), in ibid., p. 336.

12. Irving Louis Horowitz, "A Postscript to the Anarchists," in ibid., p. 601.

13. Edwin M. Schur, *Crimes Without Victims: Deviant Behavior and Public Policy* (Englewood Cliffs, N.J.: Prentice-Hall, 1965); Norval Morris and Gordon Hawkins, *The Honest Politician's Guide to Crime Control* (Chicago: University of Chicago Press, 1970).

14. Peter Kropotkin, "Property and Law," in *Movements of Social Dissent in Modern Europe*, ed. J. Salwyn Schapiro (Princeton: Anvil Press, 1962), p. 136.

15. For an extensive analysis of Kropotkin's ideas on communities and small city-states, see his *Mutual Aid: A Factor of Evolution* (New York: McLure, Philips, 1902).

16. Karl Marx, *Selected Writings in Sociology and Social Philosophy*, trans. and ed. T. B. Bottomore (New York: McGraw-Hill, 1956), p. 51.

17. Georg Rusche and Otto Kirchheimer, *Punishment and Social Structure* (New York: Columbia University Press, 1939).

18. Barrington Moore, Jr., *Social Origins of Dictatorship and Democracy: Lord and Peasant in the Making of the Modern World* (Boston: Beacon Press, 1966), pp. 21–22.

19. W. E. Tate, "Members of Parliament and the Proceedings upon Enclosure Bills" (1942), quoted in ibid., p. 22. Moore's italics.

20. Marx, *Selected Writings*, p. 158.

21. George Herbert Mead, "The Psychology of Punitive Justice," *American Journal of Sociology* 23 (1917–18): 577–602; Karl Menninger, *The Crime of Punishment* (New York: Viking, 1968); Kai T. Erikson, "Notes on the Sociology of Deviance," *Social Problems* 9 (Spring 1962): 307–14.

22. Howard S. Becker, *Outsiders: Studies in the Sociology of Deviance* (New York: Free Press, 1963), p. 156.

23. Henry Steele Commager, *The American Mind: An Interpretation of American Thought and Character Since the 1880's* (New Haven: Yale University Press, 1954), p. 229.

24. See Holmes's dissenting opinion in Lochner v. New York, 198 U.S. 45 (1905): "The Fourteenth Amendment does not enact Mr. Herbert Spencer's *Social Statics*."

25. Charles A. Beard, *An Economic Interpretation of the Constitution of the United States* (2nd ed.; New York: Macmillan, 1935), p. 324.

26. Ibid., p. 13.

27. James Madison, *The Federalist #10*, quoted in ibid., pp. 14–15.

28. Beard, *Economic Interpretation*, p. 292.

29. Forrest McDonald, *We the People: The Economic Origins of the Constitution* (Chicago: University of Chicago Press, 1958).

30. Robert E. Brown, "Reinterpretation of the Formation of the American Constitution" (1963), in *Essays on the Making of the Constitution*, ed. Leonard W. Levy (New York: Oxford University Press, 1969), p. 112.

31. Howard R. Smith, *Economic History of the United States* (New York: Ronald Press, 1955), p. 301.

32. Ibid.

33. Oliver Wendell Holmes, *Collected Legal Papers* (New York: Harcourt, 1920), p. 184.

34. Karl Mannheim, *Ideology and Utopia: An Introduction to the Sociology of Knowledge* (New York: Harcourt, 1936); *Man and Society in an Age of Reconstruction: Studies in Modern Social Structure* (New York: Harcourt, 1940).

35. Henry W. Edgerton, "The Incidence of Judicial Control over Congress," *Cornell Law Quarterly* 22 (1937): 346–48.

36. Smith, *Economic History*, p. 457.

37. Charles O. Gregory, *Labor and the Law* (New York: Norton, 1946), p. 27.

38. Ibid., p. 464.

39. From the *Chicago Times Herald*, quoted in Richard T. Ely, *Property and Contract in Their Relations to the Distribution of Wealth*, vol. 2 (New York: Macmillan, 1914), p. 652.

40. Ibid., p. 653.

41. Quoted in Robert K. Carr, *The Supreme Court and Judicial Review* (New York: Farrar & Rinehart, 1942), p. 209.

42. Ely, *Property and Contract*, p. 783. My italics.

43. Carr, *Judicial Review*, p. 105.

44. E. S. Corwin in *American Bar Association Journal* 12 (March 1926): 171.

45. Pollock v. Farmers' Loan and Trust Co., 158 U.S. 601 (1895).

46. Thomas R. Powell, "From Philadelphia to Philadelphia," *American Political Science Review* 32 (February 1938): 24.

47. Carr, *Judicial Review*, p. 147.

48. Roscoe Pound, "Static Assumptions of Contractual Freedom," in *Current Economic Problems*, ed. W. H. Hamilton (Chicago: University of Chicago Press, 1914), p. 781.

49. Edwin H. Sutherland, *White Collar Crime* (New York: Holt, 1967), p. 9.

50. Gustavus Myers, *History of the Great American Fortunes* (Chicago: Charles H. Kerr, 1908); Matthew Josephson, *The Robber Barons* (New York: Harcourt, 1934).

51. Myers adduces evidence to prove that "the bulk of Vanderbilt's original millions were the proceeds of extortion, blackmail, and theft" and that "the real beginning of J. Pierpont Morgan's business career" grew out of a fraudulent deal with the government (Myers, *Great American Fortunes*, p. 174). During the Civil War Morgan bought 5,000 condemned carbines from the government for $17,000, and sold them for $109,000, sight unseen, to a distant garrison in desperate need of arms. It is interesting to note that this deal received judicial support. When the government discovered the fraud, it refused to pay the full price and offered Morgan $55,000 as a compromise. He rejected the offer and sued for full payment, and his plea was upheld in court. Thus, the government, having failed to prosecute Morgan for fraud, now found itself obliged to pay full recompense for worthless goods.

52. Sutherland, *White Collar Crime*, pp. 8–9.

53. See, for example, Paul W. Tappan, "Who Is the Criminal?" *American Sociological Review* 12 (February 1947): 96–102.

54. Sutherland, *White Collar Crime*, p. xii.

55. Donald J. Newman, "White-Collar Crime," *Law and Contemporary Problems* 23 (1958): 746.

56. Sutherland, *White Collar Crime*, p. 47. Clarence Darrow expressed similar sentiments in a famous 1902 address to prisoners at the Cook County Jail in Chicago. The following excerpt is taken from Arthur Weinberg, ed., *Attorney for the Damned* (New York: Simon and Schuster, 1957), pp. 14–15: ". . . It's easy to see how to do away with what we call crime. It is not so easy to do it. I will tell you how to do it. It can be done by giving the people a chance to live—by destroying special privileges. So long as big criminals can get the coal fields, so long as the big criminals have control of the city council and get the public streets for streetcars and gas rights—this is bound to send thousands of poor people to jail. So long as men are allowed to monopolize all the earth, and compel others to live on such terms as these men see fit to make, then you are bound to get into jail.

"The only way in the world to abolish crime and criminals is to abolish the big ones and the little ones together. Make fair conditions of life. Give men a chance to live. Abolish the right of private ownership of land, abolish monopoly, make the world partners in production, partners in the good things of life. Nobody would steal if he could get something of his own some easier way. Nobody will commit burglary when he has a house full. No girl will go out on the streets when she has a comfortable place at home. The man who owns a sweatshop or a department store may not be to blame himself for the condition of his girls, but when he pays them five dollars, three dollars, and two dollars a week, I wonder where he thinks they will get the rest of their money to live. The only way to cure these conditions is by equality."

57. See Black's dissenting opinion in Betts v. Brady 316 U.S. 455 (1942), 476.

58. A 1964 survey in New York showed that 35% of all defendants could not even post bail of $500, i.e., raise about $25 as surety for the bondsman.

59. Patricia M. Wald, "Poverty and Criminal Justice," *Task Force Report: The Courts, Appendix C*, President's Commission on Law Enforcement and Administration of Justice, 1967.

60. *Report of the Attorney General's Committee on Poverty and the Administration of Federal Criminal Justice*, 1963.

61. *The Challenge of Crime in a Free Society: A Report by the President's Commission on Law Enforcement and Administration of Justice* (Washington, D.C.: Government Printing Office, 1967), p. 131.

62. Patricia M. Wald and Daniel J. Freed, *Bail in the United States: 1964: A Report to the National Conference on Bail and Criminal Justice* (Washington, D.C.: Department of Justice and the Vera Foundation, 1964), p. 21.

63. Justice Owen Roberts, delivering the majority opinion in Betts v. Brady. This decision, it should be noted, ran directly counter to the position already obtaining in the federal courts, where counsel was provided, and led the dissenting justices to decry the existence of a double standard of justice. The progressive policy in the federal courts only served to emphasize the denial of rights in the state courts.

64. Roger N. Baldwin, in his Introduction to William M. Kunstler, . . . *And Justice for All* (Dobbs Ferry, N.Y.: Oceana Publications, 1963), p. viii.

65. Kunstler, ibid. The trials dealt with in Kunstler's book are those of Leo Frank, "an outsider and a Jew charged with a particularly heinous crime"; the Scottsboro boys, "southern blacks accused of raping two white women"; Sacco and Vanzetti, "immigrant Italians whose anarchistic views had made them anathema to . . . society"; Mary Surratt, Alger Hiss, and Corliss Lamont, all "in one way or another, enemies of the State"; Tom Mooney, a "labor agitator in an era of antiunionism"; Scopes, "a threat to the Bible"; and the Herricks school prayer case "against God." In his intro-

duction Kunstler claims that all these "pariahs had to run the gamut of a hostile climate of opinion which militated strongly against their chance of success."

66. John P. Roche, *Courts and Rights: The American Judiciary in Action* (2nd ed.; New York: Random House, 1966), p. 103.

67. For examples of exchanges between the judge and the defendants see Mark Levine, George McNamee, and Daniel Greenberg, *The Tales of Hoffman: From the Trial of the Chicago 7* (New York: Bantam, 1970).

68. Gustavus Myers, *History of the Supreme Court of the United States* (New York: Burt Franklin, 1912), pp. 137–38.

69. Fred Rodell, *Nine Men: A Political History of the Supreme Court from 1790 to 1955* (New York: Random House, 1955), p. 46.

70. Ibid., p. 47.

71. Ibid., p. 48.

72. Myers, *History of the Supreme Court*, p. 145.

73. Rodell, *Nine Men*, p. 48.

74. Myers, *History of the Supreme Court*, p. 146.

75. Rodell, *Nine Men*, p. 49.

76. Myers, *History of the Supreme Court*, p. 9.

77. Commager, *The American Mind*, pp. 374–75.